The Buddhist Literature of Ancient Gandhāra

Classics of Indian Buddhism

The flourishing of Buddhism in South Asia during the first millennium of the Common Era produced many texts that deserve a place among the classics of world literature. Exploring the full extent of the human condition and the limits of language and reason, these texts have the power to edify and entertain a wide variety of readers. The *Classics of Indian Buddhism* series aims to publish widely accessible translations of important texts from the Buddhist traditions of South Asia, with special consideration given to works foundational for the Mahāyāna.

CLASSICS OF INDIAN BUDDHISM

The Buddhist Literature of Ancient Gandhāra

An Introduction with Selected Translations

Richard Salomon

Wisdom

Wisdom Publications, Inc.
199 Elm Street
Somerville MA 02144 USA
wisdomexperience.org

Library of Congress Cataloging-in-Publication Data
Names: Salomon, Richard, 1948– author.
Title: The Buddhist literature of ancient Gandhara: an introduction with selected translations / Richard Salomon.
Description: Somerville, MA: Wisdom Publications, 2018. | Series: Classics of Indian Buddhism | Includes bibliographical references and index. |
Identifiers: LCCN 2017026919 (print) | LCCN 2017057567 (ebook) | ISBN 9781614291855 (ebook) | ISBN 1614291853 (ebook) | ISBN 9781614291688 (pbk.: alk. paper) | ISBN 1614291683 (pbk.: alk. paper)
Subjects: LCSH: Buddhist literature, Gandhari Prakrit—History and criticism. | Buddhist literature, Gandhari Prakrit—Translations into English.
Classification: LCC BQ1029.G362 (ebook) | LCC BQ1029.G362 S25 2018 (print) | DDC 294.3/82—dc23
LC record available at https://lccn.loc.gov/2017026919

ISBN 978-1-61429-168-8 ebook ISBN 978-1-61429-185-5
26 25 24 23 22 6 5 4 3 2

Cover and interior design by Gopa & Ted2, Inc. Typeset by James D. Skatges. Author photo by Anna Schnell. Set in DGP Regular 11.75/15.75.

Wisdom Publications' books are printed on acid-free paper and meet the guidelines for permanence and durability of the Production Guidelines for Book Longevity of the Council on Library Resources.

Printed in the United States of America.

MIX
Paper from responsible sources
FSC® C011935

Please visit fscus.org.

This book is dedicated to the memory of Carol Goldberg Salomon
(July 28, 1948–March 13, 2009)
זיכרונה לברכה

Publisher's Acknowledgment

The publisher gratefully acknowledges the generous help of the Hershey Family Foundation in sponsoring the production of this book.

Contents

List of Illustrations

Figures

Maps

Preface

THIS BOOK IS a distillation of the results of twenty years of concentrated work by my many collaborators and me on the Gandhāran Buddhist manuscripts that were discovered during that period. These manuscripts and fragments, which now number in the hundreds, date from the early centuries before and after the beginning of the Common Era. Written in the Gāndhārī language in Kharoṣṭhī script, they have brought to light the previously unknown literature of Gandhāra, a major center of early Buddhism in the northwestern frontier of the Indian subcontinent. Gandhāra had previously been familiar mainly from archaeological remains, especially its world-renowned tradition of sculpture.

Until now, our findings have been published mostly in scholarly books and articles designed for an audience of specialists in academic Buddhist studies and Indian linguistics. A preliminary book, *Ancient Buddhist Scrolls from Gandhāra: The British Library Kharoṣṭhī Fragments* (Salomon 1999), introduced the first group of Gandhāran manuscripts to be discovered in a semi-technical format, while scholarly editions and translations of individual manuscripts from this and other collections have been published by the University of Washington Press in the volumes of the Gandhāran Buddhist Texts (GBT) series. These books are not intended for general readers. They are meant to enable those who work with Buddhist literature in more widely known languages such as Sanskrit and Pali to understand the Gāndhārī texts.

But almost from the very beginning of this project, I have also been aware of our obligation to avoid burying these discoveries in technical publications for specialists and to meet what I consider a scholar's duty to present new knowledge to interested readers in an accessible format. This book is an attempt to meet that obligation by making the newly found Buddhist literature of ancient Gandhāra accessible to a wider audience, be they students of Buddhism or readers with a general interest in ancient religions, languages, or literature.

In addition to translating and explaining the contents of the manuscripts themselves, I have tried to give the reader some sense of the scholar's agonies and ecstasies involved in studying fragmentary, decrepit manuscripts that have lain unread for nearly two millennia. Each of these translations is a distillation of countless hours of labor by one or, more often, several scholars. In some places, I have presented a degree of technical explanation of the methods and techniques of decipherment to give the reader a sense of not only what has been done but also how and why.

The texts presented here were selected on a variety of criteria. First, an attempt has been made to sample each of the main genres of Buddhist texts now known in the Gāndhārī language. These are grouped together under five main rubrics: prose sūtras, poetry, legends and stories about previous lives, scholarly treatises, and Mahāyāna literature. Within these categories, the specific texts were chosen on the basis of factors such as the amount of material preserved in the fragments, legibility and accessibility, and overall interest and significance. Most of the texts have either been previously published in scholarly editions or at least studied in detail by my colleagues and myself, though not yet fully published. Some of the texts (nos. 1–3, 5–6, 8, 12) are presented in full; these are generally the shorter and/or better-preserved specimens. The rest are representative selections from longer texts, most of them not previously published. From these, I have chosen passages that are relatively comprehensible, interesting, and representative of the text as a whole.

Readers will notice, and perhaps be surprised, that in many cases the introductory material and commentary is longer—sometimes much longer—than the translated text itself. This is a product of the special character of this literature. Nearly all of the texts are incomplete, and in many cases only a small fraction of the entire work survives. I have therefore tried to make up the deficiencies in the surviving material by explaining in some detail their meaning, their context within Buddhism in Gandhāra and beyond, and especially their relationships with parallel or similar texts in other Buddhist languages and traditions that help to clarify their meaning and importance. I hope that in doing so I will be contributing to, rather than distracting from, the reader's understanding and appreciation of the texts themselves.

Although nearly half of the texts presented here have already been translated in GBT volumes or elsewhere, the translations have been completely revised here and transformed into what I hope will be a more natural and readable style. The previous translations were designed primarily to help scholars and specialists compare them with the original texts and the parallels in other languages, and therefore they are strictly literal, with no pretension to literary qualities or readability. In the new translations I have, however, still stayed as close as possible to the structure if not the individual words of the originals, in the hope of giving the reader a sense of their style and rhythm. Thus, for example, I have translated in full all of the repetitions, sometimes quite extensive, that are so characteristic of Buddhist literature; see, for example, the introduction to translation 12.

Two of the translations presented here (nos. 3 and 5) are based on my own previously published work, and two others (8 and 12) have not been translated before. The rest of the translations are revised, in whole or in part, from the work, published or unpublished, of their original editors, namely Mark Allon (1), Stefan Baums (10), Collett Cox (11), Andrew Glass (2a), Meihuang Lee (2b), and Timothy Lenz

(4, 6, and 7), on whose labors I have heavily relied and to whom I am heavily indebted.

In a deeper sense, though, all of the work in this and in the prior publications has been essentially collaborative in nature, representing, for the most part, the combined efforts of members of the research group of the University of Washington Early Buddhist Manuscripts Project (EBMP, formerly called British Library / University of Washington Early Buddhist Manuscripts Project), which was constituted in 1996 to sponsor and coordinate the publication of the then newly discovered Gandhāran manuscripts. The founding members of the group were Professor Collett Cox, the then-graduate students Timothy Lenz and Jason Neelis, and myself, who were joined in the following years by Mark Allon, Stefan Baums, Andrew Glass, Meihuang Lee (Tien-chang Shih), Joseph Marino III, Michael Skinner, and Fei Zhao, among many others. From the very inception of the project and up to the present, members and visitors have attended weekly meetings every Friday afternoon of what has come to be known as the Kharoṣṭhī Klub, in which the texts are read and interpreted in a collaborative effort. Thus the principal author of the definitive edition of each manuscript serves as the leader, compiler, and final authority, but the results reflect, to a considerable extent, the work of all of the members. The work is slow and painstaking; it is not unusual for a single difficult or incomplete word to be discussed for several hours as we explore all possible options for its interpretation, which usually involves searching through a multitude of Buddhist texts in a variety of languages, with each participant contributing on the basis of his or her area of expertise. Sometimes a long afternoon's work yields only the solution to a single problematic word, but even this much can be a satisfying experience for all concerned.

I therefore must express my debt and appreciation not only to the primary authors mentioned above but to all the many others—far too many to name—who have participated in our discussions over the last twenty years. Here I can mention only a few of the prominent scholars, most of whom have visited Kharoṣṭhī Klub at least once, who have made particularly significant contributions to EBMP studies: Daniel Boucher, Jens Braarvig, Harry Falk, Charles Hallisey, Paul Harrison, Jens-Uwe Hartmann, Oskar von Hinüber, Chanida Jantrasrisalai, Seishi Karashima, Kazunobu Matsuda, Jan Nattier, K. R. Norman, Gregory Schopen, Jonathan Silk, Peter Skilling, Ingo Strauch, and Klaus Wille. It has been a source of deep satisfaction and pleasure for my colleagues and me to have had the opportunity to work closely with so many great scholars of the past, present, and future. The participants in the Hwei-tai Seminar at Stanford University in October 2015, including Luis Gomez, Jan Nattier, and especially Paul Harrison, provided many helpful comments on the interpretation of texts, particularly for the *Perfection of Wisdom Sūtra* presented in translation 12 below.

I also wish to thank colleagues and others who have read various sections of this book and offered many helpful comments and suggestions: Collett Cox, Robin Dushman, Timothy Lenz, Alan Senauke, and especially Jason Neelis. I must also express my gratitude to the many institutions and individuals who have sponsored, facilitated, or otherwise promoted the work of the EBMP for so many years. Principal among these are the British Library, Centre for Advanced Study at the Norwegian Academy of Science and Letters, Dhammachai International Research Institute, Henry Luce Foundation, International Research Institute for Advanced Buddhology at Soka University, National Endowment for the Humanities, and the University of Washington (including the University of Washington Press). Among many individual supporters, Cris Cyders and Melinda Upton Cyders, along with another generous donor who prefers to remain anonymous, have been reliable friends of the EBMP over many years. We are also deeply grateful to the private owners and public curators who have generously and freely made the manuscripts available to us for study and publication, and thereby made this entire enterprise possible: Martin Schøyen, Robert Senior, the British Library, the Bibliothèque nationale de France, and the Library of Congress. Finally, I wish to thank my friends Tom Lowenstein and Bridget MacCarthy, who offered hospitality and good company during my many early visits to London in connection with this project.

Last but not least, I thank the two editors who helped me with this book. The first is David Kittelstrom, who made innumerable changes small and large that will make this book much better than it would have been without him. The second is my father, George Salomon, who though he died many years ago remains the ever-vigilant editor inside my head, reminding me always to think of the reader and to make every sentence clear, concise, and cogent.

Technical Notes

I have tried as far as possible to minimize untranslated words, but I have retained terms such as *arhat*, *tathāgata*, *dharma*, *nirvāṇa*, *brahman*, *saṃsāra*, *saṅgha*, and *stūpa* on the assumption that these will be familiar to readers with a modest background in Buddhism. I have also left unexplained some of the most basic Buddhist principles and concepts, such as the four noble truths or the eightfold path, on the assumption that the reader will be familiar with them or able to easily track them down.

In general, I have striven for consistency, translating each word the same way each time it occurs. But I have avoided a rigid mechanical application of this principle in connection with certain common words with wide ranges of meaning or with complex technical terms such as *saṃskāra*, which cannot be reduced to a single equivalent in all contexts. In the case of the untranslatable *dharma*, I have differentiated "Dharma" in the sense of the Buddhist doctrine from "dharma" as phenomenon, quality, element, and so on. Some of these decisions and alternatives are clarified in the glossary. Choosing such primary translations for important words often involves difficult and sometimes more or less arbitrary decisions; thus, for example, I have decided to translate *bhagavān*, the usual honorific title for the Buddha, as "lord," but this is only one of several possible choices, including "exalted one" or "master," no one of which is obviously superior. In choosing translations for technical vocabulary, I have often followed the example of Bhikkhu Bodhi's translations of the Pali *Saṃyutta-* and *Aṅguttara-nikāya*s.[1]

Because of the several languages involved in this material, it is difficult to maintain perfect consistency in citing Indian names and untranslated Buddhist technical terms that have different forms in Gāndhārī, Sanskrit, and Pali. In general, I have used the Sanskrit form as the default, except where a Gāndhārī or Pali term is specifically being presented or discussed. Thus, for example, I use *sūtra* with reference to texts in all languages, even in some cases where it might seem odd to refer to a Pali *sutta* this way. In the case of important terms, I have generally supplied both the Sanskrit and Pali forms, noted as "Skt" and "P" respectively, since one or the other of them may be more familiar to readers, depending on their backgrounds. Where no alternate form is offered, as for words like *buddha* or *vinaya*, this means that the form is the same in Sanskrit and Pali.

Presenting comprehensible translations of these sometimes very fragmentary texts often requires that missing words or phrases be filled in, either internally on the basis of repeated patterns in the manuscript itself or from external sources such as parallel or related texts in other languages. All such supplementary elements in the translations are indicated in square brackets.

Source Texts

1. Three Numerically Grouped Sūtras: British Library fragments 12+14
2. Five Thematically Grouped Sūtras: Senior scrolls 5 (translations a–d) and 19 (translation e)
3. The *Rhinoceros Sūtra*: British Library fragment 5B

4. A Chapter from the Gāndhārī *Dharmapada*: "The Monk": Khotan Dharmapada + British Library fragments 16+25
5. *Songs of Lake Anavatapta*: British Library fragment 1
6. Stories of Previous Lives and Other Legends: British Library fragment 16+25
7. Avadāna Legends: British Library fragment 1
8. The *Many-Buddhas Sūtra*: Library of Congress scroll
9. A Commentary on the *Sūtra of Chanting Together*: British Library fragment 15
10. A Commentary on Canonical Verses: British Library fragments 9 and 13
11. An Abhidharma Treatise on Time and Existence: British Library fragment 28
12. The *Perfection of Wisdom Sūtra*: Split collection, fragment 5

Introduction

The Rediscovery of Gandhāran Buddhist Literature

The Gandhāran Buddhist scrolls first came to my attention in 1994, when I received a set of blurry black-and-white photographs of some old manuscripts that had recently been acquired by the British Library. Having worked for many years on Buddhist dedicatory inscriptions in stone or on metal plaques from the ancient region of Gandhāra in modern northwestern Pakistan, it was immediately clear to me that these were genuine Buddhist manuscripts written in the Kharoṣṭhī script and Gāndhārī language of that region, dating from about the first or second centuries of the Common Era. This made them the oldest surviving specimens of original Buddhist texts in the world, as well as the oldest Indian manuscripts of any type, and the discovery was widely reported in media worldwide. Subsequent studies have confirmed that these and the other similar materials that were discovered in the following years date from between the first century BCE and the third century CE.

In July 1995 I took the first of many trips to London to see the collection itself, which turned out to consist of twenty-nine fragments of scrolls made of extremely brittle birchbark.[2] I spent my first few days in London surveying the material in a combined fog of excitement, puzzlement, and jet lag, and the more I pored over the scrolls, the larger loomed the intimidating dimensions of the work that would be

Figure 1. The clay pot (British Library pot D) that contained the British Library Kharoṣṭhī scrolls.

involved in reading and translating them. The prospect was daunting not only in terms of the large amount of material but also its generally poor condition, for all of the scrolls were fragmentary in some degree, and some of them were little more than loose scraps. At some time in antiquity they had been rolled up into tight, cigar-shaped packages, packed into a clay water jug, and buried underground. The jug itself provided an important clue as to their sectarian affiliation in the form of an inked inscription recording it as a gift "To the universal community, in the possession of the Dharmaguptakas," referring to one of the traditional eighteen *nikāya*s, or "schools," of Indian Buddhism.[3]

The circumstances of the burial and subsequent rediscovery of the scrolls are unfortunately unknown, as they had already passed through the antiquities market in Pakistan by the time they became known to the scholarly world, and the only information available about their original provenance consisted of unreliable second- or third-hand rumors. Nevertheless, all indications are that they were found

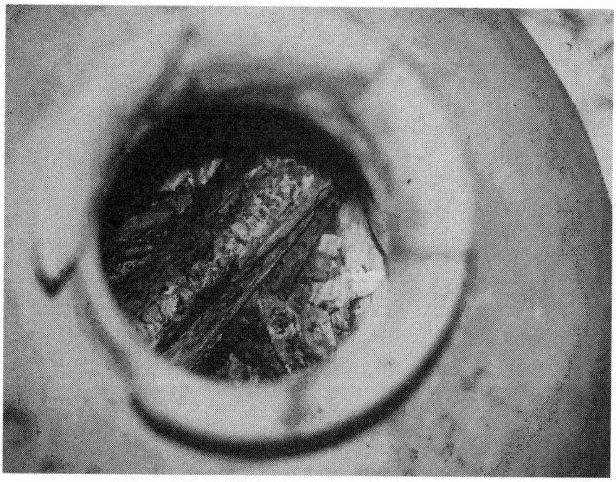

Figure 2. The British Library scrolls in their original position inside the clay pot.

in a Buddhist stūpa or monastic complex in the area of Haḍḍa, near modern Jalalabad in eastern Afghanistan, which had been one of the great centers of Buddhist intellectual life in the early centuries of the Common Era. The scrolls had evidently been interred in a ritual burial similar to that accorded to the bodily remains of deceased monks. For from a Buddhist point of view, monks and manuscripts are analogous in that they are both keepers of the Dharma; that is to say, they serve to protect and transmit the precious words of the Buddha. The practice of ritually burying manuscripts may also have been motivated by a desire to insure the survival of the Dharma in future centuries, since the Buddha is said to have predicted that his teachings would be forgotten in the centuries following his earthly decease and entry into nirvāṇa.[4] At least some of the scrolls were apparently already old and decrepit when they were interred, and several of them had secondary notations such as "All has been written today," apparently indicating that they had been recopied onto new scrolls and were ready for interment.

But after nearly two thousand years underground, they had suffered a great deal of damage. Birchbark, when new and fresh, is supple, tough, and attractive. But as it dries out, it becomes extremely brittle,

Figure 3. British Library fragments 16–19 before unrolling and conservation.

so that many of the scrolls, especially those that had lain at the bottom of the pot, had degenerated into flat stacks of horizontal strips. The osmosis of groundwater through the walls of the pot also caused the portions of the scrolls that had been in contact with the sides to decompose, so that in many cases their edges, and often larger sections, had disintegrated completely. By the time I first saw them, the scrolls had already been painstakingly unrolled by the conservation staff of the British Library's Oriental and India Office division and permanently mounted between glass sheets in fifty-six separate frames.

Despite my awe at seeing this collection of dozens of Buddhist texts in Gāndhārī, I was not entirely surprised that it had come to light. For, almost exactly one hundred years earlier, a single specimen of a similar Gandhāran manuscript had been discovered, under unclear circumstances, in the region of the Central Asian city of Khotan in the modern Xinjiang Uyghur Autonomous Region of China. The Khotan scroll contained a previously unknown version in Gāndhārī

Figure 4. British Library conservators unrolling the scrolls.

language of the popular Buddhist verse anthology entitled *Dharmapada* ("Words of the Dharma"), one chapter of which is presented as translation 4 in this book. For the next century, this manuscript constituted virtually the only known specimen, except for a few other tiny scraps, of Buddhist literature in the ancient language of the Gandhāra region. But on the basis of this unique manuscript it had been hypothesized that there must have once existed a more extensive Buddhist literature, perhaps even an entire canon, in Gāndhārī. Now, a century later, this hypothesis was about to be confirmed.

The first task was to identify the texts and to determine their relationship to other previously known Buddhist literature. After a few days of random grazing through the texts, the first breakthrough came after I noticed that in one of them an unfamiliar word, *kharga*, recurred in each line. At the time, I was camping out in the living room-cum-library of the London home of an old friend, the independent Buddhist scholar Tom Lowenstein. While randomly scanning his bookshelves one evening, my eye fell on a book by the great British Pali scholar K. R. Norman entitled *The Rhinoceros Horn and Other Early Buddhist Poems*, which consists of a translation of the Pali

Figure 5. A Gandhāran birchbark manuscript unrolled.
Senior scroll 19, recto, "The Parable of the Log" (translation 2e).

anthology of verse sūtras called *Suttanipāta* (*Collection of Sūtras*). I then immediately realized that the repeated word *kharga* must be the Gāndhārī equivalent of Pali *khagga*, "rhinoceros," and that the manuscript consisted of a Gāndhārī version of the well-known *Rhinoceros Sūtra* (*Khaggavisāṇa-sutta*), which is one of the poems incorporated into the *Suttanipāta*. Since each verse of this poem concludes with the refrain "Wander alone like the rhinoceros," the repetition in each line of the corresponding word in its Gāndhārī form removed any doubt about its contents. This poem would soon become the focus of my first major project of editing, interpreting, and translating a Gāndhārī manuscript. The results of that project, in the form of a scholarly edition and study,[5] are summarized here in translation 3.

A second breakthrough came in connection with another scroll in which I noticed the repeated phrase *anodate mahasare*. Gradually it dawned on me that must correspond to a Sanskrit phrase, *anavatapte mahāhrade*, "at the great Lake Anavatapta," which is the refrain of another well-known poem, the *Anavataptagāthā* or *Songs of Lake*

Anavatapta. This text describes how the Buddha and his disciples revealed, while seated on giant lotuses in the sacred Lake Anavatapta in the high Himalayas, the karmic factors from their past lives that led them to their present condition. A little further checking quickly confirmed that this was an early Gāndhārī version of this popular poem previously known in Sanskrit, Tibetan, and Chinese versions. This was to be the topic of my second editing project, published in 2008, which is presented in this book as translation 5.

Gradually several other texts were identified, at least as to their genre if not their precise contents. They proved to embrace a wide variety of contents, styles, and subjects: poems, sūtras and commentaries on sūtras, compilations of legends about the lives of famous figures in Buddhist history, commentaries and scholastic treatises on the fine points of Buddhist doctrines, hymns in praise of the Buddha, as well as quite a few unidentified and unclassifiable pieces. It also became evident that the manuscripts were the work of some twenty different scribes, many of whose works could be easily recognized from their distinctive hands. We had, in short, what seemed to be a random selection or culling of the contents of a monastic library, or perhaps of a personal manuscript collection, probably dating from the first century CE.

As work went on in the course of this and many subsequent trips to London, it became abundantly clear to me that the complete study of the British Library scrolls would occupy far more than one lifetime of one scholar. Deciphering fragmentary manuscripts in an incompletely known language requires special expertise in each of the various genres involved, and it was obvious that this was a job for a team, not an individual. For this, I turned first to my colleague and collaborator of many years, Professor Collett Cox, an expert in scholastic works of the *abhidharma* class, which happened to be abundantly attested among the British Library scrolls, and which were also one of the areas of Buddhist literature that I felt least qualified to work with. The two of us then teamed up, and with the generous support of officials of the British Library and of our home institution, the University of

Washington, established in September 1996 the British Library / University of Washington Early Buddhist Manuscripts Project (EBMP), dedicated to the study and publication of the British Library Kharoṣṭhī scrolls. Early on in the project an agreement was reached with the University of Washington Press to publish in a dedicated series entitled Gandhāran Buddhist Texts (GBT) the results of research by EBMP members and associated scholars.[6]

The majority of the manuscripts presented in this book (translations 1, 3, 5–7, and 9–11) belong to the British Library collection, mainly because that group, being the first to be discovered, is the one that has been most intensively studied to date. But in the years and decades following the discovery of the British Library scrolls, several more major groups of similar and equally important manuscripts, as well as some isolated individual texts, were discovered. By now over two hundred significant bodies of text are available for study. The majority have been made available for scholarly research and are being studied and published under the auspices of the University of Washington Early Buddhist Manuscripts Project and the parallel project Buddhist Manuscripts from Gandhāra at the Bavarian Academy of Sciences and Humanities in Munich. The complete detailed study of this material is a huge job that will take many years to complete, but in the meantime Gāndhārī literature has already been established as a separate subfield of Buddhist studies, and from it a steady flow of scholarly publications can be expected to continue for a long time to come.[7] These new materials are described in chapters 2 and 3, but first we turn to the historical and cultural background of these manuscripts and the world that produced them.

PART I

Contexts

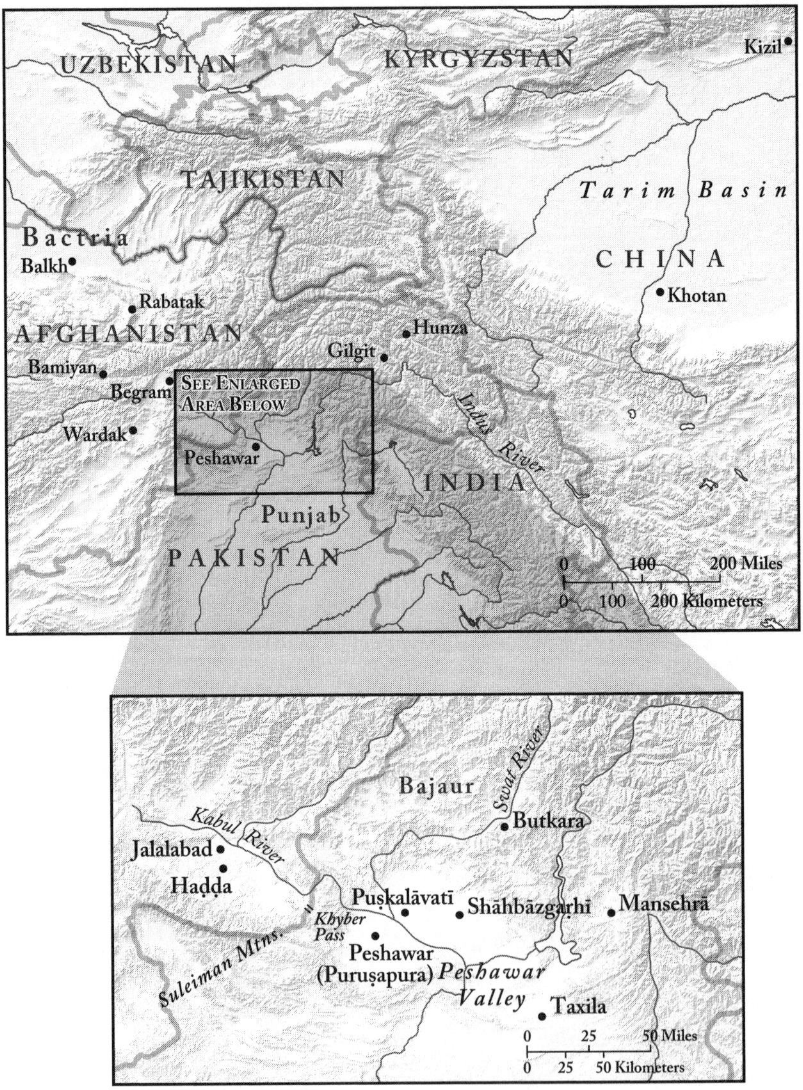

Map 1. Greater Gandhāra.

1. The World of Gandhāran Buddhism

Gandhāra and India's Northwest Frontier

Gandhāra is the ancient name, attested since the time of early Vedic texts dating back at least three thousand years, for the Peshawar Valley and adjoining regions along the Kabul River, stretching for about one hundred miles between the Suleiman Mountains on the edge of the Iranian plateau to the west and the Indus River on the east. In modern terms, Gandhāra corresponds to the area around Peshawar, capital of the Khyber Pakhtunkhwa Province (formerly North-West Frontier Province) of Pakistan.

But the term Gandhāra—or more accurately, Greater Gandhāra—is also applied more broadly to surrounding areas. This territory includes the Swat Valley to the north, the western Punjab including the ancient metropolis of Taxila to the east, eastern Afghanistan to the west, and in the north Bactria (modern northern Afghanistan and southern Uzbekistan), and even parts of the region around the Tarim Basin in Central Asia in the modern Xinjiang Uyghur Autonomous Region of China. All of these regions came under the cultural influence of Gandhāra during its glory days in the early centuries of the Common Era and thereby adopted the Gāndhārī language as a literary and administrative medium and Gandhāran Buddhism as their dominant religion. Thus Greater Gandhāra can be understood as a primarily linguistic rather than a political term, that is, as comprising the regions where Gāndhārī was the indigenous or adopted language.

With the spread of Gandhāran cultural and political power into Central Asia, particularly under the Kuṣāṇa emperors in the first and second centuries CE, Gandhāra came to be directly linked into the commerce of the silk roads, tapping into the lucrative trade in luxury goods between China and the Western world. This source of wealth was no doubt one of the major factors in the power and prosperity of the Kuṣāṇas. Besides the economic benefits that the silk road traffic brought to Gandhāra, it also provided cultural and artistic stimuli leading to the development of an eclectic Buddhist culture incorporating Central Asian and Hellenistic ideas and imagery, while also opening the way for the exportation of Buddhism into Central Asia and China.

The Bloody History of Paradise

In 1978, a Japanese rock group called Godiego recorded in English a song called "Gandhara" as the theme song for the television drama *Saiyūki*, or "Monkey." These lyrics read in part:

> A long time ago when men were all babes,
> there was a land of the free.
> Fantasy and dreams
> were its untouched wealth,
> and goodness and love were real.
> Each man desires to reach Gandhara,
> his very own utopia.
> In the striving, in the seeking soul,
> man can see Gandhara.
> In Gandhara, Gandhara,
> they say it was in India.
> Gandhara, Gandhara,
> the place of light, Gandhara.

Here we see the image of Gandhāra as it was, and still is, imagined

Figure 6. The Manikiala stūpa.

by East Asian Buddhists: a magical holy land of peace and harmony. The television show *Saiyūki* was based on a popular Chinese novel of the sixteenth century, an imaginative account of the famous Buddhist monk Xuanzang's pilgrimage to Gandhāra and other parts of India nearly a millennium earlier. This idealized presentation of Gandhāra is a distant reflection of the glory days of Gandhāran Buddhism in the early years of the Common Era. Even by the time of Xuanzang's epic journey to India in the early seventh century, Buddhism had largely declined in Gandhāra. But he was still able to see its legacy in the form of stūpas and other monuments, many of which still dot the landscape today, especially in the Swat Valley, and to collect the legends of its splendors and wonders in the centuries before his time.

The situation in this region today could hardly be more different. It is currently the epicenter of an ongoing bitter struggle between radical Islamists on one side and the ruling powers of Pakistan and Afghanistan on the other, each side fueled by foreign supporters. The willful destruction of the colossal Buddhas of Bamiyan, Afghanistan, by the Taliban in 2001 and the assassination of Osama bin Laden by American military forces in Abbotabad, Pakistan, in 2011, both within the territory of Greater Gandhāra, are only two of the most widely publicized battles in this war between the forces of fundamentalism and modernism. Viewed from a broad historic perspective, these conflicts are a sequel to the three Anglo-Afghan wars of the nineteenth and early twentieth centuries, and to the Great Game, the struggle throughout the nineteenth century between the expanding British and Russian empires for control of Afghanistan.

But even then, strife was nothing new to this region. Throughout history, from the earliest recorded times, Gandhāra has been the scene of frequent wars and invasions from the west into the Indian subcontinent. This turbulent history is the inevitable outcome of its geographical and cultural setting. Gandhāra is an archetypal frontier region situated on a fault line between major geo-cultural zones. Lying on the seam between the Iranian world to the west, the Indian world to the east, and Central Asia to the north, it is the place where, again and again throughout history, these and sometimes other worlds have collided. The passes linking the Iranian plateau and the plains of the Punjab and northern India, including the fabled Khyber Pass, which leads directly into Gandhāra proper, have served for thousands of years as a geographical funnel into India, whose fertility, vast population, and fabled luxuries have enticed conquerors and settlers since the very dawn of history. It was through this funnel that, some four millennia ago, speakers of Indo-European languages began entering northern India, where they would establish the Sanskritic culture that has predominated in the Indian cultural world ever since.

In view of its role as a frontier region and zone of transit between several cultural regions, it is not surprising that Gandhāra has always had a distinct and complex cultural identity. On the one hand, Gandhāra has usually been culturally more part of India than of the Iranian world, despite the constant influence of and frequent political domination from the west, whether Hellenistic, Iranian, Afghan, or Central Asian. In this regard, the rugged mountains that define the western border of Gandhāra proper have also functioned as a cultural boundary, if a porous one. But on the other hand, even within the Indian cultural zone

Gandhāra has always stood apart as a land on the fringe, with its own distinct ways and identity, and relationships between Gandhāra and the Indian heartland often seem to involve a certain ambivalence. Even in the early Vedic culture some three millennia ago, which was centered in the neighboring Punjab region to the east, Gandhāra was viewed as a foreign land at the outer limits of the known world, strange and vaguely threatening. The earliest Vedic text, the *Ṛg Veda*, barely mentions Gandhāra, referring only once to wool from Gandhāra, and also, more or less in passing, to the Kabul (*Kubhā*) and Swat (*Suvāstu*) Rivers. The somewhat later *Atharva Veda*, datable to around the early first millennium BCE, mentions Gandhāra only in a charm intended to dispel fevers to the far distant lands to the west and east: "We send the fever to the lands of Gandhāri, Mujavat, Anga, and Magadha."[8] In a later stage of Vedic literature, the *Chāndogya Upaniṣad* contains a parable of a man from Gandhāra who must find the way back to his distant homeland.[9]

But as the cultural purview of the heartland Indian culture in the Gangetic plain expanded in subsequent centuries, Gandhāra began to be brought within the pale. Early Buddhist literature contains several lists of the sixteen great countries of India in the Buddha's time, and these usually include Gandhāra along with Kamboja (Afghanistan) as the westernmost places. Taxila (Skt *Takṣaśilā*, Pali *Takkasilā*) is mentioned frequently in the prose commentaries on the *jātaka* stories of the Buddha's past lives as a center of learning to which young men were sent for their education. In the Brahmanical/Hindu tradition of the post-Vedic period, too, Gandhāra seems no longer to be perceived as a foreign land. For example, Pāṇini, the revered supreme grammarian of Sanskrit, was said to have come from the town of Śālātura in the eastern fringe of Gandhāra. Gandhāra is also within the purview of the Mahābhārata epic, in which its king, Subala, and especially his daughter, Gāndhārī—whose name means "woman of Gandhāra"—play major roles. Moreover, the first complete recitation of the entire epic was said to have taken place at Taxila.

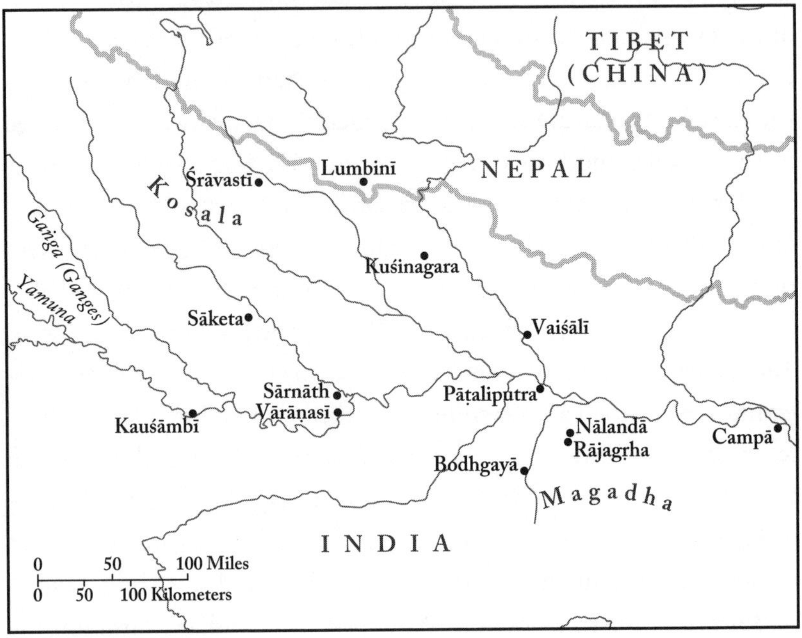

Map 2. The World of Early Buddhism

Early Buddhism and Gandhāra

The geographic footprint of early Buddhism was determined by the regions in which the Buddha wandered during his lifetime, sometime between the sixth and fourth centuries BCE.[10] During and shortly after the Buddha's lifetime, Buddhism was limited to the central Ganges-Yamuna Valley and the surrounding regions of north-central and northeastern India, hundreds of miles distant from Gandhāra. This can be seen from the locations of the four most sacred sites of Buddhism: Lumbinī, the Buddha's birthplace in Nepal's Terai region, near the Indian border; Bodhgayā in Bihar, where he attained enlightenment; Sārnāth, near Vārāṇasī in eastern Uttar Pradesh, where he first preached the Dharma; and Kuśinagara in the northeastern corner of Uttar Pradesh, where his last life ended in his *parinirvāṇa.* A similar picture emerges from a study of the names of the places mentioned in early Buddhist literature, especially the locations where he was said to have expounded the various sūtras. By far the most common references—nearly 60 percent according to a representative sampling of Pali texts[11]—are places in and around the city of Śrāvastī, the capital of the Kosala kingdom in central north India. After Śrāvastī, the most frequently mentioned location is Rājagṛha, the capital of the kingdom of Magadha, to the southeast of Kosala. Other commonly cited cities are Sāketa, Vaiśālī, Kauśāmbī, Vārāṇasī, and Campā, all of which lie in adjoining territories in and around the central and eastern Ganges Valley. The kingdoms of Kosala and Magadha were ruled during the Buddha's lifetime by Kings Prasenajit and Ajātaśatru, and the prestige and material support afforded by their patronage was no doubt a major reason that the Buddha and his followers spent so much of their time in their capitals. The crucial importance of royal patronage for the maintenance and expansion of Buddhist monastic communities is a consistent pattern throughout the subsequent history of Buddhism in India and elsewhere, as we will see in connection with the two other prototypical royal patrons of Buddhism, Aśoka and Kaniṣka.

Gandhāra, in contrast, is still at the margins in early Buddhism. It is mentioned only in the conventional listings of the sixteen great countries of India, and even there it is absent from some versions. Although Taxila, the great metropolis of the northwest, is frequently referred to in the prose commentary on the *Jātakas* and in other Pali commentaries, it is never mentioned in the early sūtras. Thus we can conclude that Gandhāra was a distant land that was probably known only faintly and indirectly to the Buddha and his followers.

Aśoka and the Mauryan Empire

Very little is known of the history of Gandhāra until the time of the Achaemenid Empire of Iran, which conquered Gandhāra and adjoining territories and incorporated them into its eastern flank between the sixth and fourth centuries BCE. After Alexander the Great destroyed the Achaemenid Empire in 331 BCE, he went on to conquer Gandhāra en route to his long-cherished goal of incorporating the wonderland of India into a realm that would embrace the entire known world. But soon after this, his enterprise failed as his army, weary after eight years of fighting, refused to go on beyond the rivers of the Punjab. His dream shattered, Alexander had to turn back westward and died three years after leaving India.

Within a few years after Alexander's incursion, Gandhāra was incorporated into the newly born Indian empire of the mighty Mauryan dynasty, which rapidly grew into the first great transregional empire that controlled the majority of the Indian subcontinent. Under its founder, Candragupta Maurya, who ruled from approximately 324 to 300 BCE, Gandhāra and adjoining regions, along with most of northern and central India, came for the first time under the rule of an Indian power based far to the east in Pāṭaliputra (modern Patna, Bihar), in northeastern India. Chandragupta Maurya's grandson Aśoka (ca. 273–232 BCE) was to become the greatest royal patron of Buddhism, "the Constantine of Buddhism," under whose sponsorship Buddhism spread in all directions, far beyond its early strongholds in north and eastern India, and began to develop into a pan-Indian and ultimately into a world religion. It is at this point that Gandhāra became part of the Buddhist world.

We know precious little about the historical development of Buddhism between the lifetime of the Buddha and the reign of Aśoka. There are no inscriptions or other primary historical sources to guide us. The only information comes from the Buddhist texts themselves. But Buddhist canonical texts are uniformly ahistorical, in the sense that they are never dated and mention historical circumstances, if at all, only in passing and only with reference to some point of Buddhist teaching or doctrine. Although a sūtra must, in order to be considered authentic and authoritative, be prefaced with a *nidāna*, that is, a statement of when and where it was preached, this preface never includes a date. The time is invariably stated only as "Thus have I heard: at one time . . . " (Skt *evaṃ me śrutam: ekasmin samaye . . .*), but that "time" is never located in a historical sequence. As a result, the chronology of early Buddhist literature, and thus the history of early Buddhism, can be deduced only by internal comparisons and other indirect methods, and at best only in relative terms. We have no way to attach specific dates to any of the texts and events of early Buddhism whereby we might trace its spread and development; indeed, we do not even know with any precision when the Buddha himself lived.

This situation changes drastically with the reign of Aśoka. Aśoka was the first Indian monarch who saw fit not only to issue public proclamations to his subjects in all parts of his vast realm but, more importantly, to have them carved onto natural rock surfaces or artificial stone pillars, with the result that many of them have survived to the present day. In this, he was probably inspired by the monumental trilingual inscriptions of the Achaemenid kings whose territories he had inherited. Several of Aśoka's inscriptions are dated by the year of his reign. The absolute chronological value of those dates has been determined with reasonable certainty and precision on the basis of his reference to five contemporary Hellenistic kings of the Western world to whom Aśoka addressed his message of "conquest by dharma." Since the dates of these Hellenistic kings—Antiochus (*Antiyoka*) of Syria, Ptolemy (*Turamāya*) of Egypt, Antigones (*Antikini*) of Macedonia, Magas (*Maka*) of Cyrene (North Africa), and Alexander (*Alikasudara*) of Greece—are well attested in classical historical tradition, they allow us to correlate Aśoka's regnal years to a known chronology, and thereby to establish the dates of his rule to approximately 273–232 BCE.

With the appearance of the Aśokan inscriptions, we have the first indication, albeit indirect, of a Buddhist presence in the region of Gandhāra. The matter is complicated, however, by the ambiguous character of these inscriptions. They fall into four main classes, which in turn may be divided into two subsets: first, those with explicit Buddhist content, namely the *minor rock edicts* and the *separate pillar edicts*, and second, the non-Buddhist inscriptions, namely the *major rock edicts* and the *major pillar edicts*. In the latter set, Aśoka promulgates a neutral, all-encompassing *dhamma* (= Skt *dharma*) that was designed to appeal to all of his diverse subjects, carefully avoiding any specific sectarian terms or ideas.

In light of this scrupulous neutrality, some historians have even questioned whether Aśoka was really a Buddhist, but this skepticism is excessive. For in his explicitly Buddhist inscriptions, he speaks in a very direct and personal manner of his conviction and dedication to the Buddhist Dharma. For example, in his minor rock edicts Aśoka confesses that although he had joined the Buddhist saṅgha as a lay follower, he felt dissatisfied with his spiritual progress during the first year and was now applying himself more diligently. Also, in his rock edict at Bairāṭ in Rajasthan he addresses himself directly to the local Buddhist monastic community and recommends seven canonical texts for special attention and study.[12]

Thus there can be no reasonable doubt that Aśoka was personally a committed Buddhist. In his mixed messages, Aśoka follows the typical pattern of Indian kings who patronized multiple religions, as we shall also see in connection with the Kuṣāṇa emperors some four centuries later. In the complex religious mosaic of traditional India, it was only normal that the ruler of a large kingdom would strive to appear to be all things to all of his people.

Aśoka's fourteen major rock edicts, recorded in three different local dialects in nine places around India, include two in eastern Gandhāra at two adjacent sites, Shāhbazgaṛhī and Mansehrā. But the problem with regard to our main concern, namely the origins of Buddhism in Gandhāra, is that both of these are nonsectarian edicts and include none of his explicitly Buddhist proclamations. Therefore we cannot assume on the basis of the inscriptions alone that Buddhism had been brought to Gandhāra by Aśoka. To determine the early history of Buddhism in Gandhāra, we need to examine other types of information, namely textual and archaeological materials.

With regard to the first category, we turn to an extensive body of legends about Aśoka preserved in various postcanonical Buddhist texts, most notably in the *Mahāvaṃsa* (the ecclesiastical chronicle of Sri Lanka) and in collections of *avadāna* legends in Sanskrit and in Chinese translation that are sometimes grouped together under the heading "Legends of Aśoka" (*Aśokāvadāna*).[13] In these stories, Aśoka is presented as the ideal Buddhist emperor and lavish patron of the saṅgha, one who gave up to it everything he owned, down to his last possession—half a myrobalan fruit.

Aśoka's image is modeled on the pattern of the royal patrons of the Buddha's lifetime, Prasenajit and Ajātaśatru, but on a far vaster scale. His most important act of patronage, reported in the Legends of Aśoka, was to retrieve the relics of the Buddha, which after his parinirvāṇa had been divided and buried in eight stūpas, and to redistribute them into 84,000 stūpas, which he had caused to be constructed throughout the earth on a single day and which came to be known as the *dharmarājikā*, the stūpas "of the Dharma-king." This widespread legend about Aśoka can be understood as a symbolic or mythologized presentation of his role in promoting the spread of Buddhism beyond its original homeland in central north India and into his vast territories and sphere of influence, comprising not only nearly all of the Indian subcontinent but also adjoining areas of Afghanistan. In short, Aśoka is portrayed as the patron who changed Buddhism from a regional religion into a pan-Indian, and eventually a pan-Asian, one.

The magical multiplication of the relics and their distribution far and wide has a resounding echo in the archaeological record, albeit only from a later period. The abundant relic deposit inscriptions from Gandhāra in subsequent centuries often celebrate the foundation of relic stūpas in "a part of the earth where a relic foundation had never been made before" (*apratiṣṭhāpitapūrve pṛthivīpradeśe*). This frequent addition to the basic relic-dedication formula reflects the belief that establishing a relic in a region where this had not previously been done earns the donor or sponsor an extra share of karmic merit, a notion that is explicitly confirmed in canonical texts.[14] This shows how the cult of the Buddha's relics continued, even after Aśoka's time, to serve as both a mechanism of and a symbol for the implantation of Buddhism in new territories.

Particularly interesting for our purposes is a secondary episode in the legend of Aśoka and the relics, in which the residents of Taxila request an extra share of relics, thirty-six sets in all, one for each thousand residents of the city.[15] Aśoka responds that he could give them only one set of relics, and so to respect their wishes, he would have to kill 35,000 of them. At this point, the people of Taxila quite sensibly withdraw their greedy request. This can be understood as a mythologized reference to the special vitality of the Buddhist relic cult in Gandhāra, as shown by the abundance of Buddhist reliquaries, inscribed and uninscribed, that have been found in that region; over four hundred examples are collected in a recent comprehensive study.[16]

Aśoka's harsh response to the pious greed of the Taxilans may seem shocking in view of his portrayal in Buddhist literature as an ideal Buddhist emperor, and even more so by comparison with his self-presentation as a benevolent and gentle ruler in his inscriptions. But there is much more to Aśoka than this; he is on multiple levels a complex and enigmatic figure. Despite the veneration he receives in Buddhist texts, his character in them is ambiguous. For example, he is described as a monster of cruelty before his conversion to Buddhism. This can of course be understood as the usual hyperbolic rhetoric of the reformed convert, but even after Aśoka becomes a Buddhist, he is still viewed with some unease and ambivalence, as shown by this and other episodes.[17] In part, this is no doubt a reflection of the tense symbiosis between Buddhist institutions and secular powers that is a constant of the history of Buddhism, but it is also characteristic of Aśoka's many-faceted character. In fact, Aśoka's own inscriptions and the Buddhist legends also have little, if anything in common,[18] and even for the most part refer to him by different names. In Buddhist literature he is always called Aśoka, while in the inscriptions he almost always refers to himself as Devānaṃpiya Piyadassī, "beloved of the gods, of loving regard," except for a few places where he adds the name Aśoka.

But the evidence presented so far still does not prove that Aśoka was actually responsible for the implantation of Buddhism in Gandhāra. None of the many inscribed reliquaries is earlier than the second century BCE, at least a century or so after Aśoka. This raises the suspicion that the legends about Aśoka's role in Buddhist literature represent later fabrications that were anachronistically cast back to the time of the archetypal royal patron and credited to him. Unfortunately, other indications of Aśoka's role in the spread of Buddhism into Gandhāra are also less than conclusive. Xuanzang, visiting Gandhāra and other parts of India in the first half of the seventh century, reported that six stūpas that he saw in Gandhāra had been built by Aśoka, but this too reflects the legends current in his time, nearly a millennium after Aśoka, so that their historical accuracy is by no means beyond doubt. Some relatively early inscriptions also credit Aśoka with this achievement; for instance, an inscription of the early first century CE refers to the rededication of relics that had been taken "from a stūpa of the Mauryan time,"[19] while an inscribed statue of the Buddha of about the same period records its dedication to a *dharmarājikā* stūpa that had been established by King Aśoka.[20]

One more clue to Aśoka's role in the spread of Buddhism to Gandhāra involves a passage from the *Mahāvaṃsa*. This passage records the names of the missionaries who were sent to various regions of India after the third great Buddhist council, which had been convened by Aśoka at his capital, Pāṭaliputra. According to this account, a monk named Majjhantika was sent to the northwest, where he converted Gandhāra and Kashmir by preaching the *Āsīvisopama Sutta*. As it happens, this sūtra (in Gāndhārī, *aśiviṣaama*) is among the several dozen whose names are included in the list of texts in one of the index scrolls in the Senior collection of Gāndhārī manuscripts, although the text of the sūtra itself has not been found.[21] This could be simply a coincidence, but the presence of this sūtra in Gandhāra might also support the accuracy of the tradition recorded in the *Mahāvaṃsa* regarding the conversion of Gandhāra in Aśoka's time.

The Indo-Greeks

Even after the time of Aśoka, for about a century there is very little direct, datable evidence for Buddhist activity in Gandhāra. After the decline of the Mauryas in the early second century BCE, a succession of invaders and conquerors from the west dominated Gandhāra for four centuries. The first phase of this period involved the Bactrian Greeks and Indo-Greeks, inheritors of Alexander's Hellenistic legacy in the eastern world, who conquered Gandhāra and other parts of northern India in the second and early first centuries BCE. During this period the Buddhist presence in Gandhāra gradually becomes more distinctly visible, until it reaches a climax in the first two centuries of the Common Era. But as is typically the case in the study of ancient India, our knowledge of the history of the thirty-odd Greek kings of Bactria and India is very incomplete. The main source for the history of this period is the abundant coinage of these kings; indeed, most of them are known from coins alone. Inscriptions, especially dated inscriptions, which are typically the best source of historical information in early India, are still very rare in this phase. The result is that the sequence and chronology of the kings is known only tentatively and approximately, as it has had to be reconstructed on the basis of interpretations, often quite subjective and controversial, of the features and relationships of the various coins.

Nonetheless, one point that is generally agreed on is that Menander, the Indo-Greek king who ruled in Gandhāra and adjoining parts of northern India around the middle of the second century BCE,[22] stands out as one of the most prominent and influential of the Greek kings of India. This conclusion is based, first of all, on the abundance of his coins, which are the most numerous among all of the Indo-Greek rulers and which are found over a wide range from eastern Afghanistan to the central Ganges Valley.[23] But Menander's greatest claim to fame is the paracanonical[24] Buddhist text whose title contains the Pali rendering of his name, the *Questions of Milinda* (*Milindapañha*). This work

Figure 7. A coin of Menander.

was probably originally composed in Gāndhārī, but it survives only in Pali and Chinese translations.[25] The text is set in Menander's capital, Sāgala, whose exact location is uncertain but was probably in the Punjab. This long text (some three hundred pages in Horner's translation) consists of a series of philosophical dialogues about Buddhist ideas and principles between the king and a learned Buddhist monk named Nāgasena. The dialogues show the king to be a penetrating thinker who expresses a lively interest in Buddhism and asks Nāgasena difficult questions about the subtleties of Buddhist doctrine.

At the end of the Pali text, King Milinda declares his acceptance of the Dharma, becomes a lay follower under the guidance of Nāgasena, and renounces his kingdom, leaving it to his son. He declares, "Among the Buddha's followers, none but the elder Sāriputra compares to you for answering questions. . . . Forgive me my transgressions, Venerable Nāgasena. Accept me as a lay follower, Venerable Nāgasena, as one who goes for refuge from this day forth."[26] However, this passage occurs only in the longer Pali version and is absent from the Chinese translation. Other than his appearance in his book of questions, Menander appears hardly anywhere else in Buddhist tradition, so that the historicity of Menander's supposed conversion to Buddhism has been questioned by many historians.[27]

In many respects, including its content, style, format, and language, as well as its ambiguous status in the canon, the *Questions of Milinda* is a most unusual text. A further problem is that the Chinese translation agrees only partially with the Pali version. The extant Pali text, in seven sections, is much longer than the Chinese, which corresponds to only the first three sections of the Pali. The last four parts of the Pali version therefore are probably later additions to the original text, so that the Pali seems to be a composite of originally separate materials cobbled together by the device of attributing them to the dialogue of Menander and Nāgasena.

It has been suggested that the original text of the *Questions of Milinda* was in Sanskrit rather than Pali, but given its association with the northwest, it is more likely that its original language was Gāndhārī.[28] Recently a few small fragments have been discovered of a Gāndhārī text that has some resemblance to the *Questions of Milinda*, including a reference to Nāgasena, but they seem to belong to some related tradition rather than to the *Questions* itself.

Thus Menander's role in the implantation of Buddhism in the northwest, if any, was by no means comparable to that of Aśoka, the archetypal royal patron of Buddhism. Menander's coinage, though abundant and important for historical studies, tells us little about Buddhism; a few of his bronze coins have a wheel design, which has been taken by some as the Buddhist symbol for the wheel of the law (*dharmacakra*), but this is uncertain. Quite likely Menander, like most kings of ancient India, engaged in multiple patronage, showing himself as a Buddhist to his local Buddhist subjects while also maintaining another image as a Hellenophile Greek, as demonstrated by his selection of the image of Athena as the principal motif on his coinage.

Regardless of the historicity of his supposed dialogues with the monk Nāgasena and his alleged conversion, the unique appearance of this Greek king in a semicanonical text set in the northwest is our best indication that Buddhism was flourishing, or at least was becoming a significant presence there, by the mid-second century BCE. But other than the *Questions*, we have little information about Menander's role in the history of Buddhism. The only other archaeological information

Figure 8. The Shinkot reliquary.

about him comes from an inscription on a broken stone reliquary that was found near the village of Shinkot in the Bajaur region, which is situated along the modern Pakistan-Afghanistan border.[29] This reliquary, among the earliest of the many Buddhist reliquaries from Gandhāra, bears several inscriptions, and one of them, unfortunately very fragmentary, was evidently dated in a regnal year of Menander. The other inscriptions on the reliquary refer to a later king of the Apraca dynasty, Vijayamitra I, who ruled around the late first century BCE, so that they probably record the rededication of relics that had been previously established during the reign of Menander. But the reference to Menander in this inscription merely concerns his regnal year, according to the standard method of citing dates at this period, and does not prove that he patronized or was in any way involved in the initial relic dedication. Still, it is an important indication of the presence of Buddhism and the cult of the Buddha's bodily relics in the Gandhāra region during Menander's reign.

There is one other inscription that sheds a little further light on the Buddhism of this period. This is a reliquary found in the late nineteenth century by an Englishman in an unspecified village in the Swat Valley, "where it was employed by the local banya [shopkeeper] as a money-box."[30] The inscription is undated, but on the basis of the archaic form of the Kharoṣṭhī script, it can be attributed to the second or first century BCE. It reads "These relics of the Lord Śākyamuni are established by the meridarch Theodotos for the benefit of the populace." Here, for the first but not the last time, we have what we lacked in the case of Menander: a clear instance of a lay Buddhist patron who, to judge from his name, was ethnically and/or culturally Greek. Moreover, Theodotos was not just any Greek; he was a meridarch: literally, "ruler of a division," that is, a high-ranking government official, probably a military commander who was in charge of a territorial division of some (unfortunately unidentified) kingdom. So here we have the earliest concrete evidence of the implantation of Buddhism in the Gandhāra region and, equally importantly, its adoption by members of the non-Indian ruling elite at some point before the beginning of the Common Era.

The Age of the Scythian Kingdoms

The period of Indo-Greek domination in northwest India was followed in the first centuries BCE and CE by waves of invaders and nomads from the Iranian plateau and the Central Asian steppes, including the Indo-Scythians (a branch of the widespread Scythian nomads, also known as Sakas), the Parthians, and finally the Kuṣāṇas. This pattern of successive displacements in Central Asia and resulting invasions into India was driven by the movements of powerful tribes of nomadic herders across the steppes of Central Asia and the Iranian plateau, movements that have profoundly affected not only the history of India but also of China, Iran, and other parts of the ancient world. In India these invaders established a series of kingdoms centered in Gandhāra that set the pattern for the history of the next several centuries, an era of unprecedented prosperity and influence.

Despite the chaos of successive invasions, this era ushered in a golden age of Buddhism in the northwest, as the invaders adopted

Buddhism as their public faith and became enthusiastic patrons of monastic establishments and the associated cults of the Buddha's relics. The universalist outlook and appeal of Buddhism, open to all people regardless of their ethnicity and culture, made it equally attractive to the Greek invaders and to their successors, the Scythians, Parthians, and Kuṣāṇas, offering to all of them both a key to salvation on the personal level and a ready means of assimilating into the local cultures of their conquered territories, helping them to gain legitimacy in the eyes of their new subjects. In this phase of history, between the first century BCE and the third century CE, Gandhāra became a center of both empires and of Buddhist culture, and it was this time of efflorescence that gave rise to the mythic image of Gandhāra as a Buddhist paradise. This is the period with which we are mainly concerned in this book.

During the earlier phase of this period, around the latter half of the first century BCE, Buddhist inscriptions suddenly become very common in Gandhāra and surrounding regions. Particularly noteworthy are the relic donation inscriptions, nearly twenty in all, associated with the Apraca kings who ruled the Bajaur region, and with the kings of Oḍi in the Swat Valley adjoining it to the east.[31] One of the earliest of these Buddhist kings was Vijayamitra I, the Apraca king mentioned above in connection with the Shinkot reliquary inscription of Menander. Although the interpretation of the later inscription on the same reliquary that mentions Vijayamitra is controversial due to its fragmentary condition, it seems that the relics that had originally been dedicated during Menander's reign were reestablished by Vijayamitra in the fifth year of his reign. Several of Vijayamitra's successors followed his example by patronizing the Buddhist relic cult, and one of them, Prince Indravarma, dedicated in the early first century CE an elaborate reliquary consisting of two repurposed silver drinking cups.[32]

At about the same time, the Oḍi kings in the Swat Valley to the east were following a similar path. This dynasty is known only from three relic dedication inscriptions on sheets of gold or silver,[33] including an extraordinarily long and detailed inscription recording the

Figure 9. The silver reliquary of Prince Indravarma.

dedication of relics of the Buddha by King Senavarma. We know little about the prehistory of these kings, who burst suddenly into view in this period as enthusiastic patrons of Buddhism, but they seem to be at pains to present themselves as natives with long-standing ancestral Buddhist associations. For example, Senavarma declares himself to be a member of the ancient royal lineage of the Ikṣvākus, from whom the Śākyas, the clan of the Buddha, also claimed descent.[34] But the Oḍi kings' claim of Ikṣvāku descent is historically very doubtful, and there is reason to suspect that, like their neighbors the Apracas, they were actually invaders of Scythian or other Central Asian origin. Although for the most part the kings of these two dynasties have Indian-sounding names, their wives often have Iranian or other foreign names, such as the Apraca queen Rukhuṇaka discussed below. Other sources, such as the coins jointly issued by later members of the Apraca lineage and the Indo-Scythian king Azes, ruler of the region of Taxila, indicate that these kingdoms to the north of Gandhāra were allied, at least politically and probably ethnically, with the powerful Scythian kingdoms that were then ruling central Gandhāra.

From the evidence of this wealth of inscriptions, it is clear that these Indo-Scythians and their contemporary allies played a central role in the expansion of Buddhism in the northwest. Whether out of genuine appreciation for its tenets or owing to the appeal of political expediency, they enthusiastically accepted Buddhism and firmly established its presence in Gandhāra. Besides the sorts of inscriptions mentioned above, other evidence from this and later periods show from an entirely different point of view how Buddhism was planted and nourished in the soil of Gandhāra. For this, we turn to the voices of the Buddhist faithful, where we find abundant testimony of the process of nativization of Buddhism. These sources claim that Buddhism was implanted in Gandhāra not only in the form of the physical relics of the Buddha but also in the form of a conviction that the Buddha himself had come to Gandhāra during his last life, as well as in many of his previous lives.

Much of this information comes from later testimony in the form of the records of the Chinese pilgrims, which in this, as in so many other ways, constitute a fundamentally important source for our knowledge of Indian Buddhism. Both Faxian,[35] who traveled in India during the early fifth century, and Xuanzang[36] in the first half of the seventh century reported seeing the footprints of the Buddha embedded in a rock in the Swat Valley, and both were told by local Buddhists that these prints would appear small or large depending on the size of the viewers' merit. While these testimonials date from several centuries after the period with which we are concerned, an actual pair of footprints was found on a stone at Tīrath in the upper Swat Valley. The pair are labelled "The footprints of Lord Śākyamuni" in archaic Kharoṣṭhī script of about the first century BCE. Although images of Buddha's footprints are abundant throughout the Buddhist world,[37] it is quite possible that these were the very prints seen by those pilgrims.

This and other reports by Xuanzang are consistent with a legend, reported in various Sanskrit and Chinese texts, that shortly before his

Figure 10. The Tīrath footprint inscription.

parinirvāṇa the Buddha traveled to the northwest in the company of his guardian spirit Vajrapāṇi.[38] Such traditions provide valuable testimony as to the processes of localization and nativization of Buddhism in Gandhāra. They show how Gandhāra not only joined the Buddhist world but came to be seen as part of the Buddhist holy land where the Buddha himself lived and taught, even though it actually lay far outside the original Buddhist territories. The depth of the nativization of Buddhism in Gandhāra is illustrated, for example, in Xuanzang's report[39] of a certain bodhi tree located outside Puruṣapura (modern Peshawar), the capital city of Gandhāra. Not only had the Buddha Śākyamuni sat under it but so too had the four buddhas before him, as also will the 996 buddhas who are to be born in the future during the present "fortunate eon" (*bhadrakalpa*).

Other legends reported by the Chinese pilgrims reflect another technique of nativization. For instance, Xuanzang tells how a malevolent *nāga* serpent named Apalāla, who plagued the Swat Valley with periodic floods, was tamed by the Buddha.[40] This is a familiar type of foundational myth regarding the spread of religions into new territories. It brings to mind, for example, the legend of Saint George and the dragon, or the tale told by the Arab traveler Ibn Baṭūṭah of the conversion of the Maldives to Islam by a Muslim scholar who subdued a sea demon who had demanded the monthly sacrifice of a virgin.[41] More characteristically Buddhist, however, are the localization of stories of previous lifetimes of the Buddha; for example, Xuanzang reports that an episode of the famous jātaka of Vessantara took place in a town in Gandhāra.[42]

Yet another instance of the localization of Buddhism in Gandhāra involves the legend of two merchants, Trapuṣa and Bhallika (P Tapussa and Bhalluka), who met the Buddha shortly after his enlightenment and became his first lay disciples. When they begged him for a token to take back to their native land, he gave them some strands of his hair and cuttings of his fingernails. According to the version of this legend reported by Xuanzang, the two merchants took these relics to their home in the city of Balkh in Afghanistan, where they installed them in the first Buddhist stūpa, thus establishing a sort of relic cult in advance with bodily remnants of the still-living Buddha.[43]

Finally, and most importantly for our purposes, the flourishing of Buddhism in the northwest in the period in question is confirmed by the discovery for the first time of large numbers of manuscripts of Buddhist texts in the Gandhāra region. The earliest Buddhist texts in Gāndhārī can now be securely dated to the first century BCE, or possibly even earlier,[44] while most of the others date from the first and second centuries CE. These dates are deduced from a combination of techniques, including radiocarbon tests (when available, which is unfortunately not always the case), analysis of accompanying inscriptions, as in the case of the Senior scrolls,[45] and estimates on paleographic and linguistic criteria.

The range of dates derived from these techniques was confirmed by the discovery, quite unexpectedly, of references in manuscripts to two Indo-Scythian rulers, Jihonika and Aśpavarma, who had previously been well known to historians from inscriptions and coins. Both of these references were found among the collections of *avadānas*, or pious legends, among the British Library scrolls. The reference to Jihonika is on a small remnant of a scroll (British Library fragment 2) that is so fragmentary that its theme and contents cannot be made out, but we can here clearly read the phrases "Jihonika the Great Satrap" and "in Gandhāra."[46] This Jihonika is otherwise known from his coinage and from an inscription from Taxila datable to the early part of the first century CE. Somewhat better preserved and more revealing, though still very fragmentary, is the reference to Aśpavarma in another British Library scroll.[47] Aśpavarma, like Jihonika, is a familiar figure from the history of the northwest in the early first century CE, known from his numerous coins in which he is entitled "commander" or "governor" (*stratega*, a loan word into Gāndhārī from Greek *strategos*, "general") and from an inscription on a silver plate from Taxila. Aśpavarma was also the last known member of the Apraca lineage, which, as we know from their numerous reliquary inscriptions, enthusiastically patronized Buddhism throughout the period of their reign. As is almost always the case with the British Library avadāna scrolls, many of the details of the story remain obscure, but it seems to contain some sort of dialogue between Aśpavarma and another man named Zadamitra, who is apparently a Buddhist monk whom the governor had invited to spend the rainy-season retreat with him. The main topic of their discussions seems to concern the nature or definition of a "good man" (*sapuruṣa*).

Despite the many uncertainties surrounding the story about Aśpavarma, we appear to have here another example of a dialogue between a secular ruler and a representative of the Buddhist monastic community. Comparable in principle to the dialogue between King Menander and the monk Nāgasena, the difference is perhaps more in the structure and ultimate fate of the texts than in their essential character and purpose. Both reflect the sort of interaction between monks and secular authorities that is a recurrent and central feature of the Buddhist tradition as a whole, the focus of these discussions being typically attempts to convince the kings of the truth and superiority of the Buddhist Dharma, and therefore to win their material support for the saṅgha, as well as to persuade them to apply Dharmic principles to their statecraft.

This new Gāndhārī material is thus also essentially of a piece with the legends about Aśoka that have already been discussed, as well those about Kaniṣka and Huviṣka that will be discussed in the following section. These better-known legends came to be admitted into the formal literary corpora of the Buddhist schools, mostly in the form of narratives incorporated into the massive vinaya of the Mūlasarvāstivāda school or of literary compilations of avadānas and similar edifying stories preserved in Sanskrit or in Chinese translations. The Gāndhārī stories, in contrast, happen to have survived only in the form of what are apparently notes casually scribbled by a storyteller or preacher as memory prompts.[48] Most of these stories evidently did not make their way into any more formal literary compositions—or at least not into any such composition that has come to us, since we must always keep in mind that what has survived of Buddhist literature through the millennia is only some unknown fraction of the entirety of what must once have existed. For example, although the stories of Jihonika and Aśpavarma have not been found in any surviving literary texts, we do now know, as result of recent discoveries and identifications, that several legends about other kings of the region and time in question were preserved in the surviving corpus of Buddhist texts. For example, Uttarasena, an ancestor of King Senavarma of Oḍi, is mentioned as a patron of the relic cult in the vinaya of the Mūlasarvāstivāda school as well as in Xuanzang's account of his travels in the Swat Valley.[49] Similarly, the Apraca king Indravarma of Bajaur is mentioned both in Kumāralāta's *Collection of Examples Adorned by Imagination* (*Kalpanāmaṇḍitikā Dṛṣṭāntapaṅkti*), a major literary collection of Buddhist legends, and in the *Scripture of the Wise and Foolish* (*Xianyu jin*), an anthology of avadānas that was popular in Central Asia and China.[50]

Many of these references in Buddhist literature to kings and other historical personages of the Gandhāra region have gone unnoticed until recently, in part because their names have themselves only become known recently from inscriptions, and in part because of the chronic difficulty of recognizing and identifying Indian names in Chinese translations. It is therefore not impossible that the names of Jihonika and Aśpavarma, whom we now know to have been included in the proto-literary Buddhist literature of Gandhāra, may also lie hidden somewhere in other texts, waiting to be discovered. In any case, it is clear that their appearance in the Gandhāran scrolls are part of a wider pattern of the enshrining of patron kings into Buddhist literature. But what is particularly interesting here is to find such references in what is evidently a primitive, proto-literary form among the British Library avadānas.

Another avadāna story in the British Library scrolls concerns a character, introduced simply as "a certain Saka" (Indo-Scythian) whom a Buddhist monk sees walking along the road "surrounded by a group of women." A discussion ensues, which as usual in these texts is incomplete and obscure but which seems to concern the danger of the disappearance of the Dharma, a perennial concern in early Buddhist literature. Although the main character of this story is not a king, he is evidently a member of the Indo-Scythian ruling class of Buddhist Gandhāra. Thus this story is another manifestation of the importance to the Buddhists of Gandhāra of their relationships with the non-Indian ruling elite.[51]

The Climax of Gandhāran Buddhist Culture under the Kuṣāṇa Empire

The last and greatest of the Gandhāran empires established by the successive waves of invasion was that of the Kuṣāṇas. The Kuṣāṇas, like their predecessors, were originally nomads from Central Asia, who, driven out from what is today the Xinjiang province of China,

Figure 11. Statue of Kaniṣka from Mathurā.

migrated westward into the northern borderlands of the Iranian world and then, around the middle of the first century CE, southeastward into India. There, especially under their greatest king, Kaniṣka, who ruled from about 127 to 150 CE, they established a vast and powerful transregional empire, centered in Gandhāra but including much of north and central India, northeastern Afghanistan, southern Uzbekistan, and parts of the Tarim Basin.

As we have already seen, although Gandhāra in antiquity was essentially a part of the Indian world, it always maintained a distinct identity that set it off from the heartland culture of Brahmanical north India. In keeping with its status as a frontier region on the borders between several cultural zones, Gandhāra in antiquity was characterized by eclectic mixtures of Indian, Iranian, Central Asian, and Hellenistic cultures, and this eclecticism was never more clearly visible than during the glory days of the Kuṣāṇa Empire. For example, in the Gandhāran Buddhist sculpture of this period, donor figures, who no doubt represent

Figure 12. Donor figures with Central Asian dress.

the power elite of the time, are frequently depicted in distinctly non-Indian garb, either wearing the tunic, wide trousers, and high boots of horse-riding nomads from Central Asia or clad in the Greek *chiton* and *himation.* A visitor to Gandhāra from the Indian heartland would surely have felt far from home among such exotic foreigners.

These costumes are only one manifestation in art of the cosmopolitan character of Gandhāra in its heyday. The exceedingly abundant corpus of Gandhāran Buddhist art of this period is characterized by a Hellenistic component that has contributed to the fascination it has held for scholars, collectors, and connoisseurs, especially in the West, since its discovery in the nineteenth century. Indeed, any awareness among the general public of Gandhāra and its culture is usually based on exposure to Gandhāran Buddhist sculpture, specimens of which can be found in virtually every major museum of Asian art worldwide. Although it remains a matter of intense controversy among art historians whether the non-Indian characteristics of Gandhāran sculpture reflect a continuous Greek tradition rooted in Alexander's conquests in Bactria, subsequent contacts with later traditions of the Hellenistic east, direct communication with contemporary artists from the Roman empire, or some complex conjunction of such sources, the

Figure 13. The Trojan horse in a Gandhāran sculpture.

eclectic character of Gandhāran art is undeniable. The themes of the sculptures, such as images of buddhas and bodhisattvas, narrative scenes from the life of the Buddha, and his worship by monastic and lay followers, are in most cases quintessentially Buddhist. But their style and composition, particularly in the figuration of the buddhas and bodhisattvas, have a pronounced Hellenistic flavor in their naturalistic and personalized portraiture, the expression of facial emotion, the use of *contrapposto*, and the complex treatment of the folds of their garments. Decorative motifs such as *putti*, garland bearers, and Corinthian columns used as dividers between scenes are similarly and obviously of Western rather than Indian origin.

In some cases, not only decorative elements but even the themes of the sculptures themselves are of Hellenistic derivation, either adapted to a Buddhist context or sometimes, it would seem, merely borrowed wholesale. A particularly striking though rare instance is the paradigmatically Greek scene of the Trojan horse carved into a stone panel that once decorated a Gandhāra stūpa. Mythological figures from the European classical tradition such as Atlas, Triton, and Aphrodite are frequently seen, and sometimes Greek mythological figures are reinterpreted in a Buddhist or Indian context.[52] A remarkable and well-known instance is the assimilation of the Greek hero Herakles

Figure 14. Herakles/Vajrapāṇi from Haḍḍa, Afghanistan.

to Vajrapāṇi, the Buddha's guardian spirit, as shown in a masterpiece from Haḍḍa, Afghanistan. Here Herakles's iconic club has been converted into the thunderbolt that is the hallmark of Vajrapāṇi, whose name means "thunderbolt (*vajra*) in hand (*pāṇi*)."

The cosmopolitan character of Gandhāra during the Kuṣāṇa empire is nowhere better demonstrated than in the renowned "Begram treasure." This was an enormous hoard of luxury objects discovered by French archaeologists in 1937 in two rooms at the site of a building identified as a palace at Begram, some thirty-five miles north of Kabul. The hoard included lacquerware imported from China, exquisite carved ivories from India, Mediterranean glass, and bronze objects from the Hellenistic West, all testifying to the wide-ranging trade networks, vast wealth, cultural diversity, and appetite for luxury goods of the Kuṣāṇa Empire at its peak.

This picture of a multiethnic society whose common unifying factor was the Buddhist faith is further illuminated by the evidence of

Figure 15. Roman glass from the Begram treasure: the rape of Europa.

the many inscriptions recorded during this period on objects donated to the Buddhist monasteries, particularly on reliquaries that contained the purported remains of the cremated body of the Buddha. In many inscriptions of this type we find donors with distinctly non-Indian names, usually of Greek or Iranian origin. For instance, a reliquary inscription of the latter half of the first century CE records the dedication of relics by one Helaüta, son of Demetria.[53] The father's name is obviously a rendering into Gāndhārī of the Greek Demetrios, while that of the son seems to be a hybrid of Greek Helios and a common Indian name suffix meaning "protected by" (Skt *-gupta*, Gāndhārī *-(g)uta*). The donor's sons are then listed as Adura, Arazada, Adramitra, Adravharṇa, Demetria, and Mahasaṃmada; thus the first four have names of Iranian derivation, the fifth a Greek name after that of his grandfather, and the sixth a distinctly Indian Buddhist name (= Skt/P *Mahāsaṃmata*). It is also significant that this inscription is dated on "the thirteenth day of the month of Gorpaios, [when the moon was] in the constellation Uttara-proṣṭhapada." Here too we see a merging of cultures in that the name of the month is given according to the Greek (Macedonian) calendar, as in many inscriptions of the period, while the lunar constellation is specified according to Indian astronomical terminology.

Names of Iranian derivation are especially common among the Buddhist inscriptions of this period. One particularly prominent donor, whose name appears in several reliquary inscriptions, was the aforementioned Apraca queen Rukhuṇaka. Her name as given in these inscriptions is a Gāndhārī rendering of the common Iranian female name Rokhshāna, meaning "luminous," which is familiar in European tradition from its Greek form Roxane, the Bactrian noblewoman whom Alexander the Great married in 327 BCE. We can assume that Rukhuṇaka/Roxane and many other Buddhist patrons with Iranian names, including Zadamitra who figures in two of the avadānas presented here,[54] belonged to the elite immigrant class frequently depicted on Gandhāran sculpture in the garb of the Central Asian nomads.

The diversity and complexity of Gandhāran culture in and around the Kuṣāṇa era is also manifested in the coins, which along with the many inscriptions are our main source for the history of this period. Particularly striking is the vast variety of the coinage issued in the second century by Kaniṣka, the greatest of the Kuṣāṇa kings, and by his successor Huviṣka. Their coins typically bear a portrait of the king on the obverse, while the reverse shows the figure of a divinity whose name is spelled out in Greek letters. More than thirty different deities are represented, including the gods of the Roman and Hellenistic pantheon such as Herakles, Helios, and Hephaistos, Zoroastrian deities of Iran like Ardoxsho, Mao, Mithra, and Nana, and Indian Hindu gods such as Śiva, the war god Mahāsena, and Skanda-Kumāra (Kārttikeya).

There are also a few specimens of Kaniṣka's coins with representations of the Buddha, labeled in Greek script as Buddha (*Boddo*) or Śākyamuni Buddha (*Sakamano Boudo*), as well as of the future Buddha Maitreya (*Metrago Boudo*). These depictions of the Buddha are however proportionally quite rare among the vast coinage of Kaniṣka

Figure 16. A coin of King Kaniṣka.

and Huviṣka, which may seem surprising in view of the prominence of Buddhism in the archaeological and epigraphic record. But this can be understood in view of the vast extent and wide cultural diversity of the Kuṣāṇa realm, which included populations speaking many different languages and practicing many religions. Kaniṣka and Huviṣka, like Indian monarchs throughout history, pursued a policy of acceptance of religious diversity and patronage of multiple religions. As a result, it is hard to know what their personal beliefs might have been; in public, they tried to be all things to all people, and coinage was one of the most effective and powerful propaganda tools for winning the acceptance and loyalty of their diverse citizenry.

A direct insight into the character of Kuṣāṇa religious diversity was provided by the discovery in 1993 of the now-famous Rabatak inscription in northern Afghanistan (ancient Bactria), which greatly expanded our knowledge of Kaniṣka's reign and of Kuṣāṇa history in general.[55] The inscription, written in Bactrian, an eastern Iranian language, records the dedication of a temple to a series of Iranian and Zoroastrian deities such as Nana, Umma, Aurmuzd (= Ahura Mazda), Muzhduwan, and Sroshard. Above the name of Sroshard an extra phrase was subsequently inserted above the line, reading "who in Indian is called Mahāsena and is called Viśākha." Here, someone evidently saw fit to clarify the identity of Sroshard with the Indian war god Mahāsena or Viśākha, the son of the supreme god Śiva. This mode of identification is characteristic of ancient polytheisms, whereby adherents of one religious tradition would identify the deities of their pantheon with the closest equivalent in another religion with which they came into contact, without any sense of contradiction or conflict; we already saw this process in the identification of Hellenistic Herakles with Buddhist Vajrapāṇi.

During the early and middle Kuṣāṇa period, inscriptions recording the construction of stūpas, dedication of relics, and various donations to the monasteries continued to be abundant in Gandhāra. Most of these, however, are the efforts of ordinary citizens; donations by Kuṣāṇa royalty themselves are rare. Although the epigraphic evidence for Kaniṣka's direct patronage of Buddhism is sparse, he is presented in later Buddhist tradition as a second Aśoka, another model of the devout and generous royal patron of the saṅgha.[56] Several Buddhist texts refer to the legend of Kaniṣka's great stūpa in Puruṣapura, which was supposed to have been the tallest one ever built, emblematic of his piety and generosity. The story told by Xuanzang[57] of the origin of the enormous stūpa that Kaniṣka built in his capital of Puruṣapura[58] is revealing in several regards. Like Aśoka, Kaniṣka was a reformed sinner who originally despised Buddhism, until one day he saw a young shepherd boy making a little stūpa. Inspired by the boy's faith, he tried to cover the small stūpa with a huge one of his own, but however big he made it, the boy's stūpa kept projecting out of it. Here we hear echoes of the legend of Aśoka, who as a child in a previous life gave the Buddha a handful of earth, as a result of which he became, in a later lifetime, the ruler of the entire earth. Although the details differ, Aśoka's and Kaniṣka's legends share the motif of the contrast between an innocent boy's naïve but sincere piety and a mighty king's arrogance. This, in turn, is an expression of the uneasy balance between royal and spiritual power that, as we have already seen, is a recurrent theme in the history of Buddhism.

Not surprisingly, the production of Buddhist manuscripts also flourished during the time of the great Kuṣāṇa kings. Although scholar-monks had already been translating earlier Buddhist texts into Gāndhārī and composing original works for some two centuries, during the high Kuṣāṇa period this enterprise reached its peak. The clearest evidence for this is the manuscripts of the Senior collection, which were found inside a clay pot bearing a dedicatory inscription dating in "the year twelve." This most likely refers to a year of the era instituted by Kaniṣka, probably in 127 or 128 CE,[59] so that this important collection of manuscripts evidently dates from the early years of his reign.[60]

Kaniṣka was succeeded by his son Huviṣka, who ruled from about 150 to 190 CE.[61] Huviṣka is mentioned in one of the few Gandhāran Buddhist inscriptions that are directly linked to the Kuṣāṇa kings. The inscription on a bronze reliquary from Wardak, Afghanistan (now in the British Museum), dating from about 178 CE, records the establishment of a stūpa and relics by one Vaga-marega, who was probably a member of a Kuṣāṇa noble line. He dedicated part of the merit of this pious act to King Huviṣka: "Through this root of good may it be for the best lot of the great king, chief king of kings, Huviṣka."[62]

Like Kaniṣka, Huviṣka's memory was also preserved in later Buddhist tradition, although he was evidently less revered than his great father. A recently discovered fragment of an unidentified Buddhist manuscript in Sanskrit from Bamiyan, dating from about the fourth century, refers to Huviṣka as having "set forth on the Great Vehicle" ([*mahā]yāna-samprasthitaḥ), that is, as a follower of the Mahāyāna.[63] This epithet is consistent with other indications that Mahāyāna Buddhism was growing and beginning to take a coherent form during the Kuṣāṇa period, most notably the recent discoveries of at least seven Mahāyāna sūtras in Gāndhārī dating from around this time.[64]

The Decline of Buddhism in Gandhāra

After the time of Huviṣka, around the late second and early third century CE, the Kuṣāṇa empire rapidly contracted. For some decades it retained its sway in its north Indian territories around their Indian capital at Mathurā, but Kuṣāṇa force in Gandhāra and Afghanistan devolved into small pockets of territory. With the decline and eventual collapse of the Kuṣāṇa Empire in the third century, Gandhāra again fell under the sway of outside powers. The dominant force in the northwest was now the new and expanding Sasanian empire of Iran, which spread into the Kuṣāṇa realm soon after its foundation in 224 CE and dominated the region for the rest of the third century. In the fourth century Gandhāra was ruled by various local potentates under the domination of greater powers from the west or east. In the later part of the fifth century, it was overrun by the White Huns, who sacked Buddhist institutions in their initial attacks but later on patronized them.

In the succeeding centuries, various dynasties, mostly based in Afghanistan, ruled over Gandhāra, including the Shahis, the Ghaznavids, Ghorids, the Mughals, and the Durranis, until it was finally incorporated into British India in 1849. Throughout this millennia-long pattern of conquest and subordination, sometimes to Iranian and Afghan powers to the west, at other times to Indian empires in the east, Gandhāra tended to be the proverbial grass on which the elephants did battle. But during the period with which we are concerned, Gandhāra was for a brief shining moment in history the center of vast empires ruling over territories stretching in all directions, rather than a mere appendage or bargaining chip for mighty powers elsewhere, and it was presumably during this time that there arose the legendary image of Gandhāra as a Buddhist paradise.

In the waning days of the later Kuṣāṇas and under their successors, Buddhism in the northwest began a gradual decline and never regained its dominant position, until it disappeared completely from view by about the ninth century. As Gandhāra ceased to be a political and cultural center, Gandhāran Buddhism lost its wealthy and powerful patrons. In Gandhāra and adjoining regions, Buddhist inscriptions suddenly became much rarer and all but disappear after the early to middle of the third century. Only among the manuscript fragments from Bamiyan, to the west of Gandhāra proper, do we continue to find substantial evidence of Buddhist textual material in Gāndhārī and Kharoṣṭhī.

Xuanzang's travelogue shows Buddhism in Gandhāra and the northwest to be alive, though not well, in the early seventh century. Over and over, he reports that monasteries are deserted or decrepit and that the remaining monks are few and often lazy and ignorant. He reports, for example, that in Gandhāra, "There were more than a thousand monasteries, but they are now dilapidated and deserted, and in desolate condition,"[65] while in Nagarahāra in eastern Afghanistan, "There are many monasteries but few monks. All the stūpas are deserted and in dilapidated condition."[66]

Particularly interesting evidence for the late phase of Buddhism in Gandhāra is a ninth-century Sanskrit inscription found in the village of Ghosrāvān, near the great Buddhist monastic and educational complex at Nālandā, far to the east in Bihar, in the traditional Buddhist heartland. The inscription is composed, in the mode of later Indian Buddhist literature, in ornate poetic style and flawless classical Sanskrit. It celebrates the career of a monk named Vīradeva, who came to be the supervisor of a monastery at Nālandā. This Vīradeva originally hailed from Nagarahāra, near Jalalabad in eastern Afghanistan, and had gone as a young man to study at the "Great Kaniṣka vihāra," that is, a monastic institution associated with Kaniṣka's great stūpa evidently in Puruṣapura. This famous monument was still known to the great Islamic scholar Al-bīrūnī, who lived in India in the early eleventh century.[67] Thus the Kaniṣka stūpa evidently remained a focal point for Buddhism in the northwest even into its last days.

The Legacy of Gandhāran Buddhism

Thus, after a few centuries of glorious preeminence, Gandhāran Buddhism retreated to a subordinate and weakened position and eventually died out completely. Had the winds of history blown in different directions, Gandhāra might have remained a Buddhist land, and pious Buddhists and Buddhist scholars might still today be learning the words of the Buddha from canons in Gāndhārī as well as in Pali, Tibetan, and Chinese. But this was not to be; instead, the Buddhist literature of Gandhāra remained unknown for the better part of two thousand years and is only now being rediscovered from some precious surviving scraps of the enormous corpus that must have once existed there.

But this does not mean that Gandhāra's role in Buddhist history was no more than a lesson in the transience of worldly glories. In another way, Gandhāran Buddhism has lived on through its crucial, though largely hidden, role in the development of Buddhism into a world religion. For it was from Greater Gandhāra that Buddhism began to spread beyond its Indian homeland into Central Asia and thence to China, Korea, and Japan, transforming itself from an Indian to a world religion. In Gandhāra's heyday, and still for several centuries thereafter, Buddhist merchants made their way through the towering peaks of the Karakoram and Hindu Kush ranges to ply their trade in luxury goods along the spur roads leading from the Indian subcontinent into the silk roads that connected China and the Western world. The lives of these travelers have been revealed in recent decades in the form of thousands of inscriptions and rock carvings left by ancient Buddhist merchants and pilgrims[68] that came to light in the course of the construction of the Karakoram Highway between Pakistan and China, rendering accessible vast areas along of the gorges of the Indus and Hunza rivers in northern Pakistan that had previously been extremely remote and all but unknown to outsiders.

Along with their silks and spices, jewels and gold, these adventurers brought the message of Buddhism to Central and East Asia, and with it came Indian manuscripts of the Buddhist scriptures. In the second century these scriptures began to be translated into Chinese in the first step in what grew to become an enormous translation project, probably the largest, most ambitious, and most difficult one ever undertaken

Figure 17. Rock carvings and inscriptions at Hodar on the upper Indus River.

in the history of the world. This project was to continue for many centuries and produce thousands of Buddhist translations into Chinese. Although it was originally assumed by scholars in the West that the Chinese translations were made from originals in Sanskrit, beginning in the 1930s a few European scholars noticed certain features of some early Chinese translations suggesting that the directly or indirectly underlying text was Gāndhārī, rather than Sanskrit. Subsequent researches have strengthened and refined this theory, which has come to be known as the "Gāndhārī hypothesis," discussed in more detail in the next chapter. Although the details of the Gāndhārī hypothesis are still being worked out, especially in light of the new manuscripts, it is now clear that China's early exposure to Buddhist literature was based in large part on texts that had been brought from Gandhāra and originally written in Gāndhārī. In this regard, Gandhāran Buddhism—like Indian Buddhism itself—gave birth to something greater than itself, even as it was itself doomed to vanish.

2. Buddhist Manuscripts, Buddhist Languages, and Buddhist Canons

Buddhist Texts and Canons

MODERN KNOWLEDGE of the early history of Buddhism, especially in its homeland in the Indian subcontinent, is derived primarily from texts and manuscripts. To be sure, other sources of information, such as archaeology, art history, and especially inscriptions, play a large part. But written texts, and especially the canonical scriptures—that is, "the words of the Buddha" (*buddhavacana*)—remain the fundamental basis of our knowledge of the early beliefs and doctrines of Indian Buddhism and their subsequent elaboration and interpretation. But what exactly are "the words of the Buddha"? This turns out to be a vast and complex question, since those words are recorded in many different languages, versions, and formats. The basic texts and collections in their various forms differ in many ways, sometimes trivially, sometimes extensively.

To understand the meaning of these different versions of the Buddhist scriptures and how they relate to each other, we must first understand why and in what form they have come down to us. Most Buddhists of the modern world, whether in Tibet, Thailand, Japan, or any of the other national and local traditions of Buddhism (including, in the modern context, the many Buddhist communities and institutions outside of Asia), learn Buddhist doctrines from scriptural canons or, more often, from a small number of texts selected or adapted from such canons. These canons are typically known as the Tripiṭaka (P Tipiṭaka), that is, the "three baskets," referring to the three major divisions of Buddhist scriptures: *sūtra*, the discourses of the Buddha; *vinaya*, the laws of Buddhist monasticism; and *abhidharma*, the technical analysis of the Dharma. Each of the local canons presents itself as the definitive and comprehensive compilation of the true and original words of the Buddha, constituting the very essence of the Dharma.

The Buddhist canons have been preserved and handed down with scrupulous care over the two and a half millennia of Buddhist history. The preservation of the words of the Buddha was a matter of the utmost concern, because those words and the Dharma that they embodied became his principal legacy when he declined to appoint a successor as leader and guide of the Buddhist community. Moreover, he had warned his followers that the Dharma would be forgotten within a period of five hundred or one thousand years (according to different traditions) after his death. This prophesied disappearance of the Dharma was a perennial cause of concern and anxiety among Buddhists, and it promoted the development of various technologies to ensure its survival as long as possible.[69]

In the first few centuries of Buddhist history, as Buddhism began to become institutionalized and to spread throughout the Indian world, the primary means of transmission and preservation of the texts was the oral-mnemonic method, that is, the chanting by communities or subgroups of Buddhist monks who had committed them to memory. This preference for oral transmission is easy to explain, since this was the normal practice in the cultural context in which Buddhism arose. This is clear in the Vedic or Brahmanical tradition of ancient India, where oral recitation was always the preferred mode of learning and preservation. In fact, it is uncertain whether writing was even known in India during the lifetime of the Buddha in or around the sixth or fifth century BCE.[70]

However, at some point in the early history of Buddhism in the Indian subcontinent, probably in the first century BCE,[71] Buddhists

Figure 18. One of 729 inscribed slabs of the Pali Tipiṭaka at Kuthodaw Pagoda, Mandalay, Burma.

began to write scriptures down as a sort of insurance policy or back-up system, lest they fall victim to the limitations of human memory and mortality and thus hasten the inevitable decline of the Dharma. Early written scriptures in peninsular India were typically written on palm leaves and strung together, whereas in the far northern and northwestern borderlands, texts were preserved on scrolls made of birchbark. In some cases, further measures were taken to ensure the survival of the sacred texts by inscribing them on stone in order to ensure their longevity. In other cases, texts in manuscript form or engraved on metal sheets were placed inside funerary pots or reliquaries and buried inside stūpas,[72] and it is this latter practice that led to the survival of most of the Gandhāran manuscripts that are the focus of this book.

The development of technologies for preserving the Dharma is an ongoing process. In modern times, beginning around the middle of the nineteenth century, Western scholars began to publish scholarly editions and translations of Buddhist texts. Printed books quickly became a widespread medium for nonacademic purposes as well, and the republication of editions of the Tripiṭaka is still today a frequent pious exercise of merit-making in parts of the Buddhist world, even though the new versions sometimes have few significant textual differences from the previous ones. More recently, the preparation of electronic editions of the canon has, like the print editions, served the interests of both Buddhist practitioners and research scholars and are now widely used by both.

The various means of preservation of Buddhist scriptures should not be viewed as mutually exclusive. In principle, no one of them is inherently better than the others, since from a Buddhist perspective anything that is conducive to the study and preservation of the Dharma is desirable, as well as productive of good karma. Just as printed and electronic copies of canons or individual texts now function side by side in a symbiotic relationship, so too in earlier times, and still today to some extent, oral recitation and written texts served to reinforce each other rather than to compete.

The three independent Buddhist canons that have come down to us in complete form are preserved in Pali, Tibetan, and Chinese. Taken together, these three canons are fundamental to most of the Buddhist traditions of today, but they by no means represent the entirety of Buddhist traditions, and neither are their contents the same. In fact, these canons differ not only in their contents but also in their overall structure and even in some fundamental conceptions.[73] The contents of the Pali Tipiṭaka and the Tibetan canon are vastly different, and the amount of overlap between them, that is, the number of individual texts that they both contain, is actually very small. The Pali canon is a conservative one, for example in the sūtra (P *sutta*) category, consisting of a core group of texts of what are agreed by all historically oriented scholars to represent some of the earliest texts of the Buddhist tradition.[74] The Tibetan canon, in contrast, contains only a small sampling of the āgama-sūtras,[75] being composed largely of texts of the Mahāyāna and Vajrayāna, or tantric, traditions. While these texts are historically much later, they are understood by the followers of those traditions as the true teachings of the Buddha himself.

The Chinese canon is yet again a different enterprise; whereas the composition of most canons, including the Pali and Tibetan, reflects a process of selection of what were considered to be authentic original texts, the Chinese canon is a comprehensive compilation of all of the Buddhist texts in Chinese that were available to its compilers. Thus it comprises not only the Chinese translations of the collections of early sūtras analogous to those in the Pali canon but also vast numbers of Mahāyāna and Vajrayāna texts. Moreover, whereas the compilers of the Tibetan canons would usually include only one translation of the same original Indian text, the Chinese canons incorporated all available translations of every text, preserving, for example, no less than six translations of the *Diamond Sūtra* (*Vajracchedikā-prajñāpāramitā*).

As vast—the printed edition of the Chinese canon, for example, comprises one hundred volumes of some eight or nine hundred pages each—and as varied as the three surviving Buddhist canons may be, they still reflect only a fraction of the entirety of Buddhist literature as it has existed through two and a half millennia and across the entirety of Asia. For these are only the canons that happen to have survived, mostly by virtue of belonging to those regions and cultural traditions where Buddhism has had a continuous tradition to the present day. But in antiquity Buddhism flourished in many areas of the world where it has long since ceased to exist. These regions include various parts of Central Asia, modern Afghanistan, and even eastern Iran, but most importantly its homeland, India. For Buddhism, like Christianity, conquered much of the world but faded away in its own home, declining in the later centuries of the first millennium of the Common Era and virtually disappearing by the thirteenth century.

Our knowledge of the lost texts and canons of these formerly Buddhist regions thus depends entirely on the accidents of the survival and discovery of ancient manuscripts. Among the earliest and most spectacular revelations of a forgotten Buddhist literature were the thousands of manuscript fragments found in Central Asia during the late nineteenth and early twentieth centuries by European, Japanese, and American explorers, most notably by Marc Aurel Stein. These finds from what was then known as Chinese Turkestan, that is, in the oases around the Tarim Basin in the present-day Xinjiang Uyghur Autonomous Region of China, brought to light a vast literature of Buddhist texts in Sanskrit, mostly belonging to the Sarvāstivāda school and dating to between the third and eighth centuries CE, as well as abundant materials in Central Asian languages such as Khotanese and Tocharian. These manuscripts included, among many other classes of texts, both āgama-sūtras and Mahāyāna sūtras. Another large corpus, involving over one hundred different Buddhist texts in Sanskrit, was found in 1931 near Gilgit in the far north of present-day Pakistan. A vast corpus of several thousand manuscript fragments in Sanskrit and Gāndhārī from the Bamiyan region has come to light more recently.[76]

From these and other similar discoveries, it has gradually become clear to scholars that the history of Buddhism is far more complex than previously realized. Early scholars of Buddhism in the West, especially in the English-speaking world, had assumed that the Pali canon represented *the* true original scriptures of Buddhism while other manifestations of Buddhism and versions of Buddhist texts were secondary derivations, elaborations, or corruptions. This view prevailed mainly because the Pali canon of the Theravāda tradition of Sri Lanka and Southeast Asia happened to be the only one that survived complete and intact in an Indian language, and because it came to the attention of Anglophone scholars at a relatively early date as a result of the colonization of Sri Lanka by England. This led to the illusion that the Pali canon was the only true Buddhist canon, and the misconception was reinforced by the self-presentation of the bearers of that tradition, who were the early European scholars' main points of contact with the Buddhist world.

But it is now clear that the seeming primacy and authority of the Pali Tipiṭaka is only an accident of history. The discovery of abundant remnants of a previously unknown Sanskrit canon in Central Asia enabled scholars to realize that there had once existed other, perhaps many other, canons in various local languages both within Buddhist India and beyond it, in the regions to which Buddhism had spread but where it had died out in antiquity. The more recent discovery of Buddhist texts in Gāndhārī emphatically confirms the view that there once existed many Buddhisms, each with its own distinctive literature and canon. Moreover, detailed studies of the Sanskrit and Gāndhārī manuscripts, particularly with a view to comparing them with their parallels in Pali, Chinese, and other languages, has further undermined the myth of Pali primacy. Comparisons of several versions of a given sūtra in the various languages concerned—for example, the Pali, Sanskrit, and Gāndhārī texts of the *Rhinoceros Sūtra*—typically show complex relationships in which no one version can be identified as the sole source or archetype for the others.[77]

For this reason, most if not all Buddhist textual scholars nowadays consider each version of a given text, and by extension each body of Buddhist literature, to have *a priori* an equal claim to accuracy and originality. This result may seem disappointing and frustrating to those who wish to discover *the* true and original "words of the Buddha," be they historically oriented scholars or practicing Buddhists. But in light of recent trends in textual scholarship, reinforced by the discovery of the Buddhist literature of Gandhāra, most scholars have abandoned the quest for a single "original" version of the canon as a wild-goose chase. For even if there ever were, in theory, a single original form of the canon, or at least of a group of individual texts as the Buddha himself uttered them two and a half millennia ago, there is no hope of finding it intact. By the time the texts were set down in writing, apparently in the first century BCE, Buddhism had already spread far and wide around India and adjoining countries, as a result of which slightly, and sometimes not so slightly, different versions had already arisen and diverged in complex and tangled ways that make it impossible to reconstruct a single original archetype.

Moreover, it is doubtful whether, even in the time of the Buddha himself, the texts existed in a single uniform shape. For example, the Buddha may have preached some sūtras several or many times in his travels and probably varied them slightly each time, for example shortening or lengthening his exposition according to the situation or the disposition of his audience. Thus different disciples could have heard, memorized, and transmitted different versions of a given sūtra, so that the textual diversity that has set in by the time of the earliest surviving written texts may have existed from the very earliest days of Buddhism. Therefore any search for the true, original words of the Buddha is doubly a quest for a will-o'-the-wisp.

For modern scholars, then, the focus has gradually shifted from a fruitless search for a single true original Buddhism to a broader understanding of the nature and interrelationships of the many Buddhisms that developed over the centuries and millennia. But where does this leave Buddhist practitioners who want to be sure that they are studying and following the true Dharma, just as the Buddha taught it? This is, of course, a matter of personal inclination and belief, but the multiple versions of texts and canons do not have to be considered a problem. In most cases, the differences between a given sūtra in, for example, Pali, Sanskrit, Gāndhārī, and Chinese are more a matter of phrasing and arrangement than of substance. If such texts are read for the spirit rather than for the letter—an attitude that is explicitly encouraged in certain sūtras[78]—the inconsistency need not be a problem for Buddhists, just as it has ceased to be a problem for most scholars.[79]

Although it has long been understood that Buddhism had numerous local manifestations in ancient India, it has now become much clearer that at least some of these local traditions had distinct versions of the fundamental texts; that is to say, they each had their own canons, or at least proto-canons. Most of these other Buddhist literatures remain hypothetical in that they will never be known to us, since they could have survived only by preservation in a continuous living tradition or by being rediscovered in an archaeological context. But the former case is ruled out since Buddhism died out in India proper many centuries ago, and the latter is hardly more promising, as there is virtually no hope that manuscripts of local traditions of early Indian Buddhism will ever be found in regions other than Greater Gandhāra. For it is no coincidence that nearly all of the old Buddhist manuscripts that have come to light were found in regions outside the heartland of the Indian subcontinent, where organic matter such as palm leaves decays rapidly in the tropical monsoon climate. Only in the dry desert climate of Central Asia or in the more moderate temperate regions of the northwestern border regions do ancient manuscripts have any chance of surviving. What we can now see of early Buddhist manuscript culture must be no more than the tip of what was once an enormous iceberg, and it is unlikely we will ever see a great deal more of it. Still, recent discoveries, particularly those of Gandhāran manuscripts, allow us to discern something of the overall shape of that iceberg.

The Languages of Buddhism

A major factor that promoted the diversity and complexity of Buddhist literature, while at the same time compounding the difficulty of recovering the original words of the Buddha, was the attitude of early Buddhism toward language and translation. For the most part, the Buddhist tradition encourages linguistic diversity and translation of scriptures. In this regard, among other world religions with strong scriptural traditions, it resembles Christianity and contrasts with religions such as Islam and Judaism, which consider the original languages of their holy books to be an intrinsic rather than an incidental feature of them. The Buddhist attitude toward language is exemplified in a well-known episode that is recorded in varying versions in the vinaya texts of several schools. In this passage, two brahman monks ask the Buddha whether they should translate his discourses into Sanskrit. The Buddha responds in the negative, telling them that his words should be learned "in one's own dialect" (*sakāya niruttiyā*), that is, in the local vernacular.[80]

In keeping with this principle, Buddhism developed into a religion of translation, and since India was then, as now, a land of great linguistic diversity, the Buddha's teachings began early on to be translated into various local dialects as they spread far and wide. The original language in which the Buddha himself is believed to have preached was Māgadhī, the Sanskrit-derived Prakrit (Middle Indo-Aryan) vernacular of northeastern India when he lived and traveled there. The problem is that no actual specimen of the Buddha's teachings in this hypothetical original language survives. Even if the teachings were written down in it at one time, we have no hope of ever finding them. This means that all the Buddhist texts we now have are in some sense translations of the originals, and this includes not only versions in non-Indian languages such as Tibetan and Chinese but also those in Indian languages like Pali, Sanskrit, and now Gāndhārī.

The overall preference for translation, however, by no means explains the entire history of the transmission of Buddhist literature, as it was counteracted by other social and linguistic factors, especially in later centuries in India. In this regard, Pali and Sanskrit hold a special position in the linguistic history of Buddhism. Pali was originally a local language of central or western India (although its exact geographical origin is a matter of ongoing controversy among linguists) that came to serve as a common language, or *lingua franca*, for Buddhists in many parts of South Asia, and it eventually became established as the canonical language of Sri Lanka. Under the influence of Buddhists in Sri Lanka, Pali also came to be the scriptural language of most Buddhist communities in Southeast Asia, where the principle of translation into local languages did not take effect. The Theravāda tradition of Sri Lanka and Southeast Asia understands Pali to be identical with the Māgadhī language and thus considers the Pali canon to represent the original words of the Buddha. Modern scholars, however, find this view untenable on linguistic and historical grounds.

In northern India, other pressures toward the establishment of a normative scriptural language eventually led to the adoption of Sanskrit by the Buddhists. By the Buddha's lifetime, Sanskrit had already been firmly established for centuries as the sacred language of the Vedic Brahmanical tradition, and therefore as the vehicle of high culture and the social elite. Thus the Buddha's explicit preference for local vernacular languages over Sanskrit was an implicit rejection or at least a critique of the standing social order, and an emblem of the openness of the new religion to followers from all levels of society. It is therefore something of a historical irony that some five or six centuries after Buddha's life, his followers began to adopt Sanskrit, at first in a hybrid form that introduced Sanskrit vocabulary and pronunciation into their vernacular texts, then gradually increasing the Sanskrit component until, by about the fourth century CE, the Buddhist language of northern India had effectively been transformed into classical Sanskrit.

This seeming paradox can best be understood in terms of the broader sociolinguistic situation. As Sanskrit remained deeply entrenched over the centuries as the language of status and scholarship, Buddhists gradually became more inclined to coopt rather than to resist it. There was an ongoing tension in Buddhist circles between, on the one hand, the vernaculars that made the Dharma more readily accessible to the common people, and on the other, the high classical language that lent it an air of respectability and venerability, especially with a view toward attracting brahman converts—always a point of pride and satisfaction among Buddhists. The situation can be broadly compared to the tension in medieval times between Latin and the vernacular languages in European Christianity, a tension that still persists today in some circles.

As a result of this gradual but pervasive Sanskritization of Buddhist literature in northern India, most of the Buddhist manuscripts discovered in Xinjiang, Gilgit, and Bamiyan are in Sanskrit. It is only with the recent discoveries of large numbers of manuscripts in Gāndhārī from an earlier period that we are beginning to get direct insights into the forms that Buddhist literature took in what may be called the vernacular period of its development. The picture, to be sure, is partial and defective, subject to the accidents of survival and discovery. Even though we now have many dozens of partial manuscripts and hundreds of smaller fragments in Gāndhārī, this is presumably still only some tiny fraction of what once must have existed, both in terms of the variety of texts and of the total number of manuscripts that must have been written and studied in Gandhāran monasteries during the period in which Buddhism flourished there.

Gāndhārī and Kharoṣṭhī

In this book, we are concerned with various languages and forms of writing, but primarily with the Gāndhārī language and the Kharoṣṭhī script.[81] Gāndhārī was in origin the local dialect of the Gandhāra region, but as Gandhāra developed into a cultural center, Gāndhārī came to serve as a *lingua franca* of the mixed population. As a result, it became the scriptural language of the flourishing Buddhist institutions of the time and thus the language of the manuscripts that are translated here.

In terms of its linguistic history and affiliations, Gāndhārī is a Prakrit language, meaning that it belongs to the Middle Indo-Aryan family of ancient vernacular languages of north and central India.[82] All Middle Indo-Aryan languages are derived from Sanskrit, or more precisely, from Old Indo-Aryan, a largely hypothetical group of ancient Indian dialects of which Sanskrit is the principal attested survivor. As such, Gāndhārī is closely related to the two other most important languages of Indian Buddhist texts, namely Sanskrit and Pali, as their daughter and sister, respectively. Their similarity and relationships are illustrated by the sample text presented in various languages in appendix 1. There, for example, the phrase "during the time of Vipaśyin" reads *vipaśyinaḥ prāvacane* in Sanskrit, *vipassino pāvacane* in Pali, and *vivaśisa praveaṇo* in Gāndhārī. This example illustrates one of the characteristic dialectal features of Gāndhārī that distinguishes it from other Middle Indo-Aryan languages, namely that it preserves all of the three sibilant sounds of Sanskrit (*ś*, *ṣ*, *s*), which in all the others are reduced to one (either *ś* or *s*). Thus the original *ś* (similar to English *sh*) in the Sanskrit name of the Buddha Vipaśyin is preserved in Gāndhārī *vivaśisa*, whereas it becomes *s* in Pali *vipassino*.

Indeed, the Middle Indo-Aryan languages, including Gāndhārī and Pali, are in some respects so close that they could be considered related dialects rather than separate languages. But the distinction between *dialect* and *language* is always a more or less arbitrary one, determined more by historical, cultural, and geographic circumstances than by objective literary criteria. Thus, for example, several different and mutually unintelligible languages are conventionally treated as "dialects" of Chinese or Arabic, while what are manifestly dialects of the same language, such as Hindi and Urdu or Croatian and Serbian, are conceived as separate languages on the basis of political circumstances and historical accidents rather than of objective linguistic analysis.[83] In the context of Buddhist languages such as Pali and Gāndhārī, however, their status as "languages" is based not on their political associations but on their status as distinct literary and canonical languages of Buddhism. Since Buddhism from the beginning encouraged the translation of its scriptures into the speech of the various regions into which it spread, those dialects into which large numbers of scriptures were translated achieved, in effect, the status of canonical "languages."

However, in another important respect the character of Gāndhārī is distinct from other Buddhist languages such as Pali and Sanskrit. Most scholars of ancient Buddhist texts are used to working with languages like Pali and Sanskrit, which have long traditions of scholastic self-analysis by which the languages have been subjected to careful grammatical study and are therefore authoritatively defined and standardized. Accordingly, the texts in such codified languages have usually been carefully edited and regularized over the millennia. In other words, they have been modeled into classical languages by more or less the same processes that have shaped the models of correctness and authority for other ancient languages such as Greek, Latin, Hebrew,

Arabic, or classical Chinese. Such classical literary languages are quite different from living, colloquial languages; they are artificially frozen, defined by scholastic, ecclesiastic, bureaucratic, or governmental authorities and held to be, in theory, immune to change and variation. In them, the lines between right and wrong are strictly and invariably defined; they embody language that has been domesticated by some authoritative elite.

But this is not the inherent nature of colloquial spoken languages. Languages in the rough are wild and unruly creatures, constantly in flux and varying in myriad ways across their subcommunities of speakers and even among individual speakers. Their standards of correctness are defined loosely and subjectively if at all, and often more honored in the breach. The Gāndhārī of the Buddhist inscriptions and manuscripts we are dealing with is more like language in the rough than a tamed classical language. For example, the inflectional ending of the singular nominative (subject form) of the commonest class of masculine nouns, which in Sanskrit is always *-as* and in Pali *-o*, may be represented by four or occasionally even five different vowels (*-o*, *-e*, *-u*, *-a*, *-i*) in Gāndhārī, and this not only in different texts but sometimes even within the same manuscript, where as many as four such forms may co-occur, at the apparent whim of the scribe. As a result, we are faced with a text where the grammatical inflections, which in theory show the syntactic function of the words, are often so ambiguous that it can be difficult to be sure whether, for example, a given noun represents the subject or object of a sentence.

Besides the ambiguity of the Gāndhārī grammar, a text editor also faces constant problems with its orthography, or spelling. For example, the word for "and" (equivalent to Sanskrit and Pali *ca*) may be spelled in no less than eleven different ways: *ca*, *ci*, *ja*, *ji*, *ya*, *a*, and so on. Likewise, the correspondent to Sanskrit *brahmacaryā*, "pure living," is written in a bewildering variety of ways, including *bramacaria*, *bramacarya*, *bramayia*, *bramayirya*, and *brahmahia*.[84] Such variations arise from various factors such as changes in the pronunciation of the word within the evolution of the language, dialect differences, and variations in pronunciation determined by the position of the word in its sentence. Thus we are faced with something like the situation that prevailed in English before its spelling and grammar were standardized, as anyone who has tried to read an English book of the seventeenth century will have noticed.

But superficially at least, the most striking difference between Gāndhārī and the other Indian Buddhist languages involves their written forms—the scripts used to represent them—rather than the structures of the languages themselves. From the time of the earliest surviving written documents of the historical period of India,[85] namely King Aśoka's inscriptions in the third century BCE, the Brāhmī script was established as the dominant form of writing everywhere in the Indian subcontinent except for the northwest, where Kharoṣṭhī script was used to represent the Gāndhārī language. The origins and relationships of both of these early Indian scripts are somewhat uncertain, although it is agreed that Kharoṣṭhī was somehow derived from, or at least based on, a form of the Aramaic script, a Semitic writing that is directly related to the Hebrew and Arabic alphabets and indirectly related to Greek, Roman, and other European scripts. Aramaic had been in use in northwestern India when it was part of the Achaemenid empire of Iran during the fifth and fourth centuries BCE, and it was apparently adapted there for the representation of an Indian language. This adaptation involved the creation of additional signs for several Indian consonants not present in Aramaic and a refinement of the method of representing vowels, which were only partially indicated in the parent script. The origin of Brāhmī script is more obscure, but the most likely explanation is that it was arbitrarily created by or under the sponsorship of Aśoka himself, apparently with Kharoṣṭhī as a partial model.[86]

The two scripts are superficially very different in that Brāhmī is written from left to right, while Kharoṣṭhī runs from right to left like its presumed archetype, Aramaic. The shapes of the individual characters are, with few exceptions, entirely different. For example, the letter for *k* is 𑀓 in Brāhmī and 𐨐 in Kharoṣṭhī. However, the difference between the two scripts is actually much less than it would seem from their surface appearance, in that they utilize the same graphic principles that are characteristic of Indian scripts in general, and that still govern the several modern Indian scripts such as Devanagari, Bengali, and Kannada, all of which are derived from Brāhmī. In this system, each graphic unit is a single syllable, usually consisting of one or more consonants, to which an extra mark may be added to specify the vowel that follows. But if the vowel of the syllable is short *a*, the most common vowel, the consonant is left unmarked. Thus, for example, in Kharoṣṭhī the syllable *ka* is written as 𐨐, while *ki* is 𐨐𐨁, with an extra diagonal stroke at the top to indicate the vowel *i*. The corresponding syllables in Brāhmī are 𑀓 and 𑀓𑀺, following the same principle despite the differences in form.

The only real systemic difference between the two scripts is that Kharoṣṭhī does not distinguish between short and long vowels, leaving the reader to interpret the quantity of the vowel on the basis of context, whereas in Brāhmī this is explicit. Thus, for instance, Kharoṣṭhī 𐨐𐨁 represents either *ki* or *kī*, while Brāhmī distinguishes *ki* 𑀓𑀺 from *kī* 𑀓𑀻. This distinction is also illustrated by the example cited above, where the Gāndhārī equivalent of Pali *pāvacane* and Sanskrit *prāvacane*, "in the time of," is written *praveaṇo* although the vowel of the first syllable was undoubtedly pronounced as long in Gāndhārī.

Thus a Buddhist monk from other parts of India who visited a monastery in Gandhāra would be unable to read a word of the manuscripts in its library until he had learned Kharoṣṭhī script. But given the underlying systemic resemblance to the scripts he would have been used to, he probably would have been able to do so with a moderate amount of training and effort. This striking though ultimately superficial difference is one of the features that sets Gandhāra off as a distinct cultural zone within the Indian world. Yet, typically enough, it does not set Gandhāra off as foreign to the Indian world but rather marks it as part of it, albeit as a frontier region with a distinctive and slightly aberrant culture.

Besides the dominant Gāndhārī-Kharoṣṭhī combination, several other languages and scripts were part of the mix that constituted cosmopolitan Gandhāra. The Greek language and alphabet was a presence, if only as an archaic legacy that was retained mostly in coin legends. In the formative period of Gandhāran Buddhist civilization, around the late third and early second centuries BCE, the Greek kings of Bactria issued coins with legends written solely in Greek language and script. But as they expanded their territories into the Indian world during the second century BCE, the Greek rulers, now known as Indo-Greeks, began to mint bilingual coins, with Greek legends on the obverse but reverse legends in Gāndhārī (see fig. 7). The use of bilingual legends on coins was continued by the Indo-Scythians, Indo-Parthians, and early Kuṣāṇas through the first centuries before and after the beginning of the Common Era, but inscriptions or other kinds of documents in Greek are virtually nonexistent in the Gandhāra region. This situation probably reflects the inherent conservatism of coinage—note, for example, that the designs of modern American and European coins are still largely based on classical Greek and Roman styles—than about any continued vitality of the Greek language in Gandhāra.

But in the time of Kaniṣka, around the second quarter of the second century, Greek and Gāndhārī coin legends were replaced by the Bactrian language written in a slightly modified form of the Greek alphabet. Bactrian, as we have seen in chapter 1, was also the language used by the Kuṣāṇa kings for inscriptions in their territories in modern Afghanistan, and its use in Kuṣāṇa coins, like most of the divinities portrayed on them, must have been primarily directed toward the northern and western parts of the Kuṣāṇa realm, in Bactria and beyond.

This is not to deny that there were still speakers of Greek, Bactrian, and probably several other languages in Gandhāra in the early centuries of the Common Era. For example, the native languages of the Central Asian and Iranian elite who are frequently portrayed as donors in Gandhāran Buddhist art would have included Bactrian and one or more dialects of Saka, the Iranian language of the Indo-Scythian immigrants from Central Asia. We have clear evidence of this influence in the form of several loan words from these languages into Gāndhārī, although no independent documents in them survive. Thus it is clear that Gāndhārī was the primary written language of Gandhāra throughout the period of our concern, whereas other languages were used only for special purposes. Nearly all of the many hundreds of inscriptions known from Gandhāra throughout the period in question are in Gāndhārī.

Deciphering Gāndhārī Documents

The story of the initial decipherment of the Gāndhārī language and its constant companion, the Kharoṣṭhī script, goes back to the fourth decade of the nineteenth century, when James Prinsep, who by then had already deciphered Brāhmī script, applied himself to Kharoṣṭhī. The key to the eventual decipherment was the abundant bilingual coinage of the Indo-Greek kings. Comparisons of the Greek and Gāndhārī legends enabled Prinsep to discern the value of many of the Kharoṣṭhī characters, although it was not until the 1850s, after Prinsep's premature death in 1840, that a nearly complete understanding of the script was achieved through the combined labors of several scholars.[87]

Like the decipherment of Kharoṣṭhī script, the interpretation of the Gāndhārī language was a gradual process to which many scholars contributed, and it is still ongoing today. Until the discoveries in the last two decades of Buddhist manuscripts, our understanding of Gāndhārī was based mainly on donative inscriptions on stone and metal objects such as reliquaries, stūpa panels, statues, and implements given to Buddhist monasteries by their patrons and visitors. The first definitive and comprehensive work on this material was Sten Konow's volume on Kharoṣṭhī inscriptions in the Corpus Inscriptionum Indicarum series in 1929, in which the hundred inscriptions then known were collected. Since then, several hundred more Kharoṣṭhī inscriptions have been discovered and published, particularly within the last thirty years, and scholars' knowledge of the Gāndhārī language has increased accordingly.[88]

While the discovery of a large number of manuscripts in Gāndhārī has vastly increased our understanding of the language, the many new texts inevitably also raise many new problems. For example, the vocabulary in the inscriptions that were until recently our main source is limited and often formulaic and repetitive, whereas the manuscripts give us vast numbers of previously unattested words. The majority of these can be interpreted with reasonable confidence on the basis of comparisons with the better-known related languages, particularly in the case of texts for which we have parallels in other Buddhist languages. Even when dealing with the many texts that do not have parallel versions, we can often understand previously unattested words by deducing their equivalents according to established patterns of grammatical and phonetic correspondence, such as the ones noted in the section above.

But there are a good many obstacles to the application of these principles. For one thing, the manuscripts are almost always fragmentary or partially illegible, so that it is often a matter of guessing how to reconstruct a word or phrase from its partial remains. Also, due to dialect variation and other random factors, correspondences between languages do not always follow the expected patterns, so that the relationship of a Gāndhārī word to those in other languages may be less than obvious. Even more problematic are those words—and they are not rare—that have no evident correspondent in other languages. In such cases, context in a sentence is usually the best guide, but when a word is attested only once, as is once again quite common, we may be reduced to educated guesses—or sometimes just stumped. Such problematic words typically reflect the local vernacular rather than the shared vocabulary of the Indian languages.[89] Occasionally clues may be found in the vocabulary of the modern dialects, the so-called Dardic languages, which are still spoken in the more isolated regions around ancient Gandhāra. These languages often contain words derived from the ancient Gāndhārī language, from which they are partially descended.

Last but not least, the bewilderingly unstandardized character of Gāndhārī, as discussed in the preceding section, is a major obstacle to a full understanding of the language. Thus, while Gāndhārī is not in any sense an "undeciphered" language, we still do not have a complete knowledge of it; our current rate of comprehension for an intact text might range between 80 and 95 percent. But such problems are, in varying degrees, the norm for the study of ancient languages and scriptures, even the most familiar and best-known ones. For example, anyone who reads the Old Testament in a nonscholarly translation would get the impression that everything in it is clear and completely understood. But in reality, there are a great many words and passages in the Bible whose meaning is uncertain or even wholly unknown. These problems are glossed over in translations designed for religious functions or popular consumption, but in a more scholarly translation the careful reader will observe frequent notes in small print at the bottom of the page along the lines of "meaning of Hebrew uncertain."

In this perspective, after nearly two hundred years of scholarly work, our knowledge of Gāndhārī is still less comprehensive than that of more prominent and copiously attested classical languages of antiquity, Buddhist or otherwise. But we do understand it far better than many other incompletely deciphered languages of the ancient world, for example Etruscan, to say nothing of totally unknown tongues like Cretan linear A or the language of the Indus Valley inscriptions. "Decipherment," in short, is a relative, not an absolute term.[90]

Scholars working on these and similar materials may take some comfort in knowing that such problems plague not only modern scholars but also ancient Buddhist scholars who dealt with multiple versions of their scriptures in various languages. This is illustrated in a remarkable passage from the vinaya of the Mūlasarvāstivāda school as preserved in Chinese translation, according to which the Buddha's disciple Ānanda once heard another monk reciting a well-known verse from the *Dharmapada* as, "If a man were to live for a hundred years and not see a water heron, it were better that he live for only one day and see a water heron." Ānanda explains to the monk that the verse rather should be, "If a man were to live for a hundred years and not see [i.e., understand] the coming into being and the passing [of all things], it were better that he live for only one day and see the coming into being and the passing [of all things]." The key term would be (in a hypothetical Sanskrit original of this passage, which is not extant) *udaya-vyaya* "coming into being and passing," a basic pair of Buddhist doctrinal concepts. But one of the several possible ways of spelling the equivalent of this phrase in Gāndhārī would be *udaya-baka*, which could also mean "a water heron." Thus the anonymous monk's ridiculous rendering of this verse is actually based on a mistranslation. Like many of the episodes in the *Mūlasarvāstivāda-vinaya*, it has a humorous tinge, and superficially it serves as a dialect joke of the sort that people amuse themselves with all over the world.[91]

The problems and limitations of modern knowledge of Gāndhārī vary considerably from text to text and from genre to genre. Some texts, especially the better-preserved ones with multiple parallels in other Buddhist literatures, are almost completely understood, though even here there usually remain a few problems with regard to particular words or phrases. In some other manuscripts, especially very fragmentary ones and those without parallels, numerous uncertainties prevail. In this book I have tried to spare the reader the agonies of doubt that tormented their original editors, presenting, as far as possible, straightforward translations in which some of the problematic passages are rendered as accurately as possible. But the reader should be aware that many renditions are only the most likely ones and are by no means certain. A few cases particularly interesting or illustrative of the types of problems involved are addressed in the introductions to the translations or in the notes.

The Destiny of Gāndhārī and the Triumph of Sanskrit

As the Kuṣāṇa empire began to decline around the end of the second century CE, political and cultural dominance in northern India began shifting to the southeast, particularly to the area of Mathurā, where Sanskrit and Brāhmī script were dominant. As a result, Gāndhārī documents began to adopt spellings resembling those of Sanskrit. For example, the normal Gāndhārī word for "seven," *sata*, may be spelled in late Gāndhārī as *sapta*, exactly as in Sanskrit. In this way, Gāndhārī and Kharoṣṭhī script gradually assimilated to the pan-Indian styles of language and script, and by the late third or early fourth century they had been mostly supplanted by Sanskrit and various local forms of Brāhmī script. At this point, Gāndhārī effectively ceased to exist as a written language and a canonical language of Buddhism.

In effect, Gāndhārī was reabsorbed into its own mother. But this seemingly paradoxical development is part of a larger pattern of gradual Sanskritization that affected Buddhist literature and culture in northern India in the early centuries of the Common Era. This phenomenon is best attested in the form of Buddhist Hybrid Sanskrit, the partially re-Sanskritized Prakrit that prefigured the complete Sanskritization of northern Buddhist literature, which was accomplished by the fifth century. The factors underlying this development are a subject of some speculation. Was it the perennial status and prestige of the Sanskrit language, which caused a certain embarrassment in Buddhist circles about their use of the less-sophisticated Prakrit dialects?[92] Or did Buddhist monks from different parts of India need a common language of communication as their vernacular dialects became increasingly different from one another?[93] Whatever the causes, Buddhists ironically ended up adopting the Sanskrit language earlier prohibited by the Buddha himself.

The Gāndhārī Hypothesis

It was mentioned at the end of chapter 1 that there is strong evidence that some of the early Chinese translations of Indian Buddhist texts reflect originals in Gāndhārī rather than in Sanskrit, as had once been assumed. With the preceding introduction to the relevant languages, we are now equipped to understand exactly how this conclusion has been reached. Clues to the Indian source languages of Chinese translations are sometimes discernible from the forms of the transliteration into Chinese characters of Indian names or Buddhist technical terms. Several of these have been found to reflect Prakrit rather than Sanskrit forms, and in particular, the distinctive pronunciation of Gāndhārī. A classic example is a word for "monk," which was transliterated in the Chinese translation of the *Dīrghāgama* (the collection of longer sūtras) as *ṣa-muən*; this was evidently based on the Gāndhārī form of the word, *ṣamaṇa*, rather than on Sanskrit *śramaṇa*.[94] These and other similar observations gave rise to the aforementioned Gāndhārī hypothesis.[95]

There are many cases among the earliest generation of Chinese translations, dating from the second to fourth centuries, of what seem to be obviously wrong or incomprehensible renderings. This is understandable for a time in which the translators were still struggling to establish methods and standards to bridge the huge gap between Indian languages and Chinese, which are as different as any two languages can be in their sound system, grammatical structures, and conceptual foundations. But if mistakes are the bugaboo of translators, they are often the linguist's best friend, because they may reveal facts about the language, such as variant pronunciations due to sound changes or dialect differences, that the correctly written standard language tends to hide. Some such apparent errors in the early Chinese texts can only be explained by reference to features of an underlying Gāndhārī archetype. For instance, in one passage in the *Lotus Sūtra* the Sanskrit text has *lokanātha*, "lord of the world," where the earliest

Chinese translation by Dharmarakṣa has in its place "roars of the world." This must reflect an underlying original text not in Sanskrit but in Gāndhārī, where the words *nātha* "lord" and *nāda* "roar" can (in some varieties of the language) be pronounced similarly.[96]

Besides such errors revealing an underlying Gāndhārī pronunciation, there are also several cases of copying errors indicating that the Indian archetype texts were written in Kharoṣṭhī script, and therefore presumably in Gāndhārī rather than in Sanskrit and Brāhmī. For example, another *Lotus Sūtra* passage is addressed in its Sanskrit version to Ajita, which is the personal name of the future Buddha Maitreya. But this word is rendered in Dharmarakṣa's Chinese with the word for the number "eighty." This makes absolutely no sense if one assumes that the Chinese version was translated from Sanskrit, but in Gāndhārī the equivalent of the Sanskrit name Ajita is *ayida*, while the word for "eighty" is *aśidi* (Skt *aśīti*). Now, in many styles of Kharoṣṭhī script the letters for *y* and *ś* are very similar, sometimes even identical. Thus the translator, or some previous scribe, must have misread or miscopied *ayida* as *aśida* and then interpreted it as the word for "eighty."[97] The only reasonable conclusion in such a case is that the Chinese translation was based, directly or indirectly, on an archetype in Kharoṣṭhī and Gāndhārī, where the two words concerned could look identical, whereas in Sanskrit and Brāhmī they would have had no such similarity.

In truth, the issues involved are considerably more complex than they are presented here. For instance, other Indian or Central Asian languages may have served as intermediaries for the translation teams. Nevertheless, it is now widely agreed that Gāndhārī texts played a significant, if not solitary, role in the formation of the early Chinese Buddhist texts. For our purposes, it is especially significant that much of the data adduced in the relevant studies comes from the Chinese collection of long sūtras, the counterpart of the Sanskrit *Dīrghāgama* and the Pali *Dīgha-nikāya*, one of the five principal canonical sūtra collections.[98] The Chinese version of the *Dīrghāgama* has been studied in detail with regard to the Indic language that underlay the translation.[99] Despite various degrees of dialect mixture and contamination, it is quite clear that a Gāndhārī substratum was involved, if not solely, at least in part.

The centrality of the *Dīrghāgama* for the Gāndhārī hypothesis is a fortunate coincidence, because one of the most interesting and unexpected discoveries among the British Library Gāndhārī scrolls was a commentary on the *Sūtra of Chanting Together* (*Saṅgīti Sūtra*),[100] one of the most important texts in the *Dīrghāgama*. The *Sūtra of Chanting Together* is one of many texts in early Buddhist literature that were arranged on a numerical scheme, which functions as a mnemonic device for arranging and organizing the basic principles, concepts, and terms of the Dharma. It is divided into ten sections, each of which consists of statements by the Buddha concerning sets of single items, pairs, triads, fours, and so on. The importance of the Gāndhārī manuscript lies in the ordering of the sets in the sūtra; it agrees almost exactly with that of the Chinese version, which is quite different from the orderings of the Pali and Sanskrit versions.[101]

This direct correspondence establishes a structural linkage between the Gāndhārī tradition of the *Sūtra of Chanting Together*, and by implication of the *Dīrghāgama* collection as a whole, with their Chinese versions, thus corroborating the linguistic connection. This linkage, moreover, is reinforced by what is known of the sectarian affiliations of the texts in question. The Chinese *Dīrghāgama* is in all probability a product of the Dharmaguptaka school, whereas the Gāndhārī manuscript in question was found, together with the other British Library scrolls, in a clay pot bearing an inscription marking it as a dedication to "the Dharmaguptakas."[102]

Thus there is a strong convergence of textual, linguistic, and sectarian data to support the hypothesis that the early introduction of Buddhism and Buddhist literature to Central Asia and China was carried out, in part at least, in Gāndhārī rather than in Sanskrit. This theory is further supported by the clear influence of Gāndhārī on other Central

Asian Buddhist languages such as Khotanese, Manichaean Parthian, and Sogdian.[103] But until recently, this theory rested on a foundation that was itself mostly hypothetical, since only one actual manuscript of a Buddhist text in Gāndhārī, namely the Khotan *Dharmapada*, had been known to exist. Now, with the discovery of large numbers of Buddhist canonical and extracanonical texts, the existence of an extensive corpus of Buddhist literature, and possibly even of an entire organized canon, in Gāndhārī[104] has become a matter of fact. Thus, despite its rapid decline and eventually disappearance, Gandhāran Buddhism has had a profound effect on the history of Buddhism. Although the patterns of history often seem to make Gandhāra the passive recipient of events caused by external forces, in reality it was a two-way street: Gandhāra gave to world culture as well as it got.

Further Discoveries of Gandhāran Manuscripts

Though the majority of the manuscripts presented here belong to the British Library collection, the selections are by no means limited to that corpus, for soon after the discovery of British Library scrolls, several other collections and single specimens of similar Gandhāran texts began to come to light. The Robert Senior collection, first announced in 2003, consists of twenty-four scrolls comprising over forty individual texts, dating from around the middle of the second century CE.[105] Like the British Library manuscripts, the Senior scrolls are believed to have been found in the region around Haḍḍa, Afghanistan, although once again this cannot be confirmed.

This group is of extraordinary significance for two reasons. First, it contains a few scrolls that, unlike the highly fragmentary ones in the British Library collection, are mostly intact and nearly completely legible, although the majority are, as usual, fragmentary. Second, its contents and overall character are as different as can be from the very diverse and miscellaneous British Library group, in that the Senior collection is a coherent set of manuscripts, nearly all belonging to the sūtra genre and all written by the same scribe. The set of scrolls had apparently been conceived and written down as a single unit with the express intention of being interred as a sacred relic, as explained in detail in the introduction to translation 2, where five sūtras set down on two separate scrolls from the Senior collection are presented.

A few years after the discovery of the British Library manuscripts, an enormous collection of Buddhist manuscript material from Afghanistan became available for scholarly study. This material, involving over ten thousand fragments in all, ranging in date from about the second to the eighth centuries, was reportedly found in caves near Bamiyan, the site of the giant Buddhas that were destroyed by the Taliban in 2001. Like most other later Buddhist manuscripts that have been found in northern India and Pakistan, Nepal, and Central Asia, the majority of the Bamiyan fragments are in Sanskrit and in local forms of Brāhmī script. But they also include some 250 small fragments of older manuscripts in Gāndhārī and Kharoṣṭhī. Although the Gāndhārī fragments represent the earliest phase of the Bamiyan manuscripts as a whole, they are somewhat later than most other Gāndhārī manuscripts, dating from about the late second to the late third centuries of the Common Era.[106] As such, they represent the later phase of Buddhist literature in Gāndhārī and provide interesting insights into the fate of Gāndhārī as a Buddhist literary language, as has been discussed above.

Like the British Library manuscripts, and unlike the Senior collection, the Bamiyan Gāndhārī fragments comprise an extraordinarily wide variety of texts, genres, and styles. For this reason, and especially because of their extremely fragmentary condition, they pose daunting challenges to the scholars studying them. In most cases we have only small pieces of scattered leaves, and there are no continuous texts of any great length. Nevertheless, it has proved possible to interpret and identify many of the texts represented, including such important ones as the *Great Nirvāṇa Sūtra* (*Mahāparinirvāṇa Sūtra*),[107] the *Sūtra of the Fortunate Eon* (*Bhadrakalpika Sūtra*), and two other Mahāyāna sūtras.

Unfortunately, none of the Bamiyan texts can be represented in this anthology because they are all too fragmentary to permit a coherent translation, but they have proven extremely important for research on the development of Gāndhārī literature and of Buddhist literature and canons in general. Particularly important is the recent discovery of some twenty-five fragments of what is evidently a complete manuscript of the *Ekottarikāgama* collection of numerically arranged sūtras. This, as will be explained in the following chapter, is the first example of a complete manuscript in Gāndhārī of one of the fundamental sūtra compilations.

Another major set of Gāndhārī manuscripts, the Bajaur collection, was reportedly found in the Bajaur Tribal Area of Pakistan near the Afghan border. Like most of the other similar groups, the Bajaur collection is a diverse collection of nineteen scrolls written by eighteen different scribes.[108] The scrolls include some twenty-five texts of miscellaneous genres, including, as usual, some familiar works as well as many previously unknown ones, most notably an exceptionally long and important Mahāyāna sūtra and some rare specimens of vinaya manuscripts, which will be described in the following chapter.

Another mixed collection, introduced by Harry Falk in a 2011 article, seems to have been split up and is now in the hands of several different private collectors, whence its nickname, the "Split collection." This group contains, among other interesting items, a third Gāndhārī fragment of the *Dharmapada* in addition to the Khotan and British Library manuscripts and, most importantly, a very early manuscript of a Perfection of Wisdom (*Prajñāpāramitā*) sūtra, one of the foundational works of Mahāyāna Buddhism, which is presented here as translation 12.

Several other smaller groups of Gāndhārī manuscripts or individual items are known. A small set of fragments of unidentified texts now in the Bibliothèque nationale de France from the region

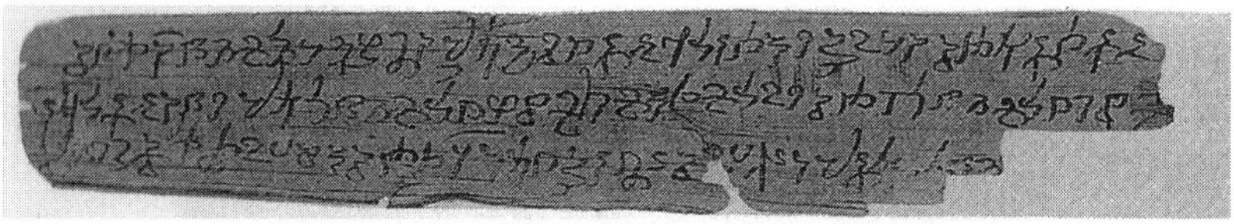

Figure 19. Fragment of a palm-leaf folio from Bamiyan: the *Great Nirvāṇa Sūtra.*

of Subashi on the northern rim of the Tarim Basin testifies to the existence of Buddhist literature in Gāndhārī in the oasis cities along the northern silk route in Central Asia.[109] A single Gandhāran scroll acquired by the United States Library of Congress in 2004, which probably dates to as early as the first century BCE, proved to contain the *Many Buddhas Sūtra* (*Bahubuddhaka Sūtra*), which is presented here in translation 8.

The Character of the Scrolls

Most of the manuscripts with which we are concerned are scrolls written on birchbark, which was the usual writing material in the Himalayan fringe of the South Asian continent. Among the several collections of Gāndhārī manuscripts, only the Bamiyan texts use the format that was customary in sub-Himalayan India, namely palm leaves trimmed into a long rectangular shape and strung together through one or two holes in each folio. In both formats, the texts are written in a black carbon-based ink, usually with little or no decoration or calligraphic ornamentation beyond the occasional small floral or geometric designs marking the divisions between text sections. On the whole, the scribes show little concern with the visual aspect of the manuscripts, which have a strictly utilitarian aspect. Although they were sacred objects, they were not conceived as works of art or as calligraphic displays but as practical tools to facilitate the teaching, learning, and preservation of the Dharma.

Figure 20. Senior scroll 24 as found, rolled up and folded in half lengthwise.

For storage, the birchbark scrolls were rolled, or sometimes folded, from the bottom upward, and the resulting packet was often folded in half lengthwise. The scrolls come in two formats. Shorter texts, such as the *Rhinoceros Sūtra* in the British Library collection (translation 3) and the *Saṃyuktāgama* sūtras (thematically grouped sūtras) from the Senior collection (translation 2), were written on a single sheet of bark, either roughly square or rectangular with the length (i.e., height) somewhat greater than the width. The height and width of these small scrolls are typically between about twenty to thirty centimeters (for an example of this type, see figure 26 on page 130). Longer texts, such as the *Dharmapada* (translation 4) or the *Songs of Lake Anavatapta* (translation 5), were inscribed on composite scrolls, typically about twelve to twenty centimeters wide. In some cases these may have originally been as much as several meters long, although no complete examples survive. These scrolls were made up of separate sheets of bark, typically between about twenty and forty centimeters long, which were glued together and sometimes also stitched to prevent separation. They also usually had a thread sewn along the vertical margins, intended to maintain the integrity of the entire scroll.

The text was written horizontally, that is, across the shorter length, from top to bottom of the recto (front) side. In many cases, the text

Figure 21. A portion of British Library fragment 1, the *Songs of Lake Anavatapta*, showing the blank area between segments that were originally glued together.

was continued on the verso (rear) side, which was turned upside down so that the writing proceeded from the bottom to the top. But in many scrolls the rear was left blank because its surface, the inner side of the bark, was rougher and darker than the soft and smooth outer side. In some cases, though, manuscripts with blank verso sides were recycled by later scribes who used them to record other texts, unrelated to the original one on the recto, as in the case of the several collections of avadānas and previous-life stories (*pūrvayoga*) in the British Library collections (translations 6 and 7).

The length of a scroll was limited by practical considerations, so that texts that were too long to record on a single scroll must have been written in multiple scrolls or "volumes."[110] In many cases, for example the *Dharmapada*, the *Songs of Lake Anavatapta*, and the *Perfection of Wisdom Sūtra*, we have only one scroll out of what should have been a set of several or many that comprised the entire text. Surprisingly, though, in only one case have we found more than one scroll of such a set. Even more surprisingly, in nearly every case, including the three presented here and several others, the surviving scroll was the first one of the set.[111] This can hardly be a coincidence, although the reason for this consistent pattern is uncertain. It could be that in such cases only the first volume was actually written, perhaps intended to serve as a symbolic representation of the whole, as an act of merit-making. Alternatively, if we are correct in assuming that some of the scrolls were interred because they had become decrepit from age and use, the pattern could result from the first volume of a set being the one that was most frequently read or recited from, and therefore the one that had to be recopied most frequently.

3. The Buddhist Literature of Gandhāra

The Scope of Gandhāran Buddhist Literature

IN ALL, OVER two hundred texts in Gāndhārī are now known.[112] The Gāndhārī texts include materials from all three of the traditional "baskets" (*piṭaka*) that comprise the Buddhist canon, though by no means in equal proportions. Most notably, the five subsets of the sūtra basket are well represented in several of the manuscript groups, while vinaya texts are rare throughout. The third basket, the abhidharma, is represented by a considerable number of manuscripts, but its scope and composition is more difficult to define, for reasons that will be explained below. There is also a great deal of new material that does not fit neatly into the structure of canons as we know them from other Buddhist traditions. Some of these texts are "paracanonical," that is, marginally or disputedly canonical, while others are distinctly post-canonical material consisting of later analytic, commentarial, and compilatory texts.

In order to understand the range of Gandhāran Buddhist literature and its relationship to other Buddhist literatures and canons, it is convenient to divide the texts into those that have parallels in one or more other Buddhist literatures, and those that, as far as we can tell, are unique to and were presumably originally composed in Gandhāra. Each of these two classes has its own special value for our enterprise of deducing the overall scope and significance of Gandhāran literature. The texts with parallels,[113] most notably sūtras, permit us to compare the Gandhāran versions with corresponding ones in Pali, Sanskrit, Chinese, and occasionally other languages such as Tibetan, in order to determine how these different versions relate to and differ from each other. But the texts without parallels[114] are at least equally and perhaps ultimately more important in that they reveal something of how Gandhāran Buddhism was, on the one hand, distinct from other local Buddhisms, and how on the other hand it may have influenced the formation of later schools of Buddhism.

Canonical and Paracanonical Sūtras

In the Pali canon, which is the most conveniently accessible and best-documented specimen of a traditional Buddhist canon,[115] the sūtra basket is subdivided into five collections, or *nikāyas* (Skt *āgama*), which are categorized either according to the length of the texts they contain, or by their internal organizational principles. These are:

1. *Dīgha-nikāya*: "long sūtras" (34 in all)
2. *Majjhima-nikāya*: "medium-length sūtras" (150)
3. *Saṃyutta-nikāya*: "grouped sūtras," i.e., short sūtras (several thousand in all) arranged according to common themes or topics[116]
4. *Aṅguttara-nikāya*: "increasing sūtras," i.e., short sūtras (several thousand) arranged in numerical sets from one to eleven, according to the number of points addressed in each sūtra[117]
5. *Khuddaka-nikāya*: "short sūtras," comprising fifteen texts of very diverse contents, including several subcollections of short sūtras[118]

Specimens of each of these five sūtra categories have been found among the Gāndhārī manuscripts but in widely differing proportions.[119] Only two items from the collection of long sūtras (Skt *Dīrghāgama*) are known: the *Sūtra on the Fruits of the Life of Striving*

(*Śrāmaṇyaphala Sūtra*) in the Robert Senior collection and the *Great Nirvāṇa Sūtra* (*Mahāparinirvāṇa Sūtra*) among the Bamiyan fragments. The British Library collection also includes a commentary on the *Sūtra of Chanting Together* from the long sūtras.

Five medium-length sūtras (Skt *Madhyamāgama*) have been identified, most of them in the Senior collection, which unlike the other collections consists almost entirely of sūtra texts. But the majority of the sūtras in the Senior collection (twenty-nine out of forty-one) belong to[120] the thematically grouped sūtras (Skt *Saṃyuktāgama*), samples of which appear in translation 2.

Specimens in Gāndhārī of the numerically grouped sūtras (Skt *Ekottarikāgama*) consist of a fragmentary British Library manuscript with three sūtras of this class (translation 1), and most importantly, a set of small fragments from Bamiyan of what was probably a complete manuscript of this collection, as will be explained below (pages 97–99).

The British Library collection also contains two important texts of the short sūtras (Skt *Kṣudrakāgama*) class: the *Dharmapada* and the *Rhinoceros Sūtra*.[121] The "Meaningful Sayings" (Skt *Arthapada*) or "Groups of Eight" (P *Aṭṭhakavagga*)[122] is represented by a small fragment in the Split collection;[123] a much larger fragment of the same manuscript is known to exist. In the case of two other important texts, the *Songs of Lake Anavatapta* (*Anavataptagāthā*) and the *Many Buddhas Sūtra* (*Bahubuddhaka Sūtra*),[124] it is difficult to determine their status and position within a hypothetical Gandhāran canon. They do not appear as such in the Pali canon but do have parallels in Buddhist Sanskrit literature from India and Central Asia, and they were probably included in one or more of the lost Sanskrit canons. Most likely, they too would have been included in the miscellaneous *Kṣudrakāgama* collection.

In general, the broad similarity of the contents and modes of arrangement of the Gandhāran sūtras with the corresponding ones in other canons shows that, as would be expected, this was the most stable and consistent part of the three sections of the Tripiṭaka.

Vinaya Texts

In contrast to the comparatively well-attested sūtra literature, vinaya texts are extremely rare in Gāndhārī. In fact, to date only two certain examples are known, both in the Bajaur collection. One of these contains a section of the *Prātimokṣa Sūtra*, the basic set of two hundred plus rules for monks that constitutes the foundation of the vinaya. Strangely enough, the set of rules is written out twice, in slightly different versions, on the front and back of the scroll. This arrangement is most unusual, but it has been surmised that this text might have served as a reference source for a monk who was studying the relationship of the different versions of the *Prātimokṣa* as it was known to different schools or Buddhist communities.[125]

Abhidharma and Scholastic Literature

Among the three "baskets" of the Buddhist canon, the abhidharma is the most prone to variation among the different schools. The abhidharma, in focusing on the systemic analysis, codification, and systematization of Buddhist thought as presented in the sūtras, is distinctly secondary to the sūtra and vinaya both in terms of historical sequence and, in some communities at least, of the authority of its contents; in fact, there were some schools in antiquity that denied canonical status to the abhidharma.[126] Among the majority of schools that did have an Abhidharma-piṭaka, the contents could be entirely different, although they do, broadly speaking, address similar issues in similar terms.

For this reason, it is impossible to define the boundaries of the abhidharma category in a corpus of literature of which we have only random surviving scraps. But there are a good number of texts, especially among the British Library and Bajaur scrolls, that partake of the characteristic features and subject matter of abhidharma and that can thus be tentatively categorized as such. Since all of these lack direct parallels in other canons, and because they often treat subtle and abstruse points of doctrine and philosophy, they present one of the most daunting challenges to interpretation; see, for example, the extract from a polemic treatise presented in translation 11.

There are also several specimens, again mostly in the British Library and Bajaur collections, of scholastic texts and commentaries that address concerns similar to those typically found in abhidharma literature but that may not have been conceived of as part of a canonical abhidharma collection. Two especially noteworthy examples, both in the British Library group, are the commentary on the *Sūtra of Chanting Together* (translation 9) and the set of analytic commentaries on canonical verses selected (on grounds that remain obscure to us) from various sūtras belonging to the *Kṣudrakāgama* collection (translation 10). As will be explained in detail in the introductions to the relevant translations, these texts employ a distinctive analytical technique of "mapping" or "categorial reduction" that seems to have been a specialty of Gandhāran Buddhist scholarship but that also influenced other Buddhist traditions. This distinctive analytic method is one of the strongest indications of an independent and influential intellectual tradition within Gandhāran Buddhism.

Edifying Narratives

Two related genres with a distinct local flavor, represented mainly in the British Library collection, are legends about the previous lives and deeds of important figures in the Buddhist tradition: *pūrvayogas*, or previous-life stories, and avadāna legends. The legends address a wide variety of topics concerning the Dharma, Buddhist ethics, and the interactions of Buddhists with other members of society.[127] Most of the surviving Gandhāran stories were recorded by a single scribe who worked as a scavenger of empty space among the British Library scrolls, writing them on the blank portions of scrolls that had been previously inscribed with other texts. These stories usually present severe difficulties of interpretation, among other reasons because they are written out in an extremely terse outline form that was apparently intended to jog the memory of the scribe himself rather than to communicate the story directly to other readers.

The local character of these legends becomes clear from their references to historical figures of the Gandhāra region in the first century CE as well as to other features of the Gandhāran cultural landscape, as mentioned in chapter 1. Less clear is the status of these texts vis-à-vis the Buddhist canon. A few of the stories have close or partial parallels in other Buddhist literatures, most notably the story of Sudaṣṇa (in translation 6c), which corresponds to the *Vessantara-jātaka*, the last, longest, and best-known story in the Pali *Jātakas*, the popular collection of stories about the previous lives of the Buddha. But the majority of these stories are otherwise unknown, although in their themes they seem to prefigure the postcanonical collections of avadānas, which became a highly developed genre in later Buddhist literature in Sanskrit.[128]

Mahāyāna Texts

Among the most important material in the Gāndhārī manuscripts are the several Mahāyāna sūtras. As mentioned in chapter 1, at least seven Mahāyāna texts[129] in Gāndhārī have now been identified among the manuscripts of the Bajaur, Split, and Bamiyan collections. Three of them, the *Bodhisattvapiṭaka Sūtra*,[130] the *Sūtra of the Samādhi of the Collection of All Merits* (*Sarvapuṇyasamuccayasamādhi Sūtra*),[131] and the *Sūtra of the Fortunate Eon*[132] are among the Bamiyan fragments, which generally represent the later phases of Gāndhārī literature, but four more examples have also been identified among older groups. Especially noteworthy is a text of the *Perfection of Wisdom Sūtra* that has been radiocarbon-dated to a period between the middle of the first and middle of the second centuries CE, and that presents an early form of one of the most foundational sūtras of Mahāyāna Buddhism.

Another early Mahāyāna sūtra from the Bajaur collection, whose title unfortunately does not survive, is of extraordinary significance. At nearly six hundred lines, this is the longest Gāndhārī manuscript known to date. It records the Buddha's teachings to 84,000 divine beings (*devaputra*) about the training and career of a bodhisattva. The discourse includes a description of the world where the divine beings will ultimately be reborn, the pure realm of an otherwise unknown Buddha Vipulaprabhāsa or Mahāprabha, which is likened to the more familiar Abhirati paradise of the Buddha Akṣobhya.[133] In form and content it is broadly similar to several other Mahāyāna sūtras, but it has no direct parallels in previously known Buddhist literature. This sūtra represents an early manifestation of Pure Land Buddhism, which focuses on the attainment of rebirth in the paradise of a buddha in a distant universe and which would become one of the most prevalent forms of Buddhism in East Asia. But it differs from other Pure Land sūtras in several important regards. For example, it lacks references to the Perfection of Wisdom and the doctrine of emptiness, to devotional "shortcuts" that can lead worshipers directly to the paradises of the buddhas, or to the cult of the book. Instead, it stresses the development of "forbearance toward dharmas" or "patient acceptance with regard to the factors of existence" (*dharmakṣānti*) as the primary goal of the teaching. This contrasts with Mahāyāna sūtras in general, where this practice is typically not so central.[134]

Thus it is now clear that there was an extensive body of Mahāyāna literature in Gāndhārī, although it cannot be assumed that Gāndhārī was the original language of these sūtras, since they could well have been translated from or existed in parallel to versions in other Middle Indo-Aryan dialects. The radiocarbon dating of the *Perfection of Wisdom Sūtra* to the first or second century CE is consistent with other indications of the development and expansion of Mahāyāna beliefs and practices in and around the Kuṣāṇa period. The Bajaur Mahāyāna sūtra, which is datable to around the same period, has thus been appropriately described by Ingo Strauch, who, together with Andrea Schlosser, is preparing a comprehensive edition of it, as an "early example of a

Mahayana sutra which leads into a stage of Mahayana which is nearly unknown to us," and which has the potential to "offer a glimpse into the true 'Early Mahayana.'"[135]

Most of the Mahāyāna texts in Gāndhārī that have been identified so far were previously known only from translations into Tibetan and/or Chinese,[136] so that for them the Gāndhārī remnants are the only original Indic-language version. But since the Bajaur Mahāyāna sūtra has no parallel in any language, this raises the possibility that this is only one of several or perhaps many early Mahāyāna texts that were once extant in Gandhāra but were never translated into Tibetan or Chinese and disappeared in India.[137] The further study and complete publication of this sūtra thus promises to provide groundbreaking insights into the origin and early history of Mahāyāna Buddhism, and we may hope that more such unknown Mahāyāna sūtras might come to light in the future.

Miscellaneous Texts

Besides these major genres, specimens of a few other classes of texts have been identified among the various collections, particularly among the very diverse Bajaur scrolls. This collection includes a text of the "protective" (*rakṣā*) class in which the serpent king Manasvī presents the Buddha with a magic spell (*dhāraṇī*).[138] This manuscript provides a unique insight into the early formation during the first centuries of the Common Era of the *dhāraṇī* genre, which was to become very prominent in later Buddhist literature.

The Bajaur collection also yielded an acrophonic poem in which each half-verse begins with a letter in the sequence of the Kharoṣṭhī alphabet, which is known as the *arapacana* after the first five characters (*a*, *ra*, *pa*, *ca*, *na*, etc.). Although other types of mnemonic teachings according to the *arapacana* sequence are known in later Buddhist literature, this is the first instance of an *arapacana* poem in its original Gāndhārī form.[139]

Both the Bajaur and the British Library collections include early specimens (not yet published) of poems or hymns in praise of the Buddha.[140] This too is a genre that was to become very popular in later Buddhist literature.

What Did Gandhāran Buddhists Read?

The manuscripts summarized here are merely a small fraction of what in Gandhāra's heyday during the early centuries of the Common Era must have been a vast literature, and the various groups of texts come from different times and places in and around Gandhāra. They do nonetheless constitute something approaching a critical mass in which some meaningful patterns can be discerned, if only in a tentative fashion. In such situations, the existence of multiple manuscripts is the most obvious indication of the importance of a particular text or genre. Given the relatively small number of texts (some 200 in all) and manuscripts known so far, we cannot expect too much help from this technique, but there are at least two cases of multiple versions of a text. One is the *Songs of Lake Anavatapta*, which is extant in one manuscript from the British Library collection and another among the Senior scrolls. This confirms its popularity, which is also indicated by the existence of several other versions in Sanskrit, Chinese, Tibetan, and, in the form of partial quotations, in Pali.[141]

But the case of the *Dharmapada* is even more revealing. Three Gāndhārī manuscripts of it are now known. Besides the Khotan manuscript that was the first Gāndhārī scroll to be discovered, fragmentary versions are now also available in both the British Library and Split collections.[142] This is consistent with the great popularity of this text throughout the Buddhist world, and it parallels the pattern seen in the Sanskrit manuscripts from Central Asia, among which the *Udānavarga* ("groups of inspired verses"), the Sanskrit correspondent to the *Dharmapada*, is by far the most common text.

The evident popularity of the *Songs of Lake Anavatapta* and the

Dharmapada is also consistent with a broader pattern among the Gāndhārī materials and in Indian Buddhist literature in general, wherein the short verse sūtras of the *Kṣudraka* class tend to be among the most widely known and frequently copied texts. In the Pali canon, the *Khuddaka-nikāya* includes, besides the *Jātakas* and the *Dharmapada*, the compilation called *Suttanipāta* ("collection of sūtras"), which itself is a composite of five smaller anthologies.[143] Although this compilation exists as such only in the Pali canon, some of its five components, especially the set of short verse sūtras called *Aṭṭhakavagga* ("groups of eight"), are widely attested as independent texts in other Buddhist traditions. The *Aṭṭhakavagga* is attested in two ways in the Gāndhārī corpus: first as a separate manuscript of the text (as noted above, page 85), and second in the form of nine verses from it that are quoted in a commentary on canonical verses in the British Library collection.[144] Another of the five component texts of the Pali *Suttanipāta*, the *Pārāyanavagga* ("the ultimate way"), is also quoted six times in the same commentary.

The reason for the frequency among the Gāndhārī manuscripts of texts of the *Kṣudraka* class is elucidated by a passage in a vinaya text of the Mahāsāṅghika school, preserved in Chinese translation, containing a list of five texts that "serve for the instruction of novices." Of these five texts, correspondents to four have been identified among the Gāndhārī manuscripts in the British Library and other collections: the *Aṭṭhakavagga*, the *Pārāyanavagga*, the *Songs of Lake Anavatapta*, and the *Rhinoceros Sūtra*.[145] This is hardly likely to be a coincidence; rather, their presence among the relatively small number of known Gāndhārī texts probably means that they were part of the basic curriculum in Gandhāran monasteries. Although the *Dharmapada* is not included in the aforementioned curriculum for novices, in view of its prominence among the Gāndhārī collections as well as in Buddhist literature everywhere, we can reasonably assume that it too was part of the basic training of young monks, perhaps even at a more elementary level than that represented by the list in question.

These texts, as will be seen from the samples presented here in translations 3, 4, and 10, teach the basic principles of Buddhist morality and practice, with little discussion of the subtler points of doctrine and theory. The *Songs of Lake Anavatapta*, for example, teaches by means of simple stories the karmic results across lifetimes of good and bad deeds. Thus Bharadvāja, who in a past life told his mother to "eat rocks," now suffers from a strange compulsion to chew on pebbles, while Kusuma, who long ago gave a single flower to the Buddha Vipaśyin, dwelt in heaven for a billion years and is now destined to attain nirvāṇa at the end of this, his last life. To this day, similar texts serve as introductory guides to Buddhist ethics for lay followers as well as for novice monks and nuns.

This is all in stark contrast to the subtle intellectualism of many of the other Gandhāran texts. Although on the whole we know little about the curriculum of study at ancient monasteries, we can suppose that the sort of complex argumentation presented in the polemic abhidharma treatise in the British Library collection must have been written by and for advanced scholar monks.[146] The agonistic format of that text, as of similar philosophical and doctrinal treatises, must reflect the formal debates between followers of different schools that were a prominent feature of Buddhist intellectual life. Such texts were no doubt studied not only for their own sake but also in order to inculcate the necessary debating skills.

Other texts, such as the commentary on the *Sūtra of Chanting Together* and the two commentaries on canonical verses (translations 9 and 10), occupy an intermediate position. They presume knowledge of the basic terms and concepts of Buddhist doctrine but seem to be designed to clarify their interrelationships and to elucidate them on a practical and pedagogical rather than an analytic or philosophical level.

The presence and distribution of Mahāyāna texts among five separate collections of Gāndhārī manuscripts is also worthy of special note. All of them were found within collections containing a wide variety of texts of different genres, and in each case the Mahāyāna text or texts were a small minority of the complete group. In the Bamiyan group, for example, small fragments of three Mahāyāna sūtras were found along with a large number of other non-Mahāyāna texts in Gāndhārī. The Bajaur collection contained, besides the important Mahāyāna sūtra described above, about twenty-four texts, the vast majority of them non-Mahāyāna.[147] This pattern is consistent with a recent trend of thinking about the shape of the early Mahāyāna, according to which the new movement originated within the circles of traditional or "mainstream" Buddhism and only later developed into a distinct institution that perceived and presented itself as in opposition to the more traditionalist schools.[148] Within the Gāndhārī manuscripts, which are now our earliest direct evidence for the emergence of Mahāyāna Buddhism, we find no evidence of separation from or hostility toward the more traditional schools. If the collocation of manuscripts of miscellaneous types in these deposits has any significance at all, it suggests that the inhabitants of Gandhāran monasteries shared and studied Mahāyāna and non-Mahāyāna scriptures together.

The Bajaur Mahāyāna sūtra also supports recent theories about the early development of Mahāyāna. As mentioned above, this sūtra, or at least the surviving portions of it, lacks any reference to several of the doctrines that are often thought of as essential to and definitive of the Mahāyāna, such as the Perfection of Wisdom, devotional cults of buddhas and bodhisattvas, and the cult of the book. But it has been argued, for example by Jan Nattier,[149] that these features became definitive of the Mahāyāna only at a relatively late stage of its development, and that a failure on the part of modern scholars to recognize this has hindered an accurate understanding of the origins and true nature of Mahāyāna Buddhism. Although we must be cautious in dealing with a fragmentary text, the new Bajaur sūtra appears to provide support for this view of early Mahāyāna. It also supports an emerging view, influentially formulated by Gregory Schopen, that the Mahāyāna, "rather than being a single identifiable group, was in the beginning a loose federation of a number of distinct related cults."[150]

Oral and Written Texts and Canons

Having surveyed the contents of Gandhāran Buddhist literature as it is now known, we can now turn to the question of the nature, contents, and structure of the much larger body of literature to which it once belonged—a body of literature that will be referred to here, as a matter of convenience, as the Gandhāran canon. This question can be best addressed by reference to the non-Mahāyāna sūtra texts, the āgamas, this being the division of the Tripiṭaka that is typically most stable across Buddhist traditions and hence most convenient and revealing for comparative study.

Although the total number of āgama sūtras in Gāndhārī is still rather small, it is nonetheless significant that, but for one important exception that will be mentioned below, all or most of the relevant manuscripts contained individual sūtras or partial anthologies rather than complete collections of larger groupings, such as one of the five divisions of the Sūtra-piṭaka. One such example is the sūtras in translation 1, three sūtras of the numerically arranged type of the *Ekottarikāgama*, each concerning a group of four items. Due to its fragmentary condition, we cannot be completely sure of the textual status of the manuscript. It could have been part of a complete *Ekottarikāgama* text, but this is quite unlikely, first because it would require an impractically large number of scrolls—many hundreds—to encompass this vast corpus, and secondly because its arrangement and organizational principles for the most part[151] do not correspond to those of the corresponding collections in Pali, Sanskrit, and Chinese.[152] Therefore this scroll is more likely to have belonged to a selective anthology, or perhaps to a partial manuscript of the *Ekottarikāgama* comprising only the "fours" section.

Particularly important and revealing in this regard is the Senior collection. Unlike all the other collections, its contents are homogeneous in terms of genre, consisting for the most part of thirty-five sūtras, far outnumbering the total number of sūtras in all other known

Gāndhārī manuscripts. The collection is apparently a selective anthology of sūtras, in which twenty-nine of the thirty-five sūtras correspond to texts that are classed in other canons as part of the thematically arranged *Saṃyuktāgama*, along with a few from the *Dīrghāgama* and *Madhyamāgama* classes. Similar selective anthologies consisting of a few dozen sūtras from the *Saṃyuktāgama* and *Ekottarikāgama* are extant in Chinese translation.[153]

Although the twenty-nine *Saṃyuktāgama* sūtras of the Senior collection are definitely part of a selective anthology rather than a complete *Saṃyuktāgama* text, their selection and arrangement show that they must have been extracted from a preexisting complete *Saṃyuktāgama* whose structure resembled that of the corresponding collections in the Pali and Chinese canons.[154] For example, one of the Senior scrolls contains fourteen short sūtras that correspond to a subset entitled the "Forest Group" (P *vanasaṃyutta*), which is found in both the Pali *Aṅguttara-nikāya* and the Chinese *Saṃyuktāgama*. This makes it clear that the Gandhāran Buddhists were familiar with complete sūtra compilations that were generally similar in content and structure to those preserved in other parts of the Buddhist world. Thus we can be confident that we are not dealing with a precanonical stage before the standard arrangements of sūtras had been formulated nor with a hypothetical period in which such compilations had been established elsewhere but were not known in Gandhāra.

This finding supports the traditional view that the central sections of the canons were common to all branches of early Indian Buddhism and that they represent the oldest and most fundamental teachings. The question, then, is not whether these collections existed in Buddhist Gandhāra, but rather in what form they existed and how they were preserved and taught. The texts described above are suggestive of a system that was largely oral and only secondarily written, and this is hardly surprising in light of what we know of the Buddhist canonical tradition as a whole. The words of the Buddha were preserved only in oral form for several centuries, and they began to be set down in writing only around the period of the earliest Gāndhārī manuscripts, that is, the first century BCE. In the centuries that followed, preserving texts in writing became more widespread, but it never entirely supplanted orality. Memorization and the communal chanting of scripture remains to this day a cornerstone of Buddhist monastic life, in which oral and written texts sometimes continue to coexist in a symbiotic fashion.

Thus on the basis of the information that has been available until now, it would seem that in the earlier phase of the Gandhāran manuscript tradition, from about the first century BCE to the second century CE, individual texts or selective anthologies from the massive sūtra collections were already being set down in writing, but not the entire collections. The Gāndhārī sūtras from the *Dīrghāgama* are instructive in this regard. Only three such sūtras have been found to date, one each in three separate manuscript groups. But it is surely no coincidence that the three are among the most prominent and frequently studied *Dīrghāgama* texts in Buddhist tradition generally. The *Great Nirvāṇa Sūtra* and the *Sūtra of Chanting Together*, for example, are both privileged in the Sanskrit *Dīrghāgama* as part of a special set of six foundational sūtras placed at the beginning of the anthology,[155] while the *Sūtra on the Fruits of the Life of Striving* is the second sūtra of the Pali *Dīgha-nikāya* and is extant in no less than eight different versions in Pali, Sanskrit, Chinese, Tibetan, and Gāndhārī.[156] This and similar patterns suggest that manuscript preservation was at this stage being used primarily if not exclusively for sūtras of particular importance, perhaps because they were singled out for special attention in the monastic curriculum.

But this picture changes when we look at the later Gāndhārī manuscripts from the Bamiyan group, most of which date from the late second century or the third century. Here, a set of some twenty-five small fragments has been recently determined to be a miniscule remnant of what was probably a complete manuscript of the numerically arranged sūtras of the *Ekottarikāgama* in Gāndhārī.[157] With the help of comparisons with the corresponding complete collections preserved in Pali and Chinese, as well as with some surviving fragments of a Sanskrit version, nearly all of the Bamiyan fragments can be identified with sūtras from the sections of the sixes, nines, tens, and elevens. Among the Bamiyan fragments we are lucky enough to have five instances of a juncture between two separate sūtras, thus revealing their sequence; and in all five cases, the sequences are similar, though not identical, to the corresponding sequences in the Pali *Aṅguttara-nikāya*.[158] This means that the fragments probably belong to a complete *Ekottarikāgama* in Gāndhārī whose structure was, as would be expected, similar but not identical to the Pali version.

Such a complete manuscript would however have had to be huge, to judge by the size of the corresponding Pali collection, which contains several thousand sūtras and covers some 1,800 pages in printed form. It would have had to comprise many hundreds if not thousands of leaves, but this is not impossible. For, unlike all of the older Gāndhārī manuscripts written on birchbark scrolls, the Bamiyan manuscripts are on separate palm leaves, a format much more convenient for recording long texts. In fact, some of the incomplete later Sanskrit manuscripts found at Bamiyan do consist of several hundred pages at least. This contrasts with the Gāndhārī scrolls, where we have found only one clear specimen of a text spanning multiple volumes, leading to the suspicion that at least some of the long texts were never actually copied out in full. Thus the difference between the contents and format of the earlier and later groups of Gandhāran manuscript implies that they belong to a transitional period during which Buddhist institutions were beginning to record comprehensive rather than partial or representative written copies of their textual corpora. This movement toward exhaustive written texts may have been promoted or at least facilitated by the adoption of the technology of separate leaves instead of the cumbersome and fragile scrolls.[159]

The discovery of an apparently complete manuscript of the *Ekottarikāgama* in Gāndhārī implies that the other component collections of the Sūtra-piṭaka, and perhaps also of the other two main divisions of the canon, were also beginning to be written out in full at this time, although as yet we have no direct evidence for this. This reconstruction of the gradual shift toward written canons is admittedly provisional, and it is not at all unlikely that future discoveries and deeper analyses of the manuscripts already known will modify, perhaps even discredit, this scenario. But this is a risk that scholars must take when all they have to work with are the random scraps of information that happen to have survived from antiquity; in such situations, hypotheses are made to be broken.

Was There a Gāndhārī Canon?

Up to now, I have been using the term *canon* in a loose sense. In the strictest sense of the term, a canon of sacred scriptures is an authoritatively standardized and unchangeable corpus, such as the Qur'an or the Bible. This is what historians of religion refer to more specifically as a fixed or closed canon, as opposed to an open canon, reflecting a situation in which a religious community deems a certain set of texts to be authoritative but without ruling out the possibility of further additions. The history of the development of scriptural religions typically involves an earlier period when the canon is more or less open and flexible, followed by a point at which it is definitively deliminated and declared closed for all time to come. The establishment of a canon, and particularly of a closed canon, is typically associated with the intervention of some authoritative person or body, whether one within the religious institution itself or, not infrequently, a king or other secular authority. The fixation of the final shape of a canon may also be determined or influenced by the composition of definitive commentaries. In the Buddhist case, the communal recitations (*saṅgīti*) of the words of the Buddha by his followers after his parinirvāṇa theoretically represent the initial establishment of a corpus of sacred texts, while the commentaries of Buddhaghosa and others defined the final shape of the Pali canon. The intervention of King Parakkamabāhu I of Sri Lanka in the twelfth century in declaring the canon of the Mahāvihāra Monastery as the only legitimate Theravāda canon is a typical example of the interference of secular authorities in canon formation.[160]

But we are not so well informed about the development and fixation of the other Indian Buddhist canons, which survive only in fragments if at all. In fact, we know next to nothing about the historical circumstances involved. A report by the Chinese pilgrim Xuanzang, however, gives some idea of how a canon may have been established in northwestern India. According to Xuanzang, Kaniṣka, the great Kuṣāṇa emperor and patron of Buddhism in the second century CE, was frustrated by the conflicting explanations of the Dharma that he heard from various teachers representing different schools. He therefore convened a council of monks in Kashmir to establish definitive versions of the texts and compose commentaries on them. These final texts were then engraved on metal plates and buried within a stūpa.[161]

Although the historicity of this report is open to doubt, since it was reported by Xuanzang some five centuries after the fact and it is not corroborated by any other source, it nevertheless does ring true insofar as it is consistent with the typical pattern of the standardization and closing of scriptural canons under the influence of secular powers. Thus there may be at least a kernel of historical truth underlying this legend, and if so, the establishment of a definitive canon under Kaniṣka would coincide neatly with the scenario presented in the previous section, according to which manuscripts of complete textual corpora, rather than of individual texts or selective anthologies, seem to first appear soon after the time of Kaniṣka's reign. If this is correct, the practice of writing out complete manuscripts of sūtra collections would have coincided with or at least developed under the influence of the impetus toward standardization of the canon. Of course, matters were no doubt not nearly this simple, but at this point we can at least say that there is a convergence of evidence pointing toward the development in

Gandhāra of authoritative canons and of complete written versions of them in and around the latter part of the second century.

The Problem of School Affiliation

I have referred here to "canons," in the plural, because we should not assume that there was only one canon of Buddhist scriptures in Greater Gandhāra; nor I do not wish to imply that all of the manuscripts belonged to a single tradition. Later Buddhist texts typically refer to eighteen lineages or schools (*nikāya*), but the presentations of their histories, internal relationships, textual corpora, and doctrinal characteristics are often contradictory and obscure.[162] The contents of and distinctions between their canons is also an area of much uncertainty and controversy, in large part because, except for the intact Pali canon of the Theravāda tradition, we have in original Indian-language texts only some fragments, mostly quite meager, of the scriptures of a few of the schools.[163] Something of the overall structures of the different canons can be deduced from these fragments and from references to and quotations from them in various texts, especially in Chinese translations of the vinayas of the several schools. But in many cases it is impossible to determine the school affiliation of a fragmentary text, especially in the case of sūtras, which typically differed less across school boundaries than the other classes of canonical literature.

But in certain cases we can find useful clues, a particularly important example being the commentary on the *Sūtra of Chanting Together*, with its clear and distinctive correspondence with a Chinese version of the text attributed to the Dharmaguptaka school. Moreover, since the British Library manuscripts were found in a jar bearing an inscription recording its dedication to a Dharmaguptaka institution, there is reason *a priori* to think that at least some, if not most or even all of these manuscripts belong to that school. Moreover, some texts from other collections, notably the *Great Nirvāṇa Sūtra* from Bamiyan and a few of the scrolls in the Senior collection, also resemble the corresponding versions in the Chinese translations of Dharmaguptaka texts.[164] A strong presence of Dharmaguptakas in Gandhāra is confirmed by the evidence of Gandhāran inscriptions contemporary with the manuscripts, many of which specify this school as the recipient of pious donations.[165] This is also consistent with the prominence of the Dharmaguptaka school during the early phases of the introduction of Buddhism in China during a period of Gandhāran prominence.

But this is not to say that all known Gandhāran manuscripts belong to the Dharmaguptaka tradition. Much more likely, they represent multiple schools. The Sarvāstivāda school is, after the Dharmaguptakas, the one most frequently mentioned in Buddhist inscriptions from Gandhāra and adjoining regions. The abhidharma manuscript in translation 11, which is likely to be a Dharmaguptaka text, argues against the Sarvāstivādins, and this can be taken to confirm that they were a significant presence. As yet, however, no Gāndhārī texts have been found that can be clearly attributed to them. Nor can we rule out other schools that are known from epigraphic evidence to have been present in Gandhāra, such as the Mahāsāṅghikas, Mahīśāsakas, and Kāśyapīyas.

Thus we do not know whether each of these schools had complete independent canons, and if so, how different they were from each other. And we also cannot be sure whether the various Gāndhārī texts now known come from a single such sectarian canon, or from two, or several. But we do at least have by now some broad notion of the contents of such a Gandhāran canon or canons. We can hope that future discoveries and studies will someday clarify these issues.

PART II

Texts

1. Three Numerically Grouped Sūtras

THESE THREE SŪTRAS[166] are recorded on a scroll in the British Library collection, of which two separate fragments[167] from the lower section survive. Like most Gandhāran scrolls, this manuscript had been rolled up from the bottom so that the upper part was on the outside of the rolled scroll and disintegrated over the millennia while it was buried underground. As a result, the introductory portion of the first surviving sūtra is lost due to decay. The third sūtra, at the bottom of the scroll, is also incomplete, lacking its last paragraph, though not because of damage but apparently because the scribe saw that he did not have enough room to fit it in the remaining space. Judging by what can be deduced about the original length of the scroll, the preserved portion probably represents at most half of the original and probably considerably less than that. Therefore it might have originally contained as few as six and as many as twelve sūtras of similar length.

The same scribe who wrote this scroll also wrote two other scrolls in the British Library collection, the *Dharmapada* and the *Songs of Lake Anavatapta*, which are presented below in translations 4 and 5. This is obvious from the distinctive features of his handwriting, with its uniformly thick strokes and upright orientation. As with his two other scrolls, he wrote this one only on the recto side, which consisted of the smooth white outer surface of the birchbark, leaving the rougher and darker inner surface blank. But in all three of his scrolls, a later scribe used the empty parts of scroll to record separate, unrelated texts of the avadāna and pūrvayoga genres, beginning with the small remaining space at the bottom of the recto and continuing on the blank verso.

The three surviving sūtras all involve the numerical element four, either explicitly or implicitly. In the third sūtra, the Buddha informs his disciples that four kinds of efforts are found in the world. In the first and second sūtras, the number four is not directly mentioned, but in each one there is a four-part narrative element. In the first sūtra, the brahman Dhoṇa asks the Buddha four questions, while the second sūtra is structured around the four bodily positions (walking, standing, sitting, lying down). This pattern of enumeration indicates that this manuscript belongs to the *Ekottarika* (P *Aṅguttara*) class of sūtras, which are grouped together according to the number of topics or narrative elements they contain.

This sort of ordering by number is a reflection of the underlying oral component of Buddhist literature, in which lexical or thematic associations often serve as mental triggers to remind the reciters of a textual sequence. Such a system must, in earlier stages of its development, have allowed for a high degree of variation and flexibility in the contents and sequence of the sūtras, but once the collections came to be standardized into a official canon, such variations were eliminated and a single version was defined as the correct order for a particular school.

An important example of this organizational principle is the *Sūtra of Chanting Together* (*Saṅgīti Sūtra*). One of the foundational texts of early Buddhism, this sūtra consists of sets of fundamental Buddhist concepts and categories, 205 in all according to the Pali version, arranged according to the number of items in each set in ascending order from one to ten. Among larger groupings of texts arranged by the numerical principle, the most prominent is the compilation known in Sanskrit as *Ekottarikāgama* and in Pali as *Aṅguttara-nikāya*, both titles meaning approximately "The collection [that increases] one by one." As we saw in part I, this huge collection is one of the five divisions of the Sūtra-piṭaka according to the arrangement of the Pali canon. It consists of several thousand short sūtras[168] arranged according to their numerical components, from one to eleven.

The manuscript in question here is certainly part of such a numerically arranged sūtra collection, if not part of a complete *Ekottarikāgama*; indeed, two of the three sūtras have more or less direct parallels among the corresponding collections in Pali, Sanskrit, and/or Chinese. Although the second sūtra on the manuscript under discussion here, "The Words of the Buddha,"[169] has no exact parallel in the sūtra collections in other languages, its structure, themes, and wording are generally familiar. This is characteristic of the relationships among different linguistic, geographical, and sectarian versions of Buddhist texts in general, which more often than not cannot be easily reduced to clear groupings and lineages; their relationships are more typically intertwined and fluid. It is very much the exception to be able to discern direct lines of development or affiliation, so that it is impossible to reconstruct an original urtext intended to retrieve the true, original words of the Buddha. Indeed, this sort of variability and flexibility seems to have been built into the Buddhist tradition from the very beginning, or at least as far back as we can ever hope to trace it. The value of the newly discovered Gāndhārī manuscripts, as of the other Buddhist manuscript finds of recent and earlier times, thus lies not in bringing back a "true" original version but rather in illuminating the variety, complexity, and richness of the many Buddhist traditions while confirming the essential unity underlying the vast diversity.

The incomplete third sūtra at the bottom of the scroll, in omitting the explanation of the last of the four efforts and the conclusion to the sūtra as a whole, leaves a space of about seven centimeters blank at the bottom.[170] This would seem to imply that the scribe finished, or at least had intended to complete this sūtra, on a second scroll and that the surviving scroll was one member of a multivolume set; but this is by no means the only possible explanation. As noted above (pages 81–82), there are several other cases of Gandhāran scrolls that from their contents would seem to have been part of a multivolume set, but in almost no cases have more than one scroll from the same set been found. This pattern suggests that such single scrolls may have been symbolic representatives of the entire text, perhaps for ritual use, and were never actually written out in full.

The Buddha and the Brahman Dhoṇa

This sūtra, which is also extant in a Pali version and in three Chinese translations, consists of a dialogue in which a brahman named Dhoṇa asks the Buddha four questions: "Would you be a god?" "Would you be a *gandharva*?" "Would you be a *yakṣa*?" and "Would you be a human being?" The Buddha answers each of Dhoṇa's questions in the negative, because the point of the sūtra is to express the uniqueness of a buddha. A buddha is neither human, nor divine, nor some kind of supernatural being such as a yakṣa or a gandharva; his perfected wisdom makes him something qualitatively different from, and above and beyond, all other classes of beings. Although a buddha is biologically a human being, his great store of good karma from previous lives, his elimination in this life of the harmful "depravities" or "taints," and his attainment of enlightenment are physically manifested in his body. A buddha is said to be distinguished by thirty-two major marks and eighty minor marks,[171] and it is the second of the major marks, namely the image of a wheel with a thousand spokes on the bottoms of his feet, that makes Dhoṇa suspect that the Buddha is something other than an ordinary human.

This sūtra also shows the characteristic Buddhist attitude toward the gods. It is not accurate that Buddhism is an atheistic religion, as is sometimes said. In fact, the texts of early Buddhism are filled with references to the gods, especially Śakra, the king of the gods, but also to innumerable minor deities. The existence of a vast array of gods and demigods was simply assumed in the cultural context of early

Buddhism in ancient India. Buddhism sets itself apart from the belief system of the Vedic or Brahmanical religion in whose milieu it arose not by denying the existence of the gods but by devaluing and even mocking them. Although the gods are stronger, healthier, happier, and longer-lived than human beings, they are nonetheless, like all living things, bound by the workings of karma and the suffering that it inevitably causes. It is only a buddha who is able to overcome karma and to help others to do so, and he is thereby far superior to the gods. In this context, it is understandable why Buddhist texts often describe deities as subservient to the Buddha.

Like a great many Buddhist sūtras, this one involves an encounter between the Buddha or his disciples and a member of the brahman class, the bearers of the elite traditions that were Buddhism's main rival for royal patronage and popular adherence. The brahman Dhoṇa senses that the Buddha is somehow different from other human beings but does not understand why and is initially mystified by his unique appearance. But after the Buddha recites three verses explaining how he attained buddhahood, Dhoṇa is inspired and expresses his conversion by the traditional formula of the three refuges: "I go to the ascetic Gautama, and to the Dharma, and to the monastic community." Thus this sūtra, like a great many others, emphasizes Buddhism's rivalry with and claimed superiority to the Brahmanical religious tradition.

The dialogue format, consisting of a series of questions and answers followed by a verbatim summation ("When I asked you, 'Sir, would you be a god?' you said 'No, brahman, I would not be a god'") before the climax of the conversation is typical of the quasi-oral style of Buddhist sūtras. The same is true of the three verses that the Buddha recites to describe his own spiritual triumph. In general, the juxtaposition of prose and verse is a common stylistic feature of sūtra literature, and very often, as here, the verses come near the end of the text by way of summary or climax.

The Words of the Buddha

This brief text apparently teaches that even though it is normally difficult to do good actions, with the help of the words of the Buddha,[172] a wise man but not a fool can perform good actions with ease. However, the key term, here translated as "good" (*sato*), is ambiguous; it could mean either "good" (= Skt *sat* / P *santo*) or "attentive, mindful" (= *smṛta*/*sato*), both of which would fit the context. The latter interpretation would mean that a wise person could perform actions mindfully, which is entirely appropriate, but it is doubtful on linguistic grounds, since the expected Gāndhārī form for "mindful" would be *śpada* rather than *sato*. Mainly for this reason, I have translated this key term as "good," but the reader should keep in mind that for each instance of the phrase "good acts," "mindful acts" is also a possible translation. Perhaps the author even intended the ambiguity, by way of a pun that would work only in Gāndhārī and not in Pali or Sanskrit.

In cases such as this, parallel texts in other languages are often the only way to conclusively determine the meaning of a problematic Gāndhārī word (of which there are many). But this sūtra, unlike the two others on the same manuscript, lacks a parallel. Such interpretive problems are all too common in Gāndhārī texts without parallels, due to factors such as the incomplete and defective state of the manuscripts, the lack of standardization in the Gāndhārī language, and our still-imperfect understanding of that language.

In any case, the point of this brief sūtra is to urge its hearers to be constantly aware of the words of the Buddha, which will make it easier for them to engage in wholesome (or "mindful") activities—but only if they are wise and not fools. The word for "action" (*kamatu* = Skt *karmānta* / P *kammanta*) suggests one of the components of the eightfold path, "correct action," although this may not be specifically referred to here. In any case, this direction to act according to the Buddha's words is repeated four times, with reference to activities done while walking, standing, sitting, or lying down. These four "postures" (*īryāpatha/īriyāpatha*), frequently mentioned in Buddhist texts, are intended to encompass all types of conscious activity. Thus, in effect, the Buddha is telling his followers to keep his words in their minds during every waking moment.

The first sūtra in this manuscript was an example of a common type of sūtra recording a dialogue or debate between the Buddha and another person, often a brahman, who is humbled or converted in the end. The present sūtra belongs to an even more frequent class in which the Buddha preaches to his assembled followers. In both cases, at the end of the sūtras the interlocutors express their delight in the Buddha's words with the standard conclusion, "Thus spoke the Lord. They were delighted and rejoiced at what the Lord had said."

The Four Efforts

In this sūtra the Buddha enumerates and explains to the monks an important set of concepts known as the four "efforts" or, according to an alternative interpretation in some texts, the four "abandonments" (G *prasaṇa* = Skt *pradhāna* or *prahāṇa*). These "efforts," namely restraint, protection, cultivation, and abandonment, are four techniques that enable a monk to maintain self-control and improve his meditative practice by subduing harmful thought patterns and encouraging beneficial ones, and thereby to eventually "achieve an end to suffering," as the concluding verse says.

The efforts are frequently enumerated in various Buddhist texts, but in two different ways. The first presentation, which is followed in our text, describes each of the efforts in terms of specific processes and techniques, whereas the other one defines them in general terms. Thus, for instance, in our text the first effort, restraint, is described with examples of restraining each of the sensory faculties from becoming attached to its objects, whereas in the alternative presentation restraint is simply defined as the effort to prevent any harmful *dharmas*, or mindstates, from arising in the meditator's mind. In this latter presentation, the four efforts are reduced to two simple contrasting pairs:

a. The two efforts whereby one prevents harmful dharmas from arising and subdues harmful dharmas that do arise, corresponding to "restraint" and "abandonment" respectively.
b. The two efforts whereby one produces beneficial dharmas and maintains them, corresponding to "cultivation" and "protection" respectively.

The order of enumeration of the four efforts varies widely in different sūtras, with five different sequences attested. In most texts, the four are grouped together in terms of the desirable and undesirable factors, either paired or contrasted; for example, restraint—abandonment—cultivation—protection. The order in our text is in fact the only one in which the ordering does not follow such a logical sequence.[173] In this regard, as is often the case, the Gāndhārī text reflects a relatively early stage of the development of written scriptures in which they have not been subjected to the processes of editing, polishing, and standardization that is reflected in later manuscripts and in the modern canons.

The structure of this sūtra embodies the numerical and categorizing character that is so characteristic of Buddhist canonical texts. It consists of a head term, *efforts*, that embraces a list of four sub-items. Two of these items are in turn cited repeatedly in connection with the members of other relevant sets of categories. Thus the first effort, *restraint*, is described with reference to the six sensory faculties (sight, hearing, smell, taste, touch, and mind), the description of the process of restraining each of them being formulaically repeated in full each time with only the relevant key word being changed (eye ~ form; sound ~ ear; etc.). Similarly, the third effort, *cultivation*, is described with respect to each of the seven enlightenment factors (G *bujaghu* / Skt *bodhyaṅga* / P *bojjhaṅga*), each one characterized by a stock epithet, "which is based on seclusion, based on dispassion, based on cessation, and results in release," repeated in full each time. This list of the seven enlightenment factors is presented in many other sūtra texts, for example in the *Sūtra of Chanting Together*,[174] so that the reader's or hearer's memory and understanding of such categories and their complex interrelationships would be constantly reinforced by the various texts. The Gāndhārī commentaries in translations 9 and 10 develop this method to a higher level, seeking to integrate the fundamental lists of Buddhist concepts into a seamless interlocking web.

A. The Buddha and the Brahman Dhoṇa

[Thus have I heard: at one time,] after traveling for a while along the road, [the Lord] stepped off the road [and sat] at the root of a tree to pass the afternoon there.

At the same time, a brahman named Dhoṇa [had set out] on that road. [He saw] in the Lord's footprints a wheel with a thousand spokes, complete [with rim and nave,] brilliant and resplendent. [Following the wheel-marked] footprints, [he saw the Lord] who had stepped off the road and sat at the root of a tree. He looked [attractive] and pleasing, his senses and mind calm. He had achieved absolute self-control and calm and supreme [self-control and calm]; guarded, his senses suppressed, masterful, he was like a clear, clean, calm lake.

Dhoṇa approached the Lord and said:

"Sir, would you be a god?"[175]

"No, brahman, I would not be a god."

"Sir, would you be a gandharva?"

"No, brahman, I would not be a gandharva."

"Sir, would you be a yakṣa?"

"No, brahman, I would not be a yakṣa."

"Sir, would you be a human being?"

"No, brahman, I would not be a human being."

[Dhoṇa then said], "When I asked you 'Sir, Would you be a god?' you said 'No, brahman, I would not be a god.' When I asked you 'Sir, would you be a gandharva?' you said 'No, brahman, I would not be a gandharva.' When I asked you 'Sir, would you be a yakṣa?' you said 'No, brahman, I would not be a yakṣa.' When I asked 'Sir, would you be a human being?' you said 'No, brahman, I would not be a human being.' What, then, sir, would you be?"

"Brahman, I am a buddha, I am a buddha."

After saying this, the Lord, the Well-Gone One, the Teacher, further uttered [these verses]:

> I have eliminated, eradicated, cut off [those afflictions] whereby I would be reborn as [a god] or as a gandharva flying in the sky, or become a yakṣa, or be born as a human being.
>
> Just as a blooming lotus [is not touched] by water, so I am untouched by the world. Therefore, brahman, I am a buddha.
>
> I have realized what must be realized; I have developed what must be developed; I have eliminated what must be eliminated. Therefore, brahman, I am an all-knowing, all-seeing buddha.

[Dhoṇa exclaimed]: "Wonderful, Sir Gautama, wonderful! Just as, Sir Gautama, one might set upright what had been overturned, uncover what had been covered, show the path to someone who was lost, or bring light into the darkness so that anyone with eyes might see what is there, just so has the ascetic Gautama declared, revealed, and explained dharmas, both bright and dark. I go to the ascetic Gautama as my refuge, and to the Dharma, and to the monastic community. May the ascetic Gautama accept me as his follower from today onward for as long as I live, until my last breath, [going] to him for refuge with sincere faith."

Thus spoke the Lord. The brahman Dhoṇa [was delighted] and rejoiced at what the Lord had said.

B. The Words of the Buddha

Thus have I heard: at one [time] the Lord was staying in Śrāvastī, at Anāthapiṇḍada's park in the Jeta forest. The Lord addressed the monks there, and they responded to him. [Then] the Lord said:

"Monks, it is easy for a wise man to follow the words of the Buddha, but not for a fool.

"It is not easy to perform good acts while walking. But with the words of the Buddha, monks, it is easy for a wise man to do them while walking, but not for a fool.

"It is not easy to perform good acts while standing. But with the words of the Buddha, monks, it is easy for a wise man to do them while standing, but not for a fool.

"It is not easy to perform good acts while sitting. But with the words of the Buddha, monks, it is easy for a wise man to do them while sitting, but not for a fool.

"It is not easy to perform good acts while lying down. But with the words of the Buddha, monks, it is easy for a wise man to do them while lying down, but not for a fool.

"Monks, it is easy for a wise man to follow the words of the Buddha, but not for a fool."

Thus spoke [the Lord]. The monks were delighted and rejoiced at [what the Lord had said].

c. The Four Efforts

Thus have I heard: at one time the Lord was staying in Śrāvastī, at Anāthapiṇḍada's park in the Jeta forest. The Lord addressed the monks there, and they [responded to him. Then the Lord] spoke.

Monks, these are the four efforts that exist, that are found in the world. [Which four?] The effort of restraint, the effort of protection, the effort of cultivation, and the effort of abandonment.

What, [monks], is the effort of restraint? With regard to that, monks, when a monk sees a form with his eye, he does not grasp at its general features [nor at its secondary features].[176] [For] when one lives with the faculty of sight unrestrained, covetousness and unhappiness, which are evil and harmful dharmas, afflict his mind. Therefore he practices restraint; he guards his faculty of sight, restrains his faculty of sight.

When [a monk] hears a sound with his ear, he does not grasp at its general features nor at its secondary features. For when one lives with the faculty of hearing unrestrained, covetousness and unhappiness, which are evil and [harmful] dharmas, afflict his mind. Therefore he practices restraint; he guards his faculty of hearing, [restrains] his faculty of hearing.

When [a monk] smells a smell with his nose, he does not grasp at its general features nor at its secondary features. For when one lives with the faculty of smell unrestrained, covetousness and unhappiness, which are evil and harmful dharmas, afflict his mind. Therefore he practices restraint; he guards [his faculty of smell], restrains his faculty of smell.

When [a monk] tastes a taste with his tongue, he does not grasp at its general features nor at its secondary features. For when one lives with the faculty of taste unrestrained, [covetousness] and unhappiness, which are evil and harmful dharmas, afflict his mind. Therefore he [practices] restraint; he guards his faculty of taste, restrains his faculty of taste.

When [a monk] feels a touch with his body, he does not grasp at its general features nor at its secondary features. For when one lives with the faculty of touch unrestrained, covetousness and unhappiness, which are evil and harmful dharmas, afflict his mind. Therefore he practices restraint; he guards his faculty of touch, restrains his faculty of touch.

When [a monk] cognizes an idea with his mind, he does not grasp at its general features nor at its secondary features. For when one lives with the faculty of mind unrestrained, covetousness and [unhappiness, which are evil] and harmful dharmas, afflict his mind. Therefore he practices restraint; he guards his faculty of mind, restrains his faculty of mind.

This is what is called the *effort of restraint*.

What, monks, is the effort of protection? With regard to that, monks, a monk [firmly takes hold of] one or another object of concentration, such as observing a blackened corpse, a putrid corpse, a skeleton, or a worm-eaten corpse. With that protection, he perseveres [in his concentration].

This is what is called the *effort of protection*.

What, [monks], is the effort of cultivation? With regard to that, monks, a monk cultivates the enlightenment factor of mindfulness, which is based on seclusion, based on dispassion, based on cessation, and results in release.

He cultivates [the enlightenment factor] of the discrimination of dharmas, which is based on seclusion, based on dispassion, based on cessation, and [results in] release.

He cultivates the enlightenment factor of energy, which is based on seclusion, based on dispassion, based on cessation, and results in [release].

He cultivates the enlightenment factor of bliss, which is based on seclusion, based on dispassion, based on cessation, and results in release.

He cultivates the enlightenment factor of calming, which is based on seclusion, based on [dispassion], based on cessation, and results in release.

He cultivates the enlightenment factor of concentration, which is based on seclusion, based on dispassion, based on cessation, and results in release.

He cultivates the enlightenment factor of equanimity, which is based on seclusion, based on dispassion, based on cessation, and [results in] release.

This is what is called the *effort of cultivation*.

[What, monks, is the effort of abandonment? With regard to that, monks, a monk does not tolerate a sensual thought that arises in his mind; he abandons it, he banishes it, he abolishes it, he eliminates it.

He does not tolerate a malicious thought that arises in his mind; he abandons it, he banishes it, he abolishes it, he eliminates it.

He does not tolerate a cruel thought that arises in his mind; he abandons it, he banishes it, he abolishes it, he eliminates it.

He does not tolerate any evil and harmful dharmas that arise at any time in his mind; he abandons them, he banishes them, he abolishes them, he eliminates them.

This is what is called the *effort of abandonment*. And these are the four efforts:

> Restraint, abandonment, cultivation, and protection: these are the four efforts of the Heir of the Sun,[177] by which a diligent monk achieves an end to suffering.]

2. Five Thematically Grouped Sūtras

The manuscripts presented in this section come from the Robert Senior collection of scrolls. This collection comprises twenty-four birchbark scrolls found inside a sealed clay pot that had been buried in the precincts of a Buddhist monastery, probably in eastern Afghanistan. But its contents are unique among the several groups of Gandhāran manuscripts in that it consists of a unified set of texts belonging to the same genre, namely sūtras, that had all been written by the same scribe at the same time. Moreover, a few of the scrolls are very well preserved, almost completely intact. This means that the scrolls were new or nearly new when interred, which in turn suggests that the set was expressly made up for the purpose of being buried.

If so, the motivation for this project was presumably the desire to generate merit. The act of burying texts containing the Buddha's words is no different in principle from that of interring his bodily relics, since the Buddha is embodied in his teachings as well as in his physical remains. Thus copying and preserving sūtras is a prime means of gaining good karma, and although this theme is particularly strongly stressed in Mahāyāna sūtras, there is no reason to think that it was not prevalent in the pre-Mahāyāna tradition as well. An additional, or rather concurrent, motivation may have been to ensure the preservation of the Dharma as embodied in the Buddha's words into the far

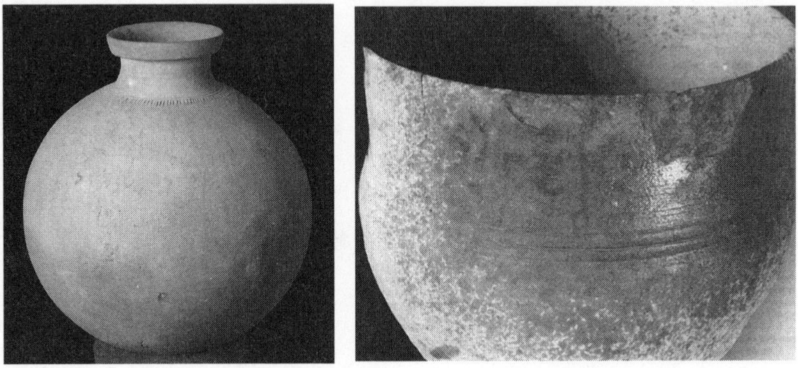

Figure 22. The pot (left) in which the Senior scrolls were found, and its lid.

future, since the loss of the Dharma was a pervasive source of anxiety in earlier Buddhist traditions.[178]

In the case of the Senior manuscripts, unlike that of the other collections, we know who was responsible for the interment, and even more importantly, when they were interred. For the pot in which they were buried bears an inscription (also recorded in an abridged form on the lid) recording their donor's name and the date: "Day 5 of the month Avadunaka, year 12: (this) was established in the stūpa by Rohaṇa, son of Ma̱sumatra, in honor of all beings." This inscription follows the typical formation for the donation and ritual establishment of relics, so we can assume that the unstated subject of this inscription is the scrolls themselves.

The date of the inscription refers to a "year 12," without specifying which of the several eras that were used in ancient Gandhāra it refers to. However, we can be reasonably confident that it refers to the year inaugurated by the great Kuṣāṇa emperor and patron of Buddhism Kaniṣka. Among the clues for this is that the citation of the month as Avadunaka, which is the Gāndhārī rendition of the Macedonian month name Audunaios. The use of the Macedonian calendrical system is characteristic of the Kuṣāṇa period. The Kuṣāṇas adopted it from the Arsacid kings of Iran, who in turn had inherited it from

Figure 23. Senior scroll 8: the index scroll.

the preceding Seleucid dynasty of Syria. Since Kaniṣka's era probably began in or around 127/28 CE, his twelfth year would correspond to approximately 140 CE.[179] Such a date for the manuscripts is consistent with radiocarbon tests[180] and with the paleographic and linguistic characteristics of the scrolls.

The unity of the Senior scrolls is established on various grounds. With regard to their contents, most if not all of the texts are of the sūtra genre, with the large majority corresponding to sūtras found in the *Saṃyuktāgama* collections. The handwriting reveals that all or nearly all of the scrolls were written by the same scribe, and they share generally similar physical characteristics.[181] Moreover, the collection includes two scrolls (numbers 7 and 8) that constitute a sort of index or guide to the collection as a whole. These two "index scrolls" contain lists of individual texts, referred to in the form of brief citations of their initial words or of one or more distinctive key words. At the end of the list, in a separate line set off near the bottom of one of the index scrolls, is a summary, reading "In total, fifty-five sūtras."

One might expect that this list would correspond to the texts actually contained in the other scrolls found together with it, but strangely enough, it does so only partially and in a confusingly inconsistent way. It is not just that the collection as we have it is incomplete. This is in fact almost certainly true, since there are several cases where a scroll that broke in half lengthwise after being folded is missing one half. Other scrolls may be missing entirely, whether because of disintegration while they were buried or because of mishandling or pilfering after they were dug up by unknown persons in modern times. But this still does not suffice to explain the mismatch with the index scrolls, because we also have as many as twenty-two actual texts—more than half of the total of forty-one texts—for which no corresponding reference could be found in the index scrolls.

One might be tempted to conclude that the index scrolls have nothing to do with the other texts at all; but this too is not the case. There are at least twelve cases, and possibly as many as nineteen, in which sūtras referred to in the indices do correspond to those actually found. For example, the first four sūtras translated below, recorded on scroll 5, are all cited on the index scrolls. There, for instance, the first sūtra is cited in the form of abridged versions of the four questions that head each of its topics, while the second sūtra is referred to by the phrase "The grass, wood, branches, leaves, and foliage here in the Jeta forest," which is the distinctive wording of its central simile.

However, even these correspondences raise further questions, because although all four sūtras on scroll 5 are cited in the index scrolls, they are not listed there in the same sequence and grouping. In index scroll 7, the third and second sūtras on scroll 5 are first listed together, but in that reversed order, while the first and fourth sūtras are listed one after the other in index scroll 8. This apparent inconsistency might be explained in terms of the technology involved. When writing on sheets of birchbark of which he presumably had only a limited stock, the scribe would have had to arrange his material carefully so that he would have enough room to complete his assignment. One clue to this concern is seen in the way that the scribe first wrote the opening settings (*nidāna*) for the four sūtras on scroll 5, estimating the length of each one before writing out the full texts. We know that he did this because, in both the first and third sūtras, he did not estimate the available space accurately, so that the last word or few words had to be squeezed into the right margin when he ran out of space before the opening for the next sūtra, which he had written previously.

Figure 24. Upper right corner of Senior scroll 5, with the concluding phrase of the first sūtra added in the margin.

But even such physical factors that may have affected the scribe's ordering of the sūtras are not sufficient to explain the discrepancies between the index scrolls and the text scrolls. For example, the scribe could easily have inverted the order of the second and third sūtras to make them correspond to the order on the index scrolls, but he did not do so. Thus in the end, the exact relationship between the list of fifty-five sūtras on the index scrolls and the twenty-two scrolls found with it remains frustratingly unclear. There are enough correspondences between the two sets, however, to make it certain that they are significantly related. It has therefore been suggested[182] that the list of sūtras in the index scrolls might have served as a preliminary or general guide for the recording of the other scrolls, but that the scribe or patron at some point changed his mind about the contents of the final anthology and adjusted them accordingly. Alternatively, the index scrolls may have represented a different anthology, perhaps even one that the same scribe had written out in full on another occasion or for another purpose. This preexisting anthology may have served as a rough model for the anthology that was actually contained in the pot, perhaps having been drawn up to order for a patron, presumably the Rohaṇa mentioned in the dedicatory inscription.

Whatever the details, the compilation of selected anthologies is a well-attested phenomenon around the period in question. Particularly relevant are two anthologies translated from Indian originals into Chinese in the second century by An Shigao, who was one of the pioneering early translators of Buddhist scriptures in the second half of the second century CE. One of these anthologies consists of twenty-seven sūtras from the *Saṃyuktāgama*, the other of forty-four from the *Ekottarikāgama*.[183] The Senior collection closely resembles such sūtra anthologies in scope and contents. As preserved—albeit incompletely—it contains forty-one texts, of which at least twenty-six and probably twenty-nine belong to the *Saṃyuktāgama* genre, to judge from their parallels in the Pali and Chinese canons. Among the others, three correspond to texts classified as *Madhyamāgama*, or medium-length, a category that has considerable overlap with the *Saṃyuktāgama* class, while only one, the *Sūtra on the Fruits of the Life of Striving*, belongs to the long sūtras. Of the eight remaining texts, some have parallels in vinaya texts, while the identification or classification of the rest is uncertain.

The texts brought together in the Senior collection, as in other anthologies,[184] do not focus on any particular aspect of Buddhist teachings but rather seem to be intended to present a representative sample of the fundamental teachings. They are probably personal selections, perhaps compiled by Buddhist masters in order to instruct their students and lay followers, and we can guess that many such anthologies must have existed over the centuries, a few of which happen to have survived. The complete sūtra collections would presumably have been the bailiwick of scholars and recitation specialists but hardly of ordinary monks and lay followers, who would have needed some guidance for selected study.

Since the Senior manuscripts comprise a planned collection of texts, unlike the other major groups of Gandhāran manuscripts, they are of particular value for understanding the history of Buddhist canons. While the antiquity, authenticity, and integrity of the sūtra collections may be an article of faith to be taken for granted by traditional Buddhists, historical scholars have questioned to what degree the sūtra collections of the Pali canon, the only Buddhist canon to have survived completely in an original Indian language, represents the common heritage of Indian Buddhism as a whole. The partial remnants of the basic sūtra collections that are preserved in other original Indian languages, mainly Sanskrit and (now) Gāndhārī, as well as the complete Chinese translations, do in general have a significant degree of overlap with the Pali suttas. But it is less clear how similar they were at an early formative period, especially as regards their sequencing and principles of organization. Even though the Senior collection is a small and incomplete anthology, and even though there are serious questions about the ordering of the texts within it, the distribution of the surviving sūtras does provide useful information about the shape of the presumed larger set of *Saṃyuktāgama* sūtras from which it extracted most of its material, and also about the relationship of that hypothetical Gāndhārī *Saṃyuktāgama* to its Pali counterpart, the *Saṃyutta-nikāya*.

Among the sūtras of the Senior collection, we find several striking concentrations of texts whose parallels appear within the same subsets in the Pali *Saṃyutta-nikāya*.[185] For example, the Senior texts include three sūtras that in the *Saṃyutta-nikāya* appear in the subset (*vagga*) of ten suttas called "Flowers."[186] (One of these, "The Adze Handle," is translated below). Even more remarkably, Senior scroll 11 contains fourteen sūtras that correspond to the fourteen suttas of a subset of the *Saṃyutta-nikāya* called "The Forest,"[187] although the order of the individual sūtras in the Gāndhārī version differs from that of the Pali. When the sūtras of the Senior manuscripts are compared to those of the Chinese translation of the mostly lost Sanskrit version of the

Saṃyuktāgama, the results are similar, although the details differ. For example, three sūtras referred to in the Senior collection correspond to three consecutive sūtras (nos. 269–71) in the Chinese text. These correlations between the Gāndhārī on the one hand and the Pali, Sanskrit, and Chinese on the other cannot possibly be attributed to coincidence, given the enormous numbers of sūtras—about 2,900 in Pali, 1,362 in Chinese—in the complete collection. They prove that this compiler was working from a corpus of *Saṃyuktāgama*-type sūtras whose contents and arrangement had a great deal in common with the corresponding ones in Pali and Chinese.

The validity of these conclusions is confirmed by a similar comparison of An Shigao's anthology of *Saṃyuktāgama* sūtras with the complete Chinese text of the *Saṃyuktāgama*. This yielded a very similar result: although the short anthology contains only forty-four sūtras compared to the 1,362 of the Chinese *Saṃyuktāgama*, several of the correspondents to the sūtras in the anthology are closely clustered within the complete collection; for example, sūtras 16, 17, and 18 of the anthology correspond to 661, 666, and 667 respectively in the full *Saṃyuktāgama*. Thus, the compilers of both the Gāndhārī anthology in the Senior collection and of An Shigao's anthology must have followed a similar strategy of selecting sets of closely adjacent sūtras from their source text; and this shows, beyond a reasonable doubt, that their source texts had similar contents and principles of arrangement.[188] This conclusion is supported by the recent discovery of what was probably a complete manuscript of the *Ekottarikāgama* in Gāndhārī, which as we saw in chapter 3 shows an overall agreement with the corresponding Pali *Aṅguttara-nikāya*.

Thus these materials support the view that the foundational sections of the Buddhist canons, namely the collections of early sūtras, were a common heritage of the various Buddhist schools in India. Although the parallel collections no doubt differed widely in details, the overall commonality in terms of contents and principles of organization can be seen to go back to the earliest period for which we have written testimony—that is, the early centuries of the Common Era. The new Gāndhārī material thus provides a degree of confidence in the integrity and originality of the early scripture collections.

The Four Concentrations

The four sūtras in this section[189] are all on Senior scroll 5. This manuscript is a small-format scroll, nearly square (27.6 cm long and 26.8 cm wide), and almost entirely intact except for a substantial gap running vertically down the middle. This was caused by the manuscript first being rolled up and then folded in half. As the bark dried out and become brittle, the doubly folded central portion disintegrated. The texts cover all of both surfaces, front and back, but the last sūtra is incomplete.

The first sūtra on scroll 5 introduces four meditative concentrations (*samasi* = Skt *samādhi*), each connected with a particular "perception" (*saña* = Skt *saṃjñā*) or focus that a meditating monk should cultivate in order to help eliminate his attachment to sensory pleasures. The first concentration is the one "accompanied by the perception of repulsiveness," wherein the meditator observes his own body while focusing on its thirty-six impure and disgusting components. This practice, known as "meditating on repulsiveness" (*aśubha-bhāvanā*), is prescribed in many Buddhist texts as an antidote to visual or sexual attraction.[190]

The second concentration prescribed by this sūtra is the one connected with the perception of death, in which the meditator focuses on his own mortality by reminding himself that life is short and that death is approaching quickly. This enables him to overcome his attachment to the present life. The third concentration, connected with the perception of revulsion toward food, teaches the meditator to think of what happens to his food after it is eaten, when it turns into filth and vomit. This enables him to overcome attachment toward the sensual pleasure of taste.

The fourth practice is the concentration connected with the

Figure 25. Senior scroll 5 before unrolling.

Figure 26. Senior scroll 5 after unrolling and conservation.

perception of dispassion toward the entire world. This technique, unlike the first three, involves a graded process of development. First, the meditating monk learns to disregard neutral surroundings, so that when he is, for example, in a village, it is to him as if there were no village there, so that he takes no pleasure in his surroundings. Then he extends this lack of ardor to beautiful places such as parks, forests, and lakes. At the final stage, he cultivates this attitude toward all of his surroundings, regardless of where he may be.

This sūtra embodies the quasi-oral formulaic, repetitive pattern that is typical of Buddhist sūtras in general. Each of its four subsections begins with a question, "What is the concentration accompanied by perception of . . . ?" Here it is to be understood that the Buddha is rhetorically asking his hearers this question and then providing the answer. This is followed by the description of the mode of meditation, after which each section concludes with the statement that each perception is "the undisturbed one-pointedness of mind" of the monk who meditates by means of it.

Unlike the three sūtras on the same scroll that follow it, this sūtra has no direct parallel in other Buddhist canons. Although the meditative techniques it prescribes are mentioned in other texts and are sometimes grouped together as part of larger sets of meditative perceptions, this particular grouping is nowhere else introduced as a separate set. Also with regard to the definitions and descriptions of each of the four perceptions, we find only partial parallels. The first has a close Pali parallel in *Aṅguttara-nikāya* 10.60,[191] but the definitions of the second through fourth perceptions are unique to the Gāndhārī text. This pattern is typical of the relationships between Gāndhārī texts and those of other Buddhist traditions, which often overlap but are by no means identical.

Not Yours

In this brief sūtra, the Buddha teaches the monks that the five aggregates (*khada* = Skt *skandha*), namely form, sensation, perception, volitional formations, and consciousness, which produce the illusory sense of personality and identity, are in reality no more than external, transitory features that do not truly constitute an essential "self." To make this point, he compares the aggregates to the external physical surroundings of his discourse, namely the trees, plants, and foliage of the Jeta forest in Śrāvastī, where he is preaching. The aggregates are no more a part of the monks than the trees and leaves around them, so they should leave behind those aggregates, and thereby their illusory sense of self, as readily as they would give up their physical surroundings. This, he explains, is the way to lasting satisfaction.

This sūtra has numerous parallels or partial correspondents in Pali and Chinese. In the Pali canon, the closest parallel is in the *Saṃyutta-nikāya*, where the corresponding sūtra is the first in a set of ten entitled the "Not Yours" group.[192] The second sūtra in this set is identical to the first except that it omits the example of the foliage in the Jeta forest. Such variations on a theme are typical of Buddhist literature in general and of the massive *Saṃyuktāgama* and *Ekottarikāgama* collections in particular, where minor structural variants of the same text are often presented as independent sūtras. These variant texts may reflect different versions of a sermon that the Buddha preached on different occasions, or different testimonia by the various disciples who reported their memories of what the Buddha had said. In either case, the pattern suggests a concern with collecting and preserving every word that the Buddha said, or even might have said, in keeping with the fundamental Buddhist dictum that "everything that the Buddha said is well said."

Although the Pali parallel is essentially the same sūtra as the Gāndhārī text, their wording and formulation differ. In the Gāndhārī version, the Buddha cites the first of the five aggregates, namely form, and says "Form is not yours; abandon it. Abandoning it will lead to benefit and happiness." He then combines the other four aggregates together in a single sentence: "Sensation, perception, volitional formations, and consciousness are not yours; abandon them. Abandoning them will lead to benefit and happiness." In the Pali text, however, he repeats the full sentence separately for each of the five aggregates: "Sensation is not yours; abandon it. Abandoning it will lead to benefit and happiness. Perception is not yours; abandon it. Abandoning it will lead to benefit and happiness," and so on.

But such differences in phrasing do not actually constitute different "texts" according to Buddhist conceptions of textuality. Rather, they embody the principle of "expansion and contraction" (*saṃkṣepa/ vistara*), according to which the same sūtra can be presented or "performed,"[193] whether orally or in writing, in shorter or longer forms as the situation may dictate, without changing its essential meaning. If the sūtra in our manuscript were to be presented in the form of an oral sermon, the preacher would probably have elaborated on all five of the aggregates with full expansion, as in the Pali text. In other words, the representation in this manuscript can be considered an implied abbreviation, which its intended audience would have readily understood to stand for the full text. In this, as in other regards, the line between the written and the oral version of sūtras can be a blurry one.

The principle of abbreviation also applies to the opening and conclusion of the sūtra. The opening reads simply "The setting is Śrāvastī" (*śavasti ṇiḏaṇe*). This is a standard abbreviation for the introductory formula for the great many sūtras that the Buddha preached in the Jeta forest in the city of Śrāvastī, which reads in full "Thus have I heard: at one time the Lord was staying in Śrāvastī, at Anāthapiṇḍada's park in the Jeta forest. The Lord said to the monks there, 'Monks!' and the monks responded to the Lord, 'Venerable sir.' Then the Lord said . . . " In practice, in written Pali texts as in Gāndhārī, this opening formula was usually abridged, especially in the *Saṃyutta-nikāya*. The same pattern holds in the conclusion, which in our manuscript reads simply "Thus spoke the Lord." This is to be understood as an abbreviation of the typical sūtra-ending formula "Thus spoke the Lord. The monks were delighted and rejoiced at what the Lord had said," as for example in the second sūtra of the preceding translation section.

Living Full of Disenchantment

This short sūtra resembles the preceding one in that it is intended to inculcate a sense of separation from the five aggregates that create the harmful illusion of personhood. In the "Not Yours" sūtra, the Buddha urged his followers to cultivate the understanding that the aggregates do not belong to them and are not them, whereas in this one he advises them to develop a sense of aversion, disenchantment, or disgust[194] toward them. This sense of distaste for the aggregates then produces a full understanding of them, and this full understanding in turn leads to liberation from attachment to them. The development of a sense of disenchantment with life in the world is one of the necessary steps toward enlightenment. This disillusionment can be the result of a spiritual or psychological crisis that shocks one into realizing the fragility of worldly life and its lack of deep and lasting satisfaction. Such a crisis is vividly narrated in the story of Yaśas in the *Songs of Lake Anavatapta*, when he sees the disheveled sleeping women and suddenly feels revulsion for instead of attraction to them.

Whereas the subject matter of the third sūtra on this scroll continues that of the second one, it also resembles both in theme and structure the presentation of the fourth meditative concentration in the first sūtra, where the disciples were advised first to develop dispassion toward ordinary places such as towns and villages, then to extend it to beautiful places such as parks and forests, and finally to the entire world. The sūtra translated here similarly prescribes a three-step progression from disillusionment to understanding to liberation. However, the similarities between these three sūtras are probably not related to their presence on the same scroll since, as was explained in the introductory comments, their collocation and ordering there is apparently incidental. The similarities are rather a function of the many recurring themes and structural patterns of early Buddhist sūtras in general.

The written text of this sūtra is heavily abridged. The concluding formula is shortened as in the previous sūtra, and the opening formula even more drastically so, with the word for "setting," *ṇidaṇa*, abbreviation to just its first syllable, *ṇi*. The three main paragraphs, concerned with being disillusioned with, fully understanding, and becoming liberated from the each of the five aggregates, are also structured in an abridged form, whereby in each paragraph only the first phrase (for example, "He should live filled with disenchantment with form") is presented in full. The Pali parallel text in the *Saṃyutta-nikāya*[195] is similarly abbreviated, but once again we can suppose that in a formal context the sūtra would have been recited in its full form; the manuscript is simply presenting it in a sort of shorthand.

The Adze Handle

Like the two sūtras that precede it on this scroll, this one refers in its preamble to the five aggregates and the necessity of understanding their true nature. But its main focus is the necessity of continuous, assiduous meditative practice in which one cultivates beneficial dharmas (Skt *kuśala dharma*) to free the mind completely from the afflictions (*āsrava*) and thereby become an arhat. These beneficial dharmas are enumerated as the four foundations of mindfulness, the four correct strivings, the four bases of supernatural powers, the four meditations, the five faculties, the five powers, the seven factors of enlightenment, and the eightfold noble path. This list corresponds to the well-known set of "dharmas conducive to enlightenment" (*bodhipākṣikadharma*), although this collective term is not explicitly mentioned in the sūtra, presumably because it is assumed that the reader would know that it is being alluded to.

However, the total number of beneficial dharmas in this list is forty-one rather than thirty-seven as in the Pali tradition, including in the specific Pali correspondent to this sūtra.[196] The difference is that the Gāndhārī list includes the four meditations (Skt *dhyāna* = P *jhāna*), which are absent from the Pali list. This forty-one-member list is also found in the Chinese translation of the *Dīrghāgama*, which is believed to be derived from an Indian source text belonging to the Dharmaguptaka school, and it also occurs in the Chinese translation of the vinaya belonging to that school.[197] Therefore the appearance of the longer list in this sūtra is one of the clues that suggest that the Senior manuscripts may represent the textual tradition of the Dharmaguptaka school.

In the complete version of the sūtra as preserved in Pali and Chinese, the Buddha illustrates the necessity of vigilant perseverance in order to reach the goal of removing the afflictions and achieving final liberation by citing three parables that show the results of patience and persistence. But the incomplete Gāndhārī text contains only the first of these similes. This first parable is a double simile, presented in both a negative and a positive form. In the negative form, a hen forms the wish that her chicks be born alive and healthy, but she fails to carefully nurture her eggs, so that her wish does not come true. In the positive version, a hen does assiduously care for her eggs, even without consciously thinking about the desired result, and they do all hatch and emerge alive. In the same way, a meditator may form a conscious desire to remove the afflictions but will still surely fail if he does not assiduously cultivate the beneficial dharmas, whereas a monk who does cultivate them patiently and consistently will achieve the goal of removing the afflictions even if he does not have it consciously in mind while he practices.

The second parable in the Pali and Chinese parallels concerns a carpenter whose wooden adze handle gradually wears away and takes on the impression of his fingers. Even though he is not conscious of the wear from day to day, after a while he notices it. In the same way, the meditator does not notice that his afflictions are slowly wearing away day by day, but when they are gone he realizes what has happened. In the third parable, a ship is brought onto dry land for storage during the cold season after having been in the water for six months. While exposed to the elements, its binding cords gradually rot and fall off. In the same way, the persistent meditator's spiritual bonds (*saṃyojana*) gradually rot away and disappear.

In addition to direct parallels in both the Chinese *Saṃyuktāgama* and Pali *Saṃyutta-nikāya*, this sūtra also has partial parallels in other parts of those collections as well as in the numerical collections. For example, the first paragraph of another sūtra in the Pali *Saṃyutta-nikāya* (II 12.23) is identical to the first paragraph of this one, while one in the *Aṅguttara-nikāya* (7.71)[198] is identical to this sūtra except that it lacks the first paragraph. This pattern is typical of the cut-and-paste structure of Buddhist sūtras and of Buddhist literature in general, whereby standard narrative formulae and blocks of text can be stitched together in a vast number of combinations and variations.[199]

But as usual, even the closest Pali and Chinese parallels to the Gāndhārī sūtra do not correspond to it exactly. Both of them lack a correspondent to the second paragraph of the Gāndhārī text, in which an unnamed monk asks the Buddha why it is that some monks fail to free their minds from the afflictions, to which the Buddha responds that it is because they fail to cultivate the forty-one beneficial dharmas that are conducive to enlightenment. Since this response is repeated in the following paragraph in nearly identical words in all versions, little if anything is lost by the absence of this paragraph. In such cases, it is impossible to determine whether the shorter Pali and Chinese versions are abridgements of the longer one in Gāndhārī, or whether the Gāndhārī text is an expansion of an originally briefer one.

The text of this sūtra was left incomplete in our manuscript. It ends at the bottom of the verso of the scroll after the first sentence of the first parable of the hen. Of course, we cannot be sure that the full Gāndhārī text did include all three parables; conceivably, it could have lacked one or even both of the adze-handle and ship parables. But it is incomplete in any case. One might be inclined to assume that the rest of the sūtra was written on a separate scroll not available to us. However, there are numerous examples among the Senior collection as well as in other groups of Gāndhārī scrolls where only the first scroll survives, and there are few cases in which a scroll from a hypothetical multivolume set is not the first one.[200] Thus it is quite possible in this case, as in several others, that the scribe of our manuscript never actually wrote out the rest of the sūtra.

The translation presents the entire sūtra on the basis of the Gāndhārī text as far as it is available. The remainder, as indicated by square brackets, is translated from the Pali parallel, since it can be reasonably assumed that the full Gāndhārī version would have resembled it. In a few cases the Pali text has been modified or supplemented for consistency with the wording and structure of the Gāndhārī text.

The Parable of the Log

The *Sūtra of the Log* is recorded on another scroll (number 5) from the Senior collection.[201] The text covers both sides of a small scroll that was originally about 17 cm high and 21 cm wide (see figure 5, page 6). Unlike the vast majority of Gandhāran manuscripts, this one is mostly intact and nearly complete, except that, like scroll 5 translated above, it had been rolled up and folded in half so that a vertical strip running down the middle is damaged. The rest of the scroll, including the original margins on both sides, is fully preserved.

The sūtra containing the parable of the log (Skt *Dāruskandha Sūtra* / P *Dārukkhanda Sutta*) seems to have been very popular, since, besides the Gāndhārī text, it is recorded in seven other versions in Pali, Sanskrit, Tibetan, and Chinese. Three of these versions are incorporated into the Bhaiṣajyavastu section of the *Mūlasarvāstivāda-vinaya* in its Sanskrit, Chinese, and Tibetan forms, but it also is included in the Chinese translations of both the *Saṃyuktāgama* and the *Ekottarikāgama*. In the Pali *Saṃyutta-nikāya*, two versions of the text, a longer and a shorter one, occur consecutively.[202] A very abbreviated version of the sūtra is also included in the Chinese anthology *Sūtra in Forty-Two Chapters*. Its popularity is further indicated by a painting from the Buddhist caves at Kizil on the northern rim of the Tarim Basin, located along the Silk Road route that skirted the edge of the Taklamakan desert in what is now the Xinjiang Uyghur Autonomous Region of China. This masterpiece of Central Asian Buddhist art, now in the Museum für Indische Kunst, Berlin, shows the Buddha preaching to an unnamed monk, who kneels at the lower right while the cowherd Nanda listens in at the left. In the foreground, the log that functions as the central motif of the sūtra can be seen floating down the river.

Figure 27. Kizil cave painting of the *Sūtra of the Log*.

According to the Gāndhārī version, the sūtra was taught by the Buddha on the bank of the Ganges River in the city of Ayodhyā when the unnamed monk requested the Buddha to deliver a brief exposition of the Dharma that would enable him to concentrate more attentively and diligently on his meditation. Exhibiting his skill in means, the Buddha pointed to a log that happened to be floating down the Ganges at that moment and presented a parable comparing the gradual progress of the log down the river to the ocean to a Buddhist practitioner's progress toward nirvāṇa, likening the physical obstacles that might prevent the log from reaching the ocean to the mental and moral obstacles that keep a person from attaining nirvāṇa. This method of teaching by parable or simile (*upamā*) is common in the sūtras, particularly in the *Saṃyuktāgama*. A key term in this teaching technique is "metaphor" or "metaphorical expression" (*asivayana* = Skt/P *adhivacana*), which is used to link the metaphor to its literal referent, as in "The 'nearer bank,' monk, is a metaphor for the six internal sense bases."

The Gāndhārī text, like some but not all of the parallel versions, contains a postscript according to which a humble cowherder named Nanda happens to be standing by and listening as the Buddha delivers his sermon. Merely by hearing it, he attains the purified state of an arhat and asks the Buddha to initiate him. The Buddha agrees to do so, but only after Nanda personally returns the cows he is tending to their several owners, even though the cows would be able to find their own ways home. This episode is revealing about the social situation of early Buddhism. On the one hand, the instant conversion of the cowherd exemplifies the Buddha's egalitarian attitudes by showing that a lowly person is as capable of realizing the truth as, for example, a learned brahman; anyone who listens to the Dharma attentively and with an open mind and heart can understand the Buddha's teaching and become a member of his community. On the other hand, the Buddha's condition that Nanda himself return the cows to their owners shows the concern of early Buddhist community with maintaining a good reputation and relationship with the surrounding communities, upon whose material support they were dependent. The intention here was to avoid any possible suspicion that Nanda had stolen the cows or, in becoming a Buddhist, had neglected his social duty.

An interesting further addition to the side story of the cowherd appears in the *Mūlasarvāstivāda-vinaya* version of the sūtra. In this episode (translated in the supplement below), the cowherd sets his staff on the ground to lean on it while listening to the Buddha, inadvertently impaling a frog. The frog, although being crushed by the staff, realizes that if it moves or makes any noise it would distract Nanda from the Buddha's teaching, and so it remains silent until it dies. Since the frog dies with a mind that is pure and filled with faith toward the Buddha, he is reborn in the heaven of the four divine kings. This extra episode, which is illustrated in the Kizil painting, is one of many legends showing how animals as well as human beings can be inspired by the Buddha's charisma and wisdom. Although animals cannot achieve liberation, they are subject to the same karmic laws as human beings and thus can be rewarded for virtuous acts and thoughts by being reborn in a higher state, which can eventually lead them to nirvāṇa.[203]

Comparisons of the Gāndhārī and the other versions of this sūtra provide numerous examples of the types of variations that are typical of the different versions of a particular sūtra. In general, the Gāndhārī text tends to be closer to the Sanskrit version in terms of its overall structure but more like the Pali with regard to the specific wording of key passages. This sort of complex relationship is typical of what we find when comparing parallel texts in these and other Buddhist languages,[204] but in this case the variations are more numerous and more tangled than usual, probably due to its broad popularity and consequent diversity of versions in different languages and regional traditions. These versions differ in various respects such as the location of the discourse, its overall structure, the ordering of the events, and the inclusion or exclusion of some of them, as well as in their specific wording.

The differences between the versions are visible from the very beginning, in the specification of the setting or occasion. In the first Pali version the location is usually given as the city of Ayodhyā, as in the Gāndhārī and Sanskrit, but a textual variant in some manuscripts cites Kosambī rather than Ayodhyā. And in the second Pali version which immediately follows the first in the *Saṃyutta-nikāya*, the sūtra is set in the city of Kimbilā, while one of the Chinese texts places it in Magadha.[205] The two Pali versions also differ in that the first one includes the episode of the cowherd Nanda, whereas he is not mentioned in the second. Another difference involves the explanation of the implication of "rotting from within," the last of the eight metaphors that make up the parable.

An important difference in the overall structure of the several versions of the *Sūtra of the Log* involves the consequences of the Buddha's discourse for the two principal listeners. In some texts, such as the first Pali version and one of the Chinese translations, it is Nanda who realizes the Dharma and becomes an arhat, whereas in the Sanskrit and the corresponding Tibetan and Chinese *Mūlasarvāstivāda-vinaya* versions both the monk and Nanda attain enlightenment, in that order. In the Gāndhārī text both characters become arhats, but in the opposite order. Also, the description of Nanda's enlightenment experience, "As the cowherd Nanda listened to this explication of the Dharma, his mind became liberated without clinging from the afflictions," is entirely different from those of all the other versions.

This is one of several places where the Gāndhārī text stands out as unique among the several versions of the sūtra. Another example is the sentence "Because, monk, nirvāṇa is a metaphor for right views," which has no parallel. Here "right views" is probably a shorthand reference to the eightfold noble path, but the statement that nirvāṇa is a "metaphor" for right views is unexpected, and the wording here is rather unusual. This sentence therefore might have originally been a marginal comment or gloss that came to be incorporated into the text itself at some point in its history. This is a common phenomenon in the history of Buddhist texts, as in manuscript traditions generally, and is one of the common mechanisms by which texts develop and diverge.

Another revealing contrast involves the explanation of the metaphor of the whirlpool. Here the Sanskrit and Chinese versions read "Getting pulled into a whirlpool is when someone renounces the training and turns back to the lower life," while the Pali has "Getting pulled into a whirlpool is a metaphor for the pleasures of the five senses." In the Gāndhārī version the two explanations are combined: "'Getting pulled into a whirlpool' refers, monk, to one who renounces the training and turns back to the lower life. The whirlpool is a metaphor for the pleasures of the five senses." This is another example of the cut-and-paste method of composing sūtras.

Another case where the Gāndhārī text has a fuller presentation than the others is in the explication of "the farther bank" as a metaphor for the six external sense-bases. Here the Gāndhārī spells out all six bases ("the form sense-base, the sound sense-base," etc.), whereas the Pali and Sanskrit simply say "the six external sense-bases," on the assumption that the readers would know what they are. In the same paragraph, we also have a good example of the type of mistakes and corruptions that inevitably arise in manuscript texts. Here, in the listing of the six external sense-bases, the last one is given as "the mind sense-base." But this is actually the last member of the preceding set, the internal sense-bases; the last external sense-base should certainly be "the dharma sense-base." Here the copyist's eye must have strayed from the end of the second list in his archetype to the end of the first list, a common sort of copying error; compare the similar eye-skipping error mentioned in note 210 below.

Finally, this sūtra contains a classic case of what is known in textual criticism as a "crux": a very difficult—often insoluble—textual problem. This involves the phrase *asuci sakapa spera samayara*, which is tentatively translated as "has impure intentions, memories (?), and behavior." This phrase and its equivalents in Pali, Sanskrit, and other languages have troubled Buddhist scholars, ancient and modern, for millennia. The various texts in which it occurs include a vast number of variant readings, and the commentaries and dictionaries propose an equally wide range of suggestions as to what it means,[206] but the truth is that no one knows for sure. This, like many other problematic words and expressions in Buddhist literature (as in other ancient scriptures), is probably an archaic or regional idiom—going back to a very early phase of the transmission of the scriptures—whose real meaning and etymological basis has been forgotten.

It is probably no coincidence that precisely at this point there are two irregularities in the manuscript. One of the syllables in the first word of the phrase (*asuci*, "impure") was originally miswritten as *asuṣi* and then secondarily corrected with the addition of the correct syllable *ci*, but without cancelling the incorrect syllable, so that the final reading is a garbled *asuciṣi*. The first syllable of the second word (*sakapa*, "intention") is written is a peculiar fashion, apparently because the scribe was uncertain as to its correct form. This is not surprising, because the reading and interpretation of this word presents a particularly difficult problem. It is variously presented in different versions as "doubt" (= Skt *śaṅkā*), "conch shell" (*śaṅkha*), or "irresolute" (*saṃkasuka*); only the Gāndhārī text has the reading "intention" (*sakapa* = Skt *saṅkalpa*).

The preceding examples are part of a recurrent pattern in Gāndhārī manuscripts whereby problematic or obscure words and passages often show graphic irregularities or alterations. This tells us that many of the interpretive problems that modern Buddhological scholars face are nothing new, and that ancient scribes and scholars were also puzzled by them. Unfortunately, this also means that, in many cases, the problems are simply not soluble. Although the newly found Gāndhārī sources may not provide clear and simple solutions to such problems, they do sometimes present new data or opinions, or at least clarify the nature of the problems.

A. The Four Concentrations[207]

What is the concentration accompanied by perception of repulsiveness? Here, a monk sitting at the foot of a tree or in an empty house or in an open space examines his own body as it is placed and as it is positioned, upward from the soles of his feet and downward from the hair on top of his head, all enclosed by skin, [full of all sorts] of impurity: head hair, body hair, nails, teeth, tendons, veins, outer skin, inner skin, bone, marrow, [flesh, sinews, kidneys, liver], heart, pleura, spleen, lungs, small intestine, large intestine, anus, bladder, feces, tears, sweat, saliva, mucus, pus, blood, [bile, phlegm, fat, grease], joint fluid, skull, and brain. It is the undisturbed one-pointedness of mind of such a person that is meant by "the concentration accompanied by perception of repulsiveness."

What is the concentration accompanied by perception of death? Here, a monk sitting at the foot of a tree or in an empty house or in an open space . . . [thinks] "I will die. I will not live long, I will pass away, I will die, I will disappear." It is the undisturbed one-pointedness of mind of such a person [that is] meant by "the concentration accompanied by perception of death."

What is the concentration accompanied by perception of revulsion toward food? "Food" here refers to rice and gruel. The monk . . . conceives it as feces, as saliva, as vomit, as a lump of vile secretions, as black filth. It is the undisturbed [one-pointedness of mind] of such a person that is meant by "the concentration accompanied by perception of revulsion toward food."

What is the concentration accompanied by perception of displeasure toward the whole world? Here, when a monk views a village as if it were no village, a city as if it were no city, the countryside as if it were no countryside, then he is dissatisfied with them, he ponders them, he does not enjoy them, he takes no pleasure in them. He tames and controls his mind toward them; he makes it [soft] and pliable. If, after he has tamed and controlled his mind toward them and has made it soft and pliable, he sees at another time a beautiful park, a beautiful forest, a beautiful pond, a beautiful [river], a beautiful land, or a beautiful mountain, then he is dissatisfied with them, he ponders them, he does not enjoy them, he takes no pleasure in them. He tames and controls his mind toward them; he makes it soft [and pliable]. After [he] has tamed and controlled his mind [toward them] and has made it soft and pliable, then at another time, [whatever he sees,] whether above and below, across, all around, everywhere, he is dissatisfied with it, ponders it, [does not enjoy it, takes no pleasure in it]. It is the undisturbed one-pointedness of mind of such a person that is meant by "the concentration accompanied by perception of displeasure toward the whole world."

B. Not Yours

The setting is Śrāvastī. [The Buddha said:] "Monks, abandon[208] what is not yours. Abandoning it will lead to benefit and happiness. Now, [what is it that is not] yours? Form is not yours; abandon it. Abandoning it will lead to benefit and happiness. Sensation, perception, volitional formations, and consciousness are not yours; abandon them. [Abandoning] them will lead to benefit and happiness.

"Here is an example: suppose someone were to cut down the grass, wood, branches, leaves, and foliage here in the Jeta forest, or were to take it away or burn it, or do whatever he wished with it. What do you think? Would you think 'That person is cutting us,' or 'taking us away,' or 'burning us,' or 'doing whatever he wished with us'?"

[The monks answered,] "Of course not, [Venerable Sir]."

"And why is [that]?"

"Because this [forest], Venerable Sir, is not ourselves; nor does it belong to us."

"In just the same way, abandon what is not yours. Abandoning it will lead to benefit and happiness. [In just the same way], form is not yours; abandon it. Abandoning it will lead to benefit and happiness. Sensation, perception, volitional formations, and consciousness are *not* yours; abandon them. Abandoning them will lead to [benefit] and happiness."

Thus spoke the Lord.

c. Living Full of Disenchantment

[The setting is Śrāvastī. The Lord said:] "This is in accordance with the Dharma, monks, that a good faithful man who out of faith has left his home and renounced the world for the homeless life should live full of disenchantment with regard to form. He should live [full of] disenchantment with regard to sensation, perception, volitional formations, and consciousness.

"As he lives full of disenchantment with regard to form, he comes to completely understand form. As he [lives full of] disenchantment with regard to sensation, perception, volitional formations, [and] consciousness, he comes to completely understand [sensation, perception, volitional formations, and] consciousness.

"Fully understanding form, fully understanding sensation, perception, volitional formations, and consciousness, he is liberated from form, he is liberated from sensation, perception, and volitional formations, he is liberated from consciousness. He is liberated from rebirth, old age, disease, and death, from grief, lamentation, [misery, depression, and despair]. He is liberated from suffering; so say I."

Thus spoke the Lord.

D. The Adze Handle

The Lord was staying in Śrāvastī. [He said:] "I say, monks, that the destruction of the afflictions is for one who knows and who sees, not for one who does not know and does not see. I say that the destruction of the afflictions is for one who knows in what way and sees in what way? I say that the destruction of the afflictions is for one [who knows] and sees as follows: 'This is form, this is the arising of form, this is the [passing away] of form. This is sensation. . . .[209] This is perception. . . . This is volitional formations. . . . This is consciousness, this is the arising of consciousness, this is the passing away of consciousness.'"

Then a certain monk asked the Lord: "You say that the destruction of the afflictions is for one who knows in this way and sees in this way. Then, in this regard, why is it that the minds of some monks do not become liberated without clinging from the afflictions?"

[The Lord answered,] "That is because they did not cultivate [this]."

"Because they did not cultivate what?"

"Because they did not cultivate beneficial dharmas."

"Because they did not cultivate which beneficial dharmas?"[210]

"Because they did not cultivate the four foundations of mindfulness, the four correct efforts, the four bases of supernatural powers, the [four] meditations, the five faculties, the five powers, the seven factors of enlightenment, and the eightfold noble path—[because they did not cultivate] these beneficial dharmas. Although a monk who lives without continuously devoting himself to cultivating [these beneficial dharmas] might conceive the desire 'O, that my mind might be liberated without clinging from the afflictions!' still his mind is not actually liberated without clinging from the afflictions. Why is that? It is because he did not cultivate [this]."

"Because he did not cultivate what?"

"Because he did not cultivate beneficial dharmas."

"Because he did not cultivate which beneficial dharmas?"

"Because he did not cultivate the [four] foundations of mindfulness, the four correct efforts, the four bases of supernatural powers, the four meditations, the five faculties, the five powers, the [seven] factors of enlightenment, and the eightfold noble path. It is because he did not cultivate these beneficial dharmas.

"Here is an example: Suppose a hen had eight or ten or twelve [eggs], but the hen did not properly sit on the eggs at the right time,[211] did not properly warm them at the right [time], and did not properly nurture them at the right time. [Although that hen might conceive the desire, 'O, that my chicks might break open their shells with the tips of their claws or their beaks and be safely hatched!' it would still be impossible for her chicks to break open their shells with the tips of their claws or their beaks and be safely hatched. Why is that? It is because that hen did not properly sit on her eight or ten or twelve eggs at the right time, did not properly warm them at the right time, and did not properly nurture them at the right time.

"In just the same way, monks, although a monk who lives without continuously devoting himself to cultivating these beneficial dharmas might conceive the desire, 'O, that my mind might be liberated without clinging from the afflictions!' still his mind is not actually liberated without clinging from the afflictions. Why is that? It is because he did not cultivate this."

"Because he did not cultivate what?"

"Because he did not cultivate beneficial dharmas."

"Because he did not cultivate which beneficial dharmas?"

"Because he did not cultivate the four foundations of mindfulness, the four correct efforts, the four bases of supernatural powers, the four meditations, the five faculties, the five powers, the seven factors of enlightenment, and the eightfold noble path. It is because he did not cultivate these beneficial dharmas.

"Although, monks, a monk who does live continuously devoting himself to cultivating [these beneficial dharmas] might not conceive the desire, 'O, that my mind might be liberated from the afflictions without a remainder!' still his mind is actually liberated without clinging from the afflictions. Why is that? It is because he did cultivate this."

"Because he did cultivate what?"

"Because he did cultivate the four foundations of mindfulness, the four correct efforts, the four bases of supernatural powers, the four meditations, the five faculties, the five powers, the seven factors of enlightenment, and the eightfold noble path. It is because he did cultivate these beneficial dharmas.

"Here is an example: Suppose a hen had eight or ten or twelve eggs, and the hen did properly sit on the eggs at the right time, did properly warm them at the right time, and did properly nurture them at the right time. Although that hen might not conceive the desire, 'O, that my chicks might break open their shells with the tips of their claws or their beaks and be safely hatched!' it would still be possible for her chicks to break open their shells with the tips of their claws or their beaks and be safely hatched. Why is that? It is because, monks, that hen had eight or ten or twelve eggs and she did properly sit on the eggs at the right time, did properly warm them at the right time, and did properly nurture them at the right time.

"In just the same way, monks, a monk who lives continuously devoting himself to cultivating these beneficial dharmas might not conceive the desire, 'O, that my mind might be liberated without clinging from the afflictions!' still his mind is actually liberated without clinging from the afflictions. Why is that? It is because he did cultivate this."

"Because he did cultivate what?"

"Because he did cultivate the four foundations of mindfulness, the four correct efforts, the four bases of supernatural powers, the four meditations, the five faculties, the five powers, the seven factors of enlightenment, and the eightfold noble path. It is because he did cultivate these beneficial dharmas.

"Here is an example: You can see the impressions of the fingers and thumbs of a carpenter or a carpenter's apprentice on the handle of his adze. But he is not aware that 'O, this much of my adze handle has worn away today, this much yesterday, and this much the day before yesterday.' But when it has been worn away, then he becomes aware that it is worn.

"In the just the same way, monks, a monk who lives continuously devoting himself to cultivating the beneficial dharmas is not aware that 'This much of my afflictions has worn away today, this much yesterday, and this much the day before yesterday.' But when they have been worn away, then he becomes aware that they are worn.

"Here is an example: After sailing in the water for six months, an ocean-going ship that is bound together with reeds[212] is pulled up onto dry land in the wintertime, so that its bindings are exposed to the wind and the sun. The bindings are rained on by monsoon clouds until they are easily loosened, and then rot away.

"In just the same way, monks, when a monk lives continuously devoting himself to cultivating the beneficial dharmas, his spiritual bonds (*saṃyojana*) are easily loosened, and then rot away."]

E. The Parable of the Log

Thus have I heard: at one time the Lord was staying at Ayodhyā, on the bank of the river Ganges. At that time, a monk approached the Lord, bowed at his feet, and sat down to one side. When he had sat down to one side, that monk said to the Lord: "May the Lord please explain the Dharma in brief, so that upon hearing it I might be able to live alone, independent, careful, diligent, and dedicated."

At that time, a large log was being carried along by the current of the river Ganges. The Lord saw that large log that was being carried along, and said to that monk: "Monk, do you see that large log being carried along by the current of the river Ganges?"

"Yes, venerable sir."

"Well, if that log does not get stuck on the nearer bank, if it does not get stuck on the farther bank, if it does not sink in the middle, if it does not land on an island, if it does not get pulled out by a human being, if it does not get pulled out by a nonhuman being, if it does not get pulled into a whirlpool, and if it does not rot from within; then, monk, this log will gradually head toward the ocean and end up in the ocean. Why is that? Because, monk, the current of the river Ganges [flows toward] the ocean."[213]

When the Lord had said this, the monk asked him, "Venerable sir, what is the nearer bank? What is the farther bank? What is sinking in the middle? What is landing on an island? What is getting pulled out by a human being? What is getting pulled out by a nonhuman being? What is getting pulled into a whirlpool? What is rotting from within?"

"The 'nearer bank,' monk, is a metaphor for the six internal sense-bases: the eye sense-base, the ear sense-base, the nose sense-base, the tongue sense-base, the body sense-base, and the mind sense-base.

"The 'farther bank,' monk, is a metaphor for the six external sense-bases: the form sense-base, the sound sense-base, the smell sense-base, the taste sense-base, the tangible-sense base, and the mind[214] sense-base.

"'Sinking in the middle' is a metaphor for pleasure and desire.

"'Landing on an island' is a metaphor for egotism.

"'Getting pulled out by a human being' refers, monk, to one who shares joys and sorrows with householders, who is happy when they are happy and unhappy when they are unhappy, and gets involved in various people's affairs.

"'Getting pulled out by a nonhuman being' refers, monk, to one who practices the pure life after making a solemn resolution to attain rebirth among one or another group of gods, [thinking] 'By this behavior or austerity or vow or pure life, I will become a god or one of the [lesser] gods.'[215]

"'Getting pulled into a whirlpool' refers, monk, to one who renounces[216] the training and turns back to the lower life. The whirlpool is a metaphor for the pleasures of the five senses.

"'Rotting from within' refers, monk, to one who behaves badly, has an evil nature, has impure intentions, memories (?), and behavior,[217] holds wrong views, and conceals his actions.

"In just the same way, monk, if one[218] does not get stuck on the nearer bank, if one does not get stuck on the farther bank, if one does not sink in the middle, if one does not land on an island, if one does not get pulled out by a human being, if one does not get pulled out by a nonhuman being, if one does not get pulled into a whirlpool, and if one does not rot from within, so too you, monk, will gradually head toward nirvāṇa and end up in nirvāṇa. And why is that? Because, monk, nirvāṇa is a metaphor for right views."

At that same time, Nanda, a cowherd, was standing near the Lord, leaning on his staff. As the cowherd Nanda listened to this explication of the Dharma, his mind became liberated without clinging from the afflictions. Then the cowherd Nanda set down his staff and approached the Lord, bowed at his feet, and sat down to one side. Then he said to the Lord: "Venerable sir, I do not get stuck on the nearer bank, I do not get stuck on the farther bank, I do not get pulled out by a human being, I do not get pulled out by a nonhuman being, I do not get pulled into a whirlpool, I do not rot from within. May I receive initiation from the Lord, and may I receive ordination?"

"Nanda, have you returned the cows to their owners?"

"Sir, yearning for their calves, the cows will go [by themselves] and will know the way to their respective homes."

"Nanda, even though the cows, yearning for their calves, will go [by themselves] and will know the way to their respective homes, still, Nanda, you must go to return the cows to their owners and then come back."

Then the cowherd Nanda bowed at the Lord's feet, circumambulated him, and departed from his presence. Then, after returning the cows to their owners, he approached the Lord, bowed at his feet, and sat down to one side. Then he said to the Lord: "Venerable sir, the cows have been returned to their owners. Now may I receive initiation from the Lord, and may I receive ordination?" And the cowherd Nanda did indeed receive initiation and ordination from the Lord.

Then, having been instructed in this way, the monk very quickly, by supernormal knowledge, here in this world directly realized for himself and entered into that unsurpassed culmination of the pure life, for the sake of which a good man properly leaves his home and goes forth to homelessness. And there he stayed, [thinking,] "I have done what was to be done, I know of nothing beyond this," and quickly became one of the arhats.

Thus [spoke] the Lord. The monk and the venerable Nanda were delighted and rejoiced at what the Lord had said.

Supplement: The Story of the Frog[219]

At that same time, the cowherd Nanda was standing near the Lord. Having set his cows out to pasture, he put down his staff. But he put the staff down on a frog, so that its skin was ripped off and it was torn limb from limb. [The frog] realized, "If I move my body or make a sound, it might cause the cowherd Nanda to be distracted from [the Lord's] words." And so, purifying his heart toward the Lord, he died and was reborn among the four divine kings.

Sequel

In a further sequel to this story in the *Mūlasarvāstivāda-vinaya* version,[220] the god who had formerly been the frog came to visit the Buddha in the middle of the night. The Buddha preached to him, making him understand the four noble truths, and the god became his lay follower. Then the Buddha explained to the monks the karmic background of the frog: in a long-ago lifetime, during the time of the previous Buddha Kāśyapa, he had been a solitary ascetic monk who was annoyed by monks who chanted communally all night long and disturbed his meditation. He became angry and cried out, "Kāśyapa's monks croak all night long like frogs!" As a result of the bad karma generated by his rage, he had been born as a frog five hundred times, but because he had now purified his heart toward the Buddha, he was released from the bad karma and became a god.

3. The Rhinoceros Sūtra[221]

The Rhinoceros and His Horn

THE *Rhinoceros Sūtra* is a poem in forty verses, all but one of which contain the identical refrain, "Wander alone like the rhinoceros," whence the title. Besides the Gāndhārī text presented here, it is known in a Pali version incorporated into the *Suttanipāta* and in an abridged Sanskrit text that is quoted in the *Mahāvastu*. The poem's theme is the distractions and entanglements that social relationships inevitably involve and the consequent advantages of the solitary life, symbolized by the rhinoceros. The Indian rhinoceros is a quintessentially solitary beast that does not travel in a herd; in the words of one naturalist, "The rhino is distinctly an unsociable animal. Two adults are never seen together except during a fight or when mating. . . . At certain times of the year the rhinoceros appears to wander far away from its haunts. . . . An individual may leave its territory and embark on a wandering migration."[222] In Indian literature, the rhinoceros is "the archetypal solitary beast."[223] It is thus a perfect symbol for the solitary life in which one is to "wander alone."

There is however a long-standing controversy about the interpretation of the title (Skt *Khaḍgaviṣāṇa Sūtra*; Pali *Khaggavisāṇa Sutta*), because it can be understood as meaning either the *Rhinoceros Sūtra* or the *Rhinoceros Horn Sūtra*.[224] In either interpretation, the symbolism is appropriate. *Rhinoceros Sūtra* is appropriate in view of the rhinoceros' solitary habits, but *Rhinoceros Horn Sūtra* is equally apt, since

Figure 28. An Indian rhinoceros.

the Indian rhinoceros (*Rhinoceros unicornis*) has, unlike most horned animals, only a single horn, which therefore can also serve as a symbol of solitude. While scholars and commentators, both ancient and modern, have argued for millennia about which interpretation of the title is the "true" or "original" one, I see no need to consider the issue in terms of mutually exclusive alternatives. Both translations are philologically justifiable and symbolically appropriate, so it is entirely possible that the original author, or perhaps rather the editor who first combined these verses into a single text under this title, intended the ambiguity, thereby creating a title with a simultaneous double referent.[225]

Reconstruction of the Manuscript

The *Rhinoceros Sūtra* was the first of the Gāndhārī manuscripts to be identified at the British Library in 1995. The manuscript (British Library no. 5B) was a badly decayed scroll of the single-sheet, smaller format type, which had originally been about 42 cm high and 24 cm wide. Due to its extremely fragile condition, when the scroll was unrolled, it separated into twelve large pieces, more than fifty small fragments, and a multitude of miniscule bits. The correct positions of the pieces could not be immediately determined, so that in the glass frame in which it is now permanently preserved in the British Library, they are

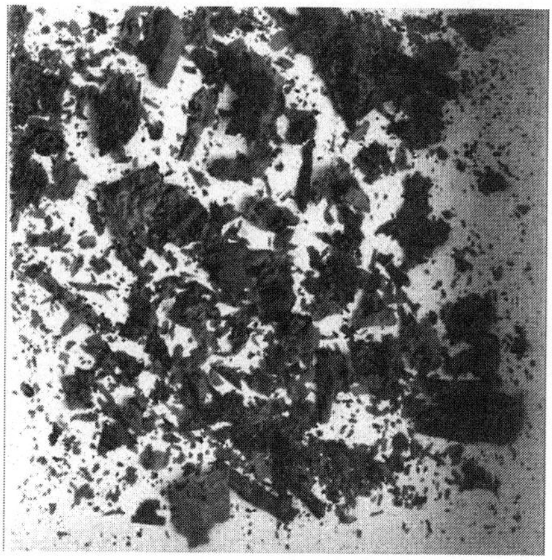

Figure 29. The *Rhinoceros Sūtra* scroll: the debris box.

arranged more or less randomly. It was only through a complex process of internal and external textual study that the original sequence of the fragments, and hence the proper order of the verses, could be determined.[226] In the course of this process, it became clear that the text had originally been laid out in an orderly fashion (which is by no means always the case in Gandhāran manuscripts), with each verse corresponding to one line, carefully arranged so that the four quarters or "feet" of each verse lined up vertically, with small spaces marking the division between the quarters. Like many birchbark scrolls, it had been double folded, causing severe damage to a vertical strip running down the scroll to the left of the center. As a result, the third quarters of each verse were mostly lost, rendering the reconstruction process all the more difficult. But in the end, approximately two-thirds of the original scroll was recovered, and the correct sequence of nearly all of the fragments could be determined.

Themes and Images: Solitude and Companionship

Although the refrain "Wander alone like the rhinoceros" repeatedly emphasizes the virtues of solitude, the poem as a whole does not deny the benefits of human company absolutely; a series of verses in the middle of the sūtra (24–27) allows for the possibility of desirable company. The first verse of this sequence reads in part, "Cultivate a friend who is inspired, learned, faithful to the Dharma, noble." The next verse says, "If you should find yourself a wise companion, a well-behaved and trustworthy fellow, together you may overcome all dangers. So wander with him, satisfied and mindful." This verse, the only one in the collection whose final quarter does not have the usual refrain, is contrastively paired with the following one: "But if you cannot find a wise companion, a well-behaved and trustworthy fellow, then, like a king who leaves behind his kingdom, wander alone like the rhinoceros."

Up to this point, this set of verses explains that a good companion is a desirable thing, although one is better off without a companion than with an unworthy one. The final verse of this subsection explains exactly what a desirable friend is: "Truly, you may delight in all of your companions; stay with the ones who are like you or better." Here the commentaries on the Pali version explain that this refers to companions who are equal or superior in terms of virtuous conduct and spiritual understanding. Such friends are desirable, even in large numbers, because unlike ordinary worldly friends they will not waste your time in idle chatter but will speak only of worthy, beneficial matters.

But if worthy friends are to be sought, then why does the poem as a whole focus on avoiding companions and the virtues of the solitary life? The answer is provided in the penultimate verse of the entire sūtra: "They like you and they help you for a motive. It's hard to find a true friend nowadays." The point is that even though the company of true—that is, spiritually uplifting—friends is beneficial, such company is rare, and in its absence one is better off with no company at all. The sūtra then concludes, "So if I were to spend my days with others, I'd waste my time in chatter or in quarrels. Seeing this danger lurking in the future, I wander alone like the rhinoceros."

Besides the central theme of the drawbacks of companionship, the *Rhinoceros Sūtra* addresses some other related points. It particularly stresses the common Buddhist theme of the danger of all kinds of attachments, including family ties: "Forsaking sons and friends and even mother . . . " (v. 18). These attachments not only inevitably lead to suffering in the end—"Dreading separation from dear ones, wander alone like the rhinoceros" (7)—but more importantly, they distract a person from more worthwhile pursuits: "In sympathizing with friends and companions, the mind gets fixed on them and loses its way" (3). All of the verses on this theme are in the first half of the poem (though they are mixed in with verses on other topics), as if to set the stage for the central theme of good and bad companionship.

In contrast to this negative theme, the sūtra also includes many verses that extol the benefits and satisfactions of the solitary life, its power and simplicity, and the freedom from fear and entanglements it offers. Verses on this theme tend to be located in the second half of the sūtra (for instance, verses 20–23), as if to counterbalance the negative theme of the first half. Many of the verses on these themes employ contrasting images and symbols from the natural world, representing bondage and entanglement on the one hand and freedom and independence on the other. Verse 4, for example, juxtaposes a large bamboo tree that has become "thick and tangled" with a young bamboo that grows separately and untangled, while verse 19 urges the reader to shed the finery of the worldly life "like the ebony tree that sheds all of its leaves." Images from animal life abound as well; besides the central symbol of the rhinoceros, other animals symbolize the life of unlimited freedom: the lion "who wanders where he will" (21–22), the deer "wandering free in the forest" (5), and the elephant "who shuns the herd" and "dwells in the forest, wandering at his will" (32). Other natural images represent breaking the bonds of attachment that keep the ordinary person chained to the worldly life: the bird that "tears right through a heavy net" (20) and the wind that "cannot be caught in a net" (21). Both are universal symbols that will be immediately familiar from modern expressions like "free as a bird" and "try to catch the wind."

The Solitary Buddhas

All Buddhist traditions agree that the *Rhinoceros Sūtra* is a collection of inspired utterances (*udāna*) that were spoken by various "solitary buddhas," or *pratyekabuddhas*, at the moment they achieved enlightenment. Solitary buddhas, frequently and prominently mentioned in early Buddhist literature, are human beings who discovered the truths of the Dharma and achieved enlightenment through their own insight rather than by being taught it by others. This achievement qualifies them as buddhas—that is, as self-enlightened beings. But since they do not go on to reveal the Dharma to other beings, they remain solitary (*pratyeka*) buddhas in contrast to "fully enlightened buddhas" (*samyak-sambuddha*), that is, buddhas *par excellence*, such as Gotama/Śākyamuni, who dedicate themselves to teaching the Dharma. According to the principles of (non-Mahāyāna) Buddhist cosmology, solitary buddhas can only appear at times where no fully enlightened buddha is living in the world. But unlike fully enlightened buddhas, solitary buddhas can coexist at the same time, and they are often described as dwelling together in assemblies.

Thus solitary buddhas function as a sort of substitute, or consolation prize, in the absence of teaching buddhas. Although one cannot study the Dharma and achieve liberation directly from them, one can gain inspiration from contact with them and win great merit by feeding or caring for them. Many texts describe how persons who encounter a solitary buddha feel a sense of awe, inspiring them to utter solemn resolutions[227] that lead to desirable rebirths and eventually to liberation.[228]

According to the frame story that introduces the abridged Sanskrit version of the *Rhinoceros Sūtra* in the *Mahāvastu* (a massive compilation of materials concerning the life of the Buddha and associated topics according to the textual traditions of the Mahāsāṃghika-Lokottaravāda school), five hundred solitary buddhas learned from the gods that the Buddha Śākyamuni was soon to be born on earth. Therefore they knew that that they would have to "die," that is, pass into nirvāṇa, since they could not coexist with a fully enlightened buddha. The solitary buddhas assembled at a park near Vārāṇasī, where each one spoke a verse about the solitary rhinoceros.

A different account of the origin of the rhinoceros verses is given by the commentary on the *Suttanipāta*, where the solitary buddhas are said to have recited them to each other at their periodic assemblies on the mythical Mount Gandhamādana. According to this source, the sūtra as we have it was recited to his attendant Ānanda by Śākyamuni Buddha, who knew the verses by his omniscient powers even though he had not been present when the verses were originally recited by the solitary buddhas. The Pali commentary provides for each verse a story explaining the circumstances that led the solitary buddha to utter his inspired verse. For example, it gives the following explanation for the verse corresponding to verse 16 of the Gāndhārī version:

> Seeing two bracelets, gleaming bright with gold,
> perfectly crafted by the skillful smith,
> clanging and banging together on one arm—
> wander alone like the rhinoceros.

> How did this verse arise? One summer day the king of Benares was taking his afternoon nap. Nearby, a servant girl was grinding sandalwood paste. She had a single gold bangle on one arm and a pair of them on the other. The pair made a jangling noise while the single one was quiet. Seeing this, the king continued to stare at the servant, thinking, "This is like the noise that arises when one lives among a group. But when one lives alone, there is no noise."
>
> At the same time, the king's queen was standing by fanning him, all dressed up in her finest jewelry. Thinking that the king's mind was fixed on the servant girl, she dismissed her and began grinding the sandalwood herself. But the many gold bangles on her arms banged together and raised

> a great clatter. The king become completely disgusted and, laying down on his right side, practiced insight meditation until he achieved solitary enlightenment. While he lay there experiencing this supreme bliss, the queen approached him and said, "May I anoint you with the sandalwood paste?" But he answered, "No, go away and leave me alone." When she asked him, "Why, great king?" he answered, "I am no longer a king!" Then the ministers heard their conversation and approached, but when they addressed him as king, he said "Listen to me: I am no longer a king!"

The point of the story is clear enough: in solitude a person enjoys silence, while two people waste their time together in idle chitchat that is no more meaningful than the sound of two bangles clashing on one arm; and larger groups produce even more useless noise. Therefore it is best to live alone. This insight came to the king in a flash as he listened to the servant woman and then his wife grinding sandalwood paste, whereupon he achieved enlightenment and became a solitary buddha. The story is typical of the solitary buddhas, who are often said to have been inspired by some trivial incident that provoked a sense of disillusionment with the world and led them to sudden enlightenment.

Besides explaining the circumstances and implications of the verse, this commentary also ties in related themes from other verses in the poem. For example, the king's shocking remark, uttered twice, "I am no longer a king," echoes the image "like a king who leaves behind his kingdom, wander alone like the rhinoceros" (v. 26); both phrases express the ultimately unsatisfactory nature of worldly power and luxury. Similarly, the queen's mistaken concern that "the king's mind was fixed on the servant girl" contains the same expression (*paṭibaddhacitto*) that occurs in verses 3, "the mind gets fixed on them and loses its way," and whose opposite appears in verses 12 and 39, "Don't fix your mind on this house or on that one." Here, the fundamental Buddhist principle of nonattachment to things of the world, including friends and loved ones, is emphasized in both its positive and negative aspects. There is a profound irony in the queen's misunderstanding of the king's state of mind; in her jealousy, she thinks that he is obsessed with the servant girl, when in fact his only feeling toward her is annoyance with the noise she is raising. The contrast illustrates the vast gulf between the unenlightened and the enlightened mind.

It will be less obvious to the casual reader that this story also cleverly combines the two possible understandings of the term *solitary buddha*, which are the object of a long-standing controversy in both traditional and modern Buddhist scholarship (an issue that is quite similar to the argument over the title of the *Rhinoceros [Horn] Sūtra*).[229] Due to the mixture and confusion of dialects that underlie even the earliest surviving strata of Buddhist texts, the word that is typically rendered as "solitary buddha" (Skt *pratyekabuddha*) can be also be understood as meaning "buddha from a cause" (*pratyayabuddha*). In the latter interpretation, the term refers to the momentary stimulus or inspiration—the "cause"—such as the sound of the jangling bangles, that can lead a person to achieve sudden enlightenment and become a "buddha from a cause." In its explanation of the verse, the commentary both embodies and justifies both possible meanings of the term: the emphasis on the desirability of solitude and quiet alludes to the first interpretation as "solitary buddha," while the reference to the jangling of the bangles as the "cause" of the king's enlightenment suggests the second, "buddha from a cause." Thus, as in the case of the title of the poem itself, it is unnecessary and perhaps even pointless to insist on the correctness of one or the other etymology. They are in a sense both correct, and the ambiguity may have been intended right from the beginning. This is entirely in keeping with a strong tendency in Buddhist rhetoric toward the creative and provocative use of ambiguity and paradox, a tendency that eventually developed to an extreme in some Mahāyāna sūtras in which the reader is bombarded with what seem to be bewildering paradoxes.[230]

Text and Context

Although the association of the *Rhinoceros Sūtra* with the inspired words of the solitary buddhas is unanimously accepted by all Buddhist commentators, it is nowhere explicitly stated in the text itself. Only the commentaries explain the backstory of the verse, as in the example cited above. While historically oriented modern scholars may question the originality of the stories, this mode of understanding texts that consist of compilations of verses is a typical one in Buddhist literature, and indeed in traditional Indian literature generally. In such cases, the text proper consists only of the verses, strung together without any narrative frame, whereas their original context and the circumstances of their origin are explained, if at all, in commentaries. A classic example is the *Jātaka* collection in the Pali canon, in which the previous lives of the Buddha are recounted in verses alone, whose narrative context and connection only become evident from the accompanying commentary in prose.

An even closer parallel to the *Rhinoceros Sūtra* is the *Dharmapada* literature in its various manifestations in Pali, Sanskrit, Gāndhārī, and other languages.[231] These texts consist of verses, grouped together under topic headings, that were thought to have been uttered by the Buddha on various occasions. The commentaries explain, sometimes at great length, the circumstances or events in reference to which the Buddha spoke the verses.[232] Whereas a modern scholar might be inclined to assume that these texts are merely anthologies of verses expressing Buddhist principles that had been collected by some ancient editor from various sources, the traditional reader understands them as an authoritative compilation of the Buddha's sayings whose authenticity is guaranteed by the commentator's report of their origin. The source of the commentator's knowledge of these origins are neither cited nor questioned; they are simply taken on faith.

This type of literature reflects the strongly oral character of early Indian tradition, where texts were preserved and transmitted primarily by memorization, for which verse texts were particularly well suited. We can suppose that these verses were from the beginning accompanied by some sort of informal, unwritten framing narrative in prose, probably varying according to the various reciters' traditions. Such traditions were eventually collected and set down in writing at some later date by formal literary commentators, who thereby established the authoritative interpretations. Be this as it may, the *Rhinoceros Sūtra* is the only text of this kind that is attributed to solitary buddhas, and regardless of whether this association is historically primary, it is eminently appropriate to their theme and content. In any case, we can be quite sure that the scribe who wrote out the manuscript translated here would never have doubted that these verses were the genuine words of the solitary buddhas.

Solitude and Society

While it is agreed by all that, in principle at least, a monk should live apart from secular society, there has been a perennial tension in Buddhism between the communal monastic life and the life of the forest monk who spends his time meditating alone in the wilderness. Not surprisingly, support for both ways of life can be found in the canonical teachings. The vinaya literature deals at great length with the rules and regulations of communal life. But the benefits of the solitary life were extolled by the Buddha in many sūtra texts, such as the *Longer Sūtra on Emptiness* (*Mahāsuññata Sutta*),[233] where he teaches that "It impossible that a monk who delights in company, takes delight in company, and devotes himself to delight in company, who delights in society, takes delight in society, and rejoices in society, would attain and remain in the liberation of mind that is temporary and beautiful or [the liberation of mind] that is lasting and unshakeable. But it is possible that a monk who remains alone and away from society would attain and remain in the liberation of mind that is temporary and beautiful or [the liberation of mind] that is lasting and unshakeable." Here, not only do the general sentiments of the discourse agree with the central message of the *Rhinoceros Sūtra*, but even the specific wording corresponds closely to verse 15: "It cannot be that one who loves companions would reach liberation, even for a moment." The *Rhinoceros Sūtra* was by no means the only text espousing the solitary path toward wisdom and enlightenment, but it was probably one of the most eloquent and widely read among them.

The *Rhinoceros Sūtra* in Buddhist Literature: Versions and Variations

The discovery of a Gandhāran manuscript of the *Rhinoceros Sūtra* confirms the popularity of this sūtra, which was already evident from its previously known versions. The *Rhinoceros Sūtra* appears in no less than three different places in the Pali canon, in each case incorporated into one of the several texts and compilations that constitute the *Khuddaka-nikāya*. As we saw above, the *Khuddaka-nikāya* is a miscellaneous grab bag of fifteen texts of very diverse contents, including some of the most popular and important material, such as the *Dhammapada* and the *Jātaka* stories. One of its most interesting components is the *Suttanipāta*, an anthology of seventy short sūtras, including some of the earliest specimens of Buddhist literature. The *Rhinoceros Sūtra* is the third sūtra in this compilation, and its presence there is one of the indications of its relative antiquity.

The *Rhinoceros Sūtra* is also preserved as part of another *Khuddaka-nikāya* compilation, namely the *Apadāna*, or "Karmic Stories." This text, which belongs to the later stratum of the Pali canon, consists of 614 short recitations by the Buddha and his disciples in which they explain the karmic factors from previous lives that led them to their present fortunate states.[234] Here too, as in the *Suttanipāta*, the *Rhinoceros Sūtra* is set in a prominent position near the beginning of the text, immediately following the introductory chapter containing the recitation of the Buddha himself. The text of the *Rhinoceros Sūtra* recorded in the *Apadāna* is identical to the one in the *Suttanipāta* except for the addition of one verse and the different title, which is given here as "The Karmic Histories of the Solitary Buddhas" (*Paccekabuddhāpadāna*).

The third appearance of the *Rhinoceros Sūtra* in the *Khuddaka-nikāya* is as the object of a commentary called the *Niddesa* that elucidates certain parts of the *Suttanipāta*. The *Niddesa* is the only commentarial text that was admitted into the canon itself, in contrast to the many later commentaries by Buddhaghosa and others, which are considered authoritative but postcanonical. The fact that the *Rhinoceros Sūtra* is the subject of a major portion of this unique canonical commentary is yet another index of its antiquity and popularity in early Buddhist literature.

The three Pali versions of the *Rhinoceros Sūtra* are virtually identical, and they are not radically different from the Gāndhārī version. The Pali versions have forty-one or forty-two verses, while the Gāndhārī has forty (not counting the four mnemonic summary verses, which are absent from the Pali texts). Of these forty-odd verses, some thirty-five are more or less common to both versions, and in most cases the wording of these common verses shows only minor variations. By way of example, below are presented the translations of the first verse in the Pali, Gāndhārī, and Sanskrit versions:[235]

Gāndhārī

Shunning violence toward all beings,
never harming a single one of them,
compassionately helping with a loving heart,
wander alone like the rhinoceros.

Pali

Shunning violence toward all beings,
never harming a single one of them,

one should not desire a son, much less a companion;
wander alone like the rhinoceros.

Sanskrit

Shunning violence toward all beings,
never harming a single one of them,
rejecting violence toward beings moving and unmoving,
wander alone like the rhinoceros.

The verses are virtually the same except for the third quarter, which is completely different in each version, this being a common pattern of variation in this poem. The verses typically open with two lines closely linked in theme and syntax, and always conclude with the refrain "wander alone like the rhinoceros." The third quarter, however, is usually a supplementary statement, less tightly linked conceptually with the opening half, which therefore was prone to float among different positions in different versions of the poem. For example, the third quarter of the first verse in the Pali version, "one should not desire a son, much less a companion," appears in the Gāndhārī text as the third quarter of verse 14.

Besides the majority of the verses that are more or less parallel in the Pali and Gāndhārī versions, there are five verses in Gāndhārī (6, 14, 18, 23, 38) that are completely or largely different from the Pali text. The two versions also differ considerably in the ordering of the verses. In general, the sequences of verses near the beginning and end are relatively similar, but in the middle of the poem their order has little in common.

All in all, the Gāndhārī and Pali sūtras are variant recensions of what is essentially the same text. But the situation is quite different—or at least superficially seems to be so—in the case of the Sanskrit version in the *Mahāvastu*.[236] The frame story there introduces the sūtra as the words of five hundred solitary buddhas who assembled near Vārāṇasī when the Buddha Śākyamuni was about to be born, but the following text actually quotes only twelve such verses, plus a concluding statement to the effect that "All of the verses of the *Rhinoceros Sūtra* are to be recited at length, one verse for each of the five hundred solitary buddhas." Although five hundred is a conventional expression for any large group, this statement is more than mere rhetorical exaggeration. The idea that this text could be expanded "at length" (*vistareṇa*) reflects the Buddhist conception of texts of this type, including the *Dhammapada* and the *Apadāna*, as open-ended compilations of variations on a theme, this being another manifestation of the pattern of expansion and contraction of Buddhist texts. This further implies that not only the short version with only twelve verses in the *Mahāvastu* but also the longer Pali and Gāndhārī versions with forty-one and forty verses respectively can be conceived as a representative sampling of many more verses of this type that theoretically could be thought to have existed, or may even have actually existed in texts that have not come down to us.

Moreover, the Sanskrit version of the *Rhinoceros Sūtra* in the *Mahāvastu*, despite containing only twelve verses, shows exactly how the sūtra has a potential for nearly infinite expansion. For example, the sixth verse reads "One keeping company nurtures affection, and from affection suffering arises. Recoiling from one who keeps company, wander alone like the rhinoceros." This verse corresponds closely to the second verse of the Gāndhārī version, but the following verse in the Sanskrit text repeats almost exactly the same words, except that instead of "Recoiling from one who keeps company" (*saṃsevamānaṃ*), the third quarter—always the most unstable part of these verses—reads "Recoiling from excessive affection" (*priyātisnehaṃ*); here in the original text only one compound word has been changed. In the otherwise identical following verse (8), "excessive affection" is changed to "separation from one's beloved" (*priyāviyogaṃ*), once again involving the change of a single word in the third line. The ninth and tenth verses are similar variations on the same theme, and in fact, among the twelve verses recorded in this version of the sūtra, there are only six that are substantially different, the others being such minor variants on them. Thus the Sanskrit version of the sūtra is explicitly presented as a template for unlimited expansion.

The *Rhinoceros Sūtra* as an Independent Text

All of the previously known Pali and Sanskrit versions of the *Rhinoceros Sūtra* were imbedded in later texts or anthologies, but in the Gāndhārī manuscript, the text stands alone. There is nothing surprising about this, as it has long been suspected that in this and similar cases, the later canonical compilations that have come down to us in various traditions embrace many texts that were originally treated as independent. Several other Gāndhārī manuscripts similarly preserve independent versions of texts that were previously known only as parts of larger corpora. For example, the Gāndhārī *Many Buddhas Sūtra* (translation 8) is an independent text whose closest parallels are found in subsections of larger texts in other languages. Similarly, we now have two freestanding Gāndhārī manuscripts of the *Songs of Lake Anavatapta* (translation 5), which hitherto had been best known as a component of the vinaya of the Mūlasarvāstivādins.

In this way, these manuscripts reveal a clearer picture of the state of Buddhist literature at a period before formal canons had been fully and finally formulated. Around the beginning of the Common Era in Gandhāra, and presumably elsewhere in the Buddhist world, these texts, and undoubtedly many others that have not yet been found, still had a separate identity and were copied and studied as individual sūtras before they were swallowed up into larger compilations and ceased to be separately preserved.

The Summary Verses

Below the forty lines, each containing one verse, that comprise the text proper, four additional verses are marked off by two small wavy lines at the right margin. These extra verses are mnemonic summaries (*uddāna*)[237] that provide a key to memorizing the contents and sequence of the sūtra. Each of the four summary verses contains ten words or short phrases that quote or paraphrase the first word or a key phrase of the corresponding ten verses. For example, the first summary verse reads:

> Toward all, keeping company, friends;
> thick bamboo, free deer;
> sons and wives, play;
> demands, to please, games.

Here "toward all" represents the first word (*sarveṣo*) of the first verse of the poem, "(Shunning violence) toward all (beings)"; "company" (*saṃsevaṇa*) refers to the opening of the second verse, "One keeping company"; and so on.

Such mnemonic summary verses are commonly found in Buddhist texts, particularly in large sūtra compilations such as the *Saṃyukt-āgama*. But these verses usually record the names or topic headings for entire sūtras or sections of sūtras comprising the collection. The mnemonic verses here in the *Rhinoceros Sūtra* are unique in that they summarize the individual verses of a poem. Since the order of verses varies considerably among the different versions of the *Rhinoceros Sūtra* in Gāndhārī, Sanskrit, and Pali, this unusually detailed mnemonic summary may have been intended to guarantee what its redactor considered to be the correct order. In this, we see a hint of a growing tendency toward the standardization of texts, symptomatic of the incipient formation of formal closed canons.

As fate would have it, the summary verses on the *Rhinoceros Sūtra* scroll have served another function, albeit not one that was intended by the scribe who wrote them. For they proved to be instrumental in the reconstruction of the very fragmentary scroll itself. As mentioned above, when the decayed scroll was unrolled, the twelve large fragments and many dozen smaller ones came out in a more or less random order, so that in many cases it was impossible to determine on purely physical grounds the original position and relationships of the fragments. Moreover, it became clear from comparing the order of verses within each fragment that the sequence of the Gāndhārī text was significantly different from that of the Pali and Sanskrit versions, so that they could not serve as reliable guides to the reconstruction of the scroll. Here the sequence of verses presented in the mnemonic summary verses came to the rescue.

But the matter was not nearly as simple as it might sound, for the summary verses themselves were split up between several fragments of the scroll. In practice, therefore, the process ran in two directions: sometimes a sequence of full verses preserved together on one fragment would guide the reconstruction of the summary verses, and this reconstruction of summary verses would in return help to establish the order of the main text. In the end, it proved possible to establish with reasonable certainty the original positions for all of the twelve major fragments and most of the small ones, so that the order of verses presented here can be considered nearly definite.

The Rhinoceros Sūtra

1. Shunning violence toward all beings,
never harming a single one of them,
[compassionately] helping with a loving heart,
[wander alone like the rhinoceros].

2. One keeping company [nurtures affection],
and from affection suffering [arises.
Realizing the danger arising from affection,
wander alone like the rhinoceros.]

3. [In sympathizing with] friends and companions,
the mind gets fixed on them and [loses] its way.
[Perceiving this danger in familiarity,
wander alone like the rhinoceros.]

4. Concerns that one has for one's sons and wives
are like a thick and tangled bamboo tree.
[Remaining untangled like a young bamboo,
wander alone like the rhinoceros.]

5. Just as a deer, wandering free in the forest,
goes wherever he wishes as he grazes,
[so a wise man, treasuring his freedom,
wanders alone like the rhinoceros.]

6. Leave behind your sons and wives and money,
all your possessions, relatives, and friends.
[Abandoning all desires whatsoever,
wander alone like the rhinoceros.]

7. Among companions you waste time in play,
and for sons you develop strong [affection.
Dreading separation from dear ones,
wander alone like the rhinoceros.]

8. The crowd will always make demands on you,
[wherever you live or stay or walk or wander.
Treasuring freedom, which they do not value,
wander alone like the rhinoceros.]

9. Even some renunciants are hard to please;
[so too the family men who live at home.
Have no concern about the sons of others;
wander alone like the rhinoceros.]

10. Games, [delights, and pleasures of the senses:
see no value in them—disregard them.
Ignore the fashions, speak only the truth;
wander alone like the rhinoceros.]

11. Be resolute [to reach your final goal,
be never faint of heart, and be not lazy.
Strong and firm in your determination,
wander alone like the rhinoceros.]

12. Do not crave tasty food [and be not fickle;
nourish yourself as you make your rounds alone.
Don't fix your mind on this house or on that one;[238]
wander alone like the rhinoceros.]

13. Avoid at any cost wicked companions,
who follow the wrong course, intent on evil.

[Don't get involved with men obsessed or careless;
wander alone like the rhinoceros.]

14. Seek out the Dharma that is right for you,
is praised by wise men, and brings happiness.
Do not desire [a son], much less a companion;
[wander alone like the rhinoceros.]

15. "It cannot be that one who loves companions
would reach liberation, even for a moment."[239]
Heeding these words of the Heir of the Sun,
wander alone like the rhinoceros.

16. [Seeing two bracelets,] gleaming [bright with gold],
perfectly crafted by the skillful smith,
[clanging and banging] together on one arm—
wander alone like the rhinoceros.

17. Pleasures are attractive, sweet, and charming,
but with their many forms [they confuse the mind].
Behold the danger [in all kinds of pleasures];
wander alone like the rhinoceros.

18. Forsaking sons and friends and even mother,
abandoning all desires whatsoever
[and wealth and property and also friends],
wander alone like the rhinoceros.

19. Cast off the garments of a family man,
like the ebony tree that sheds all of its leaves.
[Go forth clad in the mendicant's saffron robe,
wander alone like the rhinoceros.]

20. Break out from all the bonds of family life,
like a bird that tears right through a heavy net.
[Like a fire that does not return to its own ashes,
wander alone like the rhinoceros.]

21. Like the lion who never startles [at a sound,]
like the wind that cannot be caught in a net,
[like the lotus that is unstained by dirty water,
wander alone like the rhinoceros.]

22. [And like] the lion [with his mighty fangs,
the king of beasts who wanders where he will,
frequenting lonely spots to sit and sleep—
wander alone like the rhinoceros.]

23. Keeping your vows, be perfect in your conduct,
behaving gently, aware of traps and dangers,
[do not desire] a son, much less [companions:
wander alone like the rhinoceros.]

24. Cultivate a friend who is inspired,
learned, faithful to the Dharma, noble.
[Understanding Dharma,] dispelling doubts,
[wander alone like the rhinoceros.]

25. If you should find yourself a wise companion,
a well-behaved and trustworthy fellow,
together you may [overcome] all dangers.
So wander with him, satisfied and mindful.

26. But if you cannot find a wise companion,
a well-behaved and trustworthy fellow,

then, like a king [who leaves behind his kingdom,]
wander alone like the rhinoceros.

27. Truly, you may delight in all of your companions;
stay [with the ones who are like you, or] better.
But if you have none [such, guard well your behavior];
wander alone like the rhinoceros.

28. Walk in a village with your eyes cast down,
control your senses, always guard your mind.
[Uncontaminated and unburned by passion,
wander alone like the rhinoceros.]

29. Remain in solitary meditation,
behave by the Dharma in all ways.
[Recognizing the perils of rebirth,
wander alone like the rhinoceros.]

30. Passing beyond the errors of false views,
reaching the course, attaining to the way,
[I have attained true knowledge; none need lead me;
wander alone like the rhinoceros.]

31. Heat and cold, hunger and thirst,
[sun and wind, insects and serpents:
when you have overcome all of these,
wander alone like the rhinoceros.][240]

32. Like a mighty elephant who shuns the herd,
high in the shoulder, lotus-spotted, noble,
[who dwells in the forest, wandering at his will,
wander alone like the rhinoceros.]

33. Free of greed, deception, faults, delusion,
free of every stain and jealousy,
[free of concern for the entire world,]
wander alone like the rhinoceros.

34. At home in the world, everywhere unimpeded,
satisfied with whatever comes your way,
overcoming [dangers], never trembling,
wander alone like the rhinoceros.

35. Abandon passion, anger, and delusion,
desire and all the bonds of ignorance.
[Feeling no alarm at deadly] danger,
wander alone like the rhinoceros.

36. Cultivate kindness, equanimity,
compassion, and joy,[241] each at its proper time.
[Unimpeded by the entire world,]
wander alone like the rhinoceros.

37. Abandon the five obstructions of the mind[242]
and cast off all of the defilements.
[Overcoming] dangers of all kinds,
wander alone like the rhinoceros.

38. Gratitude is rare nowadays in this world;
devious and foolish are all of its people.
[Free yourself of all concerns] toward it—
wander alone like the rhinoceros.

39. They like you and they help you for a motive.
It's hard to find a true friend nowadays.

Don't fix your mind [on this house or on that one];
wander alone [like] the rhinoceros.

40. So if I were to spend my days with others,
I'd waste my time in chatter or in quarrels.
Seeing this [danger lurking in the future,]
I wander alone like the rhinoceros.

Summary Verses

1. Toward all, keeping company, friends;
thick bamboo, free deer;
sons [and wives, play;]
demands, to please, games.

2. Resolute, not craving tastes;
wicked [companions], right for you;
[cannot be], gleaming, pleasures;
[sons], cast off, break out.

3. Lion twice, vows, cultivate a friend;
if you should find, but if you cannot find, [truly];
walk in a village [with your eyes cast down];
solitary, the errors of false views.

4. And cold, like an elephant, free of greed;
at home in the world, desire, [kindness, equanimity];
[obstructions] of the mind, gratitude;
they like you; and, finally, with others.

4. A Chapter from the Dharmapada

The *Dharmapada* in Buddhist Tradition

THE *Dharmapada* (Sanskrit and Gāndhārī) or *Dhammapada* (Pali), "Words of the Dharma," is among the most widely read of all Buddhist scriptures. It serves as a general guide to Buddhist principles that is recognized and highly regarded across regional, sectarian, and linguistic divides. The *Dharmapada* is an anthology of several hundred verses grouped together under topical chapter headings (Skt *varga*, P *vagga*) such as "Mind," "Flowers," "Fools," and "Wise Men." All of the verses are traditionally believed to have been uttered by the Buddha at various times and in response to various events, the circumstances of which are explained in detail in a Pali commentary but not mentioned in the verses themselves.[243]

The verses summarize, briefly and eloquently, the central moral, psychological, and philosophical principles of Buddhism. They are expressed in relatively straightforward nontechnical terms that can be easily understood by anyone with a basic knowledge of Buddhism. The ideas expressed are not always exclusive to Buddhism, and some of the verses also appear in non-Buddhist texts such as the *Mahābhārata*.[244] Such verses must have been proverbial sayings that were common to the culture of ancient India as a whole, independent of sectarian traditions.

The *Dharmapada* is best known from the Pali version, which consists of 423 verses in twenty-six chapters. In the Pali Tipiṭaka, the *Dhammapada* is one of the fifteen texts of the *Khuddaka-nikāya*. It is a perennial bestseller among Buddhist readers in many parts of the world, and its immense popularity is also reflected by the huge number of translations into European and Asian languages.[245] That the *Dharmapada* enjoyed a similar popularity in antiquity is attested by the existence of a great many versions and recensions in other languages, including Sanskrit, Prakrit, Gāndhārī, Chinese, and Tibetan.[246] The importance of the Sanskrit equivalent of the *Dharmapada*, known as the *Udānavarga*, "Groups of Inspired Verses," is attested by the extremely large number of copies of it that have been found among the fragments of Buddhist manuscripts from Central Asia.[247] This long collection, comprising nearly one thousand verses in thirty-three chapters, was evidently part of the basic curriculum in the Buddhist communities in antiquity.[248]

Among versions of the *Dharmapada* genre in other languages, the so-called Patna *Dharmapada*, known only from a single manuscript found in Tibet, is composed in an unusual hybrid language with a mixture of Sanskrit and Pali features. The *Udānavarga* is preserved in Tibetan translation as well as in Sanskrit. There are also four versions of the *Dharmapada* in Chinese translations, which are based in varying degrees and combinations on the Pali *Dhammapada*, the Sanskrit *Udānavarga*, and another unidentified source text.[249]

The *Dharmapada* in Gāndhārī

The wide circulation of the *Dharmapada* is further confirmed by the discovery of three manuscripts of it among the still relatively small corpus of Gāndhārī texts. It is the only other text beside the *Songs of Lake Anavatapta*, known from two manuscripts, for which multiple Gāndhārī versions have been identified. The Gāndhārī version translated here is from a famous scroll that was discovered in 1892 near Khotan in Central Asia. For over one hundred years, this remained the only known manuscript of a Buddhist text in Gāndhārī. The *Dharma-*

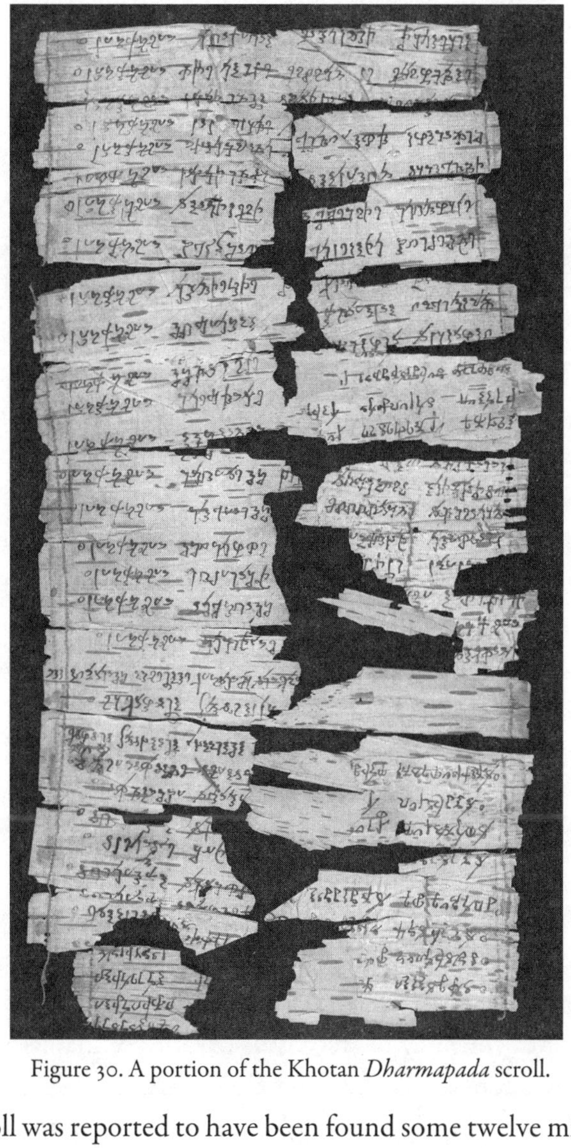

Figure 30. A portion of the Khotan *Dharmapada* scroll.

pada scroll was reported to have been found some twelve miles southeast of Khotan city, in a cave atop a mountain that is nowadays a Sufi Muslim shrine known as Kohmari Mazar. In antiquity this was a holy Buddhist holy site known as Cow's Horn Peak (Gośṛṅga), visited and described by the Chinese pilgrim Xuanzang in the seventh century. It is suspected, however, that this was not the true find-spot but rather a decoy used by its sellers to keep the real location a secret; the truth of the matter remains unknown.

The manuscript was apparently complete and in nearly perfect condition when it was found, having been protected over the millennia by the dry Central Asian climate, but it was torn into three pieces by the unknown discoverers. One part was sold to a Frenchman and now resides in the Bibliothèque nationale de France in Paris, while a second part went to a Russian and is now kept in the Institute of Oriental Manuscripts of the Russian Academy of Sciences, Saint Petersburg. The third section, sad to say, has never been located. The two surviving portions contain 344 verses, each written neatly with one verse on each line. The entire extent of the original text can be reliably estimated by reference to other versions of the text and with the help of a summary verse (*uddāna*) that marks the midpoint and lists the first thirteen chapters. The full text would have comprised twenty-six chapters, of which nineteen survive in full or in part, and about 540 verses. The complete scroll would have been approximately five meters long.

It remains uncertain whether this manuscript was originally written in Central Asia or had been imported there from the Indian subcontinent, that is, from Gandhāra or the adjoining regions. On the one hand, the text shows certain dialect features that are more typical of the Central Asian dialect of Gāndhārī[250] than of the subcontinental mother tongue; on the other hand, the material and format of the scroll resemble those of Indian documents more than Central Asian ones. However this may be, recent discoveries of manuscripts both from northwestern India and from Central Asia confirm that Buddhist literature in Gāndhārī flourished in both regions in and around the early centuries of the Common Era.

The twenty-six chapters of the Khotan manuscript of the *Dharmapada* are arranged (unlike the Pali *Dhammapada*) according to the number of verses that they contain, in descending order. For example, the first chapter, "The Brahman," has fifty verses, while the last chapter (number 21) that is completely preserved, "What Is to Be Done," has only nine. Although the Pali version of the *Dharmapada* agrees with the Gāndhārī text in having twenty-six chapters, the subject groupings are different in three cases, and more importantly, the ordering of the chapters is almost entirely different. It is especially notable that the first three chapters of the Gāndhārī text, namely "The Brahman," "The Monk," and "Thirst," are the last three, in reversed order, in the Pali. This could be interpreted as a deliberate strategy on the part of their compilers or editors to differentiate the two versions of the text, perhaps in order to establish their respective sectarian identities.[251]

The second manuscript of the *Dharmapada* in Gāndhārī is a small fragment containing the last thirteen verses of the chapter "The Monk." Two separate fragments of the left and right halves of this scroll were found in the clay pot that contained the British Library manuscripts. Only 40.5 centimeters of the bottom of the right half of the scroll survive and 29 centimeters of the left. The two fragments preserve only the last fifteen lines of the text, and all of them are more or less incomplete.

The *Dharmapada* text was written by the same scribe who wrote the scrolls of the numerically grouped sūtras and the *Songs of Lake Anavatapta*. As in those scrolls, he left a space of about twenty-five centimeters blank at the bottom of the recto when he had reached what he felt was an appropriate stopping point in the text; and again as in the two other scrolls, a different scribe used the blank space at the bottom of the recto and then the entire verso to record an entirely unrelated text. In this case, the secondary text was a set of previous-life stories (see translation 6).

Since the first scribe ended the text with the last verses of the chapter "The Monk," which we know from the more complete Khotan text to have been the second chapter of the text in the Gāndhārī version of the *Dharmapada*, we can assume that the British Library scroll originally contained the first two chapters before the top disintegrated. This allows us to estimate the original length of the British Library scroll, on the assumption that it would have contained more or less the same set of ninety verses that these two chapters comprise in the Khotan scroll. This calculation indicates that the original scroll would have been about 130 centimeters long, so that the surviving portion is less than one third of the original. As is the case with several other Gandhāran scrolls, including the *Anavatapta* scroll by the same scribe, we have reason to suspect that the full text was never actually written down.

A third Gāndhārī manuscript of the *Dharmapada* in the Split collection has recently been published by Harry Falk (2015). This text preserves ninety verses from six different chapters—"Behavior," "Miscellaneous," "Old Age," "Filth," "Flowers," and "Thousands"—some of which are nearly complete.

Relationships among the Versions

Broadly speaking, the several versions of the *Dharmapada* and cognate texts such as the *Udānavarga* all show a familial relationship but vary greatly in terms of their contents, arrangement, and extent, and their interrelationships are complex, often involving not only different versions of the *Dharmapada* genre but also overlapping with other texts of related genres. For example, out of the 344 verses in the surviving portions of the Gāndhārī scroll from Khotan, only about 225 have direct correspondents in the Pali *Dhammapada*, and many of them are placed under different section headings there. But many of the Gāndhārī verses absent from the Pali *Dhammapada* do have parallels in other Pali texts. For example, in the chapter translated below, twenty-four of the forty verses have direct parallels in the Pali *Dhammapada*, and sixteen of these twenty-four are in the corresponding chapter "The Monk."[252] But nearly all of the sixteen Gāndhārī verses that are not found in the Pali *Dhammapada* do have correspondents in other Pali collections of verses such as the *Jātaka*, the *Itivuttaka* ("Thus It Was Said"), the *Theragāthā* and *Therīgāthā* ("Songs of the Elder Monks/Nuns"), and the *Suttanipāta*.

Comparisons among the Gāndhārī *Dharmapada* manuscripts also reveal complexities. Even from the meager remnants of the British Library scroll, it is obvious that it is closely related to the Gāndhārī version from Khotan and that these two texts represent a recension that is entirely distinct from the Pali, Sanskrit, and other versions. For example, the order of the thirteen surviving verses in the British Library scroll is very similar to that of the corresponding part of the Khotan manuscript, with only minor variations. This brief passage includes in both texts a set of ten verses with the identical refrain "A monk . . . leaves behind this world and the next as a snake leaves behind its old worn-out skin." This set is entirely absent from the Pali *Dhammapada*, and it appears with substantial variants and in different sequences in other *Dharmapada* texts such as the *Udānavarga* and the Patna *Dharmapada*.

Despite this overall agreement in contents and order, the variation in the wording of the verses between the Khotan and British Library manuscripts is considerable and sometimes bewildering. Both texts, but particularly the latter one, have many readings that are very difficult to interpret, suggesting that they do not represent a fully edited and standardized text but rather two local versions of the same tradition at a still-fluid period of development. Indeed, the new manuscript has raised at least as many new questions about this difficult portion of the text as it has answered, and it is all too clear that there are deep underlying problems, which can probably never be solved, about the original meaning of such obscure verses.[253] At least some of these problems, which have been pondered by both traditional commentators and modern philologists without any satisfying answers, result from the processes of translation from an original, now-lost eastern dialect, Māgadhī, in the preliterate period, which have left the ultimate meaning obscured if not completely lost. In some cases, this situation involves what seem to be old dialect puns, some of which can still be comprehended, whereas others have been hopelessly obscured by the translation process; see, for example, note 276 on verse 36.

The remnants of the third Gāndhārī *Dharmapada* from the Split collection do not include the chapter "The Monk," so we cannot make a detailed three-way comparison of the contents and structure of the Gāndhārī versions. But the new version does overlap partially with the Khotan scroll, and there we find—not surprisingly in light of what has been said above—as much variation as similarity. Five of the six chapters preserved in the new text also occur in the Khotan manuscript but in an entirely different sequence. Moreover, the contents and internal sequencing of these chapters in the two scrolls are far more different than they are similar.[254] But this should not be too surprising, for as we have already seen, clear and direct textual relationships among Buddhist manuscripts, especially in the earlier period, are the exception rather than the rule.

The Illusion of an Underlying Urtext

Given the extreme complexity of the relationships among the several versions of the *Dharmapada* texts, there is no possibility of reconstructing an underlying original text by means of traditional methods of textual criticism. Such methods were developed in connection with written as opposed to oral traditions, and the processes of formation, transmission, and variation of oral texts are very different. Oral texts are typically much more fluid and flexible and tend not to follow predictable patterns of change and variation. In any case, their prehistories in the period before they were set down in writing are, in most cases, entirely lost. Thus it is not illuminating, and in fact it is illusory, to think of *Dharmapada* texts as stemming from a single original oral text. Rather, what the various local and scholastic traditions of early Buddhism seem to have shared was the *concept* of a corpus of inspirational and didactic verses believed to have been spoken by the Buddha, and the notion of organizing them in topical chapters. Within those different Buddhist traditions, and to some extent even within the individual traditions, these anthologies developed different contents, arrangements, and dimensions, even while retaining a common though variable core of material as well as a common conception of the nature and purpose of the text.

Viewed objectively, therefore, no one version of the *Dharmapada* can be considered to be more original, more authoritative, or more authentic than any other one. Although the Pali *Dhammapada* is often thought of as "the" *Dharmapada*, this is a misunderstanding resulting from a series of historical accidents which created the illusion that the Pali canon represented the unique and original record of the words of the Buddha.[255] It was the discovery in 1892 of the Khotan *Dharmapada*, more than any other single document, that laid the seeds of doubt about the myth of Pali primacy, and the many subsequent discoveries of Buddhist literature in Sanskrit, Gāndhārī, and other languages have confirmed the "many Buddhisms" point of view, which is now widely accepted by most academic scholars.

The *Dharmapada* as Literature

Although the Pali *Dhammapada* and the *Dharmapada* texts in general are highly revered in the Buddhist world, the genre was harshly criticized by John Brough, who in his definitive edition of the Khotan *Dharmapada* laid, more than anyone else, the foundation for the subsequent study of Buddhist literature in Gāndhārī. He had little appreciation for the *Dharmapada* as literature, characterizing it as consisting of "vast accumulations of insipid mediocrity" and criticizing the "reckless manner in which praise has been awarded" to it.[256] Brough was put off by the constant repetition of clichés, which in such Buddhist poetry often take the form of sequences of verses that vary only slightly, even by as little as one word, from one to the next. We see this pattern, for example, in the last ten verses of the passage translated below, which all share the same second half. Admittedly, this hardly meets the standard of originality and variety that one expects in high literary poetry; but this is the poetry of faith and inspiration, where imitation is the rule rather than the exception. This pattern is very common in early Buddhist literature and is carried to great length in, for example, the *Udānavarga*, where the set of verses containing the aforementioned refrain is extended to twenty-six, including three separate sets of six verses, each of which differ only by a single word.[257] Brough understood that this "serial repetition" was "highly esteemed as a mechanism for expanding the volume of sacred texts" (page 197), but he disapproved of it on literary grounds, a judgment that I find irrelevant. To understand it in its own context one may compare, for example, the Pali *Apadāna*, which contains the inspired orations of some four hundred disciples of the Buddha in which they explain the actions in past lives that made it possible for them to attain enlightenment. Many of these recitations are nearly identical to the ones that precede them, but this need not considered a defect. To the contrary, the repetition is a mark of reverence and piety, and the oral recitation of such poems is conducive to a quasi-hypnotic effect. In this regard, they serve their purpose and suit their environment, and it is in this spirit that they can best be read and appreciated.[258]

THE MONK[259]

1. A monk who is restrained in his body, who is restrained in his speech, and who is restrained in his mind will escape bad rebirths.

2. Control of the body is good; control of speech is good; control of the mind is good; control in everything is good. A monk who is controlled in everything will escape bad rebirths.

3. Controlled in his hands, controlled in his feet, controlled in his speech; his senses restrained, delighting within himself, concentrated, satisfied in solitude—him they call a monk.

4. A monk who restrains his mouth, who teaches without pride and in measured speech the Dharma and its meaning—sweet are his words.

5. A monk who dwells with a calm mind in an empty room attains superhuman bliss, with true insight into the Dharma.

6. Whenever he ponders the rising and passing of the aggregates, he attains delight and joy. This is immortality[260] for the wise.

6a. A monk who dwells with a calm mind in an empty room attains superhuman bliss, with true insight into the Dharma.[261]

7. The bliss one gets from exquisite music does not compare to that of the one who has a focused mind and true insight into the Dharma.

8. There is no meditation for one who lacks wisdom, and there is no wisdom for one who does not meditate. But one who has wisdom and meditates is close to nirvāṇa.

9. For a monk who is wise in this way, the beginning of that[262] is control of the senses, contentment, and [attention] to the monastic rules.

10. [A monk] should cultivate suitable friends,[263] pure in livelihood and conscientious.[264] Be attentive to hospitality [and] virtuous in behavior. Then, O monk, with your virtuous behavior, you will live happily.

11. [A monk] should neither despise what he has gotten for himself[265] nor envy what belongs to others. A monk who envies what belongs to others cannot achieve [true] concentration.

12. But a monk who has but little and does not despise what he has gotten—him the gods praise, pure in livelihood and conscientious.

13–14. A monk who delights in desire, takes pleasure in desire, thinks about desire, and remembers desire—he loses the true Dharma.[266] A monk who delights in the Dharma, takes pleasure in the Dharma, thinks about the Dharma, and remembers the Dharma—he does not lose the true Dharma.

15–16. Not by merely following rules and observances, nor by great learning, nor even by achieving concentration, nor by sleeping alone do we achieve the bliss of freedom from desire that cannot be enjoyed by ordinary men. A monk may not be content until his afflictions are destroyed.[267]

17–18. One does not become a monk merely by begging from others; as long as he lives a domestic life, he is no monk. But when he roots out evil, keeping his observances and living the pure life, wandering through the world attentively, then he is called a monk.

19. A monk who abides in kindness, content in the teaching of the Buddha, shakes off bad dharmas as the wind shakes the leaves off a tree.

20. A monk who abides in kindness, content in the teaching of the Buddha, may attain the place of peace (i.e., nirvāṇa), the blissful cessation of volitional formations.

21. A monk with focused mind who overcomes likes and dislikes can attain the place of peace that an inferior man never reaches.

22. A monk who is full of joy, who overcomes likes and dislikes, can attain the place of peace, satisfying and liberating.[268]

23. A monk who takes pleasure in his attentiveness and is aware of the dangers of inattentiveness cannot lose his way; he is very close to nirvāṇa.

24. A monk who takes pleasure in his attentiveness and is aware of the dangers of inattentiveness burns away the bonds both light and heavy, moving on [toward nirvāṇa] like a fire.

25. Meditate, monk! Do not be inattentive! Do not let your mind roam among the pleasures! Do not by inattention swallow a [hot] iron ball[269] and cry out "Oh, the agony!" as you burn!

26. Bail out this boat, monk; when bailed it will sail all the faster. When you cut out your desire and anger, it will take you to nirvāṇa.[270]

27. Avoid [women, who are] prone to anger, ungrateful, and deceptive. Live the pure life, monk, in the teaching of the fully enlightened buddhas.

28. Cut off five, get rid of five, develop five especially. The monk who passes beyond the five attachments is said to have crossed the flood.[271]

29. He who has no sense of possession toward names and forms, and who, being unattached, knows no grief[272]—he is the one who is called a monk.

30. He who, though adorned,[273] practices the Dharma, who is controlled, calmed, restrained, who lives a pure life, shunning violence toward all beings—he is a brahman, he is an ascetic, he is a monk.

31. A monk who has found no real essence in successive lives, like one who searches for a flower [on fig trees,][274] leaves behind [this world and the next][275] as a snake leaves behind its old worn-out skin.

32. [A monk] who removes anger as soon as it arises, as one removes [snake venom with herbs as it spreads through the body, leaves behind] this world and the next [as] a snake leaves behind its old worn-out skin.

33. A monk who plucks out every trace of pride, [as] one might snip off a lotus with its stalk and [flower], leaves behind this world and the next as a snake leaves behind its old worn-out skin.

34. A monk who has completely cut off thirst, drying up [the fast-flowing] river [of desire], leaves behind this world and the next as a snake leaves behind its old worn-out skin.

35. A [monk] who has smashed his defilements, as a mighty flood smashes [a flimsy bridge] of reeds, leaves behind this world and the next as a snake leaves behind its old worn-out skin.

36. A monk who neither moves away nor moves toward, [but] has passed beyond this entire [developed world][276] leaves behind this world and the next as a snake leaves behind its old worn-out skin.

37. A monk who neither moves away nor moves toward, realizing that everything in this world is false, leaves behind this world and the next as a snake leaves behind its old worn-out skin.

38. A monk who has no negative proclivities at all to cause him to return to this world leaves behind this world and the next as a snake leaves behind its old worn-out skin.

39. A monk who has no desires at all to cause him bondage and rebirth leaves behind this world and the next as a snake leaves behind its old worn-out skin.

40. A monk who [eliminates the five obstructions,[277] who is unafflicted], rid of doubts, and freed from the [five] pains[278] leaves behind this world and the next as a snake leaves behind its old worn-out skin.

5. Songs of Lake Anavatapta

THE *Anavataptagāthā* or *Songs of Lake Anavatapta* consists of a series of recitations in verse by the Buddha's most prominent disciples and finally by the Buddha himself. The number of recitations ranges from thirty to thirty-seven in the various versions. In each recitation, the speaker describes one or more karmically important act that he had performed in a previous life and explains how the karma from that action led him to his current exalted state as an arhat and disciple of the Buddha. The individual recitations are set inside a frame story that opens in the city of Śrāvastī in northern India, where the Buddha often preached. On this occasion, he announced to his five hundred disciples that they were to fly with him to the sacred Lake Anavatapta, the Cool Lake,[279] high in the Himalayas. There they all sat on giant lotuses provided by the guardian spirits of the lake and recited their karmic histories. After all the disciples had spoken, the text concludes with the Buddha's own much more elaborate explanation of his own karma, which is presented in combined verse and prose rather than in verse only like all the others.

The *Songs of Lake Anavatapta* is attested in two fragmentary Gāndhārī manuscripts, one from the British Library collection and one from the Senior collection. This confirms the popularity of this text in northern India and Central Asia, which was already apparent from the many manuscripts, versions, and translations of it that were previously known, including two Sanskrit and two Chinese versions and a Tibetan translation. The Tibetan text and one each of the Sanskrit and Chinese versions are all preserved in the massive vinaya of the Mūlasarvāstivāda school,[280] while the other versions are independent texts. Although the *Songs of Lake Anavatapta* is not included as such in the Pali canon, some parts of it are incorporated into or quoted in other Pali canonical or paracanonical texts, showing that the text was familiar to southern Buddhists as well.

Principal Themes

The intention of this text is to explain and exemplify the essential laws of karma in a straightforward and nontechnical way that any Buddhist can readily understand. However, contrary to what one might expect in view of the exalted status of all of the speakers, by no means are all of the acts that they recount virtuous. Several of the recitations contain confessions of past sins, and in the climactic final section even the Buddha himself reveals his own bad karma. Thus the stories show that no one, not even the Buddha himself, is exempt from the laws of karma and that everyone's karma is a complex mixture, in varying degrees, of good and bad.

In this spirit, the recitations variously concern good karma, bad karma, and mixed karma. Although the majority (about two thirds) of the stories exclusively or primarily concern virtuous actions that caused the speakers to become arhats who received direct teaching from the Buddha, several others reveal evil deeds or combinations of good and bad. One such story of mixed karma (not available in the surviving fragments of the Gāndhārī texts) applies to as prominent a figure as Mahāmaudgalyāyana, one of the Buddha's most prominent disciples. It was his virtuous act of providing initiation to a mendicant who later became a solitary buddha that led him to his present exalted position, but he is nevertheless doomed to be beaten to death by opponents of Buddhism at the end of his current lifetime because in a previous life he had a fantasy of beating his parents.[281] Even more striking is the final recitation by the Buddha himself, in which he reveals that he had committed ten evil acts in his past lives, as a result of which he still suffers both psychological pain from the vicious rumors spread by his enemies and physical pain from headaches, backaches, dysentery, and a wounded foot.

In the fifth recitation translated below, Piṇḍola Bharadvāja reveals his bad karma in a previous life from refusing to feed his mother and letting her go hungry even though he was a wealthy man. Even worse, he spoke harshly when she complained to him and insulted her by saying "You can eat rocks!" As a result, he still suffers, eons later, from a peculiar compulsion—what would nowadays be called an eating disorder—to eat rocks: "Yet even now . . . although I am a victorious arhat with supernatural powers, I must live in a cave and eat rocks."[282] Although Bharadvāja's story, like that of Nandika in the seventh selection presented here and like several others in the complete texts of the *Songs*, refers only to bad karma, it goes without saying that he, like all of the reciters in the text, must have also accumulated enormous amounts of good karma in past lives in order to have finally become a direct disciple of the Buddha. The point of the recitations is not to explain the entirety of the speakers' karma, which is impossible in any case since their past lives are infinite in number. Rather, each speaker chooses one or sometimes a few incidents that were particularly influential in determining his future state and that vividly illustrate how karma functions.

It is thus all the more striking that the final recitation of the text by the Buddha himself (preserved only in Chinese and Tibetan translations but not in the fragmentary Gāndhārī and Sanskrit texts) concerns *only* his bad karma, which he presents in far greater detail than that of the other speakers, enumerating ten instead of only one, two, or at most three events. This is the clearest indication of the underlying concern that motivates the text as a whole: the problem of why the Buddha and other enlightened beings must still suffer. The question is, of course, an ancient and universal one, as paradigmatically exemplified in Western tradition by the book of Job: why do the righteous suffer while the wicked prosper? But in a Buddhist context, this has nothing to do with the inscrutable will of an omnipotent being and everything to do with the immutable laws of karma. Specifically, the implied question here is why noble arhats who have achieved that status (note that Bharadvāja, like many of the speakers in the *Songs*, explicitly states that he has done so) and severed the bonds of saṃsāra must still suffer from the after-effects of karma; and why, especially, must the Buddha, who discovered and revealed the secret of enlightenment, still suffer worldly pain?

The solution that the *Songs* proposes involves the concept of the "remnant of karma" (Skt *karmāvaśeṣa*), which is explicitly referred to by Nandika and also clearly implied, although the term is not directly used, in Bharadvāja's story. In both cases, the reciters committed a terrible sin—poisoning a holy man and starving his mother, respectively—and paid the karmic price by spending eons in hell worlds, and then, after being reborn in the human world, starving to death five hundred times. But even after having paid off the bulk of their karmic debt and becoming arhats, they continue to suffer: Bharadvāja from his bizarre urge to chew stones, Nandika with chronic severe indigestion. These later effects are said to be the result of a persistent remainder of bad karma, like the lingering interest on an old debt, that will not leave them until they enter final nirvāṇa at the end of this, their last lifetime.

With this theory of the lingering effects of karma, the apparent problem of the suffering Buddha and the psychically ill or psychologically troubled arhat is explained. Although to a non-Buddhist the concept of karmic remainder may seem a tendentious and *ad hoc* solution, according to Buddhist principles it is the logical explanation of what has been empirically observed; since the basic concept and principles of karma are beyond doubt, seeming contradictions and problems raised by it can only be explained by proposing refinements in the interpretation of those principles.

The second key theme of the *Songs* is the karmic power of a pure and sincere heart. This is expressed in a refrain verse appearing in the recitations of Vāgīśa and Kusuma: "For no gift is small when given by one whose heart is pure, whether to a buddha tathāgata or to a buddha's disciples." The key term here is the word translated as "pure" (Skt *prasanna*) and the corresponding noun "purity" (*prasāda*), which also occurs frequently in this and other versions of the *Songs*. These words are sometimes translated as "faithful" and "faith" respectively, but the range of their meaning is broader than that, connoting a state of mental clarity and an open heart full of trust, benevolence, and receptivity toward a suitable object, such as the Buddha or one's parents. Thus Bharadvāja, having learned the hard way the importance of respecting one's parents, reminds his listeners to "purify[283] your minds toward your mother and father." One of the several meanings of the verbal stem (*pra-sad*) from which these words are derived is "clarify," as used, for example, to describe the process whereby turbid water becomes clean and transparent when it is left standing undisturbed. This in turn is an extension of the base sense of the underlying verbal root *sad*, which means "sit";[284] for the sense of the image, compare English "settle down." This underlying image of clear water serves as a metaphor for the pure and tranquil mind that Buddhist practice seeks to inculcate—whence my decision to translate the words in question as "pure" and "purity."[285]

Thus the message of the stories of Vāgīśa and Kusuma, as well as that of Mahākāśyapa in the Gāndhārī text and many others in the complete versions of the *Songs*, is that any act of veneration, piety, or generosity carried out in this state of mental purity will have especially powerful and beneficial results; as they both say in their refrain verse, "No gift is small when given by one whose heart is pure." Vāgīśa and Kusuma were rewarded with many fortunate rebirths as gods or humans and eventually attained liberation simply because they offered the most trivial gifts—three pennies or a single flower—to a stūpa with pure and loving hearts. This principle that "It's the thought that counts" is of course common to many religious and ethical systems; compare, for example, the widow's mite of which Jesus said, "This poor widow has put in more than all the others."[286] What is distinctive in the Buddhist context is that the principle takes the form of karmic law, whereby the merit earned derives from the spirit rather than the nature of the act, whether positive as in the case of Vāgīśa and Kusuma or negative in the case of Mahāmaudgalyāyana, who went to hell just for thinking about beating his parents.

A third key concept of the *Songs of Lake Anavatapta* is the "solemn resolution" or "pious vow" (Skt *praṇidhi*, *praṇidhāna*). This is a formal utterance by a person who has done a good deed in which that person declares the karmic result or results he or she hopes to gain from that act. Such resolutions are typically inspired by an encounter with a buddha or a solitary buddha and usually consist of a desire to encounter another buddha or other saintly being in the future. The resolution also often includes a secondary wish, as in Nanda's resolution to meet a buddha and to be handsome in his future life. Such resolutions are a prominent feature in many avadānas and similar genres concerned with previous lives and karmic explanations. The emphasis on these resolutions must have been intended to encourage readers or hearers of the text to undertake similar aspirations and to remind them that they themselves are the sole creators of their own karmic futures.

The encounters with buddhas or solitary buddhas that typically provoke persons to make such solemn resolutions is often connected with a gift of food or act of homage to the buddha, which ensures that their wishes will come true, as in the case of Mahākāśyapa's story. This karmic process is often phrased in terms of an agricultural metaphor, according to which the buddha or solitary buddha is a field of merit (*puṇyakṣetra*) in which the supplicant plants the roots of good karma (*kuśalamūla*). In a future life these seeds will ripen (*vipāka*) and bear their fruit (*phala*) in the form of the fulfillment of the agent's desires.

Avadānas and Related Genres

The *Songs of Lake Anavatapta* belongs to a genre, or rather a complex of related genres, of Buddhist literature that explains and illustrates the relationships between past and present (and sometimes also future) lives and the workings of karma that determine those relationships. Within this broad category, the most prominent genres are *jātaka* "birth stories" and *avadāna* "legends," which include some of the most widely read texts of the southern and northern Buddhist traditions respectively. In the jātakas, which are contained in the Pali canon in an authoritative collection of 547 stories, the Buddha relates his own previous lifetimes as a human or as various animals, revealing the accumulated good karma that enabled him to eventually discover the secret of enlightenment. In contrast, avadānas, which are mostly preserved in various compilations in Sanskrit and Chinese, typically consist of stories in which the Buddha reveals the previous lives of other persons in order to explain their circumstances in the present.[287]

Although the *Songs of Lake Anavatapta* serves the same didactic function as jātakas and avadānas, it does not follow the typical pattern of either genre, since here the speaker is not the Buddha throughout but rather the individual disciples, who are able to remember their own karma back into the infinite past because they are arhats with *jātismara*, the power to recall their own previous lives. In this respect the *Songs* resembles the Pali *Apadāna*, or "Karmic Stories,"[288] with which it has some direct textual connections, as will be discussed below. In the *Apadāna*, as in the *Songs*, various disciples of the Buddha reveal the good deeds that they had performed in previous lives that led them to their present happy condition.[289]

A hint as to the background of the composition of texts of the karmic-revelation genre can be gleaned from the introductory setting of the well-known *Sūtra of the Great Legend* (*Mahāpadāna Sūtra*),[290] one of the foundational sūtras of the *Dīrghāgama*, in which the historical Buddha—that is, Śākyamuni of the present eon—describes the lives of the six buddhas who preceded him. This text opens with a scene in which the members of a large group of monks are talking about their previous lives, suggesting that such discussions were a common subject among ancient Buddhists.[291] It is not hard to imagine how this pastime might have given rise to texts recording the testimonies of the Buddha's renowned disciples.

Style

The *Songs of Lake Anavatapta* is composed in a simple poetic style. With the exception of the first chapter, the verses are in the *anuṣṭubh* or *śloka* meter, consisting of four quarters of eight syllables each, which is the shortest and simplest Indian meter and the easiest one to compose and understand. The style consists mostly of straightforward narration with virtually none of the poetic elaboration, florid imagery, and complex syntax that characterizes much of Buddhist literature. The content matches the style in its simplicity; there is nothing of abstruse philosophy or deep scholastic scrutiny of the sort found, for example, in the treatises presented in translations 9 and 11. The relationships between the karmic causes and effects are simple and easily understood by any listener, Buddhist or otherwise.

In short, the *Songs* would serve well as a simple practical introduction to the workings of karma for the uninitiated or newly initiated, and it probably was widely used as a preaching tool; indeed, we have already seen an indication of this in a list of basic texts that is recorded in the *Mahāsāṅghika-vinaya*.[292] Buddhist teachings are typically arranged in a series of graded levels (*anupūrvikā kathā*) that provide a gradual approach to the subtleties and complexities of the Dharma. The most introductory level of teaching typically focuses on two simple ethical principles, generosity (*dāna*) and good conduct (*śīla*), and presents rebirth in the heavens as a result of their practice. The *Songs* is in large part concerned with just these elementary principles, illustrating through simple stories the rewards of following them and the punishments for violating them. It provides, in short, a simple introductory course in Buddhist morality in the context of the fundamental laws of karma.

Manuscripts and Versions

The individual narrations that make up the *Songs of Lake Anavatapta* are labeled in some versions (though not in the surviving Gāndhārī texts) as "webs" or "weavings of karma" (*karmaploti*). This metaphorical designation can be understood to refer either to the inextricable interweaving of past deeds and their present or future effects, or to the complex combinations of good and bad karma that affect every living being. Each recitation concludes with a statement by an unspecified third-person narrator that the speaker had "thus explained" his own karma at Lake Anavatapta. Here the verb translated as "explain" (Skt *vyā-kṛ*) literally means "to analyze" or "take apart," the sense being that the speaker has through his insight "taken apart" or "unraveled" and thus explained the fabric of his karma. This verb, and also the noun of action derived from it, "explanation" (*vyākaraṇa*), is frequently used in Buddhist texts to refer not only to an explanation of karma from the past but also to a "prediction" or "prophecy"—normally by the Buddha—of the future results of present acts.[293] Although from a non-Buddhist point of view an explanation and a prophecy seem to be very different things, in a Buddhist context they are simply the present and future manifestation, respectively, of the same phenomena, namely the inexorable laws of karma and the capacity of a buddha and other enlightened beings to discern the workings of karma in both directions.

As far as we can tell from their often fragmentary remains, all of the versions of the *Songs* in various languages have a similar structure, but—as usual—they vary considerably in the details. The most complete version is the one incorporated into the encyclopedic

Mūlasarvāstivāda-vinaya. The original Sanskrit text of this version is partially preserved among the large cache of Buddhist Sanskrit manuscripts dating from about the seventh century that were discovered near Gilgit in northern Pakistan, while the entire text is preserved in the canonical Tibetan and Chinese translations of the vinaya. In the Mūlasarvāstivāda text, thirty-six disciples speak before the Buddha's climactic recitation. The only other complete text of the *Songs* is a Chinese translation completed by the renowned translator Dharmarakṣa in 303 CE, apparently on the basis of an independent Indian original in Sanskrit. This version is generally similar to the *Mūlasarvāstivāda-vinaya* text except that contains only thirty, rather than thirty-seven, recitations by the disciples and the Buddha.

Besides these more or less intact texts, several remnants of other versions of the *Songs* have survived in manuscript fragments from Central Asia and Gandhāra. The Central Asian fragments are parts of three originally separate Sanskrit manuscripts that contained the *Songs* along with other texts. These were part of a huge library of Buddhist Sanskrit texts that were discovered at the ancient oasis city of Kizil. Because these manuscripts are very incomplete, we cannot determine whether they had thirty-seven chapters like the Mūlasarvāstivāda version, thirty as in Dharmarakṣa's Chinese translation, or some other number, but we can tell from the sequence of the surviving chapters that they were arranged in a different order than the other two versions.

Finally, of the two Gāndhārī versions of the *Songs*, the more substantial one is on fragment 1 of the British Library Kharoṣṭhī collection, preserving seven chapters, six of them complete or nearly complete. It was written by the same scribe who wrote the numerically grouped sūtras presented in translation 1 and the very fragmentary manuscript of the *Dharmapada* discussed in the introduction to translation 4. As usual only the lower portion of the scroll survives, but it is the best-preserved scroll in the entire British Library collection. This is because it had lain on top of the pile of scrolls and hence was not subject to

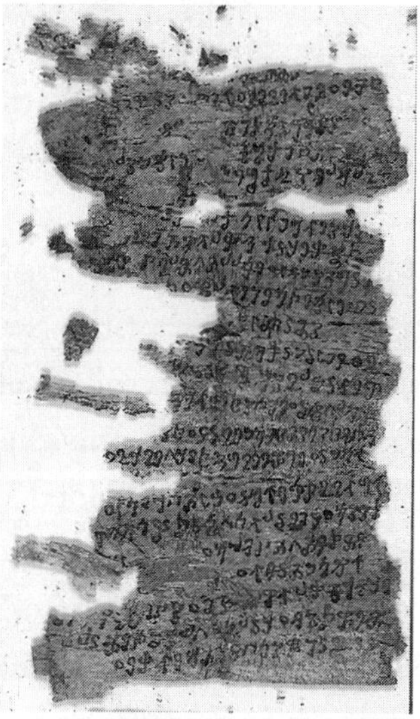

Figure 31. The *Songs of Lake Anavatapta*: Portion of British Library scroll 1 before conservation.

Figure 32. The *Songs of Lake Anavatapta*: British Library scroll 1 as originally found in the pot.

damage from compression by others, and it also was not in contact with the surface of the pot, preventing damage due to moisture.

The surviving portion is about 137 centimeters long, but comparisons with other versions of the text indicate that the original length of the scroll must have been about 250 centimeters, and that four or five chapters were probably lost in the vanished upper part. Since this scroll probably originally contained eleven or twelve chapters, whereas the complete texts of the *Songs* in other languages have either thirty or thirty-seven chapters, a complete manuscript of the Gāndhārī version probably would have taken up three or four scrolls, had it been written out in full. However, we have already noted[294] that this is one of a surprising number of cases where only the first volume survives of what should have been a multivolume text, leading us to suspect that the rest of the text was never actually written out.

The second Gāndhārī manuscript of the *Songs* is scroll 14 of the Robert Senior collection. This small scroll, twenty-eight centimeters long, is nearly complete vertically, with only the first two verses missing at the top, but it had been double-folded, causing it to break in half, and only the right half of the scroll has been discovered, so that we now have only about 40 percent of the original text. The scroll originally contained the introductory frame story and the recitation of Mahākāśyapa, which is the first one in all complete versions of the *Songs*. But even this single chapter is incomplete, as the text ends at the intact bottom with the nineteenth verse, leaving at least one concluding verse unwritten. Thus we have another instance of the first-scroll-only pattern, and in this case, as also in the sūtra scroll presented in translation 1, the text ends abruptly in the middle of a text section.

In this case, however, the question is complicated by a notation on one of the index scrolls that were found together with the Senior manuscripts.[295] Here, seven Anavatapta recitations, labeled *aṇodatie* (= Skt **anavaptikā*), or "Anavatapta story," are listed, namely those of Śāriputra, Maudgalyāyana, Mahākāśyapa,[296] Anuruddha, Śroṇa, Kauṇḍinya, and the Buddha. It is surely no accident that these seven are among the most prominent and revered disciples, so this list suggests that the anthologist who compiled the Senior collection had in mind only a selection of the "greatest hits" from the *Songs*. But other than Mahākāśyapa's, no trace of these or any other recitations from the *Songs* was actually found among the Senior scrolls, so that, whether the intended text was the complete *Songs* or more likely a selected anthology from it, it would seem that, once again, the rest of it was never written out.

Some features of the fragments of the Central Asian Sanskrit manuscripts of the *Songs* suggest that they too may have contained extracts or samples rather than the complete text. One fragment, for example, preserves the beginning of a set of Anavatapta stories starting with the ones corresponding to numbers 4 and 20 of the *Mūlasarvāstivāda-vinaya* version, while another one begins with numbers 2 and 35. These are unlikely to be parts of complete texts, since all indications are that the ordering of the recitations in the complete texts was generally consistent, though not identical. These highly aberrant sequences are therefore more likely to be part of abridgements or selections from a complete version, as also seems to have been the case with the Senior text, to judge from the citation in the index scrolls.

These variations suggest that the *Songs* was not originally a strictly defined literary text but rather a loosely defined and open-ended genre model that, like much of Buddhist literature, could be presented, whether orally or in writing, in longer or shorter forms. We have already seen this pattern in connection with the *Dharmapada* and equivalent texts, which are extant in several versions with widely varying numbers of verses, and in the *Rhinoceros Sūtra*, which is attested in versions with thirteen, forty, forty-one, and, theoretically, five hundred verses. The frame story of the *Songs*, like that of the *Rhinoceros Sūtra* in the *Mahāvastu*, reports that the Buddha brought 499[297] of his disciples to Lake Anavatapta to disclose their karmic histories, whereas the longest of the extant texts actually records only thirty-seven recitations. Although the number five hundred is conventionally used in Buddhist literature to refer to a large group and is not to be taken literally, the point is that the various texts of the *Songs* can be understood as a representative sample or anthology of a potentially much larger corpus of stories. Thus a transmitter of the text who knew or remembered other such stories could feel free to insert them into the text. According to the operative standards, such additions would be understood as improvements to the text rather than as interpolations or corruptions, as modern text scholars tend to view them. Such texts were conceived, at least in earlier periods of the history of Buddhism, as subject to expansion and contraction at the speaker's will.

An even closer parallel to the case at hand is presented by the Pali *Apadāna*. The *Apadāna* has obviously been stitched together from various components,[298] and its extremely repetitive format reads like a set of themes and variations that have been continually expanded over the centuries.[299] Moreover, the two texts have a more direct, though partial connection: the *Apadāna* includes two recitations, those of Soṇa Koṭivīsa (Skt Śroṇa Koṭiviṃśa) and the Buddha himself, that agree almost word for word with the corresponding recitations in the *Songs*. There is no doubt that these two text units were borrowed from the *Songs* and incorporated into the *Apadāna* rather than the other way around, since they both conclude with a verse reporting that they were recited "before the community of monks on Lake Anotatta" (= Skt Anavatapta). This reference to the frame story, unmentioned elsewhere in the *Apadāna*, proves that these chapters were borrowed from the *Songs*.

This, along with other quotations or adaptations of passages in two other Pali texts, the *Theragāthā* and *Nettippakaraṇa* ("The Guidebook"), shows that ancient composers of Pali texts were familiar with the *Songs*. There may well have once existed a complete text of the *Songs* in Pali from which these extracts were borrowed, but if so it has been lost, presumably because it was not accepted into the canon of the Theravāda school. But the fact that the ancient Buddhists of the Pali tradition at least knew the *Songs of Lake Anavatapta* is yet another indication of both the overall popularity of this text and of the extensive communication and interaction among regional schools of Buddhism in antiquity.

The translations below comprise all of the surviving portions of the two manuscripts of the *Songs of Lake Anavatapta* in Gāndhārī. The first section, containing the introductory verses and most of the story of Mahākāśyapa, is from the Senior manuscript, and the remaining sections are from the British Library scroll. The translation is adapted from Salomon 2008. There is no English translation of the complete text of the *Songs* as preserved in the *Mūlasarvāstivāda-vinaya* in Tibetan and Chinese, but the Tibetan text has been translated into French by Marcel Hofinger (1982–90).

Mahākāśyapa

The recitation of Mahākāśyapa is distinct from the rest of the *Songs* in several respects. First of all, it is prefaced by the introductory frame story, which in the Gāndhārī version consists of six verses. This frame relates how the Buddha and his disciples flew from the city of Śrāvastī to Lake Anavatapta, where he told them to each recount their previous lives as they remember them. The last verse of this prologue introduces Mahākāśyapa's recitation, which then takes up the rest of the chapter, though it is incomplete in our manuscript.

The frame story here is presented in a brief form, similar to that found in Dharmarakṣa's Chinese version. This contrasts strikingly with the corresponding introduction in the Mūlasarvāstivāda versions of the *Songs* in Sanskrit, Tibetan, and Chinese, which includes, among other additions, an amusing story of a magic contest between Śāriputra and Mahāmaudgalyāyana, followed by the Buddha's explanation of how they similarly vied with each other in five previous lives. This lengthy insertion is typical of the encyclopedic character of the *Mūlasarvāstivāda-vinaya* as well as another instance of the expansion-and-contraction principle of Buddhist literature.

The first chapter of the *Songs* is also set off from the others by a different meter. It is composed mostly in the *jagatī* meter, with twelve syllables to each quarter verse, in contrast to the *anuṣṭubh* meter of eight syllables per quarter used for the rest of the text. The special position and style of Mahākāśyapa's recitation reflects his status as a particularly venerated senior disciple. Among his several distinctions, he exchanged robes with the Buddha at their first meeting, symbolically taking on a role as a special intimate of the Buddha and a quasi-substitute for him after his parinirvāṇa.[300] This unique role as a mediator for the buddhas is also reflected in the legend that he will pass on Śākyamuni's robe to the next buddha, Maitreya, when he is born far in the future, as well as in the legend of the parinirvāṇa, in which the wood of the Buddha's funeral pyre would not catch fire until Mahākāśyapa arrived on the scene.[301]

Mahākāśyapa is typically presented as a stern, ascetic, somewhat remote, and even forbidding individual. He was renowned for his dislike of sensual pleasures; even after he was compelled by his parents to marry, he never touched his wife, and they mutually agreed to become celibate renunciants. His strong asceticism gained him the honor of being designated by the Buddha as the foremost of the disciples who maintain strict voluntary practices (*dhutaguṇa*), as he reports at the end of his recitation.

The story of Mahākāśyapa's past life told in the *Songs*, in which he gave a small gift to a solitary buddha, is quoted in an abbreviated form in the paracanonical Pali *Nettippakaraṇa*,[302] and the frame story of the *Songs of Lake Anavatapta* is reproduced in the "Avadāna of the Robe Cloth" (*Kaṭhināvadāna*), preserved in separate manuscripts from Nepal.[303] These sources, in addition to the several versions of the *Songs* itself, are helpful in restoring the many missing portions—more than half of the whole text—in the Senior scroll, particularly with regard to the frame story, which is particularly fragmentary and which, as we have seen, varies considerably among the different versions. As a result of these special problems, the translation of Mahākāśyapa's recitation presented below is a patchwork composite of the Gāndhārī text supplemented by material from the Sanskrit, Pali, Chinese, and Tibetan materials; as usual, the parts that are supplied from these sources are indicated in brackets. In several cases the reconstruction is based on guesses as to which of the other versions would have most closely corresponded to missing Gāndhārī passages. But the Gāndhārī text also includes a few fragmentary verses that have no parallels in any of the other versions, and here it is not possible even to conjecturally reconstruct the missing parts; these missing passages are indicated by ellipses (. . .).

Nanda

Nanda was the Buddha's half-brother, a son of Buddha's father, Śuddhodana, by Queen Mahāprajāpati. Mahāprajāpati became the Buddha's adoptive mother when his birth mother, Mahāmāyā, died seven days after bearing him. Nanda was cheerful and good-natured but also frivolous, sensual, and extremely vain about his good looks, whence his nickname Handsome Nanda (*Sundarananda*). According to other legends about him, immortalized in Aśvaghoṣa's Sanskrit epic poem the *Story of Handsome Nanda* (*Saundarananda*), he was the family member the Buddha found most difficult to convert, because of his attachment to sensual pleasures and physical beauty, and especially to his wife Sundarī ("The Beauty").

Like many of the karmic histories recounted in the *Songs of Lake Anavatapta*, Nanda's story begins in the time of Buddha Vipaśyin (P Vipassi, G Vivaśi), who lived ninety-one eons (*kalpa*) ago. In this recitation, Nanda explains how his beauty was the direct karmic result of his past virtuous acts and the solemn resolutions he made in connection with them. For example, by painting a stūpa yellow, he came to have a perfect golden skin color in a later lifetime. It is further implied that his two other virtuous deeds had specific effects on his future fortunes: building a bathhouse for the monks caused him to become morally pure, and putting an umbrella on the stūpa led to his royal birth, since the umbrella is a standard Indian symbol of royalty. Nanda's story is unusual in that it explains the results of three successive good deeds, whereas the karmic biographies most often focus on one deed, either good or bad, or occasionally on one of each, as discussed above in the case of Mahāmaudgalyāyana.

The position of Nanda's recitation in the Gāndhārī text is

anomalous in comparison to the other versions. Compared to the order of recitations in the canonical Mūlasarvāstivāda version, the surviving chapters of the Gāndhārī text correspond to numbers 26 (!), 6, 11, 8, 7, 10, and 5. The placement of Nanda's recitation, chapter 26 in the Mūlasarvāstivāda text, near the beginning of the Gāndhārī text confirms that there was considerable variety in the ordering of the different recensions of the *Songs of Lake Anavatapta*. The anomalous position of Nanda's story is probably due to a preference, apparently unique to the Gāndhārī version, for arranging the stories into pairs of positive and negative examples, as we will see particularly in the four final stories translated below. The text of the *Songs* in the *Mūlasarvāstivāda-vinaya* does not follow this alternating pattern. There, stories involving bad karma tend to be grouped together. In the Gāndhārī text Nanda's story was most likely preceded by that of Svāgata, for in his recitation, Svāgata tells how he was punished for mocking the appearance of a Buddhist monk by being reborn as a repulsively deformed beggar. This story thus makes a perfect counterpart to that of Handsome Nanda.

The text of this and the following recitation is very fragmentary, as they were on the exposed outer part of the rolled-up scroll. The missing portions of the text are as usual supplied on the basis of the other versions of the *Songs of Lake Anavatapta*, indicated by brackets.

Śroṇa Koṭiviṃśa

Śroṇa Koṭiviṃśa is among the most prominent of the disciples in Buddhist literature, about whom diverse legends have been recorded. For example, the long legend about Śroṇa recorded as the first story of the "Divine Stories" (*Divyāvadāna*)[304] is entirely different from the legend told here and in the Pali *Apadāna*, where it has been borrowed from our text. But all of the legends do agree in describing him as a wealthy merchant. This is a common motif in Buddhist literature, especially in texts that are directed at lay followers. This reflects the socioeconomic position of early Indian Buddhism, in which the merchant class, along with royalty and nobles, was the main source of the financial support necessary to maintain the communities.

Yaśas

At twenty-five verses, the recitation of Yaśas is the longest among the Gāndhārī versions of the *Songs* and is also among the longest in the complete *Songs* preserved in the Tibetan and Chinese translations. Its content is also notably different from the others in that it focuses on the speaker's psychological states and their karmic results rather than on acts of external piety or lack thereof. For it was his experience in a past life of visualizing the human (especially female) body as essentially repulsive that enabled Yaśas to escape the spiritual bondage of his life of luxury in his final incarnation, and he vividly describes the existential crisis that led him to do so. Yaśas's story also differs from the others in that, although many of the other reciters allude to their great fortune in meeting the Buddha, Yaśas is the only one to describe the encounter in detail.

Of particular interest in Yaśas's story is the episode in which he sees the women of his palace fast asleep and, feeling nothing but disgust for them, flees from the palace. This is an exact counterpart to a famous episode in the life of the Buddha, right down to the details such as the gods opening the gate for him. In fact, it has been suggested that this legend actually originally referred to Yaśas and was only later incorporated into the hagiographic literature about the Buddha as it gradually developed in the centuries after his lifetime.[305]

Piṇḍola Bharadvāja, Vāgīśa, Nandika, and Kusuma

The last four recitations preserved on the British Library manuscript of the *Songs*, those of Piṇḍola Bharadvāja, Vāgīśa, Nandika, and Kusuma, form a set in that they present alternating pairs of lessons in the results of bad and good karma. Bharadvāja and Nandika both suffer from similar discomforts—a peculiar eating disorder and chronic indigestion, respectively—as a result of past misdeeds involving stinginess with food, while Vāgīśa and Kusuma both came to be personal disciples of the Buddha because of small and simple good deeds that they did when they were innocent children. As we saw above, the alternation of stories with good and bad karmic outcomes seems to be a peculiarity of the Gāndhārī version of the *Songs*.

All four of these stories illustrate the karmic importance of the intention underlying the deeds, and especially of the frame of mind in which they were performed. Nandika, for example, specifically mentions the "evil thought" that led him to refuse to feed a sage during a famine. Vāgīśa and Kusuma, on the other hand, received the reward of personal discipleship with the Buddha not so much because of the trivial acts that they performed as for the state of mind in which they did so. Vāgīśa explicitly says that he made his petty donation without any awareness of the benefits that it would bring him. He was merely imitating what he saw other people doing, yet he received the full karmic benefit of his act because he performed it with a pure heart. Kusuma too acted out of a disinterested innocence, as a child who was merely following the lead of his companions with their "pure hearts and minds."

A. Mahākāśyapa

[The Buddha, guide of the Dharma, who severs the bonds, was staying] at Śrāvastī. [His senses] subdued, [supremely virtuous, the Tathāgata himself spoke to the monks:]

"There is a beautiful [lake], frequented by wild spirits, [beautifully adorned by trees and flowers of all kinds, from which four] rivers flow in four [directions toward the vast ocean: the Ganges, Indus, Oxus, and the Tarim, which no man can cross] unless he has attained supernatural powers. Come now, let us go to [that wondrous lake.]"

[Heeding the command] of the Great Sage, the incomparable Savior, [they all flew off together, like the king of the ruddy geese leading his flock.] When they arrived there, [the Buddha encouraged them to speak of their former lives: "Let any one of you here who can recall it reveal your good and bad karma and its final happy result.]"

Then Kāśyapa, disciple of the Incomparable One, [as a lion wandering on a mountaintop confidently goes about his domain, told of his deeds in a former life:]

"I gave a gift, [just a single handful of millet,] to a solitary buddha. [His mind liberated, devoid of hostility, and free of the afflictions,] that solitary buddha [lived in peace, pure of heart]. Through him I came to understand the supreme Dharma, and in that Dharma I made this solemn resolution: ['May I encounter in a future life others who live this way,] and may I [spend] my life in the Kuru paradise.' [By the ripening of that very karma, I was born a thousand times in the Kuru paradise, among] the long-lived, [selfless beings, graceful in their movements and noble in behavior. By the ripening of that very karma, I was born] over and over, a thousand times, in the heaven of the Thirty-Three Gods, wearing wondrous garlands, [ornaments, and ointments, with a beautiful body, splendid]. Then by the ripening of that very karma, [I was born as a brahman in a great family, admired by men and women];

I was very wealthy, yet indifferent to the pleasures of the five senses. I [had never seen the Teacher], but then I saw the garment of a disciple of the Victor.[306] I made myself [a patchwork robe], and bowing [to all the arhats, I renounced the world]. After I had renounced the world, I saw the Teacher [sitting at the Shrine of Many Sons]. I bowed [at his feet and said to him], 'Lord, you are my master, and I am your disciple.' [He said:] 'So be it, [Kāśyapa], exactly as [you say: I am your teacher, and you are my disciple]. Now listen as I speak of the sweet Dharma, if you wish [to be liberated from all suffering.]'

". . . for only seven days, I was a student in training. Then [on the eighth day, I attained perfect knowledge]. . . . By the final ripening of that same (karma), I encountered Śākyamuni, the greatest of men. [For one who makes a solemn resolution with a pure mind reaches whatever it is that] he desires. By the final ripening of that karma, my mind is liberated, free of hostility, and free [of the afflictions]; I [have encountered these men who are living their final lives], who are free of hostility, and I have met the Savior. This was well spoken by the Savior, free of hostility. Thus the Savior . . . the Tathāgata. [This] excellent deed was done in previous lives. [The Tathāgata is] the highest of all, unconquered. [Whatever a virtuous person desires] comes to him. Everything [has come to me] as I properly conceived it in my heart, [and now this is my last lifetime. My births are ended, as is all desire; the bonds of rebirth have been cut completely. I am a true-born son of the king of the Dharma, and I shall attain nirvāṇa, as all my afflictions have been eliminated. The All-Seeing One has designated me as the foremost of those who live in strict asceticism.[307] I have eliminated the afflictions and cast out all my passions; I have reached the immovable place (i.e., nirvāṇa)."

Thus did the elder Kāśyapa explain his own karma before the community of monks on the great Lake Anavatapta.]

["Long ago, during the time of the Buddha Vipaśyin, I built a bathhouse for the community of monks. At that time I made this solemn resolution:] 'May I have another fortunate encounter [with such venerable ones, and may I be pure and clean,] rid of the faults and afflictions.' I also prayed: '[May I be] handsome, with a golden complexion.' [And so,] now I am charming and attractive, handsome and shapely.

"By that root [of merit] I have experienced fortunate births [as a god and a human], glorious [because of my meritorious deeds]. Once I [put a coat of plaster on the stūpa] of a solitary buddha and covered it completely [with a layer of yellow paint. Hoping to get the marks of a great man,][308] I further prayed, 'May I have a complexion like gold and be free of the faults and afflictions.' By that root [of merit], I was born in the city of Vārāṇasī as the [middle] son of Kṛkin, [the king of Kāśī]. When I saw the stūpa of Kāśyapa,[309] I [purified] my mind and placed the middle umbrella on it.[310]

"[For building a bathhouse], painting a stūpa yellow, and placing an umbrella on a stūpa, [I have experienced great happiness]. Now this is my last lifetime; I have gained human birth in the royal family of the Śākyas, as brother to the Savior, the Buddha. My body bears full thirty marks of a great man, no more, no less. The All-Seeing One [has designated] me as the foremost of handsome men.[311] I have cast out all my passions and attained [eternal] bliss."

Thus did the monk Nanda, brother of the Savior, the Buddha, explain [his own karma] on the great Lake Anavatapta.

c. Śroṇa Koṭiviṃśa

"During the time of the Buddha Vipaśyin, I made a hall for the universal community in the capital city Bandhumatī.[312] I covered the entire floor with fine carpets and donated them [to the community]. Then, with a pure mind and joyful heart, I made this solemn resolution: 'May I encounter a buddha, and may I be initiated by him. Thereafter, may I attain the calm of [supreme] nirvāṇa.'

"By that root of merit I passed through saṃsāra for ninety eons as a god or a human, glorious because of my meritorious deeds. Through the past ninety eons and now for one more,[313] I cannot [recall that I] ever set [my feet on the bare ground. Now this is my last] lifetime; I have gained human birth as the only son of a wealthy merchant in Campā. As soon as I was born, my father declared his wish for me: 'I'll give my son 200 million, no less.'[314] Soft hair grew on the soles of my feet, four finger-widths long. I was never dirty and always happy, and I became extremely rich. The All-Seeing One has designated me as the foremost of the energetic. I have cast out all my passions and attained eternal bliss. Therefore, if you wish to benefit yourself and aspire to greatness, revere the true Dharma and remember the teaching of the buddhas."

Thus did Śroṇa of Campā, a monk and disciple of the Buddha, explain his own karma on the great Lake Anavatapta.

D. Yaśas

"Once I was an ascetic living in the wilderness. As I entered a village to seek alms, I saw a woman's corpse, bloated and discolored. I sat down next to it and examined it closely. With total focus and concentration, I contemplated its repulsiveness. Then, even as I was sitting there, its stomach burst open. Hearing that dreadful noise, my concentration was broken. I saw clots of blood and heaps of excrement in its stomach, oozing all around, filthy and revolting, and the small and large intestines, the kidneys, heart, and stomach were being eaten by hundreds of maggots.

"Then I [concentrated] my mind again. While staring at the body outside me, I visualized it as my own: 'That body is really just like mine, and mine is really just like it: putrid on the inside, filthy, completely disgusting.'

"Then I arose and went back to my ashram. I stopped seeking alms and ate no food. When I finally entered a village to get something to eat, I saw attractive women there, but I cultivated the same perception: 'All physical bodies are like that corpse: putrid on the inside, filthy, completely disgusting.' As I meditated in this way, I was freed from passions and fully developed the four infinite sublime states.

"After I died and passed on from that life, I was destined for the Brahma heaven. After passing from the Brahma heaven, I was born in the city of Vārāṇasī. There, as the only son of a rich merchant, I was wealthy, spoiled, handsome, comfortable, popular, and dear to my family. I became extremely rich. But once as I was lying in bed at night after amusing myself all day, I woke with a start and saw my women lying all around me. They were [resting their heads] on their drums, tambourines, and lutes. They were splayed out, fast asleep with their hair all disheveled, snoring and mumbling in their sleep. The beneficial effect from the past manifested itself,[315] and I created a mental image of

Figure 33. The Buddha and the sleeping women in a Gandhāran sculpture.

my chambers as a repulsive cemetery. Then in a panic I cried out: 'Help me, please! I am besieged, threatened from all sides!'[316] I leaped out of bed and fled from my palace, and the compassionate gods opened the gate for me. Departing from the city, I came to the bank of a river, and there I saw an ascetic walking around on the other side. I cried out to him these words, which were few but which would have such great effect: 'Help me, please! I am besieged, threatened from all sides.'

"Then the Tathāgata addressed me with words of deathless nectar: 'Fear not, young man; come here, I am your rescuer.' At that very instant, I was freed from passions. I cast off my jeweled sandals and swam to the other shore, approaching the compassionate one, the unrivaled Master. Then the compassionate Master, understanding that I was thirsty, taught me the sweet Dharma[317] that reveals the four noble truths.

"Venerable sirs, I saw the Dharma and asked the sage to initiate me, and in his compassionate mercy, Gautama did so. Then at the end of that very night, just as the sun arose, all of my afflictions were eliminated; I was calmed and cooled."

Thus did Yaśas, a monk and disciple of the Buddha, a master of supernatural powers, explain his own karma on the great Lake Anavatapta.

"In a past life long ago, I was the son of a wealthy merchant. I was in charge of my father's household; I took good care of him, but I mistreated my mother. I gave plenty of food and drink to my father and brothers and sisters, and even to the slaves and servants, but I was stingy with my mother, and I insulted her. I gave her nothing to eat and uttered these awful words: 'You can eat rocks!' By the ripening of the karma from that deed, I passed many lives in the hells, and when I returned to life as a human being, I had to eat rocks for my food. From one lifetime to another, I could eat only rocks, and I always died in terrible pain from pangs of hunger.

"So it went for five hundred lifetimes: wherever I was born, I always died in terrible pain from pangs of hunger. Now this is my last lifetime, in which I have attained human birth and encountered the Buddha, Lion of the Śākyas, supreme among men. I have been initiated in the teaching of the Lion of the Śākyas, and have become an arhat, a serene disciple. Yet even now, venerable sirs, although I am a victorious arhat with supernatural powers, I must live in a cave and eat rocks. This will be my abode until I die; [only then] will the final ripening of my karma be entirely exhausted. Therefore you must purify your minds toward your mother and father. Serve them respectfully, lest you regret it later."

Thus did the elder Bharadvāja, a monk and disciple of the Buddha, explain his own karma on the great Lake Anavatapta.

"For the last ninety-one eons, I do not recall any bad births [but only] good births as a god or human, all because I worshiped at a stūpa. I didn't know the benefit of it, but I saw people approaching the stūpa of [the Buddha] Vipaśyin one after the other and worshiping at it, so I did the same. Laughing, I bought three pennies worth of flowers, incense, and ointment and put them on the stūpa, and I have never had a bad birth since then.

"For no gift is small when given by one whose heart is pure, whether to a buddha tathāgata or to a buddha's disciples. Had I known the virtues of the buddhas when I was paying homage to the Tathāgata, I would have worshiped at the stūpa all the more, and it would have been even better for me. Therefore, understanding the many virtues of the Master, you should worship at a stūpa. Then you will escape from bad births.

"The All-Seeing One has designated me as the foremost of poets, learned, eloquent, wise, and inspired.[318] Therefore, if you wish to benefit yourself and if you aspire to greatness, revere the true Dharma and remember the teaching of the Buddhas."

Thus did the elder Vāgīśa explain the ripening of his own karma before the community of the Master's monks on the great Lake Anavatapta.

G. Nandika

"Long ago, I was [a wealthy master merchant] in Rājagṛha. When a famine struck, all the ascetics had to be fed. Seized with stinginess, I had an evil thought: 'Who in the world would want to feed a mendicant for seven years during such a dreadful famine?' So I cooked some rice with horse's urine and fed it to a monk, and he died. By the ripening of the karma from that deed, I passed many lives in the hells. Then, because of the remnant of that karma, wherever I was born, I always died in terrible pain from pangs of hunger.

"So it went for five hundred lifetimes: wherever I was born, I always died in terrible pain from pangs of hunger. Now this is my last lifetime, in which I have attained human birth and encountered the Buddha, Lion of the Śākyas, supreme among men. I have been initiated in the teaching of the Lion of the Śākyas and have become an arhat, a serene disciple. Yet even now, venerable sirs, though I am a victorious arhat, I have to survive on gruel, always sick and dependent on others."

Thus did the elder Nandika, the companion of Anuruddha, explain his own karma on the great Lake Anavatapta.

"One day I put a jasmine flower[319] on my ear and a garland on my head, and went out to the park together with my friends. There I saw the great stūpa of the glorious Buddha Vipaśyin. A vast crowd of people had assembled there to worship and pay homage at it. My friends joined in, each taking his garland and putting it on the stūpa with pure heart and mind. Seeing them do this one after the other, I took the jasmine from my ear and put it on the stūpa myself.

"For no gift is small when given by one whose heart is pure, whether to a buddha tathāgata or to a buddha's disciples. Had I known the virtues of the buddhas when I was paying homage to the Tathāgata, I would have worshiped at the stūpa all the more, and it would have been even better for me. Therefore, understanding the many virtues of the Master, you should worship at a stūpa; then you will escape from bad births. By giving a single flower, I dwelt pleasurably among the gods for ten billion years, and now at the end of this life, I will attain nirvāṇa. This, venerable sirs, is what I remember: I gave a single flower and experienced the fruit of that deed; for karma never fails."

Thus did the elder Kusuma, a monk and disciple of the Buddha, explain his own karma on the great Lake Anavatapta.

6. Six Stories of Previous Lives and Other Legends

THE MANUSCRIPT translated here is one of seven scrolls in the British Library Kharoṣṭhī collection that record sets of summaries, often extremely brief, of stories that are labeled as *avadāna*, "legends," or in a few cases *pūrvayoga*, "previous lives." All but one of them were written by the same scribe, who has a distinctive, large flowing hand. Of these seven scrolls, four (fragments 1, 4, 12+14, 16+25) are relatively well preserved, though still very far from complete, while the others are merely small remnants.

The genre labels *avadāna* and *pūrvayoga* are familiar in Buddhist literature, especially among the texts from the north Indian tradition in Sanskrit or Buddhist Hybrid Sanskrit and in Chinese translations of lost Indian originals. There these two terms are used more or less interchangeably to refer to stories, usually narrated by the Buddha, that illustrate the workings of karma by revealing the acts of a particular individual in a previous life and the results of those actions in his or her present life. They typically consist of a "story of the past," a "story of the present," and an explanation of the karmic relationship between the two, much like what we have seen in the previous translation.[320]

But the Gāndhārī texts in question do not follow this normal pattern in that many of them consist of only a single story without explicitly alluding to karmic results and connections. The stories labeled *pūrvayoga*, of which there are only four in total, three of them in the scroll translated here, tell stories about previous lives of the Buddha and of his prominent disciples but do not directly mention their connections to their lives in the present. In each case, they are introduced as "the pūrvayoga of so-and-so," followed by a story of a previous lifetime of the characters in question, namely the Buddha, Ājñāta Kauṇḍinya, and Ānanda.

The stories that are labeled *avadāna*, of which about fifty-eight survive, are a more mixed bag. Many of them take place during the Buddha's lifetime, but others are placed in later periods of Buddhist history. One story, for example, is set in the time of Aśoka, a century or more after the Buddha's parinirvāṇa. Several others contain references to "Sakas" or other persons with Iranian names, or to places in Gandhāra such as Taxila and Puṣkalāvatī, suggesting that they represent events contemporary with or not much earlier than the time of manuscript itself—that is, in and around the first century CE. The subjects of the Gandhāran avadānas are quite diverse. Several refer to the activities of the Buddha's direct disciples, such as Śāriputra, Gavāmpati, and Mahākāśyapa. Others describe the activities of other monks and their interactions with laypeople. A recurrent theme in several stories is the problem of the predicted disappearance of the Dharma. Other miscellaneous stories include such topics as a contest between magicians and an allegorical dialogue among the personified five "faculties" or "powers" (Skt *indriya*).[321] But unlike the pūrvayogas, only a few of them have any explicit reference to the effect of karma on rebirths, which is a central feature of the avadānas in other Buddhist literatures.[322]

There are several possible explanations of why the Gāndhārī avadānas do not explicitly address the workings of karma in any detail, as we would expect. Perhaps, in view of the extremely abbreviated form in which these stories are presented, the linkage between the events described in the stories and their karmic outcomes is implied and would have been supplied in expanded versions that were delivered orally on the basis of these summaries. But there is little direct evidence for this. It may simply be that these stories reflect a broader application of the term *avadāna* than the one that is familiar to us from the Sanskrit and Chinese literary traditions, one that applies it to any interesting or remarkable story. In any case, it is clear that Gandhāra had an independent local tradition of edifying recitations called *avadāna* that is quite distinct from avadāna literature as it has previously been known.

Most, and probably all, of the seven avadāna/pūrvayoga collections are secondary texts in the sense that they were added to scrolls on which other texts had previously been written.[323] In each case, an earlier scribe had written out a text on the recto side—that is, on the smooth white outer bark—but left some part of the bottom of the recto and all of the rougher verso blank. The avadāna scribe began by filling up the small blank space at the bottom of the recto, then turned the scroll around and flipped it lengthwise to continue writing on the verso, from the bottom up. Unfortunately, since the tops of the scrolls are always lost, we do not have the ends of any of the avadāna texts. But in every case they cover the entire surviving part of the verso, so they seem to have been fairly long.

The set of stories presented here follows the *Dharmapada* text on British Library fragments 16+25 presented above in translation 4. Another set of avadānas (translation 7) was added onto British Library fragment 1 after the *Songs of Lake Anavatapta* (translation 5). Yet another set is on fragments 12+14, following the numerically grouped sūtras (translation 1), and a fourth set is on fragment 4, whose first text is a commentary on canonical verses. There are also several other groups of avadānas on small fragments whose connection with other texts cannot be determined,[324] but it is clear that the avadāna scribe was a scavenger who used the empty space on preexisting scrolls, which may have been part of his personal library, to record his stories.

Most of these groups consist of avadānas only, but the one translated here is a mixture of stories designated as *pūrvayoga* (B, D, and E) and *avadāna* (A), while two stories (C, F) are not labeled at all. One of the latter (F) resembles the type of stories that in the other scrolls are called *avadāna*, while the other, the story of Sudaṣ̣ṇa (C), corresponds to a very popular legend that in the Pali and other traditions is included in the jātaka category, namely the *Vessantara-* or *Viśvantara-jātaka*. Thus this scroll alone seems to contain a mixture of genres, but the rationale for the selection and ordering of the individual stories remains obscure, and this is unfortunately also true of the other avadāna scrolls.

Though it is not entirely clear what this scribe had in mind in recording these stories, some of their physical and textual features do provide clues. With regard to their content, the most striking feature of the pūrvayogas and avadānas is their extreme brevity and compression. Even the longest of them take up no more than twenty lines, while most fill a dozen lines or less and several as little as two or three lines. The text typically presents the barest outlines of the story, sometimes skipping entirely over important parts of it; in an extreme case, the story of Sudaṣṇa recounts in four lines a legend whose parallel version in Pali, the *Vessantara-jātaka*, covers over one hundred printed pages. The texts are often so brief that they are virtually impossible to follow if the reader does not already know the story line.

The abbreviated character of these little sketches is made explicit by the insertion at the end of most of them, and sometimes at the beginning as well, of expansion formulae such as "The whole [story] is to be told at length" or "To be told at length according to the model." Here the term "model" or "pattern" (*upamana* = Skt *upamāna*) presumably refers to some standard framework or formula, oral or written, for the complete recitation of the stories concerned, but we do not have any direct evidence of such formulae. Such notations create the impression that the scribe had written the stories for his personal use. They may have served as memory prompts or lecture notes for oral presentations, rather than being formal written texts intended to be read by others, like the primary texts on each of the scrolls.

The informal character of the pūrvayoga/avadāna texts is also discernible in their language and style. They are typically composed in a colloquial style that reads quite differently from literary texts like the

Songs of Lake Anavatapta and the *Dharmapada*, which were translations, or perhaps rather "mechanical transpositon[s],"[325] into Gāndhārī from some other (not clearly identifiable) north Indian dialects and which bear the stamp of a pan-Indian Buddhist poetic style. The language and style of the pūrvayogas and avadānas, with their limited technical terminology and formalized structure, are equally distinct from those of scholastic texts such as the commentary on the *Sūtra of Chanting Together* (translation 9). Most of the avadānas reflect an informal, vernacular register of Gāndhārī, largely free of literary and technical conventions, which must have been quite close to the colloquial language actually being spoken in Gandhāra at this time.

Another unique feature of the pūrvayoga and avadāna manuscripts is the presence in several of them of secondary interlinear notations reading "[It has been] written," "All has been written," "All of these avadānas have been written today," or the like.[326] The significance of these notations is controversial, in part because they are in a hand that is similar but not exactly identical to that of the stories themselves, so that it is hard to be certain whether they were written by the scribe who wrote the stories himself or by another person. One theory to explain these notations posits that the pūrvayoga and avadāna texts were pedagogical exercises by a scribe in training, and that the interlinear phrases indicate that the work had been checked and approved by the instructor or supervisor. But if this were the case, the supervisor must have been rather a lenient one, as the rough and ready texts are hardly of the quality that one would expect a future scribe to imitate. Another explanation is that the notations indicated that the texts had been recopied onto a new scroll by a second scribe in preparation for the ritual interment of the original scrolls, after they had become decrepit and fragmented. This theory, however, is open to question because it is hard to determine exactly what the condition of the scrolls concerned was at the time of their interment.[327]

Yet another explanation, which I consider the most likely one, is based on the theory that these cursory texts were never intended for eyes other than those of the scribe himself, who used them as lecture notes or perhaps rather as an outline for a more formal text he intended to write. If this was the case, the "written" notations might have indicated that he had finished writing out the full texts of the stories elsewhere, there filling in the portions that had been indicated here as "to be told at length." Of course, no such full texts in Gāndhārī have come to light, so this explanation, like the others, remains hypothetical. But in any case, it would seem that in these rough scraps we have the kernel of a class of literature that was to develop in later Sanskrit literature into formally structured literary anthologies such as the *Avadānaśataka* ("One Hundred Legends"), in which one hundred avadānas are divided into ten thematic groups of ten stories each.

However this may be, we find in these unusual manuscripts something quite different not only from the relatively formal texts of the other Gāndhārī scrolls but also from the sort of literature that one usually finds in ancient manuscripts. Here we are not dealing with set texts written and preserved for archival, ritual, or educational purposes that had been copied and recopied many times since their initial composition or redaction in written from. Instead, we have here rare instances of autograph manuscripts, that is, texts as originally written in their author's own hand. Thus they show us, instead of received versions of established texts, specimens of literature in the making. They provide a picture of the work in progress of a Gandhāran scholar-monk who seems to have been collecting, recording, and organizing various legends into an incipient literary compilation. In this way, these scrolls provide a peek behind the screen that typically conceals the prehistory of texts and corpora before they were established in fixed canonical forms.

However, the very qualities that make these texts so interesting also make them extremely difficult and opaque. Out of the fifty-eight stories preserved on the seven British Library scrolls, only twenty-three are comprehensible to any meaningful degree. While the colloquial character of their language and style is of considerable linguistic interest, it increases the difficulty of understanding and translating them. One often encounters in them local or vernacular words that are otherwise unattested, so that the translator is often reduced to guesswork in interpreting them. An even greater obstacle is their extremely terse style, which makes them difficult and often impossible to understand unless a parallel or related story is available in Sanskrit, Pali, or Chinese to serve as a guide; but more often than not, no such parallel exists. And finally, all of the manuscripts concerned are fragmentary throughout and in many places barely legible, if at all.[328]

Therefore it is not possible to present complete and coherent translations for all of the pūrvayogas and avadānas in British Library fragments 16+25. Translations for only the first six stories, which are relatively well preserved, can be offered here. After the sixth story, only some meager remnants of the right-hand portion of six more lines are preserved at the badly decayed top of the scroll. Virtually nothing can be made of this part beyond a few isolated words, but several abbreviation formulae and punctuation marks of the sort that usually mark the end of a story are discernible. This suggests that these six lines may have contained as many as five stories. If this is correct, they must have been set down in an extremely compressed fashion, even more so than what we have seen in the surviving parts of the text. Unfortunately, there is little more that can be said about this tantalizing remnant.[329]

a. The Story of a Rich Man

> Thus is the tradition: There was in the city of Pāṭaliputra [a certain] monk. At that time, at that moment, to a certain man . . . the rich man Mahikoḍa. Thus it is to be recited.

No parallel has been identified for this extremely brief and apparently incomplete story, so that little can be made of it. The story is in effect intact but for one or two words, and nearly all of the words are at least more or less familiar and comprehensible. But the text provides only the setting, namely the city of Pāṭaliputra, the imperial capital of the Mauryan dynasty in northeastern India, and introduces three characters: a monk, another unidentified man, and apparently a rich man named Mahikoḍa. The missing portion probably contained a verb, of which the unidentified "certain man" was the object, and the rich man perhaps the subject. But we don't know what was done to him, and for lack of any parallel or related text we have no way to guess what happened.

In any case, the presentation of this story is anomalous in several respects. It lacks a title heading at the beginning such as "The story of the previous life of so-and-so," which most stories in this and the related collections have, and at the end it has neither the usual abbreviation formula nor a story number like all the others. According to the interpretation proposed by Lenz (2003, 146), this first story reflects a false start by the author, who had begun to write a set of stories but for some reason changed his mind about its contents after the first one, discarded it, and started a different set.

B. The Previous Life of the Bodhisattva as a Merchant

> The story of the previous life of the Bodhisattva: thus it was heard. The Bodhisattva was a merchant, a great sea-going merchant. He gathered up his wares and went down to the ocean. But his ship capsized and the merchant sank to the bottom. There was a reward [?] . . . The merchant was left by himself there on the bank. He killed himself.
>
> Thus the story of the previous life is to be told at length according to the model. [Story number] 1.

The theme of a seafaring merchant who undergoes various adventures after a shipwreck is a commonplace in avadānas and other types of Buddhist narrative literature.[330] Often, as here, the hero saves his companions or sacrifices his life for them and in the end is revealed to be a previous incarnation of the Buddha while he was still a bodhisattva. The story in our text thus has several approximate parallels in various texts that help us to understand the fragmentary and severely abridged text in the Gāndhārī manuscript. Among them is the one translated below, which, like the *Songs of Lake Anavatapta* and many other originally separate texts, is preserved in the *Mūlasarvāstivāda-vinaya*.[331]

> Once upon a time, O monks, there was a master merchant named Dhanaratha ("Wheel of Wealth"). He set out for the great ocean with five other merchants. They enjoyed telling stories and chatting with that merchant and became quite fond of each other. When in due course they reached the shore of the ocean, each one prepared his own ship. As they went down to the shore, they said to the merchant Dhanaratha: "Merchant, we don't feel safe without you."

"In that case," he said, "climb up here onto my ship and leave yours behind." They climbed onto his ship, but a storm blew up. They were terrified, but Dhanaratha told them, "Have no fear, my friends. If the ship sinks, hold on to my neck, and I will rescue you."

Bodhisattvas are clever in all sorts of skills and arts. He tied his precious jewels to his side. Then the ship sank, and the merchants held on to Dhanaratha. He brought them to the shore, but he was so weary that he was barely alive. Once they reached land, they let go of him, and he died in utter exhaustion. When they pulled him up out of the water and onto dry land, they saw the precious jewels tied to his side; they took them and went on their way.

What do you think, monks? I am the one who at that time was the merchant Dhanaratha. And these five monks are ones to whom I distributed my jewels after rescuing them at that time and to whom I now distribute the jewels of the [five] faculties, the [five] powers, and the [other] factors of enlightenment after rescuing them from the wilderness of saṃsāra.

On a historical level, the prominence in Buddhist literature of stories about seagoing merchants reflects the importance of the Indian sea trade with West Asia, North Africa, and the Mediterranean world in the early centuries of the Common Era and the popularity of Buddhism among the merchant class. On a symbolic level, such stories invoke or imply the metaphor, prevalent in Buddhist rhetoric, as also in other Indian and non-Indian religious traditions, of "crossing to the other shore" of a river or ocean. In a Buddhist context, the ocean represents saṃsāra, the other shore is nirvāṇa, and the Buddha is "the great caravan leader" (*mahāsārthavāha*) who leads others across.

The story translated above is not the same one as in the Gāndhārī manuscript but rather a variation on the same familiar theme. So while this and other parallels help us to understand the Gāndhārī text and to fill in the many blanks in its outline, several uncertainties remain. For example, the passage translated as "The merchant sank to the bottom. There was a reward [?] . . . The merchant was left by himself there on the bank" is beset with uncertainties, including unfamiliar words that do not correspond to anything in the parallel text.[332]

The following sentence reads, in the typically terse style of these texts, "He killed himself," but here the sequence of actions seems to be out of order. In another similar story told in the *Mahāvastu*,[333] the merchant killed himself with a knife so that his companions could use his corpse as a float to bring them to the shore, but it is hard to see why in our text he would kill himself after he had saved the others. Evidently the author of our text knew a version of the story that differed in details from the several others extant elsewhere in Buddhist tradition.

c. The Previous Life of the Bodhisattva as Prince Sudaṣṇa

> [The story of the Bodhisattva's previous life as] Sudaṣṇa. It is to be told as an example.
>
> Since he was an all-giving king, he gave his mighty elephant to a brahman. The king also surrendered his chariot and gave away his children. Then Śakra, king of the gods, came from the sky and spoke this verse to him: "Truly this man is black, and black is the food that he eats."
>
> The whole story is to be told at length. [Story number] 2.

This brief tale in four lines of text is an extreme abridgement of the famous story of the prince, known as Vessantara in Pali and as Viśvantara or Sudaṃṣṭra in Sanskrit, who represents the paradigm of generosity throughout the Buddhist world. His story has been told and retold in a vast number of languages and versions over the millennia and illustrated in Buddhist art in many lands. The legend is best known in the Pali jātaka version, in which it is the 547th and final story of the Bodhisattva's previous lives. Among the other versions of this ubiquitous legend, one in Sanskrit is included in the same section of the *Mūlasarvāstivāda-vinaya* as the preceding story. This version is much shorter than the corresponding Pali jātaka but still far longer than our four-line summary, covering fifteen pages of printed text.[334] It is summarized as follows:

> The righteous King Viśvāmitra ruled from his capital Viśvapurī over a happy and prosperous kingdom. His son Viśvantara was also kind, righteous, and extraordinarily generous. One day Viśvantara, who was the bodhisattva in a previous life, ventured out of the city and encountered

some brahmans who asked him for his chariot. He gave it gladly, with the wish that by doing so he might attain enlightenment.

Another time, Viśvantara went out on his magnificent elephant. On the way some brahmans approached the prince and asked him for his elephant. He gave it gladly, with the wish that by doing so he might attain enlightenment.

But when King Viśvāmitra heard that his son had given away the great royal elephant, he was extremely angry. Viśvantara decided to abandon worldly life and become a forest ascetic. His wife Mādrī begged him to take her along. The king pleaded with him to change his mind, but Viśvantara was resolute, explaining that he could never control his urge to give his possessions away.

Leaving the city, Viśvantara reminded his subjects that all affectionate relationships must come to an end. Then a brahman approached him and asked him for his wagon. Mādrī berated the brahman for his lack of compassion, but Viśvantara happily gave the brahman his wagon together with its horses.

Then they went on to the forest hermitage, the prince carrying their daughter Kṛṣṇājinā while Mādrī carried their son Jālina. Then a brahman approached Viśvantara and asked him to give him his children to be his servants. Viśvantara begged the brahman to take him instead of his children, but the brahman insisted. Finally Viśvantara realized that he could not violate his vow of largess and gave the children to the brahman. At that moment the ground shook with an earthquake, as the gods in heaven marveled at Viśvantara's generosity and self-control.

Then Mādrī, feeling the earthquake, ran back toward the hermitage. When a lioness blocked her way, Mādrī commanded it to let her by. Guessing that her children had been

> given away, she rushed home. When she asked Viśvantara where they were, he told her that he had given them away.
>
> Mādrī mourned and lamented piteously, hugging the little trees that her babies had nurtured and weeping for their little pet fawns. But Viśvantara reminded her of his higher purpose of attaining the perfection of generosity. Mādrī then said that he could even give her away in order to achieve his goal of saving the world. At that moment Śakra, king of the gods, appeared in the sky and assured Viśvantara that he would attain nirvāṇa. Then Śakra disguised himself as a brahman and asked Viśvantara for his beautiful wife. Viśvantara told Mādrī to go with the brahman, rejoicing that at last he was free of all possessions.
>
> Śakra then revealed his true form to Mādrī and offered to grant her anything she desired. She asked him to free her children send them to their grandfather, King Viśvāmitra. Śakra then gave Mādrī back to Viśvantara, telling him never to give her away again.
>
> Then Śakra made the brahman take the children to Viśvapurī and offer them for sale there, where his ministers recognized them and informed the king of what had happened. He had Viśvantara and Mādrī brought back to the capital and installed as king and queen.
>
> After telling this story, the Buddha explained to the monks that he had been Viśvantara in his past life and that the greedy brahman had been Devadatta (the Buddha's evil cousin). The Buddha concludes the story by telling the monks, "You should learn to be grateful and respectful and not to forget even the smallest favor, let alone a great one."

The contrast among these three versions of the Viśvantara legend constitutes an extreme example of the principle of expansion and contraction whereby a given text can be presented in full detail as in

Figure 34. The *Viśvantara-jātaka* on a stair riser from the Jamālgaṛhī stūpa.

the Pali version, which reads like a novella, or in a form resembling a short story as in Sanskrit, or as a minimal outline as in the Gāndhārī. None of the versions is in principle more valid or authoritative than the other; it is simply a matter of which form is most appropriate to the medium of presentation, the audience, and other circumstances of a given telling. The abridged and even the extremely abridged versions must have been intended to stimulate the readers' or hearers' memory of the entire legend, which would have been already known to them.

This mode of compressed presentation for memory stimulation has analogues in Indian Buddhist art, where familiar legends such as jātakas and avadānas are often depicted in abbreviated fashion, represented by a few key scenes or personages. These scenes are designed to call to mind the entire story, just as the few brief sentences and the partial citation of a single verse in this Gāndhārī version of the Viśvantara story remind the reader of its entirety. For example, a stair-riser panel from the Gandhāran stūpa at Jamālgaṛhī shows three scenes from the *Viśvantara-jātaka*. At the right, Viśvantara is in his hut with his two children while the greedy brahman stands to the left, asking Viśvantara for them. At the center, the brahman walks away with the children, while to the left Mādrī, carrying the food she has gathered, is blocked by the lioness. Like the outline of the story in our manuscript, such sequential scenes decorating Buddhist stūpas would have stimulated pilgrims to remember the story in detail. Local monks or guides probably used them as illustrations when they recounted the legend to their visitors, expanding on the pictures as the author of our text would have expanded on it when he was presenting the story orally.[335]

Although the story of Sudaṣṇa in our manuscript is certainly a variant of the Viśvantara legend that was familiar to all Buddhists, it is anomalous in certain respects, both in comparison to the other stories in this and the other Gandhāran pūrvayoga and avadāna collections, and in comparison to the versions of the legend in other Buddhist traditions. The style of the text is distinctly more formal and literary than the highly colloquial level that is typical of the other Gāndhārī texts of similar genre, and it is the only one of the stories on this manuscript in which a verse is actually cited, although a verse is referred to, but not written out, at the end of the story of Ānanda's past life. However, the verse in the Pali jātaka collection that corresponds to the one cited here occurs not in the *Viśvantara-jātaka*, as one would expect, but in the *Kaṇha-jātaka*. Its surprising presence in the Gāndhārī Viśvantara/Sudaṣṇa story can be explained in light of the similar themes of the two stories, both of which concern a man who desired to give away everything he owns, and whose resolve was tested by Śakra. The hero of the *Kaṇha-jātaka* was born with a dark complexion, whence his name Kaṇha ("black"). Śakra tries to provoke him by uttering the verse in question, which reads in full, "Truly this man is black, and black is the food he eats on a black bit of ground; he is not pleasing to my heart." In the Gāndhārī text, the citation of this verse probably refers to the scene in which Śakra disguises himself as a brahman and asks Sudaṣṇa to give him his wife, even though this episode is not otherwise alluded to.

It might seem that this verse is less appropriate to the Viśvantara/Sudaṣṇa story than to the *Kaṇha-jātaka* where it occurs in Pali. There, the word "black" (*kaṇha*), repeated three times in the verse, alludes not only to the hero's dark complexion but also to his name. In the Viśvantara/Sudaṣṇa story there is no such direct correspondence between the verse and the narrative, so that one might be tempted to jump to the conclusion that there is something wrong with the Gāndhārī text—that its composer inserted the verse here in error, forgetting or not knowing its "correct" place. Such a judgment, however, is not appropriate, for it would reflect the now discredited model of Pali supremacy, which affords a privileged position to the Pali version of the jātakas and of Buddhist scripture in general that is not historically justified.[336] Actually, there is no reason to doubt that the Sudaṣṇa story as known to our author did include the verse "This man in black . . . ," probably spoken by Śakra to Sudaṣṇa to provoke and test him, or perhaps rather to Sudaṣṇa's wife Mādrī in order to lure her away from her husband. In any case, this variation is indicative, once again, of the independence of the Gandhāran literary tradition and the characteristic flexibility of Buddhist literature in general, in which the same material can be presented in a wide variety of forms and styles without any one being privileged as inherently more authoritative than the others.

This being said, it is still true that the Sudaṣṇa story stands out as anomalous among the relevant Gāndhārī texts in terms of its style and content. These peculiarities are presumably attributable to the special character of the story itself in Buddhist tradition as a whole, where it stands out everywhere as the jātaka *par excellence*, so that the phrasing of the Gāndhārī version might have been more strongly influenced by other versions in other languages. But here too, there is nothing problematic about this anomaly, since these Gāndhārī pūrvayoga and avadāna collections are very much a mixture of material peculiar to Gandhāra and material common to other Buddhist traditions but adapted to local traditions (as in story E below).

D. The Previous Life of Ājñāta Kauṇḍinya as a Potter

The previous life of Ājñāta Kauṇḍinya. Thus is the tradition: Ājñāta Kauṇḍinya was a potter who lived by a river. Once a solitary buddha came to that place and said to the potter: "[Grant me] a place to stay for the rainy season: [build] a house for me to dwell in for the three months of the rainy season."

The potter said, "Venerable sir, if you will stay with me the whole time, then I invite you and will make a place for you." . . .

The potter . . . [said] "As a further favor to me, please take these abundant [?] supplies here. If I may give you a residence for the [entire] rainy season, I will exert myself for you."

The solitary buddha said, "For me . . ."

The potter thought. . . . The solitary buddha knew that he was going to fall ill. . . . The potter was filled with regret. Then the solitary buddha died; his karma had ripened. Five hundred solitary buddhas came from the sky, carrying sandalwood [for his funeral pyre]. The potter focused on this[337] and made this solemn resolution: "In the future, may I encounter a buddha, may I realize the Dharma, and may I be the first of all to do so."

As a result of that solemn resolution in the past [he was reborn as] Ājñāta Kauṇḍinya. This should be [told] at length, according to the model. [Story number] 4.[338]

At sixteen lines, this is the longest of the stories in this scroll. It is also one of only two stories that is duplicated among the British Library pūrvayoga/avadāna collections; besides this relatively lengthy and intact version, the fragmentary remnants of a similar but apparently somewhat more abridged text of the same story are preserved on the badly damaged British Library scroll 3.[339] The text is relatively well preserved except for one line near the middle that is almost entirely lost. Some help is provided in a few places by the second copy of the story on scroll 3, and especially by two complete versions in Sanskrit and Chinese of what is essentially the same story. The version in a long biography of the Buddha entitled *Past Deeds of the Buddha*, extant only in a Chinese translation (*Fo benxing ji jing*), is particularly close to the story in our text. It is summarized as follows:[340]

> The Buddha addressed the disciples, telling them that there had once been a solitary buddha in the city of Vārāṇasī who became ill just before the beginning of the rainy season. He visited a potter and asked to be allowed to live in his home through the rains. The potter happily agreed and built a hut for the solitary buddha and provided him with all his needs.
>
> Once during the night the potter saw the solitary buddha sitting in meditation and emitting a fiery light, and he was in awe at his spiritual power. Throughout the rains he tried to treat the solitary buddha's illness, but he could not be healed and finally he died. While the potter bitterly mourned for the solitary buddha, a host of 499 solitary buddhas flew through the sky to the potter's home, bearing sandalwood logs with which to cremate the dead solitary buddha's body. Then they told the potter that instead of mourning the solitary buddha, he should rejoice over the merit that he gained by caring for him.
>
> The potter then invited the 499 solitary buddhas for a meal, and afterward they told him that in the future a buddha would arise in the world, and that, because of the merit

he had produced, he could encounter that buddha if he would make an appropriate resolution to do so. The potter accordingly expressed the wish that in a future life he might meet the Buddha Śākyamuni and become his senior-most monk. After assuring him that his wishes would come true, the solitary buddhas flew off into the sky.

The potter then gathered the remains of the solitary buddha's body and built a stūpa over them. He then repeated his resolution to meet Śākyamuni, to understand his Dharma, and become his senior-most disciple.

The Buddha then explained that Kauṇḍinya had formerly been that potter, who because of his great merit was now sitting at his side.

The story explains how it was that Ājñāta Kauṇḍinya (Aññāta Koṇḍañña in Pali) came to be one of the Buddha's most prominent disciples and, moreover, why he had the distinction of being the first of the disciples to understand the Dharma and thereby free himself of the defilements and become an arhat. A central theme of this story, as was the case in the *Songs of Lake Anavatapta*,[341] is the solemn resolution (Skt *praṇidhi* or *praṇidhāna*). Kauṇḍinya's wish to become the first to understand the Dharma is of course eventually fulfilled in a future lifetime, and as a result he received the honorific title Ājñāta, "the Realized," which thereafter was prefixed to his clan name Kauṇḍinya. This final outcome is not explicitly mentioned in the Gāndhārī story, no doubt because it would be obvious to the intended reader or listener, but it is prefigured there by the verb with which he expresses his desire. Here the word translated "may I realize" is *ajaneja* (= Skt *ājānīyām*), which is the first person optative form ("may I . . .") of the same verb whose past participle form *ājñāta*, "[who has] realized," becomes his honorific title Ājñāta.

The potter, although he was no doubt a poor man, was happy to invite the sick solitary buddha to spend the entire rainy season at his expense and to "exert himself" on his behalf, because he instinctively recognized his spiritual excellence and power. In fact, according to Buddhist principles, he would have felt that it was the solitary buddha who was doing him a favor by accepting his food and medicine rather than the other way around. Thus this story, like so many of its genre, illustrates the fundamental principle of Buddhist social ethics, according to which monastics and lay followers exist in a state of mutual symbiosis: the lay followers provide the monks and nuns with the economic wherewithal they need to survive and teach the Dharma, while monastics provide in return the spiritual sustenance that enables the laity to improve their own karmic futures.

E. The Previous Life of Ānanda as a Prince

> The previous life of Ānanda: The entire [story is to be told] according to the model. Gasabadhaga was a king here in Jambudvīpa. He had two sons, Sabrudidrigo and Bhano, who served as his provincial governors. . . . Sabrudidrigo renounced the world and attained solitary enlightenment.
>
> [Quote] the verses at length. [Story number] 5.

This story, like that of Sudaṣṇa, is extremely compressed, and although this part of the scroll, near the better-preserved bottom, is more complete and legible than the preceding ones, it is comprehensible only with the help of parallel texts. Fortunately, in this case we have three other versions of the story, two from the vinaya of the Mūlasarvāstivādins preserved in Sanskrit, Chinese, and Tibetan and the other from the Chinese *Past Deeds of the Buddha*. The parallel versions are more or less consistent, though as usual they differ in matters of detail. The Sanskrit parallel is summarized as follows:[342]

> Long ago there was a king of Vārāṇasī named Bhānu, who had two sons named Bhānumān and Bhānumanta. Bhānumān, the elder son, realized that if he became king, he would have to perform cruel deeds that would cause him to be born in hell. He therefore resolved to become a wandering ascetic and begged his father, the king, for his permission to leave. His father reluctantly agreed to let him go, so Bhānumān left the palace to live among the ascetics, while his younger brother was anointed as heir apparent.
>
> Bhānumān soon achieved enlightenment without a teacher and became a solitary buddha. But he became sick and in his wanderings came back to Vārāṇasī. When the

king heard that his elder son had returned, he invited him to live in his private park and assigned his younger son Bhānumanta to attend to him. Bhānumān realized that his younger brother was destined to die in seven days and urged him to become an ascetic too. Bhānumanta agreed, but this time the king refused to grant his permission. So Bhānumān went to the king and revealed to him Bhānumanta's impending doom, and the king then allowed him to become an ascetic.

Bhānumanta then began to serve his elder brother assiduously. He noticed that due to his illness Bhānumān's bowl trembled as he held it to eat, so Bhānumanta took off his gold earring and set it down as a base for his brother's bowl. Seeing the bow thus steadied, Bhānumanta was inspired to utter a solemn resolution that all those who enter into the Dharma might be equally steady in it.

Bhānumanta then asked Bhānumān why he no longer eloquently preached the Dharma as he used to when he lived in their home. Bhānumān explained that it is only the fully enlightened buddhas, as opposed to the solitary buddhas, who preach the Dharma. Bhānumanta was then moved to make another resolution to be reborn as the brother of a buddha and to serve as his personal attendant.

The solitary buddha Bhānumān then initiated his brother as an ascetic, but Bhānumanta was unable to learn the Dharma in the week of life that remained for him. Instead, he made another resolution, to be reborn as a learned bearer of the Dharma.

At the end of the story, the Buddha reveals that Bhānumanta was Ānanda in a previous life, and that it was as a result of his final resolution that he was now the brother[343] of the Buddha, served as his attendant, and was a learned bearer of the Dharma.

The story in our manuscript seems to present the bare-bones outlines of a similar, though—as usual—not identical story. For example, all of the Sanskrit and Chinese versions describe the king as ruling in Vārāṇasī, whereas the Gāndhārī simply says that he ruled "in Jambudvīpa," that is, somewhere in the Indian world. In the Gāndhārī text the two sons are described as regional governors, a detail that is not mentioned in the other versions, although this was a typical occupation for young princes. The names of the three principal characters differ among the various versions; for example, in the Sanskrit text Bhānu is the name of the king rather than of the second son as in the Gāndhārī and also in one of the Chinese versions. The name of the king in the Gāndhārī text, Gaṣabadhaga, has no parallel in any of the other versions and is not a normal Buddhist name. It appears to be at least partly of Iranian derivation, probably reflecting a local adaptation of a well-known story, like the one that follows about the monk and the Saka.

It is even possible that King Gaṣabadhaga was an actual historical figure, otherwise unknown to us, who had been incorporated into the Buddhist legends of Gandhāra, as we know to have been the case with other rulers such Aśpavarman and Jihonika.[344] In any case, like the other stories in this manuscript, it is evidently a localized version of a widespread legend in the Buddhist traditions of northern India, presented in the form of a highly compressed summary of what in the other versions is a relatively long story, covering nearly three printed pages in the Sanskrit.

An unusual feature of this story is the word "verse" (*gatha* = Skt *gāthā*) added at the end. Here the scribe no doubt had in mind one, or perhaps more than one, verse associated with the story in his memory that he didn't feel a need to write out in full. The self-directed notation seems to mean, "Don't forget to say the associated verse(s)." The verse or verses may have been equivalent or similar to the two verses spoken in the Sanskrit version by the solitary Buddha Bhānumān to his father when he was convincing him to allow his brother Bhānumanta to become an ascetic. In the first verse, for example, he says, "O

Bhānu, let Bhānumanta go; I, Bhānumān, will initiate him. For the conquerors[345] have declared that leaving the world behind is the best way." As we have seen, in the preceding story of Viśvantara/Sudaṣṇa, a key verse was actually cited in the manuscript, though it was one that in the Pali tradition belonged to a different jātaka. This suggests that some, perhaps even all, of the pūrvayogas and avadānas recorded in the British Library manuscripts were associated with one or more such floating verses. Indeed, in Buddhist literature such verses are typically considered to be the core of the text, with the surrounding prose serving only to explain the context and circumstances in which the verses were uttered, usually by a buddha. Sometimes, as in the Pali jātakas and in the commentary on the *Dhammapada*, the prose portion is explicitly presented as commentary on the verses rather than as a part of the text proper. The pūrvayoga/avadāna scribe may have been jotting down these notes with reference to a well-known verse or set of verses that accompanied each story, primarily by way of setting the context of these verses. But in most cases, he did not see the need to actually write out the verses themselves, which he undoubtedly knew by heart.

F. The Monk and the Saka

At this point, as we move higher up on the verso of the scroll, the text becomes more and more fragmentary, and no parallel text is available to serve as a guide. Therefore it is not possible to give a continuous translation for this story, though something of its subject matter and general theme can be discerned. It concerns an unnamed monk in Taxila (Skt Takṣaśilā), the great metropolis and cultural capital of northwestern India, who walks to a village and there encounters a Saka man who is surrounded by a group of women.[346] The rest of the story records a dialogue between the Saka and the monk, apparently concerning the preservation and disappearance of the Dharma, the same subject that is discussed by a monk and a Saka named Zadamitra in translation 7b.

These and a few other British Library avadānas reflect a common concern about the relationships between the Saka ruling elite of northwestern India and the Buddhist community, which probably included both local monks and those from other parts of India. The generous patronage of Buddhist institutions by Sakas and other outsiders is abundantly attested in contemporary inscriptions, in many of which the donors have Saka names, so it is not surprising that the Sakas in the Gandhāran avadānas are presented in a favorable light. What is surprising, however, is that in other Buddhist traditions, the Sakas are also associated with the disappearance of the Dharma, but in a decidedly negative way. This association is expressed by a prophecy, preserved in varying versions in many texts, according to which a war waged against three evil kings—a Greek, a Saka, and a Parthian—who persecuted Buddhists will lead to the disappearance of the Dharma.[347]

Thus Buddhist literature as a whole exhibits a peculiar ambivalence toward the Sakas and other outsiders. The avadāna texts presented here indicate a positive attitude, no doubt reflecting their widespread adoption and patronage of Buddhism. But this seems to have coexisted with negative attitudes, for which several explanations (not mutually exclusive) can be proposed. First of all, a certain suspicion and ambivalence toward secular powers is characteristic of Buddhist communities in general, to which the general xenophobia that was characteristic of traditional Indian civilization (as of all ancient cultures) may also have contributed. But perhaps more important was the damage, if not intentional destruction, that must have been inflicted on Buddhist communities in the early stages of the Saka and other invasions. This would have created a legacy of hostility that lingered even after the Sakas had adopted Buddhism and other local ways.[348]

7. Avadāna Legends

LIKE THE PŪRVAYOGA texts in the previous section, the series of avadānas on British Library scroll 1 were added to the scroll at some time after the primary text, namely the *Songs of Lake Anavatapta*, had been written on it. As usual, the avadāna scribe began writing in the small empty space left by the first scribe at the bottom of the recto then continued on the previously blank verso. Thus the surviving part of this group of avadānas consists of five lines of text at the bottom of the recto followed by eighty-one lines on the verso. As usual, we do not know how much more of this text was continued on the lost upper part of the scroll.

The surviving eighty-six lines comprise ten stories, but most of them are quite fragmentary, and even in those parts of the scroll that have survived the surface of the bark has deteriorated to the extent that the text is either very difficult to discern or, all too often, completely illegible. Moreover, unlike the pūrvayoga stories, no parallels in other Buddhist languages and literatures have been located for any of the avadānas on this scroll. Only two stories, 6 and 7, are sufficiently intact and coherent to justify a translation below.

Although better preserved than most of the ten stories on this scroll, the eighth story is more fragmentary than two previous ones, so that a full translation cannot be presented. It begins with a title line, "Also, a second avadāna of Zadamitra." The story opens with a meeting or assembly, presumably of monks, who were invited by Aśpavarma, who either is, or is accompanied by, a "commander" (*stratega*), to spend the rainy season retreat. This person is surely the commander Aśpavarman, who is known from coins and inscriptions to have ruled in Gandhāra in the early first century CE.[349] There ensues a discussion or debate concerning, apparently, the nature of a "good man" (*sapuruṣo* = Skt *satpuruṣa*), that is, of a true follower of the Dharma.[350] The surviving remnants of the dialogue are largely unclear, but we almost certainly have a discussion of Buddhist values between a representative of secular authority—this time, a historically attested individual—and local Buddhists. In any case, this story, along with the avadāna fragment concerning Jihonika, a contemporary of Aśpavarma, provide a firm chronological anchor point for the development of Gandhāran Buddhist literature.

In the case of three or four other stories on this scroll, the general themes are discernible but the details are obscure, while the rest are virtually incomprehensible.[351]

A. The Contest between the Black and White Magicians

Thus it was heard. In the city of Pāṭaliputra a magician was demonstrating his magic. There are two kinds of magic: demonic and divine. That man was demonstrating demonic magic. Then another magician came to that place and [demonstrated] divine magic. . . . He said, "Do you wish to see [my] magic?"

[The other magician said,] "Certainly."[352]

[Then] he displayed Mount Meru.

The entire story is to be told at length here, up to: Then by the force of his magic, darkness obscured the sun. The whole story is to be told at length according to the model.

[Moral of the story:] Impermanence is the countermeasure [to the illusion of permanence]. The entire story is to be told. The entire [story is to be told] with reference to the nature of impermanence.

[Avadāna number] 6.

Although no parallel to this story has been located, at least its general outlines are reasonably clear. It tells of a contest in Pāṭaliputra between two magicians, one who practices demonic or black magic, the other divine or white magic, in which the latter prevails, apparently by showing Mount Meru, the great mountain at the center of the earth, and by eclipsing the sun with darkness. The details of the contest, however, are simply alluded to by the abbreviation formula "The whole story is to be told at length here, up to . . ." In this story, the scribe uses no less than three such abbreviation formulas, leaving us to guess what might have been implied.

Elsewhere in Buddhist as well as in Vedic tradition, demonic magic is said to have originated with the demon Śambara, whence its name *śabari* (Skt *śāmbarī*), while divine magic, or *idro* (Skt *aindrī*), was created by the god Indra or Śakra. These terms are found in a cycle of myths that are recorded in Buddhist texts such as the Pali *Saṃyutta-nikāya* but that go back to ancient, pre-Buddhist Indian traditions of the endless battles between the gods and the demons. In this story, these forms of magic are being performed by human beings, with the white magician evidently using divine magic in service of the Buddhist Dharma. This is evidently the point of the concluding comments "Impermanence is the countermeasure [to the illusion of permanence]" and "The entire [story is to be told] with reference to the nature of impermanence." In both cases, however, the interpretation is less than certain. In the first conclusion, the meaning of the word translated as "countermeasure" (*parigarmo* = Skt *parikarma/pratikarma*?) is not much more than a guess based on context and on somewhat shaky etymological grounds. The second conclusion is incompletely preserved, and the translation has been filled by comparison with similar phrases in this and other avadāna collections. But it is not at all clear why the scribe recorded this similar conclusion twice in somewhat different wordings.

Perhaps this peculiarity is simply a token of the casual, unpolished style of the avadānas as a whole. But in any case, the key word in both phrasings is certainly "impermanence" (*anicada* = Skt *anityatā*), one of the most fundamental of Buddhist doctrines. Presumably the illusions manifested by the white magicians demonstrated the impermanence of all phenomena by momentarily making Mount Meru appear and darkening the sun. In any case, this is the only one of the Gāndhārī avadānas for which a specific didactic or doctrinal purpose is mentioned, although in some other collections of Buddhist avadānas and legends the stories are prefaced by a brief statement as to the lesson that they were intended to impart.[353] We can therefore imagine that our author had in mind some such specific teaching point for some or even all of his stories, though we can hardly explain why it was only here that he saw fit to write it down.

B. The Story of Zadamitra

The avadāna of Zadamitra. The sixth . . . The whole story is to expanded at length. Thus it was heard: Zadamitra went to . . . In [that] place there was a banyan tree. He said to the *kṣabura* . . . He attained a meditative trance. From this city . . .

He said to the monk: "Show me . . ."

[The monk] said, "The true Dharma has disappeared."

Zadamitra said, "If the true Dharma shall have disappeared, then I will attain solitary enlightenment."

The Teacher, an arhat, [and] a great soul.

The whole story is to be told at length according to the model.

[Avadāna number] 7.

Although the text of this story is relatively complete, there are many uncertainties about its interpretation, for the usual reasons: no parallel has been found, and the central figure, Zadamitra, is unknown elsewhere, although as we saw in the discussion of avadāna 8, we do have some idea about his historical role and position. Thus, for example, the word *kṣabura*, evidently the name or description of one of the main characters, is completely unknown, and no reasonable guess can be offered as to its meaning or etymology so that it has had to be left untranslated. In the translation above, the ellipsis dots (. . .) represent in most cases lacunae in the manuscript, but sometimes also words or phrases for which no plausible translation can be offered.

Despite these problems, we can discern at least part of the plot and theme of the story. It concerns, besides the hero Zadamitra, a *kṣabura*, who is in some way associated with a banyan tree, and a Buddhist monk. The latter half of the story, which is somewhat less opaque, consists of a dialogue between Zadamitra and the monk, though its connection with the first half remains obscure. The topic of the discussion is clearly the disappearance of the Dharma, which, as we have seen, is a common theme in Buddhist literature generally. When the monk informs Zadamitra that the Dharma has disappeared (or perhaps, is going to disappear), the latter proclaims that he will attain individual enlightenment, meaning that he will become a solitary buddha who, like the many solitary buddhas before him, discovers the Dharma for himself without being taught it and without teaching it to others.

In this story, then, we seem to have a prediction of the future rather than an explanation of past events as in the pūrvayoga stories. Although Zadamitra's self-prediction is not phrased in the typical wording of a solemn resolution like the one spoken by the future Ājñāta Kauṇḍinya in translation 6d, it does seem to imply some such formal vow. The three nouns, "The Teacher (i.e., the Buddha; or perhaps, 'a teacher'), an arhat, [and] a great soul," that follow his resolution have no syntactic connection to the preceding or following phrases, but they may be a shorthand reference to a further set of vows. As seen in the story of Ājñāta Kauṇḍinya, persons in a state of inspiration in the presence of spiritually more advanced beings are often moved to make multiple vows.

This story is also of interest with regard to the history of Buddhism in Gandhāra. The hero's name, Zadamitra, is an Indianized version of an originally Iranian name, which would probably have been pronounced Zādmihr in his native language. His non-Indian name suggests that Zadamitra belonged to the ruling elite of Saka conquerors in the first century CE, many of whom became generous patrons of the Buddhist monastic communities. It is therefore not surprising that he is shown in a favorable light as an enthusiastic follower of the Dharma who makes a vow to attain enlightenment in a future life. This calls to mind the similar theme of the story in which an unnamed Saka man speaks about the future disappearance of the Dharma in translation 6f. The composer of this text, presumably a Buddhist monk, was evidently favorably inclined toward the Saka patrons of Gandhāran Buddhism in the first century CE and was no doubt also concerned to encourage them to continue their patronage. Indeed, it almost seems as if here the Sakas were being perceived, or rather portrayed, as the future saviors of the Dharma itself.

A curious detail of this story is the word "sixth" at the beginning, immediately after the title, "The avadāna of Zadamitra." This does not seem to be a label to the story itself, which is numbered at the end as 7. It may in some way refer back to the previous story, which is the sixth of the collection. For example, it might be a shorthand notation referring to the comments at the end of the sixth avadāna, to the effect that it is to be told to explain the concept of impermanence. Since that concept is also appropriate to avadāna 7, whose main theme is the disappearance of the Dharma, this is probably the best explanation, although here, as so often, we must resort to trying to read the mind of our scribe/author, who merely jotted down notes or even just single words that hint at his intentions.

8. The Many Buddhas Sūtra

THE *Many Buddhas Sūtra* (**Bahubuddhaka Sūtra*) is preserved on a fragmentary scroll in the Library of Congress in Washington, DC, on which ninety lines of text survive. As usual with Gandhāran scrolls, the upper part of the scroll is lost, but comparisons with related texts indicate that the amount of missing text is not very large.[354]

The scroll probably originally had a title or colophon at the end, but if so, this is lost. I have attributed to it the title *Many Buddhas Sūtra* on the basis of its similarity in structure and contents to two similar texts bearing that name (*Bahubuddha Sūtra* or *Bahubuddhaka Sūtra*) that are incorporated into the *Mahāvastu*. A third close parallel for the Gāndhārī text is incorporated in the Chinese *Past Deeds of the Buddha*, another biographical compilation structured around the life of the Buddha.[355] The introductory portion of *Past Deeds* describes the previous lives of the Buddha at length, including a section that covers approximately the same set of topics as the *Many Buddhas Sūtra* in Gāndhārī and Sanskrit.

The *Many Buddhas Sūtra* presents a patterned account of the lives of fifteen buddhas: thirteen buddhas who lived in the past, beginning with Dīpaṅkara and ending with Kāśyapa; the buddha of the present time, Śākyamuni; and the buddha who will be the next to appear in the future, namely Maitreya. Their lives are presented in a strictly

Figure 35. A Gandhāran relief of the *Dīpaṅkara-jātaka*.

schematic fashion, describing for each buddha his lifespan, the eon in which he lived, his social class, the number of his followers, and the length of time before the Dharma that he taught will be forgotten. Under each topic heading, the relevant information or number is given for the fifteen buddhas in succession. Thus the text has the effect of presenting the lives of the buddhas in a parallel pattern, differing only in the details.

In this way, the *Many Buddhas Sūtra* serves to emphasize the belief that, as the title indicates, the Buddha of the current historical eon is not unique. Rather, he is one member of a lineage of buddhas who have lived in the distant past and who will live in the future. Moreover, although this sūtra describes fifteen buddhas of the past, present, and future, this is not meant to be a complete list. On the contrary, this is only a small slice of the entire lineage—which is ultimately infinite—of buddhas.

This selection of this particular sequence of fifteen buddhas was chosen for special attention by the composer of the text because it is the period of Buddhist history that most directly relates to the spiritual career of "our" Buddha, Śākyamuni. The text begins with the Buddha

Dīpaṅkara because it was he who first predicted that the Bodhisattva, that is, the being who was destined to become the Buddha Śākyamuni, would attain buddhahood in a distant future lifetime. This refers to the well-known legend in which, many eons ago, a young man named Megha or Sumedha paid homage to Dīpaṅkara by spreading his hair on the muddy ground for the Buddha to walk upon. This act of pious devotion showed Dīpaṅkara that Sumedha had the virtuous qualities that would enable him to eventually become a buddha, and his prediction to this effect was the turning point in the Bodhisattva's spiritual career.

The selection of these fifteen buddhas shows that the purpose of the sūtra is not simply to present a history of buddhas for its own sake. Rather, the narrator, namely the Buddha Śākyamuni himself, is explaining to his followers *how* he became the Buddha. The first remaining section, of which only fragments remain at the damaged top, consists of a series of verses summarizing the Bodhisattva's gifts to the previous buddhas and acts of reverence toward them in his previous lives. The second section then describes the four courses of bodhisattva training that the future Śākyamuni pursued under his thirteen immediate predecessors. Thus, although fifteen buddhas are described in this text, the focus is not so much on those buddhas themselves as on the Bodhisattva's relationship with them, and specifically on how it was that his admiration and emulation of those buddhas planted the seeds of his own future buddhahood.

But in a broader sense, this text is not really about how the Bodhisattva himself became Śākyamuni Buddha, or at least not only about this. Ultimately, the question that this sūtra addresses is "Where do buddhas come from?" and the answer is "from other buddhas." A buddha, according to this and similar texts, evolves gradually over vast eons of time and across a vast number of rebirths, but the key to the pursuit of buddhahood is encounters with the buddhas themselves. Such encounters inspire certain persons with a wish to emulate the Buddha, which they express though a solemn resolution to meet other buddhas in their future lives and ultimately to become buddhas themselves. Such initial aspirations are confirmed in subsequent encounters with later buddhas who guarantee the ultimate success of this ambition.

This periodic appearance of buddhas across vast sweeps of cosmic history can be imagined as an endless chain whereby a particular buddha whose buddhahood was conditioned by his encounters in past lifetimes with previous buddhas in turn inspires other beings to aspire to and ultimately reach buddhahood in the distant future. Since Buddhism conceived of time as beginningless and endless, the lineage of buddhas extends back infinitely into the past and will continue infinitely into the future. Thus the question of how many buddhas there are is ultimately meaningless: buddhas are infinite because time is infinite.

Nevertheless, there are many Buddhist texts that refer to and even describe in detail particular numerical sets of buddhas. The archetype of this genre is the *Sūtra of the Great Legend* (*Mahāpadāna Sūtra*), in which the present Buddha describes the careers of his six predecessors, beginning with Vipaśyin, all of which are virtually identical to his own life. Nothing here is said about buddhas before Vipaśyin or after Śākyamuni, and it is uncertain whether, at the early point in the history of Buddhist doctrine and literature that this sūtra represents, the conception of an infinite lineage of buddhas had already developed or at least had been understood as an implicit possibility.

But a later Pali text, the *Lineage of the Buddhas* (*Buddhavaṃsa*), one of the texts of the *Khuddaka-nikāya* of the Theravāda canon, presents the life stories of twenty-five buddhas from Dīpaṅkara to Gotama according to the typical patterned formula, differing only in details. At this point in the development of Buddhist doctrine, if not earlier, the concept of the lineage of buddhas had extended beyond the seven buddhas of the *Sūtra of the Great Legend*, and the existence of more buddhas beyond the twenty-five described in the new text is clearly implied. Here too, as in our Gāndhārī text, the Buddha lineage begins with Dīpaṅkara because it was he who predicted Gotama's future buddhahood; but this does not imply that Dīpaṅkara was the first buddha who ever existed.

The reader may be struck by the discrepancy between the *Lineage of the Buddhas*, which has twenty-three buddhas between Dīpaṅkara and Śākyamuni, the Buddha of our era, and our Gāndhārī text, which counts only twelve in that period. Actually, though, the lineages of previous buddhas presented in different Buddhist texts often vary widely, except for the list of seven from Vipaśyin to Śākyamuni, which is consistent. This short list constitutes a core lineage that was inherited from the early foundational sūtras by all schools and regional manifestations of Buddhism. Beyond that basic list, however, the various traditions developed their own lists of buddhas, which sometimes differ quite widely and which may be elaborated at great length. For example, the first of the two *Many Buddhas Sūtras* in the *Mahāvastu* provides a list of no less than 331,140,263 buddhas, beginning with a sequence of 300 million consecutive buddhas all named Śākyamuni, followed by 800,000 Dīpaṅkaras![356]

Rather than taking this strange list literally, perhaps it is better understood as a rhetorical allusion to the infinite number of buddhas, which is sometimes explicitly stated in other texts.[357] In any case, the notion of an infinite number of buddhas, both in the past and future, follows logically from the Buddhist concept of infinite time on the one hand, and from the authorization of the notion of multiple sequential buddhas in the foundational *Sūtra of the Great Legend* on the other. But given the glaring differences between the sequences as presented in different texts, there is little to be gained in trying to compare and reconcile them. Rather, it is more fruitful to think in terms of the purposes and functions of such texts. To the Buddhists of antiquity, this was true and meaningful history, while the stuff of history as conceived in Western terms—the kings and princes, their endless wars and conspiracies—was merely the dross of life in saṃsāra, barely worth recording and remembering except insofar as it affected the fortunes of the Buddhist Dharma and its monastic institutions.

Besides presenting a historical and chronological framework for the belief system of their intended audience, the accounts of the past buddhas, and especially of their interactions with the present and future buddhas, had even more important functions on the levels of both doctrine and practice. For the system of the continuing production of buddhas not only provided readers with a hope of having the rare and treasured chance in some future life to personally encounter a buddha, but it also encouraged them even to aspire to the ultimate goal of becoming buddhas themselves. For the problem of the missing buddha—the grief that afflicted those who had known the Buddha before he departed into nirvāṇa and the disappointment of those who were born too late to have met him—is a central problem in Buddhism that underlies, directly or indirectly, many of its doctrines and practices. Physical substitutes for the Buddha, such as relics of his body and the commemorative stūpas that enshrined them, or texts and other items associated with the Buddha that were felt to embody him, came to be major centers of devotional focus throughout the Buddhist world. But doctrines and beliefs equally served to address the problem of the absent Buddha. Thus, for example, some highly successful manifestations of Mahāyāna Buddhism invoked a doctrine of living, accessible buddhas who are dwelling at the present time in other worlds. But texts such as the *Many Buddhas Sūtra* hold out the promise that a devoted follower of the Dharma may, over the vast sweep of time and endless rebirths, encounter not only one but many buddhas, and thereby might even eventually have a chance to become one.

Besides this doctrinal function, the *Many Buddhas Sūtra* and similar texts had practical applications in the sphere of meditative practice as well as in more worldly affairs. For the names of the buddhas were felt to have great magical potency, so that the chanting of texts containing them could protect the speaker from harm. The names of the buddhas were also believed to have a more elevated spiritual power, in that repeating them would produce beneficial states of mind and favorable karma.[358] The verbal or mental repetition of long lists of the

Figure 36. Base of a *caitya* (shrine) from eastern India with rows of Buddha images.

names of virtually indistinguishable buddhas has a visual counterpart in depictions of rows upon rows of identical buddhas in Buddhist sculpture and painting. These vast sequences of buddhas, whether in written, spoken, or visual form, served as meditative tools for focusing the mind on buddhahood and wholesome mental states. A direct statement to this effect is found in *Past Deeds of the Buddha*, where, after reciting a long list of names of previous buddhas, the Buddha concludes by saying: "If one is a man of wisdom, he should seek enlightenment. He should chant these buddhas' names and will soon become a buddha."

We can also extrapolate something about the ritual uses of the Gāndhārī *Many Buddhas Sūtra* from the history of another text in the same genre, namely the *Sūtra of the Fortunate Eon* (*Bhadrakalpika Sūtra*). This long text lists no fewer than 1,004 buddhas who have lived or will live during the present world eon, the Fortunate Eon, so called precisely because so many buddhas live in it; this, in contrast to other eons, which may see one, two, or occasionally three buddhas but most often none at all. It is generally agreed in Buddhist traditions, including in the text presented here,[359] that the last four buddhas—Krakucchanda, Koṇāgamana, Kāśyapa, and Śākyamuni—have already lived in the current Fortunate Eon. It is also agreed by all schools that Buddha

Maitreya will follow within this era. In the *Sūtra of the Fortunate Eon*, however, it is further predicted that another 999 buddhas will be born within the eon after Maitreya, and all of them are listed with their names and various attributes such as their social class, the number of assemblies of their followers, and the duration of their Dharma-teaching; that is to say, following a scheme that is quite similar to that of the *Many Buddhas Sūtra* and other texts of the same genre. We know that this sūtra was extremely popular in the Buddhism of Central and East Asia on the basis of the many versions and manuscripts of it that have been found in Central Asia and of its translations into Chinese, Tibetan, Mongolian, and Khotanese.[360] Until recently no text of the *Sūtra of the Fortunate Eon* in an original Indian language was known, but now several fragments of a Sanskrit manuscript of it have been found in Khotan,[361] as has a Gāndhārī manuscript in the area of Bamiyan.[362] Thus it is now clear that this text circulated in Greater Gandhāra as well as in Central Asia.

Superficially, the *Sūtra of the Fortunate Eon* and the *Many Buddhas Sūtra* seem quite different, but the difference between them is only a matter of point of view rather than of essential character: whereas the *Sūtra of the Fortunate Eon* looks primarily to the future, with a brief account of the (relatively) recent past, the *Many Buddhas Sūtra* looks backward into Buddhist history while also providing a brief glimpse forward toward the next buddha to come. That is to say, the real difference between them involves the different slices of the infinite history of buddhas that their speaker—who is of course himself an omniscient buddha—wishes to present. While the *Many Buddhas Sūtra* focuses on the relatively recent past in order to present the karmic history of Śākyamuni as a model for the attainment of buddhahood, the *Sūtra of the Fortunate Eon* looks toward the future to provide a prophetic promise of the many saviors to come.

Conventional modern thinking sees past and future as fundamentally different in that the former is known, or at least capable of being known, while the latter is unknown and unknowable. In Buddhist thought, however, this distinction is meaningless, because buddhas are equally omniscient with regard to the endless future as to the beginningless past. Thus in a sūtra—which by definition contains the words of a buddha—there is no real epistemological difference between the recital of past events and the prediction of the future; both are equally true, valid, and real.

This fundamental principle is embodied in the Sanskrit word *vyākaraṇa*, which etymologically means "analysis" but which in a Buddhist context can mean both "explanation" and "prediction," as has been explained above in connection with the karmic "explanations" presented in the *Songs of Lake Anavatapta*.[363] Thus, whereas the *Many Buddhas Sūtra* and the *Sūtra of the Fortunate Eon* would appear in Western terms to embody history and prophecy respectively, from a Buddhist point of view there is no difference of genre between them, only a difference of application. In this context, they are both Buddhist history—the "history" of the past and of the future respectively, as revealed by the omniscient voice of the Buddha.

Status of the Manuscript and the Text

Radiocarbon dating of the *Many Buddhas* scroll suggests a date in or around the first century BCE.[364] Other means of dating such manuscripts, principally by comparative analysis of the script and language, are too approximative to yield a more precise result than this, but nothing in them contradicts such a date. Thus this scroll is among the earliest ones known to date and may represent the first phase of written texts in Gandhāra and, presumably, the rest of the Buddhist world.

Since the top of the scroll is, as usual, lost, we do not know exactly how much of the text is missing. The two other texts that most closely resemble our text, namely the second *Many Buddhas Sūtra* in the *Mahāvastu* and the similar passage in *Past Deeds of the Buddha*, are incorporated into much longer compilatory texts about the lives of the Buddha Śākyamuni. So the first question regarding the Gāndhārī manuscript is whether it too was part of some much longer biographical anthology or whether it was instead treated as an independent text. The answer is almost certainly the latter. First of all, the layout of the surviving portion of the scroll suggests that it contained only the sūtra itself because, to judge from the parallel passages in the two larger texts, the preserved part of the Gāndhārī manuscript would have been approximately the middle of the text. This is exactly what we would expect if the entire text of the entire sūtra had been written out by itself on a single scroll. Comparisons with other Gāndhārī manuscripts and their parallels in later Buddhist literatures point in the same direction. Most notably, both the *Songs of Lake Anavatapta* and the *Rhinoceros Sūtra* were previously attested exclusively or primarily as incorporations into larger texts or anthologies until independent Gandhāran manuscripts of both of them were discovered. Thus the Gāndhārī *Many Buddhas Sūtra* is another representative of an earlier stage of development of Buddhist literature in which the anthologizing tendency was not yet dominant and sūtras that were later swallowed up into compilations were still circulating independently.

The three texts in question here—the *Many Buddhas Sūtras* embedded in the *Mahāvastu* and in *Past Deeds of the Buddha*, and the new Gāndhārī version—clearly constitute a distinct subset of the many sūtras that enumerate the buddhas and their characteristics. They are not only concerned with the same sequence of buddhas, from Dīpaṅkara to Maitreya, but also count within this span approximately the same number of buddhas,[365] listed in a similar order. In this regard these three stand apart from other sūtras belonging to the same overall genre.

On the level of details, however, the three texts are by no means identical. For example, the number and order of the topics that are discussed with regard to each buddha differ somewhat in all three, and the information provided under these topic headings is often inconsistent. Moreover, some parts of the Gāndhārī text have no direct correspondent in the others, most notably the second surviving section in which the Buddha details his practice of the four bodhisattva courses under the previous buddhas (see section 2 below). Thus while these three texts constitute a distinct subgroup within the broad genre of buddha-lineage texts, they are not parallel texts in the strict sense of the term. Rather, they can be understood as separate formulations or "performances" based on a common underlying pattern and structure, once again exhibiting the characteristic flexibility of Buddhist literature.

Section 1: Śākyamuni's Encounters with Previous Buddhas

As noted above, the beginning of the scroll is, as usual, very badly damaged. It originally consisted of a set of fifteen verses, five of which are entirely lost, describing the bodhisattva's encounters with the fourteen other buddhas. The descriptions of these encounters, as in many other Buddhist texts, typically consist of an act of piety and/or a gift given to the buddha by the Bodhisattva, followed by the Bodhisattva's solemn resolution to attain enlightenment and become a buddha, and the buddha's response in the form of a prediction that the Bodhisattva will eventually attain that goal. These formulaic elements can be discerned in the fragmentary remnants of most of the verses translated below. For example, verse 3, ". . . in an incalculable eon from now, as the lion of the Śākya clan and a man of the Ikṣvāku lineage, you will save gods and men," preserves part of the Dīpaṅkara Buddha's prediction; verse 4, ". . . very precious. Placing an antelope skin before the Teacher, I asked him for ultimate enlightenment" describes the Bodhisattva's offering to a previous buddha; and verse 5, ". . . and made a resolution to attain enlightenment . . . will be a buddha . . . " is part of the Bodhisattva's resolution.

Since this passage consists of verses, it was probably preceded by a prose passage describing the same events, this being a common pattern in Buddhist Sanskrit literature, for example in the *Mahāvastu*, where a narrative prose passage is often followed by a restatement or summary in verse. Moreover, this pattern is followed in a later part of this manuscript (section 4), where the enumeration of the eons in which each buddha lived is first presented in prose and then restated in verse. Comparisons with the similar texts, especially the second *Many Buddhas Sūtra* in the *Mahāvastu*, suggest that this hypothetical prose passage would have been the first main section of the sūtra. This would have been preceded by a framing introduction (*nidāna*) in which Ānanda, to whom the Buddha addresses the entire text, asks Śākyamuni how he became a buddha. If this hypothetical reconstruction is correct, the amount of text lost at the top of the scroll would not have been too large, so that the majority of the text has apparently been preserved.

Section 2: Śākyamuni's Four Courses of Development under Previous Buddhas

In this section Śākyamuni reveals under which of the previous buddhas he pursued each of the four stages (*caria* = Skt *caryā*) of his bodhisattva career. These stages are here called the course of *natural character* (*pragidi* = Skt *prakṛti*), the course of the *solemn resolution* (*praṇisi* = *pranidhi*), the course of *development* (*vivaṭaṇa* = *vivartana*), and the course of *purity* (*śukra* = *śukra*). Many Buddhist texts enumerate the stages of a bodhisattva's progress toward buddhahood, including influential Mahāyāna works such as the *Stages of the Bodhisattva* (*Bodhisattvabhūmi*) and the *Ten Stages* (*Daśabhūmika*), but the formulations vary widely. Most of them enumerate four, seven, or ten courses or stages, and the closest parallels to the four stages enumerated in our text are found, as would be expected, in the *Mahāvastu* and *Past Deeds of Buddha*. Both of those texts contain similar lists of four stages, but their names and formulation differ considerably from those of our text.

Our text merely lists the four courses in relation to the buddhas under whom the Bodhisattva practiced them without defining or explaining them. The similar lists in the *Mahāvastu* and *Past Deeds of the Buddha* do provide descriptions of the courses, and this gives us at least an approximate idea of their meaning in the Gāndhārī text. The first course, *natural character*, is explained as referring to a period of preliminary training in which a bodhisattva manifests and exercises his inherently virtuous character by practicing the ten kinds of proper behavior, such as showing respect for his parents, elders, and religious men, honoring a buddha and his disciples, practicing generosity, and so on, even though he has not yet formulated a resolution for enlightenment.

The second course, the *resolution*,[366] is the period in which the bodhisattva utters one or more solemn vows, in one or several lifetimes, to achieve enlightenment and become a buddha.

The third and fourth courses of the Gāndhārī text differ from those listed in the two parallel texts. The third is here called *development*, presumably referring to a period in which a bodhisattva develops his moral character and wisdom in order to progress toward fulfilling his resolve and attaining his goal. In the other texts the third course is called *conformation* (*anuloma*), in which a bodhisattva conforms to his resolution by behaving in a way that will lead to success.

The fourth and final course in our text is named *purity*, presumably referring to a phase in which a bodhisattva follows a pure and chaste life, perfecting his spiritual virtues to the point that he is ready to become a buddha. In the *Mahāvastu*, however, the fourth course is called *non-returning* (*avivartana*), referring to the stage at which a bodhisattva cannot revert to lower stages and is certain to achieve his goal.[367]

While on the one hand the Gāndhārī *Many Buddhas Sūtra* lacks the definitions of the four courses that are provided by the two parallel texts, on the other hand it is the only one of them that specifies exactly which of them the Bodhisattva followed under each buddha. However, there is near the end of the corresponding *Mahāvastu* passage one verse that summarizes the number of buddhas under whom the Bodhisattva followed each of the four courses.[368] This verse closely resembles the summary verse at the end of this section of the Gāndhārī text, but since the preceding text does not mention under which buddhas the Bodhisattva practiced the four courses, the summary verse seems irrelevant and out of context in the *Mahāvastu*; so much so, in fact, that its point was not realized by previous interpreters and translators and has only become apparent in light of the recently discovered Gāndhārī text. Such internal inconsistencies are once again typical of the loose and flexible character of Buddhist texts, exemplifying the familiar principle of "expansion and contraction." The summary verse in the *Mahāvastu* implies the existence of a full exposition of the relevant material, suggesting that the composer or compiler of the *Mahāvastu* was familiar with the background of the summary verse, even though he did not see fit to include the details in his text.

One point in this section that may seem strange at first sight is sentence 14, the last one before the concluding summary verse, in which we are told that "under Lord Maitreya, Śākyamuni as a bodhisattva practiced the course of purity."[369] The reader may well wonder how it could it be that Śākyamuni, while still a bodhisattva, practiced the course of purity under another buddha who is to attain enlightenment long after him. The answer lies in the legend that Maitreya had originally been destined to become a buddha before Śākyamuni, but when Śākyamuni stood before Buddha Puṣya on one foot while chanting a verse of praise for seven days, he won so much good karma that he jumped ahead of Maitreya in the race to buddhahood. Thus the passage here apparently refers to the future Śākyamuni's performance of acts of piety and purity in the presence of the future Maitreya at a time when they were both still bodhisattvas.

This section, like all the ones that follow it, is structured according to a sequence of fourteen or fifteen pattern sentences, which in most cases are identical except for the name and the specific information about each buddha. However, there are occasional minor inconsistencies; for example, the second sentence of this section is structured quite differently from all the others and is phrased in the first rather than the third person as elsewhere. Such minor variations in wording have been retained in the translation of this and subsequent sections in order to give an accurate sense of the original, even though in most cases they have no great significance for the meaning of the text, being rather manifestations of the rough-and-ready character of many Gandhāran manuscripts.

Another surprising peculiarity in this section is the presence of the familiar expansion formula "and so on, at length" (*eva vistareṇa* = Skt *evaṃ vistareṇa*) between the sentences concerning Buddha Śākyamuni I and Buddha Tiṣya. This formula is unexpected in this position, since the text seems to be otherwise complete. However, this is precisely the position where the two buddhas, Arthadarśin and Puṣya, who are absent in the sequence of the Gāndhārī manuscript, appear in the parallel passage in *Past Deeds of the Buddha* and, with a slight variation in order, in the *Mahāvastu* parallel as well. It would seem, therefore, that the scribe was referring here to an optional expanded version of the text in which the two extra buddhas are to be inserted. This confirms that the sort of inconsistencies between different versions of such texts represent ancient variants and that the ancient scribes and scholars were aware of them and had to develop techniques to deal with them, just as modern philologists have to.

Section 3: Lifespans of the Buddhas

The lifespan of the buddhas was a matter of considerable interest to early Buddhists, not surprisingly in light of the problem of the absent Buddha discussed above. The presence of a buddha on earth is considered a rare and wondrous blessing, but it also gives rise to a pervasive anxiety about what will happen when that buddha passes into nirvāṇa. The summary verse at the end of this section states that some buddhas lived for an entire eon by means of their supernatural powers or by virtue of their karma, while others chose to "disregard" both their powers and their karma and pass into nirvāṇa before the end of the eon in which they lived. This calls to mind a much-discussed and rather mysterious passage in the *Great Nirvāṇa Sūtra* in which Ānanda fails, under the influence of the evil spirit Māra, to request the Buddha at the appropriate time to remain on earth until the end of the eon.[370] The Buddha tells Ānanda that, had he only asked him, he would have done so. A buddha who would voluntarily remain on earth thus seems to have been the ideal of early Buddhists. Within the lineage of fifteen buddhas that our text describes, the second buddha, Sarvābhibhū, did so, and probably also the first buddha, Dīpaṅkara, although the relevant passage is in a lost part of the scroll. In general, the lifespans of the successive buddhas gradually decrease,[371] from many thousands of years for the earlier buddhas to only eighty years for Śākyamuni.[372]

Most of the buddhas, at least eleven of the fourteen discussed in this regard, are said to have remained alive "together with their community of monks." But the second buddha, Sarvābhibhū, is reported to have remained only with his personal attendant, while the corresponding information about the first and third buddhas is lost. Similarly, most of the buddhas (ten of fourteen) are said to have remained alive "out of compassion for the world," but in the case of at least two of them (Krakucchanda and Kāśyapa; the information for Padmottara and Atyuccagāmin is lost) this specification is absent. The significance of these variations remains unclear, as they are not explained here or in the other related texts.

In this section, even more than in the previous one, the format of the sentences is in several regards not entirely regular. For instance, some of the buddhas, such as Dīpaṅkara and Tiṣya, are accorded a full set of titles as "tathāgata, arhat, and completely enlightened buddha," while others have only the honorific "Lord" (*bhagavān*) attached to their names. In other places, the order of the elements within the formulaic sentence is inconsistent. But again, there is no doctrinal significance in these variations.

Also unusual is the verse inserted after the first two sentences. Its significance is also uncertain, since most of it is lost.

Section 4: The Eons in Which the Buddhas Lived

This section comprises two subparts, the first providing the basic information in prose and the second restating it in verse form. The first part simply reports the eon in which each buddha lived, as counted back from the present Fortunate Eon. The intervals between buddhas in the period covered in this text are constantly decreasing: the first two lived an "uncountable" eon and ten million eons,[373] respectively, before the present eon, whereas the ninth and tenth buddhas both lived in the same eon, only thirty-one eons ago. In the present eon, three buddhas have already lived, one is presently (in narrative time) still living, and (at least) one more, Maitreya, is still to come.

The fifteen verses in the second part of this section restate the eon of each buddha along with poetic characterizations of the buddhas. In most if not all of these verses, the epithets applied to each buddha explain, directly or by some etymological hint, the significance or derivation of his name.[374] For example, in the third verse Padmottara is compared to an unsullied lotus, obviously referring to the meaning of his name, "Supreme Lotus." Similarly, in the eighth verse Vipaśyin, "Insightful," is described as "all-seeing." In several of the verses, however, the connection between the description and the name is veiled, indirect, or obscure. For instance, in verse 7 Tiṣya is said to be the "supreme among all beings" (*utamo sarvasatvaṇa*), which may be intended to suggest a punning or pseudo-etymological connection between the name Tiṣya and the word *atiśaya* "preeminence, excellence." In a few verses, there is no evident connection between the name of the buddha and his characterization. If any such etymological comments were intended here, they remain obscure due to lacunae and other problems in the text as well as our still-incomplete understanding of the Gāndhārī language.

Section 5: The Social Classes of the Buddhas

The concluding verse of this section explains that buddhas are always born in one of the two highest social classes (*varṇa*) of traditional Indian society, namely the *brahman* priests and scholars and the *kṣatriya* warriors, nobility, and royalty. All the other relevant texts agree on this point. Even though the Buddha criticized the rigid hierarchy of the brahman-dominated society of his time, it must have seemed only natural in the social context that a Buddha would belong to the higher classes. This hierarchical principle is expanded on in some parallel texts,[375] which explain that buddhas are born as brahmans during historical periods in which brahmans are considered the highest class, and as kṣatriyas when that class is at the top of the social hierarchy. In our text, two of the kṣatriya buddhas, Sarvābhibhū and Atyuccagāmin, are further characterized as "anointed king" and "wheel-turning king," respectively, to emphasize their high status.

Texts representing the point of view of the Vedic and Brahmanical tradition invariably present the brahmans as the unchallenged elite of the social hierarchy. But Buddhist texts often imply that kṣatriyas are superior, for example putting them before brahmans in their lists of the four social groups: kṣatriya, brahman, *vaiśya* (merchants and tradesmen), and *śūdra* (servants and menial workers). The Buddhist promotion of the kṣatriya class reflects a desire to win the favor of the royalty and nobility, whose patronage was crucially important for the survival and spread of Buddhist institutions, whereas the demotion of the brahman class reflects the Buddhist distaste for their ritualistic belief system, especially since it involves animal sacrifice.

Section 6: The Assemblies of the Buddhas

All texts of this genre enumerate the assemblies of followers for each buddha, but the number of assemblies attributed to each buddha and the number of monks who attended them vary considerably. Most often, each buddha is reported to have had three such assemblies, with varying numbers of disciples at each one. In our text, however, the lists of assemblies are inconsistent and somewhat puzzling. In only one case, Śikhin, is a third assembly mentioned, but here the text reports only the first and third assembly, without mentioning a second one. Two other buddhas, Dīpaṅkara and Viśvabhū, are credited with two assemblies. For all the others, only one assembly is explicitly referred to, but for six of them (Padmottara through Vipaśyin) the assembly is labeled as "his first assembly," as if to imply that there were subsequent ones.[376] It would therefore seem that the scribe was engaging here in silent abbreviation, providing only a partial listing of the data, presumably on the assumption that the reader would be able to supply the missing information from memory. This is however rather surprising, since this information is not part of the basic knowledge that all readers would be likely to know, and moreover it is subject to considerable variation in different texts. Could it simply be that the scribe was getting tired as he neared the end of his text?

Section 7: Duration of the Buddhas' Dharma

As we have seen, the duration of the teaching of the Dharma was an urgent concern for ancient Buddhists, because the Buddha had predicted that it would be corrupted and forgotten some centuries after his parinirvāṇa. It is therefore not surprising that some, though not all, of the various texts that describe past and future buddhas include among their topic headings the period during which the Dharma would be remembered after each buddha had revealed it. The Dharma itself is eternal and unchanging, and each buddha rediscovers and teaches the exact same Dharma in his time; it is only the memory of the Dharma, in the fallible mind of humans, that is unstable. The long periods in which the Dharma has been lost are the darkest of times, so that living while the Dharma is still remembered is the greatest blessing next to the even rarer privilege of living while a buddha is present on earth.

In our text, only some remnants of this section survive at the badly damaged top of the verso. All that remains are parts of the accounts for the first five buddhas, and the actual number of years that the Dharma survived is preserved in only two of them. Even the basic pattern of each sentence is not entirely clear, as the word preceding "proclaimed" is illegible in all of the sentences and cannot yet be satisfactorily reconstructed.

The approximately parallel text incorporated in *Past Deeds of the Buddha*, which for the most part agrees with our text in overall structure, concludes with this topic heading. Moreover, this topic is followed there by an overall summary verse (*uddāna*) listing the topic headings, the last of which is the duration of the Dharma. This means that the corresponding section in our text was in all probability also the last one, so that the amount of text that has been lost at the end would not have been very large. The remainder of the duration of the Dharma passage would probably have taken up some seven or eight lines, following by a typical sūtra-concluding formula along the lines of "Thus spoke the Lord. The monks were delighted and rejoiced at what the Lord had said." If this is correct, the amount of text lost on the missing part of the verso of the scroll was probably not more than ten lines in all. This is considerably less than what was lost on the top of the recto, which would have included the introductory frame narrative and a prose account of the Bodhisattva's encounters with the previous buddhas. The larger amount of text missing on the recto would mean that some part of the upper section of the verso had been left blank, perhaps about a quarter of the length of the original scroll.

The Many Buddhas Sūtra[377]

1. Encounters with Previous Buddhas

... I asked ... such an incomparable ... was done ... will be a buddha ... [2][378]

... in an incalculable eon from now, as the lion of the Śākya clan and a man of the Ikṣvāku lineage, you will save gods and men. [3]

... very precious. Placing an antelope skin before the Teacher, I asked him for ultimate enlightenment. [4]

... and made a resolution to attain enlightenment ... will be a buddha ... [5]

... placed before ... By the ripening of this act, gold rained ... [6][379]

... and made a resolution for enlightenment ... will be a buddha ... [11]

... obtained. I gave it to the sage Viśvabhū and his community ... supreme enlightenment ... [12]

... the finest food ... obtained ... [13]

... possession [?] of Krakucchanda, who knows the world ... May I attain this ultimate enlightenment. [14]

... attained supremacy in the world, the unsurpassed Lion of the Śākyas. [15]

2. The Four Courses of Development

1. [Ānanda, under Lord Dīpaṅkara, Śākyamuni as a bodhisattva] practiced the course of natural character.
2. Under Lord Sarvābhibhū, I [practiced the course of natural character.]
3. Ānanda, under Lord [Padmottara], Śākyamuni as a bodhisattva practiced the course of natural character.
4. Ānanda, under Lord Atyuccagāmin, Śākyamuni as a bodhisattva [practiced] the course of natural character.
5. Ānanda, under Lord [Yaśottara], Śākyamuni as a bodhisattva practiced the course of natural character.
6. [Ānanda,] under [Lord] Śākyamuni (I), [Śākyamuni (II) as a bodhisattva practiced the course of the resolution]; and so on, at length.
7. Ānanda, under Lord Tiṣya, Śākyamuni as a bodhisattva [practiced the course of . . .][380]
8. Ānanda, under Lord Vipaśyin, Śākyamuni as a bodhisattva practiced the course of . . .
9. Ānanda, [under Lord Śikhin], Śākyamuni as a bodhisattva practiced the course of development.
10. [Ānanda, under Lord Viśvabhū, Śākyamuni] as a bodhisattva practiced the course of development.
11. Ānanda, under Lord Krakucchanda, Śākyamuni [as a bodhisattva practiced the course of purity.]
12. Ānanda, under Lord Konākamuni, Śākyamuni as a bodhisattva [practiced] the course of purity.
13. [Ānanda, under Lord Kāśyapa], Śākyamuni as a bodhisattva practiced the course of purity.
14. Ānanda, under [Lord] Maitreya, [Śākyamuni as a bodhisattva] practiced [the course of purity.]

[Summary verse:] Regarding this, it is said:

> Under five [buddhas, the Bodhisattva practiced] the course of natural character; [under . . . buddhas, the course of the resolution; under . . . buddhas, the course of development; and under four buddhas] he grew in purity.

3. Lifespans of the Buddhas

1. Ānanda, Dīpaṅkara [remained] as a tathāgata, arhat, and completely enlightened [buddha for an entire eon, together with . . .], out of compassion [for the world].
2. Ānanda, Sarvābhibhū remained as a tathāgata in ancient times . . . for an entire eon, together with his attendant, out of compassion for the world.

[Fragmentary verse on lifespans of buddhas:]

> . . . . will be . . . Afterward, tathāgatas pass into nirvāṇa.

3. [Ānanda, Padmottara remained as a tathāgata for . . . thousand years, together with his . . . , out of compassion for the world.][381]
4. [Ānanda, Atyuccagāmin] remained [as a tathāgata] for . . . thousand years, together with his community of monks, out of compassion for the world.
5. Ānanda, Lord Yaśottara remained as a tathāgata, arhat, and completely enlightened buddha for . . . thousand years, out of compassion for the world, together with his community of monks.
6. Ānanda, Lord Śākyamuni (I) [remained] for eighty thousand years, together with his community of monks, out of compassion for the world.
7. Ānanda, Tiṣya remained as a tathāgata, arhat, and completely

enlightened buddha for five hundred years, together with [his community of] monks, out of compassion for the world.

8. Ānanda, Lord Vipaśyin remained for eighty thousand years, together with his community of monks, out of compassion for the world.
9. [Ānanda,] Lord [Śikhin] remained for seventy thousand years, together with his community of monks, out of compassion for the world.
10. Ānanda, Lord [Viśvabhū] remained for sixty thousand years, together with his community of monks, out of compassion for the world.
11. Ānanda, Lord Krakucchanda remained for forty thousand years, together with his community of monks.
12. Ānanda, Lord Konākamuni remained for [thirty] thousand years, together with his community of monks, [out of compassion][382] for the world.
13. Ānanda, Lord Kāśyapa remained for twenty thousand years, [together with] his community [of monks].
14. And I, Ānanda, will now remain eighty years, out of compassion for the world, together with my community of monks.

[Summary verse: Regarding this,] it is said:

> Some [buddhas] remained [for an entire eon] by their supernatural powers; some remained by their karma. Others, disregarding supernatural powers and karma, reached nirvāṇa during [an eon].

4. The Eons in Which the Buddhas Lived

1. [Ānanda], Lord Dīpaṅkara lived in an uncountable eon [before] the [present] Fortunate Eon.

2. Ānanda, Lord [Sarvābhibhū] lived a full ten million eons before the Fortunate Eon.
3. Ānanda, Lord Padmottara lived a full hundred thousand eons before the Fortunate Eon.
4. Ānanda, Lord Atyuccagāmin lived a full thousand eons before the Fortunate Eon.
5. Ānanda, Lord Yaśottara lived a full five hundred eons before the Fortunate Eon.
6. Ānanda, Lord Śākyamuni (I) lived a full hundred eons before the Fortunate Eon.
7. Ānanda, Lord Tiṣya lived a full ninety-five eons before the Fortunate Eon.
8. [Ānanda], Lord Vipaśyin lived a full ninety-five eons before the Fortunate Eon.
9. Ānanda, Lord Śikhin lived a full thirty-one eons [before the Fortunate Eon].
10. Lord Viśvabhū also lived [a full] thirty-one eons [before the Fortunate Eon].
11. Ānanda, Lord Krakucchanda lived in this Fortunate Eon.
12. Ānanda, Lord Konākamuni lived in this Fortunate Eon.
13. Ānanda, Lord Kāśyapa lived in this Fortunate Eon.
14. [Ānanda,] I, Śākyamuni, am living [in this Fortunate Eon].
15. Ānanda, Lord Maitreya will live in this Fortunate Eon.

[Verse restatement:] Regarding this, it is said:

> . . . lived [Dīpaṅkara] the insightful (?) buddha. [1]
>
> . . . the wise Sarvābhibhū lived as Lord Buddha, who knew
> the mental inclinations [of others]. [2]
>
> In the [one hundred thousandth] eon [before now] there

lived the unsurpassed buddha named Padmottara, who was unsullied [like] a lotus. [3]

In the thousandth eon [before now] there lived the conqueror Lord Atyuccagāmin, who attained the heights of glory[383] and spoke with the Brahma voice. [4]

In the five hundredth eon [before now] there lived Lord [Yaśottara], who called out to gods and men, the finest of orators. [5]

Five hundred eons ago there lived the unsurpassed Buddha Śākyamuni (I), the bull of the Śākyas, who bore the thirty-two excellent marks. [6]

In the ninety-[fifth] eon [before now] there lived [the Buddha] Tiṣya . . . , supreme among all beings, the finest of orators. [7]

In the ninety-first eon [before now] was born the Buddha Vipaśyin, all-seeing, the unsurpassed great man . . . [8]

In the thirty-first [eon before now] there lived the unsurpassed Śikhin, who gleamed like the moon on the fifteenth day,[384] complete and unsullied. [9]

In the [same eon] was Lord Viśvabhū, famed in every quarter,[385] who had gained control over the [ten] powers, the destroyer of defilements and impurities. [10]

In [this] eon there lived Lord Krakucchanda, the prime leader of the world, great in wisdom, . . . of Brahma. [11]

[In this eon] there lived here the supreme Konākamuni, praised . . . by the sages, [himself] the foremost sage.[386] [12]

[In this eon there lived] . . . Kāśyapa, the leader of the world, wondrous and miraculous, the guide of the community of monks. [13]

[In this eon] Śākyamuni lived as the Buddha, destroyer of Māra's army, out of compassion for the world. [14]

. . . and in the Fortunate Eon, in the time to come, there will be Maitreya, the leader of the world and the guide of the community of monks. [15]

[Summary verse:]

[The buddhas] have been proclaimed in the sequence of the eons. Those eons in which buddhas are born are the supreme eons. [16]

5. The Social Classes of the Buddhas

1. [Ānanda], Lord [Dīpaṅkara] went forth[387] from a brahman family.
2. Ānanda, Lord Sarvābhibhū, an anointed king, [went forth] from a kṣatriya family.
3. [Ānanda, Lord Padmottara] went forth from [a brahman] family.
4. Ānanda, Lord Atyuccagāmin, a wheel-turning king, [went forth from] a kṣatriya [family].
5. Ānanda, Lord Yaśottara went forth from a brahman family.
6. Ānanda, Lord Śākyamuni (I) went forth from a kṣatriya [family].
7. Ānanda, Lord Tiṣya went forth from a brahman family.
8. Ānanda, Lord Vipaśyin [went forth] from a kṣatriya family.
9. Ānanda, Lord Śikhin went forth from a kṣatriya family.

10. Ānanda, Lord Viśvabhū went forth from a kṣatriya family.
11. [Ānanda, Lord Krakucchanda] went forth from a brahman family.
12. Ānanda, Lord Konākamuni went forth [from a brahman family].
13. Ānanda, Lord Kāśyapa too went forth from a brahman family.
14. [I] went forth [from a kṣatriya family].
15. Ānanda, Lord Maitreya will go forth from a brahman family.

[Summary verse:] Regarding this, it is said:

> . . . [buddhas are always] kṣatriyas or brahmans; they never belong to any other class.

6. The Assemblies of the Buddhas

1. [Ānanda, Lord Dīpaṅkara had] a great assembly of . . . disciples and a great assembly of 5 million[388] disciples.
2. [Ānanda,] Lord [Sarvābhibhū] had a great assembly of 14 billion disciples.
3. [Ānanda, Lord Padmottara] had a great assembly of 700,000 disciples, which was his first assembly.
4. [Ānanda, Lord Atyuccagāmin] had a great assembly of 655 million disciples, which was his first [assembly].
5. Ānanda, Lord [Yaśottara] had a great assembly of 2 million disciples, which was his first [assembly].
6. [Ānanda], Lord [Śākyamuni (I)] had a great assembly of 12,500 disciples, which was his first [assembly].
7. [Ānanda, Lord Tiṣya] had a great assembly of 655 million disciples, which was his first [assembly].
8. Ānanda, Lord Vipaśyin had his first great assembly of 6.8 million disciples, his first assembly.
9. [Ānanda, Lord Śikhin] had a great assembly of 6.8 million disciples. His third [*sic*] assembly had 100,000 disciples.
10. [Ānanda], Lord [Viśvabhū] had a great assembly of 100,000 dis-

ciples. His second assembly had 9 million [disciples].

11. Ānanda, Lord Krakucchanda [had] a great [assembly] of 40,000 disciples.
12. [Ānanda], Lord [Konākamuni] had a great assembly of 30,000 disciples.
13. Ānanda, [Lord] Kāśyapa had [a great assembly of 20,000 disciples].
14. And I, Ānanda, now [have a great assembly] of 1,250 [disciples].

7. Duration of the Buddhas' Dharma

1. [Ānanda, after Lord Dīpaṅkara had entered into parinirvāṇa, for . . . years the true] Dharma remained as it had been proclaimed . . .
2. Ānanda, after Lord Sarvābhibhū had entered into parinirvāṇa, [for . . . years the true Dharma remained as it had been] proclaimed . . .
3. Ānanda, after Lord Padmottara had entered into parinirvāṇa, for ten thousand years the true [Dharma remained as it had been proclaimed . . .]
4. Ānanda, after Lord [Atyuccagāmin] had entered into parinirvāṇa, for twenty thousand years the true Dharma remained [as it had been proclaimed . . .]
5. [Ānanda, after Lord Yaśottara] had entered into parinirvāṇa . . .

9. A Commentary on the Sūtra of Chanting Together

The *Sūtra of Chanting Together* (*Saṅgīti Sūtra*) is one of the most important of the "long sūtras" collected in the *Dīrghāgama/Dīgha-nikāya*. Its special significance is indicated by its inclusion in the group of six sūtras placed at the beginning of the Sanskrit *Dīrghāgama* of the Sarvāstivāda school, constituting a special subset of "foundational sūtras" that was particularly popular in Central Asian Buddhism. The *Sūtra of Chanting Together* is extant in Pali, Sanskrit, and Chinese versions and was also the object of commentaries in these languages.

The sūtra presents a systematically arranged digest of the main principles and technical terminology of early Buddhism, structured in a way that is meant to facilitate memorization and recitation. It consists of ten sections of enumerated sets—single items, pairs, triads, and so forth, up to sets of ten. The total number of sets is 205 in the Pali version and 139 in the Chinese, while the number of sets in each section ranges from a minimum of only one in the Chinese (the nines and tens) and two in Pali (nines and tens), to 37 in Chinese (threes) and 50 in Pali (threes and fours). By way of example, the following are the topic headings for sets 7 through 12 in the section of sets of four in the Gāndhārī version: the four kinds of grasping (*upādāna*), the four bodily ties (*kāyagrantha*), the four thorns (*śalya*), the four kinds of birth (*yoni*), the four foundations of mindfulness (*smṛtyupasthāna*), and the four correct efforts (*samyakpradhāna*).

Like all sūtras, the *Sūtra of Chanting Together* begins with a narrative introduction specifying where and on what occasion it was originally spoken. But the format of the sūtra's introduction is unique. It reports that the Buddha and his followers were in the city of Pāvā, the capital of the Malla people near Kuśinagara. After being served a meal by their hosts, they went to a brand-new meeting hall, which the Buddha consecrated by preaching long into the night. After the Mallas left, the Buddha excused himself because his back was sore and asked his favored disciple Śāriputra to teach the monks about the Dharma on his behalf. This event took place shortly after the death in Pāvā of Nāthaputra, the teacher of the Nirgranthas, a rival sect to the Buddhists who are the ancestors of the Jains. Immediately after Nāthaputra's death, his Nirgrantha followers had fallen into bitter disagreements as to who understood his teachings properly, so that their community was in disarray and lost the support of its lay followers. With this negative example in mind, Śāriputra proposed that the monks should "chant together" (*saṃgāyitabbaṃ*) the Buddha's teachings in harmony and without dispute, to ensure that their pure way of life should be long-lasting and would promote the benefit and happiness of human beings and gods. They then proceeded to chant the essential terms and concepts of the Dharma according to the numerical pattern described above. The sūtra not only describes its circumstances and purpose of its original recitation, but it also became the model for the periodic communal recitations of the entire canon that took place immediately after the Buddha's death and then at various points in the later history of Buddhism, even down to modern times. Such recitations are still known by the same term as the sūtra itself, *saṅgīti*.

In practical terms, the *Sūtra of Chanting Together* serves as a mnemonic summary of and index to the basic Buddhist teachings. This method of presentation is particularly suited to and characteristic of the oral mode of teaching, learning, and preserving information that prevailed in the early centuries of Buddhism, when texts were kept in oral form only. Even after the canon began to be set down in writing at some time around the first century BCE, the oral form of the texts was retained, and communal chanting of them continued to be an important part of the life of the saṅgha. In this, as in other respects, the introduction of writing did not replace oral learning but only supplemented it.

In its reduction of the principles of the Dharma to a strategically ordered set of terms and concepts, the *Sūtra of Chanting Together* represents the Buddhist preference for structured and comprehensive formulations. In this respect, it can be seen as a forerunner of the abhidharma literature, and indeed, the Sanskrit commentary on it, the *Saṅgītiparyāya*, became one of the seven basic texts of the Abhidharmapiṭaka of the Sarvāstivādia school.

The several versions of the *Sūtra of Chanting Together* preserved in Pali, Sanskrit (incompletely), Chinese, and now, in the form of a commentary, in Gāndhārī, are broadly similar in their format and contents, but the variation in the number of sets within each of the ten numerical categories, and especially in their ordering, has provided important clues about the historical and sectarian relationships among these versions. While the contents and order of the Pali, Sanskrit, and Chinese versions are all quite different from each other, the structure of the underlying Gāndhārī sūtra is almost identical to that of the Chinese. For example, sets 7–12 of the section of the fours in the Gāndhārī manuscript, as listed above, correspond exactly to the Chinese, whereas the corresponding sets in the Pali version are numbered 35, 34, [missing], 36, 1, and 2, respectively, while in Sanskrit they are numbers 39, 40, [missing], 29, 1, and 2. The close correspondence between the Gāndhārī and Chinese versions is both a powerful argument for the attribution of the Gāndhārī text to the Dharmaguptaka school and a point of evidence in favor of the Gāndhārī hypothesis, according to which many early Chinese Buddhist texts were directly translated from or derived from Gandhāran archetypes.[389]

Comparison with Other Commentaries

Three commentaries on the *Sūtra of Chanting Together* are now known. The Pali commentary is part of Buddhaghosa's commentary on the complete *Dīgha-nikāya*, the *Sumaṅgalavilāsinī*,[390] representing the Theravāda school. The *Saṅgītiparyāya*, extant in Sanskrit in fragments[391] and in a complete Chinese translation, belongs to the Sarvāstivāda school, while the newly discovered Gāndhārī commentary presented here presumably belongs, as we have seen, to the Dharmaguptakas.

All three commentaries are entirely independent of each other. The Sanskrit/Chinese *Saṅgītiparyāya* and Pali *Sumaṅgalavilāsinī* typically explain the text word by word or phrase by phrase, defining the individual terms and expanding on them, for instance by providing examples, enumerating subtypes of the terms, or spelling out their further implications. The Gāndhārī commentary on each topic set similarly begins with explanations of the set as a whole and of each of its members. These preliminary explanations typically employ such techniques as etymologies of the terms, synonyms or glosses for them, expansion and paraphrase, and similes or metaphors.

To this extent, the Gāndhārī commentary does not differ in structure and principles from the other two. But in many cases, it also offers an additional feature that is not found in the others, an explanatory technique that can be referred to as "categorial mapping" or "categorial reduction."[392] In this technique, the members of a given set are mapped onto the members of another set, typically one of the fundamental categories such as the four noble truths, the eight components of the noble path or the three categories or divisions of the path (conduct, concentration, wisdom), the three enemies (passion, hatred, delusion), or the four infinite sublime states (loving kindness, compassion, joy, equanimity). For example, in the first text sample below, the five faculties are mapped onto the three divisions of the path as follows:

the first faculty, faith, is placed in the conduct division; the second and third faculties, energy and concentration, in the concentration division; and the fourth and fifth faculties, mindfulness and wisdom, in the wisdom division. Very often, a single set will be mapped onto several other basic sets; thus, the previous mapping of the set of five faculties onto the three divisions of the path is followed by two more mappings of the same set, first onto the individual members of the eightfold path and then onto the three forms of realization.

Beyond this mapping system that is applied to the individual members of each set, the commentary also sometimes employs a higher level mapping of the sets as a whole. According to this system, each sequence of ten sets is followed by a "summary statement" (*sakṣito maṃtro* = Skt *saṃkṣipta-mantra*) in which each of the sets is mapped onto a master category, usually one of the four noble truths. This super-mapping thus constitutes a framework for the entire commentary in the form of the four truths, into which the individual components of the Dharma are placed and linked to each other. Thus the two levels of categorial mapping serve as an edifice that not only preserves and groups together the essential elements of the Dharma but also illustrates their interconnectedness in a single integrated system.

Although the technique of categorial mapping is not used in the Sanskrit and Pali commentaries on the *Sūtra of Chanting Together*, it is not entirely without parallel in the other Buddhist canonical literatures. Most significantly, it has notable similarities in this and other respects to two paracanonical[393] Pali texts, the *Peṭakopadesa* ("Teaching of the Tipiṭaka") and *Nettippakaraṇa* ("The Guidebook"), which also construct complex systems for the interpretation of the Tipiṭaka. Previous scholars have noted that these two books are anomalous among Pali texts in various respects, and some[394] have proposed that they were translated into Pali from an archetype in a north Indian language. The discovery of Gāndhārī commentaries that employ similar exegetical techniques, including not only the present commentary but also the commentary presented in the following translation, suggests that *Peṭakopadesa* and *Nettippakaraṇa* or their archetypes may have originated in a Gandhāran tradition that specialized in this method of interpretation. In any case, it is now clear that Gandhāran Buddhism had a local school of textual exegesis that may have exerted a significant influence on other regional Buddhisms.

Description of the Manuscript

The commentary scroll, British Library fragment 15, was written in the usual fashion, first on the recto from the top of the scroll to the bottom, then continuing on the verso in the opposite direction. Also as usual, it was rolled up from the bottom to the top so that the exposed outer portion of the roll, which contained the beginning and end of the text on the recto and verso sides respectively, has suffered the most damage. As a result, the surviving part of the scroll, about 115 centimeters long, begins in the sections on groups of three, preserves all of the fours through the sevens, and breaks off in the eights. This means that some three-quarters of the text is at least partially preserved, and probably more than that, since the missing sections are among the shortest ones, judging by the Chinese parallel. However, the surviving section of the scroll is far from complete. The top and both edges of the scroll are damaged, so that all 365 or so lines are more or less incomplete. Also, the rolled-up scroll broke into horizontal segments about four centimeters high due to its having been subjected to compression for two millennia, and part of the text has been lost at each of these breaks.

The physical damage is only one of the many challenges that interpreters of this manuscript face. Even where the text is visible, the letters are very small and none too clear. The scribe was no calligrapher, and the manuscript seems to have been written hastily. But above all, the unfamiliar character of the text and its highly technical character have posed the hardest problems, and the interpretation and preparation of a complete published edition is a long-term, ongoing project. The two sample passages presented below are preliminary and tentative, representing the collective efforts over several years of several members of the Early Buddhist Manuscripts Project research team, especially Collett Cox, Stefan Baums, and Timothy Lenz. Many uncertainties about the readings and interpretations of these passages remain, but in most cases at least the overall sense is more or less clear. The passages presented here were chosen on the grounds that they are relatively complete and typical of the text as a whole.

Passage 1: The Five Faculties

The set of five faculties (*idria* = Skt *indriya*) is the sixth set of five items in the Gāndhārī and Chinese version of the sūtra and the twenty-third set in the Pali version. After quoting the root text, formatted here in bold, the commentator begins by defining the head term *faculty* as a synonym of "control" or "sovereignty" (Skt *ādhipateya*) and then applies this definition separately to each of the five faculties. He then explains the relationship among the individual faculties, whereby each one promotes the following one. This topic, which is not addressed in the other commentaries on the sūtra, is characteristic of the concern of this commentary for establishing connections at all levels.

The next topic is a set of comparisons for the attitudes or relations that a practitioner should cultivate toward the five faculties: one should relate to faith as toward one's mother and so on. This and similar comparisons in other passages are again unique to this commentary. The commentator then explains how some of the faculties are the "nourishers" of the others, again exhibiting his interest in establishing linkages among individual members of sets.

The last three paragraphs of the commentary map the faculties onto the three divisions of the path (conduct, concentration, and wisdom), then onto the individual components of the eightfold path, and finally onto the set of three forms of realization.

Sample 2: The Six Roots of Argument

The set of the six roots of argument (*vivada-mula* = Skt *vivāda-mūla*) is the ninth set of six items in both the Gāndhārī and Chinese versions of the sūtra and the fifteenth set in the Pali. The commentary first alludes to the root text, but in an extremely abbreviated form, citing only the key terms describing each of the six roots. In the Pali and Chinese versions of the sūtra, each of the six roots of argument is accompanied by a long paragraph, identical in each of the six repetitions, describing their negative effects. In all probability, the Gāndhārī *Sūtra of Chanting Together* also contained these paragraphs, but the commentator did not deem it necessary to write them out, assuming that the reader would have been able to supply them from memory.

The abbreviated quotation of the sūtra is then summarized by a brief conclusion, "These are the roots (of argument)." The commentary then discusses the six roots of argument in four passes in which each root is mapped onto other basic doctrinal sets:

a. The six roots of argument are contrasted with the practices or states of mind that act as antidotes to them.
b. The six roots are mapped onto the three divisions of the path.
c. The six roots are mapped onto the set of the "three enemies," that is, desire, hatred, and delusion.
d. The six roots are mapped onto the two types of "passionate greed," that is, passionate greed for desire and passionate greed for views.

In this way, the set of the six roots are cross-referenced in the commentary with other established sets (though not all of these sets are included in the lists of the sūtra itself) to form an interlocking grid of terms, doctrines, and principles.

In the translation below, the full text of the sūtra passage in question, from which only the key terms are actually cited in the manuscript, is restored on the basis of the Pali version,[395] with the additions indicated in square brackets. Thus in the presentation of the first root of argument in the first paragraph of the translation, the manuscript actually reads only "angry, hostile."

A. The Five Faculties

[Root text]

The five faculties: [1] faith faculty, [2] energy faculty, [3] mindfulness faculty, [4] concentration faculty, [5] wisdom faculty.

[Definitions]

What does *faculty* mean? *Faculty* means the same thing as "control." The faith faculty belongs to those who have control of faith. The energy faculty belongs to those who have control of energy. The mindfulness [faculty] belongs to those who have control of mindfulness. The concentration faculty belongs to those who have control (of concentration). The wisdom faculty belongs to those who have control of wisdom.

[Relationships among the five items]

When one has faith, energy takes hold. When energy takes hold, mindfulness attends one. When one is attended by mindfulness, one's mind becomes concentrated. When one's mind is concentrated, one knows things as they really are. [This is] the wisdom faculty. Mindfulness . . .

[Comparisons with the five faculties]

One should relate to the faith faculty as toward one's mother. One should relate to the energy faculty as toward a servant—a comparison may be made to an army for [all] five faculties.[396] One should relate to the mindfulness faculty as toward a treasurer, to the concentration faculty as toward a king, [and] to the wisdom faculty as toward a guru.

[The faculties as nourishers of each other]

[The faith faculty] (?) is said to be proper conduct. The energy faculty is the nourisher of concentration. Mindfulness is the nourisher of wisdom. That nourishment is the path (?).

[The faculties mapped onto the three divisions of the path]
The conduct division [is correlated] with the faith faculty, the concentration division with the energy and concentration faculties, [and the wisdom division] with the mindfulness faculty and the wisdom faculty.

[The faculties mapped onto the individual members of the eightfold path]
[As for] the eightfold path: Correct intention, correct speech, correct action, and correct livelihood [are correlated] with the faith faculty, correct exertion with the energy faculty, correct mindfulness with the mindfulness faculty, correct concentration with the concentration faculty, and correct views with the wisdom faculty.

[The faculties mapped onto forms of realization]
. . . as for the realization of the nature of the body, [this is correlated] with the concentration faculty. As for the realization of correct views, [this is correlated] with the wisdom faculty. As for liberation from rebirth, [this is correlated] with all five [faculties]. . . . Energy and mindfulness are the nourishers.

b. The Six Roots of Argument

The [six] **roots of argument**: [First, sirs, a monk who is] **angry and hostile** [behaves disrespectfully and rudely toward the Teacher, behaves disrespectfully and rudely toward the Dharma and behaves disrespectfully and rudely toward the community of monks. He does not fulfill his training. A monk who behaves disrespectfully and rudely toward the Teacher, who behaves disrespectfully and rudely toward the Dharma, who behaves disrespectfully and rudely toward the community of monks, and who does not fulfill his training, he creates argument in the community, and argument leads to the detriment of many people, to the unhappiness of many people, to the disadvantage of many people, to the detriment and suffering of gods and humans. If, sirs, you were to observe such a root of argument within yourselves or among others, then you should exert yourselves to eliminate that root of argument. If, sirs, you were not to observe such a root of argument within yourselves or among others, then you should behave in such a way as to avoid being infected by it in the future. In this way the root of argument is eliminated, and in this way there will be no infection by the root of argument in the future.]

[Moreover, sirs, a monk who is] **negative and contentious** [behaves disrespectfully and rudely toward the Teacher, behaves disrespectfully and rudely toward the Dharma, and behaves disrespectfully and rudely toward the community of monks. He does not fulfill his training, etc.]

[Moreover, sirs, a monk who is] **jealous and envious** [behaves disrespectfully, etc.]

[Moreover, sirs, a monk who is] **devious and deceitful** [behaves disrespectfully, etc.]

[Moreover, sirs, a monk who is] **obstinate in his own views, clings to what is wrong, and finds it difficult to concede** [behaves disrespectfully, etc.]

[Moreover, sirs, a monk who] **has false views** [**and holds extreme views** behaves disrespectfully, etc.]

These are the roots [of argument].

[The six roots of argument and their specific antidotes]

Angry and hostile: [For this root of] argument, the antidote is physical acts of loving kindness.

Negative and contentious: [For this root of] argument, [the antidote is] verbal acts of loving kindness.

Jealous and envious: [For this root] of argument, [the antidote is] mental [acts] of loving kindness.

[These] are abhidharmic argument (?).[397]

Devious and deceitful: [For this root of] argument, [the antidote is] proper conduct.

Obstinate in his own views and . . . holds extreme views:[398] [For these roots of] argument, [the antidote is] correct views.

[The six roots of argument and the three divisions of the path as their antidotes]

Angry and hostile, negative and contentious, [jealous and envious: For these roots of] argument, [the antidote is the concentration group].

Devious and deceitful: [For this root of] argument, [the antidote is the conduct group.]

Obstinate in his own views . . . holds extreme views: [For these roots of] argument, [the antidote is] the wisdom group.

[The six roots of argument and the three enemies]

Angry and hostile and **negative and contentious**: [these are] on the side of hatred.

Jealous [and] envious and **deceitful** [**and hypocritical**: these are on the side of passion].

[Obstinate in his own views] . . . and **. . . holds extreme views**: here, these are on the side of delusion.

[The six roots of argument and the two types of greed]

Because of the first four [roots of argument], there is a passionate greed for desire. Because of the last two [roots of argument], there is a passionate greed for views. Because of these, argument . . .

10. A Commentary on Canonical Verses

THE BRITISH LIBRARY collection contains extensive remnants of commentaries of an unusual type, constituting one of the genres that are unique to Gandhāran Buddhist literature. These texts comment in detail on verses that in themselves are well known. Parallels for most of the verses are found in various popular collections such as the Pali *Dhammapada*, *Suttanipāta*, and *Theragāthā* and in the corresponding texts in Sanskrit, Gāndhārī, Chinese, and other languages. But in these commentaries, these diverse verses are mixed together in a way that is not found in other Buddhist literatures.

Verses of this type present the Dharma in an accessible form, communicating the basic ideas and moral principles of Buddhism. The Gāndhārī commentaries on these verses, however, are designed to promote an understanding of these simple verses at a more advanced

Figure 37. Section of British Library scroll 9 showing the text translated in sample a.

level. The style of explanation is similar to that of the commentary on the *Sūtra of Chanting Together* presented in the preceding translation. Typically, the commentaries first present a word-by-word or phrase-by-phrase explanation of the verse and then return to a series of "passes," as many as five or six for each verse, in each of which particular words or phrases are equated with members of basic Buddhist concept sets. Typically, the first pass after the preliminary explanation is introduced with the phrase "in short," indicating that the mappings to be introduced are to be understood as summaries of the initial interpretation. The subsequent passes are introduced by phrases such as "alternatively" or "otherwise," implying that the two or more mappings were recognized as equally valid.

The verses cited in these commentaries are introduced at the beginning of each section in an abbreviated form, usually by quoting only the first quarter of the verse, sometimes even less than that. The quotation is then followed by the introductory phrase, "Thus the sūtra; [now] the explanation" (*sūtro tatra ṇideśo*). It was obviously assumed that the intended readers would already know all of the verses by heart and at least understand their superficial meaning. The purpose of the commentary seems to have been to build on this basic textual knowledge by interpreting it within a more technical apparatus. Although we have no direct information about the curriculum of study for monks in the monasteries of ancient Gandhāra, we can imagine that commentaries such as this one were used at an intermediate level, where the trainees would begin to fit the basic texts that they had memorized into a more systematic framework. In this regard, these Gāndhārī commentaries are completely different from the corresponding Pali commentaries on texts of this type. For example, Buddhaghosa's well-known commentary on the *Dhammapada*[399] is largely concerned with explaining the circumstances in which the Buddha came to utter the verses and the karmic background of those circumstances. But there is no reference to any such background material in these Gāndhārī commentaries.

A more important difference is that the Gāndhārī texts concerned are not direct commentaries on any one text. These commentaries seem to have extracted verses from various sources, with no discernible sequence or obvious connection among the verses. The commentaries are not likely to be based on some otherwise unattested collection that contained the verses in the sequence in which they appear in the commentaries, because the position of these verses in different texts is consistently attested, not only in Pali, Sanskrit, and Chinese but even in Gāndhārī literature itself, for example in the *Dharmapada* collection now known in three Gāndhārī manuscripts. Therefore we seem to be dealing not with a single underlying text that is the primary object of the commentary but rather with a selection of verses culled, presumably by the commentator himself, to serve his pedagogical purposes.[400]

We would surely have a better sense of the conception and function of these commentaries if only they were complete. But as usual, we have only fragments of them from the surviving lower portions of the scroll, so that the beginning and end at the top of the scroll, which may have contained the title, introduction, and colophons, are lost. There is however one small fragment of a colophon which, to judge from its handwriting, probably belonged to one of these commentary scrolls. This mentions the name of its owner, a monk called Saṅghaśrava, plus the notation "twenty-five verses" (*gasae pacaviśadi 25*), presumably referring to a count of verses in a particular section of the text. The colophon also contains the word "book" (*postaga* = Skt *pustaka*), and to judge by similar colophons such as that of the Gāndhārī *Perfection of Wisdom* scroll (see translation 12), we would expect the name of the text to have preceded this word; but alas, that part of the colophon fragment is lost.[401]

We have three incomplete specimens of this genre among the scrolls of the British Library collection. The longest and best preserved one, the source of the samples presented here, is partly preserved in four fragments (British Library fragments 7, 9, 13, and 18) that were probably originally parts of three separate scrolls. These surviving fragments contain the commentaries on 43 verses covering 413 lines in all, most of which, as usual, are more or less incomplete. Since there is no parallel text with which to compare this manuscript, we have no way to know what proportion of it was lost, but it is clear that the complete text would have been quite long. This is the only case where we have remnants of more than one scroll from the same Gāndhārī text, so that here we can assume that we are dealing with a formal text that was written out in full for practical use rather than an incomplete, symbolic text. In any case, the prominence among the British Library scrolls of commentarial texts of this type, along with the *Sūtra of Chanting Together* commentary, indicates that this system of explication by mapping terms played a prominent role in the monastic curriculum in Buddhist Gandhāra.

Below are three specimens of commentaries on individual verses, chosen, as in the other selective presentations in this volume, on the grounds that they are both representative of the text as a whole and relatively complete. Even so, several lacunae and other uncertainties remain, as is always the case with Gāndhārī texts that lack parallels in other traditions.[402]

Sample a: Trade What Ages

The root verse of this section reads, "Trade what ages for the ageless, what burns for what cools, the supreme calm, the rest from all exertion." But as usual, only the first two words, corresponding to "what ages for the ageless" in the translation, are actually cited. Here and in the following extracts the missing portion of the verse is supplied in square brackets on the basis of the parallel texts in Pali and Sanskrit. The original verse is shown in bold as are the citations from it in the subsequent commentary.

This verse appears, with slight variations, in the Pali *Theragāthā* (v. 32) and is also attested in the Gāndhārī *Dharmapada* from Khotan.[403]

The commentary on the verse contains three passes. The first pass explains that the four nontechnical terms in the verse actually refer to various technical categories; for example, "what ages" is explained as referring to the five "aggregates of grasping," while "the ageless" is the sphere of nirvāṇa-without-remnant.[404] The second pass identifies five terms in the verse with the four noble truths, while the third presents an alternative interpretation in which three terms are said to represent the elimination of the three "courses" (*vataṇi* = Skt *vartani*), namely defilement, action, and suffering.

Sample b: Endowed with Proper Conduct

The root verse in this passage has only partial parallels in the Pali *Dhammapada* and Gāndhārī *Dharmapada* as well as in several other texts. The only complete parallel is found in an anomalous example of the genre, the Patna *Dharmapada*, recorded in a peculiar variety of hybrid Sanskrit.[405]

After the first pass in which the commentator explains the referents of the key terms, the second pass, which is fragmentary and obscure, provides alternative explanations with reference to the development of the two paths of tranquility and insight. Here the precise significance of the terms "knowledge connected with that of others" and "knowledge that is dependent on others" are, like others in this text, difficult to determine, since they are not familiar from other Buddhist literatures. The third pass equates the terms to four "stages" (*bhūmi*): vision, development, immediacy, and accomplishment. This list is interesting in that it differs from the many other sets of levels or stages of progress that are described in both Mahāyāna and non-Mahāyāna literature.[406] Finally, in the fourth pass the terms in the root verse are connected with the three divisions of the path, namely conduct, concentration, and wisdom.

Sample c: An Angry Man

The topic verse corresponds to a verse found in the Khotan Gāndhārī *Dharmapada* (282) and in the Pali *Aṅguttara-nikāya*.[407] The commentary contains five passes, beginning with (1) a general interpretation, several parts of which are incomplete and obscure. This is followed by mappings to (2) failure with regard to the three divisions and the three sources of suffering, (3) failure with regard to the paths of good conduct and good dharmas, (4) failure to follow the noble path, and (5) failures with regard to skill in benefit and skill in the Dharma. In this last set, we once again encounter unfamiliar concepts. The commentary focuses mostly on the first half of the verse, which is the only part referred to in the last three passes.

An interesting peculiarity of this section is a reference in the third pass to a group of "sixteen items in the numerically grouped sūtras" (Skt *Ekottarikāgama*, P *Aṅguttara-nikāya*).[408] This is quite puzzling, because all extant versions of the numerically grouped sūtras, including the recently-discovered Gāndhārī one, consist of groups of sets ranging in number from one to eleven items, and no version has sets of sixteen items. Because of this, and because the phrase immediately preceding this reference is unfortunately lost, it remains, for the time being at least, a mystery.

A. Trade What Ages

10. [Trade] what ages for the ageless,
 [what burns for what cools,
 the supreme calm,
 the ultimate rest from exertion].

Thus the sūtra; now the explanation.

[First pass: Explanation of the terms]
The ageless is the element of nirvāṇa-without-remnant. **What ages** is the five aggregates of grasping. One casts them off; [for] one should seek nirvāṇa in agelessness. **What burns** refers to the three sources [of suffering, namely desire, anger, and delusion]; one should seek to extinguish them. The place where there is no burning is what is meant by **the ultimate rest from exertion**, namely the two spheres of nirvāṇa.[409] **Trade . . . for . . . the supreme calm** [means] "Take hold of the two spheres of nirvāṇa, where suffering is cast off."

[Second pass: The four noble truths]
In short: **What ages** is [the truth of] suffering. **The ageless** and **what cools** is [the truth of] cessation. **What burns** is [the truth of] arising. **Trade** means "They are to be cast off by knowledge"; this is the [truth of] the path.

[Third pass: The three courses]
Alternatively: **What cools** is the elimination of defilement. **Trade** refers to the elimination of action. **The ageless** is the elimination of suffering.

b. Endowed with Proper Conduct

29. Endowed with proper conduct and with vision,
 [rejoicing in calming within himself,
 he delights in relying on the path,
 wise and strongly concentrated].

Thus the sūtra; now the explanation.

[First pass: Explanation of the terms]

With proper conduct illustrates restraint in action. **With vision**, knowledge arises . . . is called. Or else, this refers to the quality of being unseverable, or to the quality of not being obstinate; or [it means that] he does not . . . proper conduct and observances. [**Calming within himself** is] the calming of suffering caused by the volitional formations. He is **rejoicing** in the **calming** of that very suffering caused by the volitional formations.

[Second pass: The paths of tranquility and insight]

Alternatively, **calming** is tranquility and **rejoicing** is insight; [then] **he delights in relying on the path** means that he delights in developing tranquility and insight. **Wise** means that he has arrived at knowledge connected with that of others by means of knowledge that is dependent on others. **Strongly concentrated** means that his mind is firmly fixed.

[Third pass: The four stages]

In short: **With proper conduct** refers to purity of conduct. **With vision** refers to rightful action in regard to views. This is the stage of vision. **Rejoicing in calming within himself** is the stage of development. **He delights in relying on the path** is the stage of immediacy. **Wise and strongly concentrated** is the stage of accomplishment.

[Fourth pass: The three divisions of the path]

Alternatively: **With proper conduct** refers to the conduct division. [**With vision**] refers to the concentration division. **Wise** refers to the wisdom division. **Strongly concentrated** refers to detachment from passion. . . .

c. An Angry Man

30. An angry man does not know what is good for him;
[an angry man does not see the Dharma.
When anger overcomes a man, he dwells in blind darkness.]

Thus the sūtra; now the explanation.

[First pass: Explanation of the terms]
. . . with a corrupted mind. Impermanence means the same thing as suffering. . . . He knows neither what is good for himself nor what is good for others. **An angry man does not see the Dharma**: his own . . . keeps [him] in bondage. **Blind** refers to the destruction of one's efforts. **Darkness** refers to the destruction of one's intentions. **When anger overcomes a man** refers to a man who is consumed with anger.

[Second pass: Failure with regard to the three divisions and the three sources of suffering]
In short: **An angry man does not know what is good for him** refers to failure with regard to the wisdom division [of the path]. **An angry man does not see [the Dharma]** refers to failure with regard to the concentration division. **He dwells in blind darkness** refers to failure with regard to the conduct division. The three [divisions] . . . **Blind darkness** is also applied to (?) the three sources [of suffering, namely desire, anger, and delusion] and to failure with regard to the three divisions.

[Third pass: Failure with regard to the paths of beneficial conduct and good dharmas]
Alternatively: **An angry man does not know what is good for him** refers to failure with regard to the paths of beneficial conduct. **An**

angry man does not see the Dharma means that he does not perceive beneficial dharmas . . . as in the sixteen items in the numerically grouped sūtras.

[Fourth pass: Failure to follow the noble path]
Alternatively: In **An angry man does not know what is good for him** . . . what is good for him is nirvāṇa. **He does not see the Dharma** means that he does not practice the noble path.

[Fifth pass: Failures with regard to skill in benefit and the Dharma]
Another [interpretation]: **He does not know what is good for him** refers to failure with regard to skill [in what is beneficial]. **He does not see the Dharma** refers to failure with regard to skill in the Dharma.

11. An Abhidharma Treatise on Time and Existence

Doctrinal Debates and Controversies

British Library fragment 28 preserves a large portion of an otherwise unknown polemic treatise in which the proponent, who is not explicitly identified in the surviving part of the text, argues with two separate opponents about two central topics of Buddhist ontology: (1) the question of whether past and future phenomena, or *dharmas*, can be said to "exist" in the sense that they are operative in the workings of karma, and consequently, (2) the nature of existence in the three times—past, present, and future. These are fundamental problems arising out of Buddhism's unquestioned axiom of the law of karma, namely that present and future events are determined by prior actions. This principle raises the problem of explaining how something that occurred in the past can have future effects if it no longer exists. This problem was the subject of extensive discussion for centuries in the abhidharma literature and was one of the most bitterly argued points of contention among the various scholastic camps.

The text consists of a free-flowing dialogue between the proponent and his opponents, in which the former cites the latter's opinions point by point and then refutes them by logical—or sometimes, it might seem, sophistic—arguments. At least in the portion of the text that we have, the argumentation is strongly negative; the proponent does not directly state his own views, although it can be deduced that he holds that only present factors exist, not past or future ones. Like most Buddhist and other Indian philosophical works, the text reads like the proceedings of an oral debate, reflecting perhaps the milieu in which these issues were thrashed out in monasteries or royal courts. This debate format involves highly technical terminology, stylized conventions, and abbreviated forms of expression. For these reasons, as well as because of their often abstruse subject matter, such texts can prove difficult to follow. In the case of this one in particular, which is highly fragmentary and has no direct parallel, a great many questions and problems remain. At times, it is even difficult to discern which of the debaters is speaking. Despite these difficulties, at least the overall framework and the structure of the arguments in the surviving portions can be deciphered, in part with the help of related discussions in later abhidharma texts in Pali, Sanskrit, and Chinese.[410]

The surviving portion of the manuscript contains nearly two hundred lines, though as usual many of them are incomplete or otherwise damaged. Also as usual, the remaining section is from the lower section of the scroll, so that the beginning and end of the text are missing. Because of this, and because there is no parallel to guide us, we do not know the title of the text, its overall structure or context, or how much of it is missing. But it is possible that the abstract issues discussed in the surviving portion were being presented in a broader context involving issues of Buddhist praxis, since the structure of the argument is similar to the treatment elsewhere of past and future factors in connection with the conditions for arising of the "contaminants" or "negative proclivities" (*anuśaya*).[411]

The Problem of Sectarian Affiliation

It is not possible to determine with any certainty the sectarian affiliation of the main proponent, and therefore of the text itself, nor can we be sure exactly who it was that he was arguing against. The historical origins, institutional functions, and doctrinal positions of the various schools of early Buddhism, traditionally numbered as eighteen, is a much-vexed problem, due mainly to the absence of any consistent and comprehensive tradition about their histories, as well as of early manuscript evidence.[412] On circumstantial grounds, the best guess is that we are dealing with a Dharmaguptaka text, given the apparent affiliation of the British Library scrolls with that school; this on the grounds that, first, they were found in a pot bearing an inscription referring to the Dharmaguptakas, and second, that the commentary on the *Sūtra of Chanting Together* corresponds closely with the Dharmaguptaka version of that text preserved in Chinese translation. The points of view espoused by the proponent of the treatise are, as far as we can discern them, at least not inconsistent with those that are attributed to the Dharmaguptakas in later abhidharma literature.

In the first major section of the surviving text, the proponent argues about the operations of past and future dharmas against an unidentified opponent who espouses positions that are similar to those attributed in other texts to the Kāśyapīya school. In the second section, where the participants debate the nature of existence in the three times, the opponent is explicitly labeled as a Mahāsarvāstivādin, or "Great Sarvāstivādin," an expression that is recorded nowhere else. It obviously refers to the prominent abhidharma school of the Sarvāstivādins, "Those who maintain that everything exists (at all times)," but the implication of the prefix *mahā-*, "great," is unclear. It seems to be used here in a sarcastic sense, referring to the extreme position of the opponent, who claims that "Everything exists. Everything exists at all times. Everything exists everywhere. Everything exists with every form," and so on.

At least once, the proponent labels this opponent as "one who maintains distinctions" (*vivarjavaḏa* = Skt *vibhajyavāda*)," but this is a notoriously problematic and imprecise label whose exact referent differs widely in various contexts, so that it does not help us much in determining the affiliations of the participants in this debate.

What is clear, however, is that the main proponent is arguing vociferously against the influential Sarvāstivāda school. But it is interesting that the positions espoused by the Great Sarvāstivādin opponent do not always agree with those that are attributed to the Sarvāstivādins in later treatises. For example, the opponent proposes at one point that existence is itself the three time periods of past, present, and future, a statement that contradicts the standard Sarvāstivāda position that the times do not exist in and of themselves as independent entities. The same is true of the statement (section 4) that "The past should be referred to as nothing but the past. The future should be referred to as nothing but the future. The present should be referred to as nothing but the present," since discussions in some later Sarvāstivāda texts indicate that this had been a point of contention at an earlier period of development of the Sarvāstivāda school.

Therefore this Gāndhārī text apparently provides a record of an earlier, formative stage of development of the Buddhist doctrinal schools than has previously been available. This is the particular importance of this manuscript, which, like many Gāndhārī texts, allows us to peek behind the curtain of classical canonical orthodoxy, which typically conceals the historical give and take that must have prevailed before definitive positions were developed within a given school. Thus this unique manuscript is, in the words of Collett Cox, "a witness for this crucial but poorly documented pre- and para-sectarian, transitional phase when significant doctrinal issues were emerging and the Buddhist exegetical genre was still a work in progress."[413]

About the Translation

Overview and section 1. The following translation contains a representative sample that is intended to give the reader a sense of the text as a whole. The selected passage begins with the opening of the second major topic, namely the nature of existence in the three times. This topic begins in line 66 and continues to the end of the surviving portion of the scroll. The passage is introduced with an opening statement by the Sarvāstivādin opponent, who sets forth the basic claim that "Everything exists" and then follows with seven specifications of this general statement: "Everything exists at all times. Everything exists everywhere," and so on. The rest of the selection consists of the opponent's amplification of his position in sections 2–4 and the proponent's refutation of the initial claims and of related arguments attributed to his opponent in sections 5–14. The opening statement generally determines the structure of the lengthy refutation, as the proponent takes up the points one by one for individual criticism. But it is not a rigid framework, as he also intersperses and refutes two other proposals (sections 9–10) that are not presented in the original statement. Also, the last two proposals in the opening statement (G and H) are not addressed in the surviving portions of the manuscript. They might have been discussed in a lost portion of the scroll, but in light of the wording of the discussion of point F in section 14, with the characteristic abbreviator phrase "and so on" (*peyala* = Skt *peyāla*), it is more likely that the arguments were omitted because the intended reader would have been able to anticipate them.

In this loose structure, we can see on the one hand the underlying influence of the free-flowing give and take of an oral argument. But it is also evident from the very similar presentations of debates in other abhidharma texts, most notably in the Pali *Kathāvatthu* ("Topics of Discussion"), that the arguments came to be stereotyped, almost ritualized.[414] Thus we are dealing with a discursive written style that grew out of the experiences of oral debate, whereby the opponent becomes something of a straw man who simply rehearses familiar Sarvāstivāda arguments that are refuted in the texts of their various sectarian rivals.

The principal mode of argumentation in this, as in many Indian philosophical texts, is the tactic of "undesirable consequence" or "gotcha!" (*prasaṅga*). This is the debating technique whereby one forces the opponent by logical argument to confess to an internal inconsistency within his own position, or to concede that his positions or statements lead to a patently impossible or doctrinally unacceptable conclusion.

A striking example of this technique is seen in section 7, where the main speaker manipulates his opponent's statements in such a way as to force him to contradict himself.

Section 2. In this paragraph the opponent is presented as attempting to specify the scope of "everything" and the sense of "exists," whence the statement "What exists is everything, yet what exists is not everything." He then proposes interpretations of "existence" in terms of inclusion within the twelve sense-spheres or in reference to the three times. The final statement, "The existent should be called *existence*. The nonexistent should be called *nonexistence*," sounds in translation like an empty tautology, but is perhaps to be understood in the original language as an etymological or derivational explanation: "What 'exists' (*asti*) should be called 'existence' (*astiḏa* = Skt *astitā*)," and so on.

Section 3. Here the opponent tries to clarify the relationship between existence and the time periods by way of variable "modes of being" (*bhāva*) of the dharmas, as opposed to their inherent nature (*svabhāva*), in order to avoid the contradiction of mixing together of the three time periods.

Section 4. This passage involves several problems, and the translation is at several points uncertain. For example, the precise significance of the words translated as "established" (*abhinipana* = Skt *abhiniṣpanna*) and "in order to determine" (*parinipanaṭhadae* = *pariniṣpannārthatāyai*?) remains obscure. Because of these and other problems, it is not entirely clear whether this paragraph is a continuation of the opponent's initial arguments or the beginning of the proponent's critique of them. But it is more likely that this is the conclusion of the opponent's statement, in which he tries to clarify and refine or modify his position while still maintaining the separateness of the three time periods. Beginning with the claim that "It is not the case that everything exists," he provides a concrete instance with the case of the arhat, the karmic effect of whose past defilements still "exist" but no longer have the efficacy to produce their expected effects.

In a final statement, he refers to the three essential characteristics of conditioned factors (*saṃskṛtadharma*), namely birth, aging, and impermanence, which according to abhidharma theory correlate to the past, present, and future as follows: conditioned factors on which none of these characteristics have yet had their effects are defined as "future," those on which the three characteristics have partially had their effects are "present," while those on which all three characteristics have already acted are called "past." In this connection, the opponent cites a sūtra passage from the *Larger Sūtra on the Foundations of Mindfulness* (P *Mahāsatipaṭṭhāna Sutta*) that refers to the arising of sensual desires in the past, present, and future. (As usual in Buddhist texts, the quotation is given in abridged form, citing just the first four words, on the assumption that the reader will automatically recall the entire passage.) The relevant paragraph of the sūtra text reads "If he feels sensual desire present within himself, a monk is aware that 'I have sensual desire within myself.' If he does not feel sensual desire, he is aware that 'I do not feel sensual desire.' And he is aware how future sensual desire arises, and how to abandon past sensual desire, and how sensual desire that has been abandoned cannot arise in the future."[415] Here the desire that is "present" represents the characteristic of aging, the "future" desire that may arise represents birth, and the "past" desire that has been abandoned represents impermanence.

Section 5. Here the proponent of the text begins the refutation, referring, apparently, to a statement by "one who maintains distinctions" (explained in the next section) and labeling the opponent a "Great Sarvāstivādin." The proponent challenges the Great Sarvāstivādin's notion that "everything exists" on the straightforward ground that this would mean that things that every Buddhist would agree is impossible—the existence of individual souls, a sixth aggregate, a fifth noble truth, and so on—would have to exist.

Note that the statement "What exists should be called *existence*; what does not exist should be called *nonexistence*" is a direct quotation of the opponent's words in section 2. The implication seems to be that the proponent has caught the opponent in a contradiction between this prior statement and the position attributed to the Great Sarvāstivādins that "There is absolutely nothing that does not exist."

Section 6. Anticipating that the opponent will not deny that the individual soul and so on cannot exist, he accuses him of being "one who makes distinctions," presumably meaning that he has abandoned his Sarvāstivāda absolutism and thereby contradicted himself. Then he further challenges the opponent—as usual, by turning his own statements against him—to explain how it is that, if such impossible things do not exist, one can nevertheless somehow conceive of them with the four conditions (*pratyaya*) that the Sarvāstivādins themselves consider necessary for the arising of a thought. Here he explicitly refers only to the first two of the four conditions, namely the *objective support* (*ārambaṇa*) and the *dominant condition* (*adhipati*). The other two conditions, the *immediately contiguous* (*samanantara*) and the *causal* (*hetu*), are not mentioned, perhaps because they are considered less directly relevant to the case at hand.

Section 7. The formal logic of the proponent's refutation can be understood as follows: if what exists is everything, then, since the sense-sphere of vision exists, it is everything, and since [all] twelve sense-spheres exist, they are everything; therefore the sense-sphere of vision and the twelve sense-spheres are both "everything" and thus are identical. But this is patently absurd, since the sense-sphere of vision is a member of the set of twelve sense-spheres, not identical with the set. Therefore the statement that "Everything exists" is untrue. The opponent then proposes that since visual form (the object of the sense-sphere of vision) and the sense-sphere of vision both exist, the latter is not in fact everything; but this proposal is easily dismissed by the proponent, since it obviously contradicts the opponent's original position that "What exists is everything." Finally, if the opponent tries to claim that "What exists is in some cases everything and in some cases not everything," this is again rejected as illogical, since it would mean that everything both exists and does not exist.

Section 8. Now the text proponent refutes the third proposition in the opening statement, proposition C, "Everything exists everywhere." He points out the obviously absurd consequences of this position, according to which distinct or contrary entities would be indistinguishable. Then, anticipating the opponent's retraction or modification of his absolute statement, he rejects any such modification on the ground that this would once again involve making distinctions that are contrary to the opponent's Sarvāstivāda absolutism.

Section 9. Here the proponent refutes a proposition not explicitly cited in the introductory statement: "everything exists in all (dharmas)."[416] Using the same logical tricks as in the previous paragraph, he first invokes examples of the absurd consequences of the statement[417] and then rejects an anticipated retraction or modification on the grounds that this would involve making the sort of distinctions that are contrary to the opponent's own principles. He then adds a triumphant rhetorical flourish, asking the opponent how he can still maintain his position that "everything exists"?

Section 10. Here again the proponent refutes a proposition not in the introductory statement, namely that "everything exists as belonging to everything." Once more using the logical weapon of absurd consequences, he refutes the proposition on the grounds that, were it true, it would be impossible to distinguish between different beings and their individual characteristics and attributes (dharmas).

Section 11. Here the proponent refutes the opponent's proposition B, "Everything exists at all times," by the usual strategy.

Section 12. The proponent refutes proposition D, "Everything exists in every aspect," by listing some of its absurd consequences.

Section 13. The proponent implicitly refutes proposition E, "Everything exists by every reason," but without explicitly quoting it. Here and in the following paragraph the text seems to be presenting abbreviated summaries of the arguments, assuming that the knowledgeable reader will be able to construe them; this is explicitly stated in the following paragraph. The implied point of the refutation here seems to be that proposition E would lead to the illogical consequence that past dharmas would be influenced by future ones.

Section 14. Here the proponent summarily refutes proposition F, Everything exists with all modes of being," without specifying his reasons, as in the previous passage. He also dismisses out of hand, without even citing them, the two remaining propositions G and H, with the abbreviation marker *peyala*, "and so forth." In effect, he tells the reader, "Figure it out for yourself!"

Translation

1. You say, "[A] Everything exists. [B] Everything exists at all times. [C] Everything exists everywhere. [D] Everything exists in every aspect. [E] Everything exists by every reason. [F] Everything exists with all modes of being. [G] Everything exists by all causes. [H] Everything exists by all conditions. Everything exists."

2. What exists is everything, yet what exists is not everything. [Dharmas] that are included in the twelve sense-spheres exist. Existence may be said to be [dharmas of] the three times, which are not mixed together. Or else, existence is the [three] times [themselves]. What exists should be called *existence*; what does not exist should be called *nonexistence*. The existent should be called *existence*. The nonexistent should be called *nonexistence*.

3. Or else, [existence is] past, present, and future. The past year exists. The future year exists. The modes of past and future exist as past and future. The mode of a householder exists as past and future. The mode of monastery worker (?) exists as past and future. The mode of a monk (?)[418] exists as past and future. The mode of an arhat exists as future. [In this way,] everything exists.

4. It is not the case that everything exists, nor is it the case that everything does not exist. A past [factor] exists without efficacy; [for example,] an arhat may have had desire, anger, and delusion in the past. The past should be referred to as nothing but the past. The future should be referred to as nothing but the future. The present should be referred to as nothing but the present. Just as the essential nature of the past is established as having existence in order to determine the past, so too the essential nature of futureness is established as having existence in order to determine the past; and so too, the essential nature of presentness is established as having existence in order to determine the past. This [principle] is to be applied similarly to the future and so on, down to the unconditioned [factors].

One may also say that existence is the three characteristics of conditioned factors. "Everything" in this sense [is suggested by the text] "I have sensual desire within myself. . . ."

5. The one who maintains distinctions (?) raised this issue: With regard to that, there is this point of discussion: the Great Sarvāstivādin [maintains that] "Everything exists." The Great Sarvāstivādins say, "There is absolutely nothing that does not exist; past, future, present, and unconditioned [dharmas all] exist." [But if] you say "Everything [exists]" then you have to say that the soul exists, that personhood exists, that the individual exists, that a sixth [aggregate exists], that a thirteenth sense-sphere exists, that a nineteenth element exists, that a fifth noble truth [exists]. If you say that even that which does not exist exists, that cannot be reconciled with hundreds of sūtras. What exists should be called *existence*; what does not exist should be called *nonexistence*. This can be reconciled with the hundreds of sūtras.

6. [If] you say that the soul does not exist, that personhood does not exist, that the individual does not exist, that a sixth aggregate does not exist, that a thirteenth sense-sphere does not exist, that a nineteenth element does not exist, that a fifth noble truth does not exist, well, then you are one who maintains distinctions! You recognize one thing as existence and another thing as nonexistence, so you can't say that everything exists, can you? If a fifth noble truth does not exist, a sixth aggregate does not exist, a thirteenth sense-sphere does not exist, a nineteenth element does not exist, the soul does not exist, personhood does not exist, and the individual does not exist, then what is the objective support of this consciousness that arises with reference to such [nonexistent things]? And what is the objective support of this thought-moment, and what is its dominant condition, since the very nature of that objective support whereby that thought-moment would thus arise from the four [necessary conditions] does not exist?

7. You say, "What exists is everything." Well, the sense-sphere of vision exists. Therefore, [all] twelve sense-spheres are the sense-sphere of vision. If [you respond that] visible form and the sense-sphere of vision exist, so that it is not the case that [the sense-sphere of vision] is everything, then your position that "everything exists" is not true. [If you say that] what exists is in some cases everything and in some cases not everything, then you would have to say both that in some cases everything exists and that in some cases it would not exist.

8. When you say "Everything exists everywhere," it would follow that the sense-sphere of visible form [exists] in the sense-sphere of vision and that all modes of being [exist] in the hell mode of being, and so on. Thus the essential nature of one thing would exist in the nature of another thing, and the nature of one thing would exist in the essential nature of something else. Then if you say, "We need not say that everything exists everywhere," then you would have to say that, this being the case, everything does not exist everywhere, [but rather] that some things exist and some things do not exist.

9. When you say "Everything exists in all [dharmas]," it would follow that impaired faculties would have a future faculty and hell states would have [the other] four states.[419] Thus you would have to say that the faculties are omnipresent. Then if you say, "We need not say that everything exists in all [dharmas]," then in all [dharmas] something would exist and something would not exist. How then could you say that everything exists?

10. Then if you say, "Everything exists as belonging to everything," then one being would be connected to the aggregates of others, to the sense-spheres of others, and to the elements of others.

11. When you say "Everything exists at all times," then the afternoon would exist in the morning, and the morning would exist in the afternoon. The past and the future would exist in the present, and so on with regard to other times.

12. When you say "Everything exists in every aspect," [then] the aspect of the future exists in the aspect of the past, and the aspect of the past exists in the aspect of the future; the aspect of calm exists in the aspect of emptiness, and the aspect of emptiness exists in the aspect of calm; the aspect of untruth exists in the aspect of truth; the aspect of happiness exists in the aspect of suffering; the aspect of self exists in the aspect of nonself, and the aspect of nonself exists in the aspect of self; and the aspect of not-everything exists in the aspect of everything.

13. Beneficial and harmful [dharmas] exist by reason of past, future, and present [dharmas].

14. [When you say "Everything exists with] all modes of being," this is to be refuted according to [one's] insights; and so on [for the rest of the propositions].

12. The Perfection of Wisdom Sūtra

The Perfection of Wisdom School

THE MANY SŪTRAS grouped under the category Perfection of Wisdom (*prajñāpāramitā*) constitute one of the most influential bodies of literature in Buddhism. The various Perfection of Wisdom sūtras are extant in a vast variety of forms and versions, in Sanskrit and in Chinese and Tibetan translations, and are still central to the belief system and practice of Buddhism in much of East Asia. The Perfection of Wisdom literature lies at the heart of Mahāyāna Buddhism and is usually thought of as constituting the earliest manifestation of Mahāyāna or, more strictly speaking, of the several streams of thought that eventually coalesced into the classical Mahāyāna. The primacy of the Perfection of Wisdom doctrine and texts is strongly supported by the newly discovered Gāndhārī material.

Like Mahāyāna texts in general, the Perfection of Wisdom sūtras are esoteric literature, not in the casual or colloquial sense of "obscure" or "mysterious" but in the proper etymological sense of the term. "Esoteric," from the Greek *esōteros*, meaning "interior" or "deeper within," denotes teachings that are presented or restricted to a particular limited audience and hence are to some degree hidden or secret. For Mahāyāna sūtras were understood by their followers to represent teachings of the Buddha that were not addressed to the general lay and monastic public like the "mainstream" sūtras preserved in the Pali canon but rather were reserved for select disciples, divine beings, and sometimes also lay followers whose level of spiritual awareness enabled them to comprehend these deeper teachings. Not surprisingly, as with esoteric teachings in other religions, these texts were ignored, if not positively rejected by the followers of the traditional conservative doctrines and canons, who predominate in modern Buddhism as adherents of the Theravāda school in Sri Lanka and Southeast Asia. But those who accepted the new revelations looked down upon the old ways as a lower (though not false) path, which they referred to as the Hīnayāna, that is, the "inferior" or "abandoned" vehicle, which in their view had been superseded by the new and superior Mahāyāna, or "great vehicle." Adherents of Mahāyāna Buddhism now prevail throughout Tibet and most of East Asia, including China, Korea, and Japan.

The Perfection of Wisdom literature can also be characterized as "mystical," but once again in the stricter rather than the popular or loose sense of the word. That is to say, its texts and practices focus on the ineffable experience of awakening by wisdom (*prajñā*), which cannot be directly expressed in ordinary language. The texts strive to communicate meditational experiences in which the mind transcends all contrasts and oppositions, and which can only be verbalized through bewildering statements and questions such as "Does there exist any thought such that that thought is no thought?" or "In that state that is absence of thought, does one there apprehend existence or nonexistence?" (sections A.7–8 below). Edward Conze, a pioneering scholar of the Perfection of Wisdom school, considered its essence to lie in a series of paradoxes, which he summarized in two sentences: (1) "One should become a Bodhisattva . . . i.e., one who is content with nothing less than all-knowledge attained through the perfection of wisdom for the sake of all living beings," and (2) "There is no such thing as a Bodhisattva, or as all-knowledge, or as a 'being,' or as the perfection of wisdom, or as an attainment."[420] Practitioners of the Perfection of Wisdom, however, might prefer to think of these statements as only *apparent* paradoxes, as explained by Paul Williams: "By switching between . . . two levels, ultimate and conventional, it is possible to generate apparent paradoxes for pedagogic effect, but (*pace* Conze), there are no genuine paradoxes, no real 'speaking in contradictions' in the *Perfection of Wisdom*."[421]

In any case, the central conception of the Mahāyāna sūtras, as far as it can be verbally expressed at all, can be summed up in the single concept of "emptiness" (*śūnyatā*), according to which all things and concepts, including buddhas and nirvāṇa, are ultimately illusory and devoid of any real essence (*svabhāva*). The principle of emptiness can be understood in historical terms as a radical extension of the traditional Buddhist concept of "nonself" (*anātman*), applied not only to the illusory sense of individual personality that is a fundamental principle of conservative Buddhism, but to the entire conceptual universe, in which everything is similarly unreal and empty.

In order to impress their message upon the hearer, the sūtras are full of extreme hyperbolic descriptions of the mystery of true wisdom, which are repeated over and over and, in some versions of the sūtras, expanded at enormous length. In this way, they attempt not so much to describe as to inculcate the meditational experience and insights of the Perfection of Wisdom. If evaluated by the standards that are normally applied to literature, the sūtras seem disorganized, meandering, and endlessly repetitive. But they were never intended to be read as literature in the stricter sense of the term, that is, to be analyzed according to logical principles and appreciated as aesthetic experience. Instead, the reading and especially the chanting of a Perfection of Wisdom sūtra is itself a meditative experience. With its mind-numbing repetitions, outlandish exaggerations, and jarring paradoxes, a Perfection of Wisdom sūtra is intended to lure and shock its audience out of its normal worldly state of mind and lead it toward mystical insights.

Thus Perfection of Wisdom sūtras are also not philosophical texts in the conventional sense of the term, even though they focus on ideas about the nature of reality that, in Western terms, are central to philosophy. Rather, they are meditative tools designed for the inculcation of higher states of mind; in Conze's words, "In these Sūtras we are not dealing with a series of philosophical propositions about the nature of things, but with a set of practices designed to bring about a state of complete detachment."[422] In this regard, they contrast not only with European philosophical literature but also with the analytic scholastic texts that are prominent in other genres of Buddhist literature. For example, there could hardly be a greater contrast in style and form between the loose, verbose, rambling style of the Gāndhārī *Perfection of Wisdom Sūtra* presented here and the tight logical structure and terse wording of the scholastic texts in the three preceding translations. Yet both styles are equally fundamental to the intellectual apparatus of Buddhism, the Perfection of Wisdom representing the experiential, meditative, and mystical aspect, whereas the scholastic literature embodies the analytic, intellectual stream. The two modes of thought should be understood not as conflicting and mutually exclusive but as complementary and mutually contributory toward the goal of guiding beings toward awakening.

The Characters: Śāriputra, Subhūti, and the Buddha

The contrast between these two incongruous yet complementary modes of thought is nowhere better embodied than in the persons of two of the Buddha's leading disciples, Śāriputra and Subhūti. In mainstream sūtras, Śāriputra is presented as the Buddha's wisest disciple, who was designated by the Master himself as "the foremost of those of great wisdom" among all of his followers. Śāriputra was said to have preached at the request of the Buddha the *Sūtra of Chanting Together*. He was also credited with the organization of the abhidharma system; in short, he personifies the rationalist, systematizing approach to organizing and preserving Buddhist knowledge.

Śāriputra's sober enumeration of Buddhist concepts in orderly sets of one through ten in the *Sūtra of Chanting Together* stands in contrast to the ultra-hyperbolic references to "all the living beings in as many billionfold world systems as there are grains of sand on the banks of the Ganges." But the Perfection of Wisdom texts show us a very different Śāriputra, one who, bewildered by the profundity of this esoteric wisdom, must constantly ask another disciple, Subhūti, to explain it. Instead of the Śāriputra of the older tradition, who was often called upon to explain the Dharma on behalf of the Buddha, we now meet him as a sort of "straight man," a rhetorical symbol of the inferiority of the old system to the newly revealed higher perfection of wisdom. This role reversal is evident from the very beginning of the *Perfection of Wisdom Sūtra* presented here, where the Buddha asks Subhūti—not Śāriputra—to "reveal how a bodhisattva, a great being, may become adept in the perfection of wisdom." Śāriputra then wonders whether Subhūti will do so by his own mental ability or through the Buddha's power, but Subhūti knows what Śāriputra is thinking before he even speaks and tells him that anything that a disciple says or explains is merely a reflection of the Buddha's own teaching. This frame story sets the pattern for much of the rest of the text, in which Śāriputra asks questions and either the Buddha himself or Subhūti speaking on his behalf answers them.[423]

The Perfection of Wisdom Sūtras

A peculiarity of the various Perfection of Wisdom sūtras is that although their contents and even specific wording are generally similar, they vary enormously in length and degree of detail. Although the principle of contraction and expansion, whereby the same text can exist simultaneously in shorter and longer versions, applies in varying degrees to many types of Buddhist literature, it is carried to an extreme in the Perfection of Wisdom sūtras. The various texts are often referred to by titles indicating their length in "lines" or "verses,"[424] ranging from the longest version, the *Perfection of Wisdom in One Hundred Thousand Lines*, down to a text consisting of the single syllable *a*, which is conceived to express the essence of the entire Perfection of Wisdom.[425] This contrast illustrates the ultimately mystical character of the Perfection of Wisdom, whose essence can only be pointed toward or hinted at by words, no matter how many or how few. Between these extremes, other Perfection of Wisdom sūtras include those in twenty-five thousand and eighteen thousand lines, as well as much abridged and very popular texts such as the *Heart Sūtra* and *Diamond Sūtra*. But the version in eight thousand lines (*Aṣṭasāhasrikā Prajñāpāramitā*), which the new Gāndhārī text presented here most closely resembles, was overall the most influential of the early Perfection of Wisdom texts.[426]

In comparing versions of a text of this sort, it is often difficult to determine whether the longer version is an expansion of an original shorter one or whether the short version is an abridgement of the longer one. Within the tradition, as expressed by commentators on the Perfection of Wisdom, it is assumed that the longest version in one hundred thousand lines was the original while the shorter ones were abridged to suit the needs of less-advanced audiences. Modern scholars, however, viewing the issue on the basis of historical and philological rather than functional criteria, are generally inclined to see the eight-thousand-line text as the archetype of the later versions, both expanded and abridged.

The *Perfection of Wisdom Sūtra* in Gāndhārī

The historical priority of the *Perfection of Wisdom in Eight Thousand Lines*, as well as the priority of the Perfection of Wisdom texts among Mahāyāna literature in general, have been deduced mainly from the evidence of the dates of the early Chinese translations, which, unlike their Indian originals, were dated and documented by their translators and editors. Among the earliest stratum of Chinese Buddhist translations is the rendering of the *Perfection of Wisdom in Eight Thousand Lines* made by Lokakṣema in 179 CE. The eight-thousand-line text has also been handed down for centuries in a stable, standardized Sanskrit version, which underlies the widely circulated Tibetan and later Chinese translations.

In view of these points, it is not surprising that the newly discovered Gāndhārī *Perfection of Wisdom Sūtra* corresponds most closely to the eight-thousand-line version. The existence of a Perfection of Wisdom text in Gāndhārī also accords with prior suggestions, based on testimony in much later strata of Buddhist texts, that these sūtras were originally composed in Prakrit rather than Sanskrit.[427] It has also previously been proposed that Gandhāra and the northwest were the region in which the Perfection of Wisdom originally arose, but this remains controversial, and the theory of an origin in the Andhra region of South India is favored by many authorities.[428]

Still, the discovery of a Perfection of Wisdom sūtra in Gāndhārī is a major event, first of all in that it confirms the accuracy of the overall picture of the history of early Mahāyāna literature as it had been previously constructed indirectly from Chinese sources. The Gāndhārī scroll has been subjected to radiocarbon testing, which indicated a probable range of dates between 47 and 147 CE.[429] This falls well within the range that has been generally suggested for the earliest Mahāyāna texts, namely in or around the first century CE. Until recently, the Sanskrit texts of the Perfection of Wisdom sūtras had been known mostly from manuscripts preserved in Nepal, some dating back as far as the eleventh century, but a much earlier manuscript from Bamiyan containing the eight-thousand-line version in hybrid Sanskrit and dating to about the second half of the third century has recently been identified and published.[430] This new material now gives us a much clearer view of the history of this text, revealing an early Gāndhārī version from the first centuries of the Common Era and a slightly later hybrid Sanskrit text that prefigure the stable, fixed version in standard Sanskrit that developed in the following centuries.

Lokakṣema's first Chinese version[431] from the late second century is on the whole quite similar to the Gāndhārī text, resembling it much more than it does the Sanskrit version. Thus it is quite likely, though not provable, that the archetype of Lokakṣema's Chinese translation was either in Gāndhārī or in a hybrid Sanskrit version descended from a Gāndhārī version.[432] This point, together with the discovery in the far northwest of two early manuscripts of the *Perfection of Wisdom in Eight Thousand Lines*, might seem to prove the aforementioned theory of a Gandhāran origin for the Perfection of Wisdom literature. But the matter is not so simple, and the arguments in favor of the South Indian origin are too persuasive to be dismissed out of hand, even in light of the new evidence. For similarly early (or even earlier) manuscripts could well have existed in South India, but they could not be expected to survive over the millennia in the monsoon climate. In any case, the new manuscripts do at least confirm what has also been previously suspected, namely that Gandhāra was, if not the actual place of origin, one of the focal points for the early development and propagation of Mahāyāna texts and doctrines. This, as we saw in chapter 1, was to have fateful results on the development of Buddhism throughout East Asia.

Description of the Manuscript

The Gāndhārī *Perfection of Wisdom Sūtra* is recorded on a fragmentary birchbark scroll in the Split collection, measuring about eighty centimeters, that must have been part of a long scroll. The text was published in Falk and Karashima 2012 and 2013 with Sanskrit and Chinese parallels but without a translation. The recto contains approximately the first third of the first chapter (*parivarta*), entitled "The Practice of the Knowledge of All Forms" (*Sarvākārajñatācaryā*). The verso has the end of the fifth chapter, "The Teaching on Merit" (*Guṇaparyāya*), with the surviving portion corresponding to about the last three-quarters of the Sanskrit version, though in a drastically abbreviated form.[433]

The Perfection of Wisdom scroll is unusual among Gandhāran manuscripts in two interesting respects. First, its remaining portion seems to have come from the top of the scroll, since it contains the beginning of the first and the end of the fifth chapter; the passages in between would presumably have been on the recto and verso of the lower portion of the scroll. This is in contrast to the situation of nearly all other long Gandhāran scrolls, in which the bottom, which was on the protected inside of the scroll, is the part that survives, while the top is almost always lost. Presumably in this case the scroll had been rolled from the top down, rather than the upward from the bottom, as in the other examples known so far.

This unusual arrangement is also responsible for the second special feature of this scroll, namely that its colophon, which must have originally been near the top of the verso, has survived. The colophon reads in part "The first volume of the *Perfection of Wisdom*, property of Buddhamitra, the monastic companion of Indraśava."[434] Here the title is simply given as the *Perfection of Wisdom* with no specification of the length, as is the case with the later Perfection of Wisdom sūtras. At this stage of development the Perfection of Wisdom sūtras most likely did not have specific designations in terms of their length, and the versions with drastically expanded and compressed texts may not yet have existed.

The size of the complete Gāndhārī text can be roughly estimated by comparison to the other versions. Since the Sanskrit and Chinese versions of the *Perfection of Wisdom Sūtra in Eight Thousand Lines* contain thirty-two and thirty chapters respectively, and since these chapters are broadly speaking fairly consistent in length, we can presume that the complete Gāndhārī text would have comprised about six or seven scrolls, since the surviving scroll contained the first five chapters. The portion of the first scroll that survives might have been about one fifth of the complete scroll, so that we have in total only a small fraction, less than five percent, of the entire original text. However, here again, as is so often the case with longer Gāndhārī texts that would seem to have been written out in multiple scrolls, the one that we have is the first volume, so that we cannot be certain that the rest of the text had actually been written out in full, or whether only the first scroll was actually recorded.

Relationship of the Gāndhārī Text to the Other Versions

In general, the Gāndhārī text is closer to Lokakṣema's Chinese translation of the *Perfection of Wisdom in Eight Thousand Lines* than it is to the Sanskrit version. Among these three versions, the Gāndhārī is usually the least elaborate, the Chinese somewhat expanded, and the Sanskrit much more so. For example, in the introductory passage in the first paragraph of chapter 1, the Buddha's entourage is described in the Gāndhārī version only as consisting of 1,250 monks. Here the Sanskrit version has in addition a long description of the monks as "all arhats, their afflictions all eliminated, free of defilements, self-controlled," and so forth. Lokakṣema's Chinese translation describes the audience as consisting of disciples such as Śāriputra and Subhūti and bodhisattvas including Maitreya and Mañjuśrī, and additionally specifies the occasion as the bimonthly assembly for the recitation of the monastic precepts.

Similarly in section A.4, where the Gāndhārī text has a single verb, "say," the Sanskrit version has five synonymous ones ("teach, expound, utter, clarify, elucidate"), while the Chinese has two verbs ("teach, accomplish"). The same is the case in section A.6, where the Sanskrit version has a sequence of nine verb phrases describing the discouragement that may disturb a bodhisattva's determination to pursue the perfection of wisdom, whereas the Chinese text has five, and the Gāndhārī version only three, corresponding to the first, middle (fifth), and last of the Sanskrit.[435]

In these and other such examples, we see a consistent pattern of movement from the simplest version in Gāndhārī toward a moderately expanded one in Chinese and to a much more elaborate Sanskrit text. This corresponds well to the dates of the respective texts: mid-first to mid-second century CE for the Gāndhārī, 179 CE for the Chinese, and late third century for the earliest attestation of the Sanskrit text (i.e., the Bamiyan manuscript). The surviving portion of the Gāndhārī version of chapter 5, which consists of only sixty-five lines, is drastically abridged in comparison to the corresponding Sanskrit passage, which covers twenty-five pages in a printed edition. Many of the long descriptive paragraphs of the Sanskrit text are absent or radically abbreviated in the Gāndhārī manuscript. Thus the two earliest testimonia of the *Perfection of Wisdom Sūtra*, one in Gāndhārī and the other in Chinese but likely derived directly or indirectly from a Gandhāran archetype, are much briefer than the Sanskrit versions, and this adds strong support to the modern theory that the Perfection of Wisdom sūtras grew by gradual expansion of an original relatively simple text (or texts) rather than by contraction of an original complete version, as the indigenous tradition supposes.

But these differences between the Gāndhārī *Perfection of Wisdom Sūtra* and the later versions for the most part involve only details of wording, in particular the degree of elaboration. In terms of the doctrines and ideas expressed, the distinctions are usually minor. Nevertheless, there are numerous cases where the new text provides previously unattested and sometimes unexpected variants.[436] For instance, in paragraph 6 of chapter 1, the Gāndhārī text reads "That thought, when controlled, is no thought" (*daṃtaṃ taṃ cito acito*), where the Sanskrit has "That is to say, that thought is no thought," and Lokakṣema's Chinese says "There is mind, [but] there is no mind." The Gāndhārī reading has no parallel, neither here nor in any of the other later versions of the eight-thousand-line text, and seems rather surprising, but some other Perfection of Wisdom texts do refer in other contexts to a bodhisattva as having "controlled thoughts" (*dāntacitta*). It is hard to say whether this variant might somehow clarify this crux, involving one of the most mysterious passages in the text, or whether it is to be dismissed as an unoriginal reading inserted by a scribe or editor who was trying to clarify an obscure passage. But in any case, here and elsewhere the Gāndhārī manuscript provides many textual variants, some rather surprising, that will provide a great deal of fodder for future thought by scholars of the Perfection of Wisdom.

Chapter 5: The Teaching on Merit

The fifth chapter of the *Perfection of Wisdom in Eight Thousand Lines*, missing in the Gāndhārī text, opens in the other versions with a dialogue between Kauśika—that is, Śakra, king of the gods—and the Buddha about the relative merits of studying, worshiping, teaching, and explaining the text itself. First, the Buddha explains that the person who gives the perfection of wisdom to others gains far more karmic merit than the one who uses it for his or her own benefit. He then develops this theme in a series of extravagant comparisons illustrating the superior merit of the perfection of wisdom over other virtuous acts, such as setting beings on the path of virtuous behavior or establishing them in the four meditations (*dhyāna*), the four infinite sublime states (*apramāṇa*), the five supernatural knowledges (*abhijñā*),[437] and so on. The Buddha compares the merit gained by doing each of these deeds for all the living beings in Jambudvīpa, or in the four continents, or in a thousand worlds, or in two thousand worlds, and so on, up to worlds numbering as many as the sands of the Ganges River, with the merit of preserving and spreading the perfection of wisdom. In each case, of course, the merit derived from the latter is greater.

The surviving Gāndhārī text of this chapter begins with the comparison with the merit of establishing beings in various numbers of worlds in the four infinite sublime states and the five supernatural knowledges. In order to provide the context of the incomplete Gāndhārī fragment, I have translated the immediately preceding portion of the Sanskrit text, labeled as paragraph 0, in which the Buddha compares the merit of establishing in the four meditations all the beings in as many worlds as there are grains of sand on the banks of the Ganges.

A. The Practice of the Knowledge of All Forms

[1] [Thus] have [I] heard at one time. The Lord was staying at Rājagṛha on Vulture Peak Mountain [with a vast community of monks], 1,250 monks. There the Lord addressed the venerable Subhūti:

[2] "[Subhūti], regarding the [bodhisattva's], the great being's, perfection of wisdom, reveal how a bodhisattva, a great being, may become adept in the perfection [of wisdom]."

[3] Then the venerable Śāriputra thought: "Will this Venerable Subhūti expound on this by resorting to his [own] strength or rather by the power of the Buddha?" Then Venerable Subhūti said to Venerable [Śāriputra]:

[4] "Venerable Śāriputra, whatever the Lord's disciples say is entirely the doing of the Tathāgata. Why is that? Because whatever Dharma is taught by the Tathāgata, it is by training in that Dharma teaching that they realize [its true nature]. Because it is by training themselves in whatever Dharma is taught by the Tathāgata that they realize [its true nature]. This is the outcome of the Tathāgata's Dharma teaching. Whatever those good men teach, [they do not contradict the essence of that] true nature."

[5] [Then] Venerable Subhūti said to the Lord: "In saying, 'Reveal, Subhūti, the perfection of wisdom of a bodhisattva, of a great being,' when, Venerable Sir, you speak of a bodhisattva, to what object does this term *bodhisattva* refer? Venerable Sir, I do [not] perceive any [object] that is this object [called] *bodhisattva*. And not [perceiving] this bodhisattva, not apprehending [this] bodhisattva, and not perceiving the perfection of wisdom, [how can] I teach a bodhisattva about the perfection of wisdom?

[6] "And yet, Venerable Lord, if when [he is spoken to and] taught in this way, a bodhisattva's mind does not get depressed, does not turn

away, and does not feel afraid, this very [bodhisattva, this great being], is to be instructed in the perfection of wisdom. This is the very perfection of wisdom of the bodhisattva, if he thus stands firm. [Moreover], Lord, a bodhisattva, a great being, should be instructed in such a way that, as he is being instructed, [he would] not thereby [fancy himself to be] a bodhisattva.[438] Why is that? That thought, when controlled, is no thought."[439]

[7] Then Venerable Śāriputra said to Venerable Subhūti: "[Venerable] Subhūti, does there exist any thought such that that thought is no thought?"

[8] Thus addressed, Venerable Subhūti said to Venerable Śāriputra: "[Venerable] Śāriputra, in that state that is the absence of thought, does one there apprehend existence or nonexistence?"

[9] [Śāriputra said:] "No, Venerable Subhūti, this is not the case. For if existence or nonexistence is not apprehended in that state that is the absence of thought, then is this inquiry appropriate?"

[10] Then Venerable Subhūti said to Venerable Śāriputra: "Venerable [Śāriputra], what then is this state of the absence of thought?"

[11] Then Venerable Śāriputra said to Venerable Subhūti: "Well said, well said, Subhūti! You have been designated [by the Lord] as the foremost [of those who dwell in peace].[440] Such a one [as you] should be considered as . . . and should be known as a bodhisattva who is never without the perfection of wisdom. This same perfection of wisdom should be heard even by one who is being trained [only] at the level of a disciple (*śrāvaka*). Why is that? [Because in this] perfection of wisdom the miraculous display of the Dharma[441] has been taught as it is to be studied by a bodhisattva."

[12] Then Venerable Subhūti said: "Since, Venerable Lord, I do not even know, I do not even apprehend this name *bodhisattva*, then, not knowing it and not apprehending it, which bodhisattva could I instruct in the perfection of wisdom? It [would be] a shame for me to create the name *bodhisattva* without apprehending it. Moreover, Venerable Lord, [his mind][442] is not settled, not established. For if,

as the perfection of wisdom is being taught, a bodhisattva's [mind] does not get depressed and does [not] feel afraid, that bodhisattva is established, is settled in the irreversible sphere. Moreover, Venerable Lord, [a bodhisattva] who is engaging in the perfection of wisdom should not establish himself in form. If he establishes himself in form, he engages in the production of form; and similarly [with regard to sensation, perception, and volitional formations].[443] [And] if he establishes himself in consciousness, he engages in the production of consciousness. [Why] is that? [Because one who engages in production does not] grasp [the perfection of wisdom]."

[13] Then Venerable Śāriputra spoke thus to Venerable Subhūti: "How does [a bodhisattva] grasp the perfection of wisdom?"

[14] Thus addressed, Venerable Subhūti responded to Venerable Śāriputra: "Form, Venerable Śāriputra, is not [grasped in the perfection of wisdom]. And as for the nongrasping of form, this is not [to be taken as] form; and similarly sensation, perception, and volitional formations [are not grasped]. Consciousness is not grasped. That [nongrasping] of consciousness [is not to be taken as] consciousness. This perfection of wisdom too is not grasped. Thus it is [in the perfection of wisdom] that a bodhisattva, a great being, should engage. This is the bodhisattva's concentration called the *ungrasped*, which is not shared with, not grasped by solitary buddhas. Omniscience too is not grasped. Why is that? Because it is to be eliminated (?)[444] by an outward appearance. This too, Venerable Lord, is the perfection [of wisdom] of a bodhisattva.

[15] "Moreover, Venerable Lord, a bodhisattva, a great being, who is engaging in the perfection of wisdom should consider, '[What is this] perfection of wisdom, whose is this perfection of wisdom? Is a dharma that is not known and is not attained the perfection of wisdom? [If in this way] a bodhisattva does not fear, does [not] feel afraid, he is never without the perfection of wisdom."

[16] Then [Venerable Śāriputra] said to Subhūti: "For what reason is that bodhisattva never without the perfection of wisdom?"

[17] Thus addressed, Venerable Subhūti said this [to Venerable Śāriputra]: "Form itself, Venerable Śāriputra, is without any essence of form; and similarly for sensation, perception, and volitional formations. Consciousness, [Venerable] Śāriputra, is without any essence of consciousness. And the perfection of wisdom itself, Venerable Śāriputra, is without any [essence] of perfection of wisdom."

[18] Then [Venerable Śāriputra] said [to Venerable Subhūti]: "Will a bodhisattva [who] trains himself in this [go forth to omniscience]?"

[19] Venerable Subhūti said [to Śāriputra]: "So it is, Venerable Śāriputra, [so it is.] ... A bodhisattva who trains himself in this will go forth to omniscience. Why is that? Because dharmas are not gone forth[445] [and] are not born. Omniscience approaches a bodhisattva, a great being [who thus engages]. And this bodhisattva [who thus engages] in the Perfection of Wisdom approaches [omniscience] in the perfection of wisdom."

[20] Venerable Subhūti spoke further regarding the bodhisattva: "If he engages in form, [he engages in an outward appearance. If he engages in the production of form], he engages in an outward appearance. If he engages in the destruction of form, he engages in an outward appearance. [If he engages in the thought] 'Form is empty,'[446] he engages [in an outward appearance. If he engages] in the thought 'I am engaging,' he engages in an apprehension; and so on, similarly for sensation, perception, and volitional formations. If he engages in consciousness, [he engages in an outward appearance]. If he engages in the production of consciousness, he engages in an outward appearance. If he engages in the destruction of consciousness, he engages [in an outward appearance. If he engages in the thought 'Consciousness is empty,'] he engages in an outward appearance. If he engages in the thought 'I am engaging,' he engages in an apprehension. Such a bodhisattva, such a great being, [is engaging] in nothing but an outward appearance. [And if he thinks, 'One who] engages in this way engages in the perfection of wisdom and develops the perfection of wisdom,'

[he is engaging in nothing but] an outward appearance. [This bodhisattva is to be understood as unskilled in means."]

[21] [Then Venerable] Śāriputra [said to] Venerable[447] [Subhūti: "Engaging in what way, Venerable Subhūti, does a bodhisattva, a great being, engage in the perfection of wisdom?"]

[22] [Venerable Subhūti answered Venerable Śāriputra: "If, Venerable Śāriputra, a bodhisattva, a great being, does not engage in form, does not engage in the outward appearance of form, does not engage in the thought 'Form is an outward appearance,' does not engage in the production of form, does not engage in the suppression of form, does not engage in the destruction of form, does not engage in the thought 'Form is empty,' does not engage in the thought 'I am engaging,' and does not engage in the thought 'I am a bodhisattva'; and similarly with regard to sensation, perception, and volitional formations; and if he does not engage in consciousness, does not engage in the outward appearance of consciousness, does not engage in the thought 'Consciousness is an outward appearance,' does not engage in the production of consciousness, does not engage in the suppression of consciousness, does not engage in the destruction of consciousness, does not engage in the thought 'Consciousness is empty,' does not engage in the thought 'I am engaging,' and does not engage in the thought 'I am a bodhisattva'; and if he does not think 'One who engages in this way engages in the perfection of wisdom, he develops the perfection of wisdom'—engaging in this way a bodhisattva, a great being, does engage in the perfection of wisdom. For as he engages, he does not think 'I am engaging,' he does not think 'I am not engaging,' he does not think 'I am both engaging and not engaging,' he does not think 'I am neither engaging nor not engaging,' he does not think 'I will engage,' he does not think 'I will not engage,' he does not think 'I will both engage and not engage,' and he does not think 'I will neither engage nor not engage.' Why is that? He does not think these things because all dharmas are unapproached and unattained. This is

called the 'concentration of the unattainability of all dharmas' of the bodhisattva, the great being; it is vast, superior, unlimited in scope, not shared by all the disciples and solitary buddhas. Remaining in this very concentration, the bodhisattva, the great being, quickly realizes supreme perfect awakening."]

B. The Teaching on Merit

[0] ["If a good man or a good woman were to establish in the four meditations each and every being in as many billionfold world systems as there are grains of sand on the banks of the Ganges; what do you think, Kauśika? Would that good man or good woman thereby produce much merit?"

Śakra said: "Yes, much, Lord, much, Well-Gone One."

The Lord said: "More merit than that, Kauśika, would that good man or good woman produce if he or she were to set this Perfection of Wisdom down in writing, and having faith in it, give it to one who is faithful in it; being confident of it, give it to one who is confident of it; being devoted to it, give it to one who is devoted to it; being pure of heart toward it, give it to one who is pure of heart toward it; being determined on it, give it to one who is determined on it; and, fixing his or her mind on awakening, give it with the determination of a bodhisattva to one whose mind is fixed on awakening; and similarly, if he or she were to just untiringly furnish it for writing or for recitation, and assiduously offer it, reveal it, excite and stimulate and delight with it, present it verbally and teach it and persuade with it, and clarify its meaning to someone and thereby purify his mind, free him of doubts, and say to him, 'Come, good man, train yourself in this very bodhisattva path; for as you train in it, engage in it, and exert yourself in it, you will quickly realize supreme complete awakening. And having become awakened, you will lead infinite realms of beings to the complete elimination of the substratum of attachment, that is, to the realization of the summit of existence.']

[1] ["Furthermore, Kauśika, if a good man or a good woman were to establish as many living beings as there are in Jambudvīpa] in the four infinite sublime states, [or] establish them in the five supernatural

knowledges; then what do you think, Kauśika? Would they thereby produce [much merit]?"

[2] [Kauśika] said: "Much, Venerable Lord."

[3] [The Lord said:] "More than this, Kauśika, is the merit that a good man or good woman [would produce] who would write a book of the Perfection of Wisdom and give it to other people. Furthermore, Kauśika, [if] a good man or a good woman would [recite this Perfection of Wisdom to him- or herself] and write [it as] a book and give it to another person, such a person would thereby [produce] even more [merit. Furthermore], Kauśika, if a good man or good woman would [recite] this Perfection of Wisdom to him- or herself and teach the meaning of [this] Perfection of Wisdom to another person, such a person would thereby produce [still] greater merit."

[4] [Then Śakra], the king of the gods, said to the Lord: "Venerable Lord, should this Perfection [of Wisdom] also be taught to that good man or good woman?"

[5] [The Lord] said: "[Kauśika], this Perfection [of Wisdom should be taught] even to a good man [or a good woman who does not understand it]. Why is that? There will arise, Kauśika, in [a time] to come, an imitation[448] of [this] Perfection of Wisdom. With reference to that, [one should teach the Perfection of Wisdom even to those who do not understand it,] lest a good man or good woman who wishes to realize supreme perfect awakening go astray upon hearing that imitation."

[6] Thus addressed, Śakra, [king] of the gods, said [this] to the Lord: "What, [Venerable] Lord, is this imitation of the Perfection of Wisdom?"

[7] Thus addressed, the Lord [said this] to Śakra, king of the gods: "In times to come, Kauśika, [there will be] monks who will say, 'We will teach the Perfection of Wisdom,' [but they will teach] the imitation. [And how will they teach the imitation? They will teach that form is impermanent.[449] [They will engage in] the thought that form is impermanent; they will strive after the thought that [form is impermanent]. And they will thus teach: 'He who will strive in this way

will [engage] in the Perfection of Wisdom'; and so on, similarly with regard to sensation, perception, and volitional formations. And they will teach that consciousness is impermanent. [They will engage] in the thought that consciousness is impermanent; [they will strive after the thought that consciousness is impermanent.] And they will thus teach: 'He who will strive in this way [will engage] in the Perfection of Wisdom.' [This], Kauśika, is the imitation of the Perfection of Wisdom.

[8] "But really, Kauśika, the impermanence of form [should not be] seen as resulting from the destruction of form; [and similarly with regard to] sensation, perception, volitional formations, and consciousness. Really, Kauśika, the impermanence of consciousness [should not be] seen as resulting from the destruction of consciousness. [If] one sees it in that way, one is engaging in the imitation of the Perfection of Wisdom. And therefore, Kauśika, he who will teach the meaning of the [true] Perfection of Wisdom will thereby produce more merit.

[9] "Furthermore, Kauśika, if some [good man] or good woman were to establish in the fruit of the stream-enterer all the beings in Jambudvīpa—what do you think, [Kauśika]? Would that [good man] or good woman produce much merit?"

[10] [Kauśika] said: "Yes, much, Venerable Lord."

[The Lord said:] "More than this, Kauśika, is the merit that a good man or good woman would produce who would write a book of the Perfection of Wisdom and [give it] to another person. Become one who wins [these] very dharmas, namely, those that are connected with the Perfection of Wisdom!

"Why is that? [Because], Kauśika, the fruit of the stream-enterer is produced from it [i.e., the Perfection of Wisdom]. But never mind, Kauśika, about this Jambudvīpa! Suppose, Kauśika, that someone were to establish in the fruit of the stream-enterer as many beings as there are in a billionfold world system; [what do you think,] Kauśika? Would he produce much merit?"

[11] [Kauśika] said: "Yes, much, Venerable Lord."

[The Lord said:] "More than that, Kauśika, is the merit that [a good man] or good woman would produce who would write a book of the Perfection of Wisdom and [give it] to another person. [But never mind,] Kauśika, about a billionfold world system! Suppose, Kauśika, that someone were to establish in the fruit of the stream-enterer as many beings as there are [in world systems equal in number] to the grains of sand in the river Ganges; what do you think, Kauśika? Would [that good man or good woman] produce [much] merit?"

[12] [Kauśika] said: "Yes, much, Venerable Lord."

[The Lord said:] "More than that, Kauśika, is the merit that a good man or good woman would produce who would write a book of the Perfection of Wisdom and give it to another person. Become one who wins these very dharmas, namely, those that are connected with the Perfection of Wisdom! When you shall train yourself in it, [then you] will become one who wins the dharmas of omniscience. [For] you will produce the fruit of the stream-enterer from it; and so on[450] with regard to the [fruit of] the once-[returner], the fruit of the non-returner, and the state of an arhat. Then you will produce individual awakening from it.

[13] ["Furthermore, Kauśika, if] all the beings in Jambudvīpa were to produce the thought of supreme perfect awakening, and if someone were to write this Perfection of Wisdom and give it to those [beings] who had set out toward [supreme] perfect awakening; and if someone else were to write this same Perfection of Wisdom and give it to an irreversible [bodhisattva,[451] thinking that] 'He [will] train himself in this Perfection of Wisdom, he will apply himself to it, and thus, developing the Perfection of Wisdom to the highest degree, he will attain complete fulfillment of his self-cultivation'—this [latter] person would produce more merit than that [previous] accumulation of merit.

[14] "Furthermore, Kauśika, if all the beings in the billionfold [world] systems were to produce the thought of supreme perfect awakening, and if someone were to write this Perfection of Wisdom

and give it to those beings who had set forth toward supreme perfect awakening; and if someone else were to write this same Perfection of Wisdom and present it to an irreversible bodhisattva [thinking,] 'He will train himself in this Perfection of Wisdom, [he will apply himself to it], and thus, developing the Perfection of Wisdom to the highest degree, [he will attain complete fulfillment of his self-cultivation]'—this [latter] person would produce more merit than that previous accumulation of merit.

[15] "Furthermore, Kauśika, if all the beings in world systems equal in number [to the grains of sand in the river Ganges] were to produce the thought of supreme perfect awakening, and if someone were to teach this Perfection of Wisdom in its spirit and its letter to those beings who had set forth toward [supreme] perfect awakening; [and if someone else] were to write this same Perfection of Wisdom and give it to a bodhisattva, a great being—this [latter] person would produce more merit than that [previous] accumulation of merit.

[16] "Moreover, Kauśika, if the beings in Jambudvīpa were to produce the thought of [supreme] perfect awakening and become irreversible [bodhisattvas], and if some good man or good woman were to write this Perfection of Wisdom and present it to those irreversible [bodhisattvas, those great beings, and] were to teach it [in its spirit and] its letter; what do you think, Kauśika? Would that good man or good woman [produce] much merit?"

[17] [Kauśika said:] "Yes, much, Venerable Lord."

[The Lord said:] "If another bodhisattva were to arise [and say], 'I will attain to supreme perfect awakening more quickly'; and if someone were to advise and instruct in the Perfection of Wisdom this one who wishes to attain to supreme perfect awakening more quickly, that person produces more merit than that previous accumulation of merit."

[18] Then Śakra, king of the gods, said this to the Lord: "Lord, the closer a bodhisattva, a great being, comes to awakening, all the more does one who advises and instructs [him] in the Perfection of Wisdom

and gives him his [requisite] clothing, alms bowl, bedding, and medical needs produce greater merit. Why is that? Thus, venerable sir, one should do.[452] A noble disciple who shows favor to a bodhisattva encourages him, favors him, supports him toward supreme perfect awakening. Thus you should do. For the disciples of the Lord are descended from this (?)."[453]

[19] "If this thought [of awakening] is not aroused, the bodhisattvas would not train themselves in it, and [not training themselves] in the six perfections, they would not attain to supreme perfect awakening. But since [they do train themselves,] they will attain [supreme perfect awakening]."

[Colophon]

The first volume of the *Perfection of Wisdom*, [property] of Buddhamitra, the monastic companion of Indraśava. And by this root of merit, in honor of all beings, of my mother and father . . .

Conclusions

State of the Art and Future Prospects

THE PAST TWENTY years during which the study of Gāndhārī manuscripts has burgeoned have coincided with revolutionary developments in the technology of textual scholarship. The early phases of the project, in the waning years of the twentieth century, were carried out under what seem in retrospect to be primitive conditions. Major improvements have in the meantime been developed in two regards, namely image reproduction and manipulation, and methods of textual research. In the early months of the project, the EBMP researchers had to either work from the blurry black-and-white photographs that had been originally supplied by the British Library or travel to London to study the original manuscripts housed in bulky and fragile glass frames. Later on, the British Library was able to provide a set of digital color photographs, and then a second, improved set with higher resolution, which quickly became our principal resource for studying the British Library and other manuscripts. These can now be examined on screen with graphics-editing programs that allow us to enlarge and adjust the images for maximum visibility; happily gone are the long days at the British Library of hunching over a cumbersome illuminated magnifying apparatus called the Mantis while nervously wiggling the long glass frames to try to find the right spot in the text. Image manipulation on screen not only enhances legibility but also permits us to virtually reconstruct the scroll by digitally moving the many loose fragments and broken pieces to their original position. This too is a far cry from the early days when we had to piece the manuscripts together from photocopies of the blurry black-and-white photographs, cutting out the pieces with scissors and sticking them back together in their correct location with scotch tape.

This is not to say that the original manuscripts are no longer needed. Although the researchers now do the vast majority of their work, some 90 or 95 percent, on screen, in the end there is nothing like the real thing, and the editors still must carefully examine every syllable of the original manuscripts, usually several times over, before finalizing their editions. Certain subtle visual clues can only be picked up from the original, for example distortions caused by high and low spots in the wrinkled bark that are flattened out in the digital imaging process. Also, it is sometimes possible to read portions of the text that are concealed under thin overlying pieces of bark by shining a fiber-optic light from below the glass frame, illuminating the underlying surface.

Similarly with regard to tools for textual and philological research: in the early years, EBMP researchers who needed to identify and interpret a text had to depend on a miscellany of traditional print dictionaries, word lists, and concordances in various publications. This approach had to be supplemented by slogging through endless volumes of Buddhist texts in many languages, with only memories of previous readings, or sometimes intuition or just luck, as guides. But as the project progressed, more and more sophisticated digital tools for electronically searching entire corpora of Buddhist and other relevant literatures gradually became available. Instead of laboriously tracking down a word in the dictionaries and concordances, it has become possible to compile, at the touch of a button, a complete list of its occurrences over a vast range of Buddhist texts.

While these developments have vastly improved our ability to identify fragmentary texts and to interpret the many difficult words in them, the new technology is not a magical cure-all for all of the problems that arise in an enterprise of this magnitude. The vast volume and complexity of Buddhist literature, the fragmentary condition of the manuscripts, and our still-incomplete knowledge of the Gāndhārī language mean that a complete study of each text still involves endless hours of searching, reading, and comparing texts, and despite one's best efforts in every case, some questions, and in some cases many questions, still remain. While I have for the most part spared the readers of this volume the complex problems that underlie many of the translations, I have in a few places discussed in the introduction or notes some particularly interesting or bewildering examples.

Technological advances have been enormously helpful not only in interpreting the material but also in presenting, organizing, and preserving it. Since the early stages of the project, Drs. Andrew Glass and Stefan Baums have been compiling a complete database (http://gandhari.org) featuring, among other items, an exhaustive bibliography of works on or about Gāndhārī texts; a complete catalog of known Gāndhārī texts, including inscriptions and secular documents from Central Asia as well as Buddhist manuscripts; and the only comprehensive dictionary of the Gāndhārī language. The database is continually being developed and expanded as technological capabilities and the study of Gāndhārī material progress, and it is now the primary research tool for all Gāndhārī materials, both for the Gāndhārī scholars themselves and for Buddhist scholars in other areas of specialization.

One troubling problem remains, however. Nearly all of the Gandhāran manuscripts currently available have come to light on the antiquities market in Asia and Europe, so that their true provenances, and thus their archaeological contexts, are all but unknown. This is a frustrating situation, and the dream of the scholars in this field is that at some time in the future, however distant it may be, such manuscripts will be found in the course of a professionally documented archaeological excavation. Such discoveries would vastly increase the value and importance of the material as a whole, by showing us exactly how, where, when, and perhaps even why such manuscripts were prepared, used, and interred. But for the meantime we can only wait and hope.

What Have We Learned?

During a public presentation I gave during the early years of the study of the Gandhāran manuscripts, a member of the audience asked whether they contained "a fifth noble truth." I took the question to mean, do the texts reveal anything that challenges or overturns the basic doctrines of Buddhism as they have been understood until now? I answered him in the negative. I was therefore surprised to come across, some years later, an actual reference to a "fifth noble truth" in the abhidharma treatise presented above.[454] But this initially shocking phrase must be understood in its proper context: it is part of a rebuttal to an opponent, showing that his position that "everything exists" requires that he accept, among other impossibilities, the existence of a fifth noble truth. This is intended to be absurd: the point is that there is not, and cannot be, a fifth noble truth, so that I was relieved to find that the texts themselves do confirm my response to my questioner.

The material in the new manuscripts reveal a vast amount of new information about and insight into the literature and ideas of a previously little understood but highly influential Buddhist culture, but they do not overturn our basic understanding of the history of Buddhism. To the contrary, they tend, in broad terms at least, to confirm and clarify rather than to contradict some of the theories that have been proposed in both older and more recent academic scholarship; see, for example, the comments on the history of the Perfection of Wisdom literature in the introduction to translation 12. Perhaps most importantly, the discovery of manuscripts of several Mahāyāna texts, some dating back to the second or possibly even the first century of the Common Era, supports the previous consensus that Mahāyāna ideas and texts arose at about this period. While the earlier theory was reached mostly on indirect grounds, such as the dates of the early translations of Mahāyāna sūtras into Chinese, the new material gives us direct confirmation of its general accuracy. It also confirms the suggestions made by several scholars that some of the early Mahāyāna sūtras, previously known in versions in Chinese or Sanskrit, were derived from archetypes in Gāndhārī. And while the discovery of Gāndhārī versions of Mahāyāna texts does not conclusively prove that the sūtras were originally composed in Gāndhārī, it does confirm that—as also had been previously suggested—Gandhāra was a, if not the, major locus of the emergence and spread of Mahāyāna Buddhism.

The period covered by Gāndhārī manuscripts, from the first century BCE to third century CE, is a critical phase of the history of Buddhism in other respects as well. This is the time when various Buddhist communities were adopting and expanding the use of writing as a medium for the preservation and transmission of the canon. It is also the period in which fixed, definitive canons were beginning to take shape and in which Sanskrit was beginning to supersede the regional vernaculars as the canonical language. Even more importantly for the history of Buddhism as a whole, the Gandhāran manuscripts belong to the time and place from which Buddhism began to spread beyond the Indian world, first into Central Asia and thence into China, and eventually to Korea and Japan. The long-standing "Gāndhārī hypothesis," which posited that the archetypes of early Chinese translations of Buddhist literature were in Gāndhārī, has now found a firm basis in an actual—rather than a hypothetical—body of Buddhist literature in Gāndhārī.

The rediscovery of large numbers of Buddhist texts in Gāndhārī also strengthens the recent trend in Buddhist scholarship toward thinking of early Indian Buddhism in terms of "many Buddhisms," that is, as a complex of diverse and localized traditions—many of which have left little or no trace in the historical record—rather than as a monolithic entity. Such local Buddhisms have been revealed by earlier archaeological and textual discoveries, for instance at Gilgit and in the Tarim Basin in Central Asia, which brought to light enormous corpora of Buddhist literature in Sanskrit from the middle of the first millennium. But the Gandhāran material shows us a regional vernacular form of Buddhism at an earlier and more formative stage, and what we find there is an intriguing mixture of the familiar and the unfamiliar. Most of the sūtra texts have more or less direct parallels in other Buddhist canons, and even those that lack parallels consist mainly of familiar wording, images, and ideas. This is not surprising, since the mainstream sūtras are typically the most stable part of Buddhist canons across space and time. Their relationships, however, are complex in the sense that, more often than not, a given Gāndhārī sūtra will agree more closely with one parallel text in Pali, Sanskrit, or Chinese in some respects but resemble other parallels in other respects. Rarely can we trace out consistent lines of descent or relationship between the several versions of a given sūtra.

In this regard, the emerging picture of relationships among Buddhist texts and literatures is interestingly analogous to the point of view current prevailing among scholars of human paleontology. They have abandoned the old, and in retrospect naïve, view of a linear, chain-like model in which only a missing link or two had to be found to establish the ancestry of the human race. For recent experience has made it abundantly clear that the more hominid fossils are discovered, the more complicated and messy—not clear and simple—the picture becomes. Accordingly, paleontologists now typically envision the evolutionary history of humanity not as a chain or a ladder but as a "tangled bush," with many dead ends and no clear single line of descent from primitive hominids to modern humans. In much the same way, a given Buddhist text, linguistic tradition, or sectarian canon can rarely, if ever, be traced back in a neat line of transmission through other known texts and corpora leading to a single ancestor.

Moreover, the evolutionary bush is "tangled" not only in the sense that there have turned out to be a great many more branches (i.e., lines of descent) than earlier generations of paleontologists could have imagined, but also in the sense that the lines were probably by no means always fully distinct. In many cases, it now appears, individuals of different lines interbred, making it even more difficult to trace the relationships of the species. In much the same way, as more and more specimens of old Buddhist manuscripts come to light, the picture becomes more, not less, complicated. Buddhist communities were in regular contact, trading and borrowing ideas and words—pieces of the Dharma's DNA, as it were—and incorporating them into their own texts. The result is a conflated literary tradition, comparable to the interbred lines of human ancestry, which in few if any cases can be separated into straight lines of descent, simply because such straight lines do not exist. In short, an ancient lesson has been relearned: "The more you know, the less you know."

While this might seem disappointing in that it fails to provide us with clear and simple pictures of the historical development of individual texts—something that philological scholars always hope, though often in vain, to discover—on other levels it is revealing and important. The pattern reflects, first of all, the flexible attitude toward scripture that was characteristic of early Buddhism. But other factors are involved, among them the vagaries and complexities involved in the translation policy espoused by the Buddha and the frequent and extensive interchange between the Buddhist communities throughout the Indian subcontinent. While the Gandhāran manuscripts confirm the "many Buddhisms" approach, they also show that these many Buddhisms were by no means islands unto themselves. A good example of this give-and-take among regional Buddhisms is the *Songs of Lake Anavatapta*, which is attested in several Sanskrit and Chinese versions as well as in Gāndhārī but does not appear as such in the Pali canon. Nevertheless, a Pali text of a related genre, the *Apadāna*, contains two inserted passages that were obviously borrowed from the *Songs of Lake Anavatapta*, possibly directly from the Gāndhārī version.

This pattern is sometimes even discernible among the Gāndhārī texts that have no parallel in other Buddhist languages. As explained in the introduction to the translations of the two Gāndhārī commentaries (translations 9 and 10), the hermeneutic method of categorial mapping that underlies their structure is evidently characteristic of the scholastic traditions of Gandhāra, but it is also observed in two paracanonical texts extant in Pali, the *Peṭakopadesa* and *Nettippakaraṇa*, whose uncharacteristic format had previously been suspected of betraying the influence of other regional traditions. It now becomes clear that this external source was, in all likelihood, the Buddhism of Gandhāra.

But the most distinctive local feature of the Gandhāran manuscripts are the references in the British Library avadāna collections to two local historical figures, the satraps Jihonika and Aśpavarma, who were previously known from coins and inscriptions but not mentioned elsewhere else in Buddhist literature. These references do however fall into a general pattern, observed in similar textual genres in other Buddhist traditions, of references to kings, such as Ajātaśatru, Aśoka, Kaniṣka, and Huviṣka, who patronized Buddhist establishments, or perhaps rather were being solicited for patronage. From these discoveries in the Gandhāran manuscripts, we can extrapolate that other regional Buddhist literatures, now lost, must have recorded similar historical information. The avadāna literature in which these historical names are recorded is also of special importance in that we seem to have, in these sketchily recorded outlines of stories, the kernel of what was to develop into a formal literary genre in the Sanskrit literary traditions of later Buddhism.

Although the Gandhāran documents known so far are surely only a miniscule fraction of what must once have been a vast literature, scholars are beginning to discern, with the ongoing study of some two hundred documents, some sense, if only vague and tentative, of the overall scope of that literature. The results and conclusions presented in this volume must still be considered as preliminary and incomplete, and the scholars involved are conscious of the dangers of drawing conclusions on the basis of incomplete information. But we can only work with what we have; for example, in 1999 I wrote in reference to the British Library collection that "Notably absent from the new material is any significant reference to or indication of Mahāyāna concepts."[455] But since that time, as we have seen, several Mahāyāna texts in Gāndhārī have been found among the other groups of Gāndhārī manuscripts.

No doubt some of the conclusions presented in this volume too will eventually be disproven or superseded by other discoveries and analyses. The study, translation, and publication of many Gandhāran manuscripts is currently being pursued by scholars in several countries. Moreover, besides the manuscripts and collections described in this book, it is known that a large number of others are held in private hands, and there is reason to hope that many of these will eventually become available for scholarly study. But the work is by its nature slow and painstaking, and the number of Gāndhārī manuscripts that have been fully published and translated is still only a fraction of the whole. We can, however, be sure that many more insights into the history of Buddhism will gradually emerge from these efforts, and it is to be hoped that a further anthology of translations of Gāndhārī texts will be compiled at some point in the future, which will build on this one and correct whatever needs to be corrected in it.

It only remains to put the Gandhāran manuscripts into a broader perspective. The new discoveries and the several scholarly projects involving them are only one part of a larger enterprise involving the study of a vast number of Buddhist manuscripts of all sorts that have been discovered or become newly available to scholars in recent years. Besides the Gāndhārī works, several other projects in various European and Asian countries and in the United States are studying and publishing materials such as the enormous body of Sanskrit manuscripts from Bamiyan, important new manuscripts from the Gilgit region including a complete text of the Sanskrit *Dīrghāgama*, and a large collection of previously unavailable Sanskrit texts from Tibet.[456] It is no exaggeration to say that we are living and working in a golden age of Buddhist studies, and there is every reason to hope that this golden age will continue for many years to come.

Appendix 1

SPECIMEN OF A VERSE IN VARIOUS BUDDHIST LANGUAGES

IN ORDER TO give the interested reader a closer look at the details of the texts and languages involved and their relationships to one another,[457] I have presented below the first verse from the recitation of Śroṇa Koṭiviṃśa in the *Songs of Lake Anavatapta* (see translation 5c) in seven different versions in five languages. The further details of these texts, their place in Buddhist literature, and their interrelationships are discussed in detail in Salomon 2008. The Gāndhārī and the two Sanskrit versions are extant only in fragmentary manuscripts; in them, the portions of the lost text that can be reliably reconstructed on the basis of the parallels are indicated in parenthesis with asterisks.

The several versions of the verse are all quite similar, in some cases almost identical. This is particularly the case with three versions, namely the Sanskrit text from one of the Gilgit manuscripts, the Tibetan, and the second Chinese. These are virtually the same, because they are embedded in the same text, namely the *Mūlasarvāstivāda-vinaya*, which was translated into Tibetan and Chinese from a Sanskrit original.

The Gāndhārī text is anomalous in that Śroṇa's gift to the saṅgha consists of a hall (Skt *kūṭāgāra*, more specifically a peaked building), while in all the other versions his gift was "one cave" (*ekaṃ layanaṃ*) for the monks to live or meditate in. The variant in Gāndhārī is significant in that it implies a different understanding of Śroṇa's karmic history. Most of the other versions specify that he gave only "one cave" in order to stress the point, frequently mentioned in the *Songs of Lake Anavatapta*, that a small gift made with a pure heart can create great merit. In the Gāndhārī, however (and apparently also in Chinese A), the implied connection is that it was his gift of a *kūṭāgāra* that caused him to receive from his father a birth gift of twenty *koṭi*s in a subsequent birth, whence his nickname (not actually mentioned in the text) Koṭiviṃśa, "Twenty Crores"; his karma was, so to speak, determined by a pun.

The other Sanskrit, Pali, and Chinese texts are independent versions that for the most part differ only in the ordering of the component words and phrases. This variation in word order is often an artifact of the translation process. For example, the difference in the form of words like "cave," *layanam* in Sanskrit but *leṇaṃ* in Pali, often requires that the translators rearrange these and the surrounding words in order to maintain the proper metrical scheme, which is generally the same in the Indian languages concerned.

Gāndhārī
*cadudiśami saghami kuḍ(*a)gharo maya kridu* °
*vivaśisa praveaṇo badhumadir(*a)y(*adha)ṇ(*i)e* °
During the time of the Buddha Vipaśyin, I made a hall for the universal community in the capital city Bandhumatī.

Pali (*Apadāna*)
vipassino pāvacane ekaṃ leṇaṃ mayā kataṃ
cātuddisassa saṅghassa bandhumārājadhāniyā
During the time of the Buddha Vipaśyin, I made one cave for the universal community in Bandhumā's capital city.

Sanskrit A (manuscript fragment from Gilgit)
*cātu(*rdiśasya saṃ)ghasya mayaikaṃ layanaṃ kṛtam*
bandhumatyāṃ pravacane rājadhānyāṃ vipaśyinaḥ

During the time of the Buddha Vipaśyin, I made one cave for the universal community in the capital city Bandhumatī.

Sanskrit B (manuscript fragment from Kizil)
+ + + + + + + + + + + + + + + + + +
*(*vipaśyinaḥ) prāvacane bandhumatyāṃ sukh* + + +
During the time of the Buddha Vipaśyin, in Bandhumatī, pleasant . . .

Tibetan
rnam par gzigs kyi gsung rab la rgyal po'i pho brang bshes ldan du
bdag gis phyogs bzhi'i dge 'dun gyi gnas khang gcig cig brtsigs nas ni
During the time of the Buddha Vipaśyin, I made one cave for the universal community in the capital city Bandhumatī.

Chinese A (translated by Dharmarakṣa)
惟衛佛世時 槃頭摩國土
本爲四方僧 興立一房室
Long ago, in the age of the Buddha Vipaśyin, in the land of Bandhumatī, I established a hall for the universal community.

Chinese B (translated by Yijing)
昔於親慧城 造一毘訶羅
淨心修已畢 奉施四方僧
In the past, in the city of Bandhumatī, with a pure mind I made a vihāra, and after building it I offered it to the universal community.

Appendix 2

SPECIMEN OF A GANDHĀRAN BUDDHIST INSCRIPTION: THE RELIQUARY OF ŚATRULEKA

THE INSCRIPTION of the *kṣatrapa* (satrap) Śatruleka is engraved on a circular stone bowl of gray schist decorated with horizontal lines and lotus-petal and chevron patterns engraved on the cover. The bowl is now in the collection of the Museum für Indische Kunst, Berlin. Its original findspot is unknown, but it is probably from the Bajaur region of northwestern Pakistan. It is an outstanding example of the very numerous Gandhāran reliquaries, of which more than four hundred are known, comprehensively collected and illustrated in Jongeward et al. 2012. (This one is described there on pages 97–98.) Like most reliquaries, it has two parts, a bowl and a lid with a lip that fits into the top of the base. This form appears to have been developed or adapted from boxes used to store cosmetics or jewelry. A special feature of this ornate example is the knob atop the lid in the form of a miniature reproduction of the reliquary itself.

As usual, the reliquary contained various precious objects that were intended as supplementary offerings. These include a small circular silver casket and another, even smaller, one of gold that nested inside the silver one. Also found inside the smaller caskets were flowers made of gold leaf, pearls, and other small objects and pieces of jewelry in gold and crystal. The inscription, written in five lines around the

Figure 38. The inscribed reliquary of Śatruleka.

bowl, records the dedication of a relic of Lord Śākyamuni by an otherwise unknown satrap Śatruleka, who describes himself as the nephew (*bhagineya*, specifically "sister's son") of Vijayamitra [II], king of Apraca. Therefore this inscription belongs to the family line of kings of Apraca, whose last known member was the *stratega* Aśpavarma, who is mentioned in one of the avadāna texts in the British Library Gāndhārī manuscripts. The inscription is dated in the year 77 of the era of King Azes, which corresponds either to 20/21 CE or 30/31 CE, depending on which of the proposed starting years of that era, 58/57 BCE or 48/47 BCE, one chooses.[458] Thus this inscription represents the cultural milieu from which many of the Gandhāran manuscripts presented in this book stem and is nearly contemporary with some of them.

The inscription follows, for the most part, the usual formula of relic donation records. Like many reliquaries dedicated by the Apraca royal family and their associates, it specifies that the relics are established "in a previously unestablished place," illustrating the central role of the relic cult in the spread of Buddhism to the northwest and beyond. As is also typical of Gandhāran reliquary inscriptions, it includes a declaration of "honor" to all buddhas, solitary buddhas, arhats, and their disciples, plus a list of the donor's relatives with whom he wished to share the merit of his pious act. At the end a supplementary sentence is added in which one Patrolaśiśaka claims to have also established the relic. This otherwise unknown person was probably a functionary in the monastery in whose stūpa the relic was interred who had some role in the accompanying ritual and thereby laid claim to a share of the merit. Such additions of participants' names at the end are found in several Gandhāran relic dedication inscriptions.[459]

The inscription mentions several interesting and historically significant names. The "Kāśyapīya monks," who are specified in line 2 as the recipients of the reliquary (or theoretically, its caretakers on behalf of the entire Buddhist community), represent one of the several scholastic lineages cited in Gandhāran inscriptions, along with the more frequently mentioned Dharmaguptakas and Sarvāstivādins. Of the donor's two sons (line 3), one, presumably the elder, is named Indrasena, a typical Indian kṣatriya name of the period, but the second has a Greek name, Menander. Perhaps he was named in honor of the great Indo-Greek king of that name who ruled some 150 years earlier. Finally, Rukhuṇaka, who is described in line 5 as "mother of a living son," figures prominently among the donors mentioned in the inscriptions of the Apraca rulers, where she is sometimes referred to as "wife of the Apraca king." It is not clear from the information available whether she was the wife of the current ruling king, Vijayamitra, or rather of a previous king, but in any case, her title "mother of a living son" indicates that at the Apraca court she was a figure of some authority, perhaps grooming her son as a future king.

The complete decipherment of this inscription since its initial publication in 1982 has been a gradual process, involving the work of seven different specialists.[460] Some of the difficulties arose from the procedure of engraving the text, in which a scribe first lightly scratched the text and an engraver then cut it into the soft stone. The engraver, who may have been illiterate, frequently miswrote the letters, so that it is only through a close examination of the original object[461] that the originally intended readings can usually be made out. The translation presented here is a distillation of what seem to me the best parts of the several editions.

> [1] savatsaraye sata-sa{sa}tatimaye maharajasa ayasa vurtakalasa śavaṇasa masasa divasaye catuviśaye 20 4 śatrulekeṇa kṣatraveṇa subhutikaputreṇa apracaraja-bhagineyeṇa bhagavato śakamune dhatuve [2] pratiṭhavita apratiṭhavitapurvaṃmi pradeśaṃmi aṭhayi-gramaṃmi kaśaviyana bhadaṃtana parigrahaṃmi. sarva budha pujayita sarva pracegasabudha-rahaṃta-ṣavaka pujayita. sarve [3] pujaraha puyayita. ima dhatuvi pratiṭhaviti sadha bharyayi daviliye putrehi ca iṃdraseṇeṇa menaṃdrena ca. matapita pujayita. bhrada iṃdasene iśparo [4] vijayamitro avacaraja |[5] (*iṃ)dravarmo stratego gaṃdharaśpami pujayidu. rukhuṇaka jiputra. sarva pujarahaṃ pujayita. imi dhatu pratiṭhavati patrolaśiśaka.

> [1] In the seventy-seventh year of the deceased great King Azes, on the twenty-fourth, 24, day of the month of Śrāvaṇa, [2] the relics of the Lord Śākyamuni have been established by the satrap Śatruleka, son of Subhūtika and nephew of the Apraca king, in a place where relics had not previously been established, at the village Aṭhayi, in the keeping of the Kāśyapīya monks.
>
> All of the buddhas are [hereby] honored; all of the solitary buddhas, arhats, and disciples are honored; and all (others) [3] deserving of honor are honored.

He establishes these relics together with his wife Davilī and with his sons Indrasena and Menander. His mother and father are honored. His brother Indrasena, Lord [4] Vijayamitra, the Apraca king, [5] (and) Indravarma, the commander, master of Gandhāra, are honored. Rukhuṇaka, mother of a living son, (is honored). All (others) deserving of honor are honored.

Patrolaśiśaka establishes these relics.

Notes

1 Bodhi 2000 and 2012.

2 For a detailed description of the British Library scrolls, see Salomon 1999.

3 The original text reads *saghami caüdiśami dhamaüteaṇa parigrahami* (= Skt *saṅghe cāturdiśe dharmaguptakānāṃ parigrahe*). This is an abbreviated version of the stereotyped formula for donations to a monastery. "The universal community" (literally, "the community of the four directions") refers to the theoretical ideal according to which all Buddhists belong to one saṅgha. "In the possession of the Dharmaguptakas" means that, in theory, the particular community of Dharmaguptakas concerned had the right to temporary use of the donated object. The significance of the Dharmaguptaka connection is discussed in chapter 3 (pages 101–2) and in the introduction to translation 9 (pages 297–98).

4 For discussion of the methods and motivations for the ritual interment of ancient Buddhist manuscripts, see Salomon 2009 and Strauch 2014b.

5 Salomon 2000.

6 To date, six volumes of the series have been published by Allon, Glass, Lenz, and Salomon (see the bibliography entries under these authors' names for details), and several more volumes are currently under preparation. Each volume consists of a detailed study of a particular scroll or set of scrolls, containing, besides an edition and English translation, detailed studies of the manuscript itself, its language, script, sources, and parallels. To a large extent, this book represents a summary and compilation of the material in the published and in-progress volumes of the GBT series.

7 A complete bibliography of publications on Gāndhārī texts of all kinds (Baums and Glass 2002a) is available at http://gandhari.org/a_bibliography.php.

8 *Atharva Veda* 5.22.14.

9 *Chāndogya Upaniṣad* 6.14.

10 The dates of the Buddha's life remain uncertain and controversial. Three approximate dates for the Buddha's passing, his *parinirvāṇa*, which occurred in the eightieth year of his life, have been proposed: 543 BCE, 486 (or 483) BCE, and ca. 373–368 BCE. For a brief summary of the issue, see Errington and Cribb 1992, 11 and 12n3.

11 Gokhale 1982.

12 An authoritative translation of this inscription is given in Hultzsch 1925, 173–74. For a scholarly analysis, see Schneider 1982.

13 For the *Aśokāvadāna* literature, see Strong 1983.
14 Salomon and Schopen 1984.
15 Strong 1983, 220.
16 Jongeward et al. 2012.
17 Strong 1983, 113–15.
18 Strong 1983, 5–15.
19 *Muryakaliṇate thubute*; Falk 2005, 348–49.
20 Salomon 2007. A few other inscriptions at the major stūpa sites at Taxila and Butkara (in the Swat Valley) also refer to *dharmarājikā* stūpas, though without explicit mention of Aśoka. But these inscriptions date from around the first century CE and thus do not prove that these stūpas were actually founded by Aśoka, and indeed the visible structures there are clearly post-Mauryan. Yet this too is not the whole story, because, like many ancient stūpas, these had been rebuilt and expanded, as many as five times in the case of the Butkara stūpa. It has been plausibly suggested that the inner core of the Taxila and Butkara stūpas could have been original Aśokan stūpas on the grounds, for example, that early punch-marked coins of the type that are believed to date from the Mauryan period were found at the Butkara stūpa. (On the dating of the Butkara stūpa, see Faccenna 1964, 27–39, especially page 32.)
21 On these index scrolls and their relationship to the other Senior scrolls, see the introduction to translation 2. The sūtra in question has a Pali parallel, the *Āsīvisopama Sutta*, at *Saṃyutta-nikāya* IV 172–75.
22 On Menander, see Lamotte 1988, 419–26, Bopearachchi 1990, and Fussman 1993.
23 See, e.g., Fussman 1993, 90–91, and Bopearachchi 1990, 39–40.
24 This text is "paracanonical" in the sense that it is included in the *Khuddaka-nikāya* in the Theravāda Pali canon in Burma but not in Thailand and Sri Lanka.
25 The Pali *Questions of Milinda* is translated in Horner 1963. For the Chinese version, see Demiéville 1924.
26 Horner 1963, 2:304.
27 Menander was known to several historians of the Western classical world. Most interestingly, the Roman historian Plutarch, writing in the early second century CE, reported a curious legend according to which, after Menander was killed in battle, various cities claimed his ashes. They then had to be divided into equal parts among them and were interred in separate monuments in each place. The obvious resemblance of this story to that of the destiny of the relics of the Buddha after his parinirvāṇa has led some to take it as evidence that Menander was a Buddhist, but this is speculative at best; it is perhaps more likely that it results from some misunderstanding or dislocation of the Buddha legend. For discussion, see Fussman 1993, 65, Bopearachchi 1990, 48n47, and Neelis 2011, 105–6.
28 This possibility is mentioned in Fussman 1993, 66.
29 For an authoritative presentation of this inscription, see Fussman 1993, 95–111. The text and an English translation is also given in Baums 2012, 202–3. It has been proposed (Falk 2005, 349–53) that some of the inscriptions on the reliquary (though not the reliquary itself) are modern forgeries, but I do not agree with this theory.
30 Konow 1929, 1; see also Salomon 2012, 197–99.
31 All of these inscriptions are compiled with text and translation in Baums 2012. One

of them, the relic bowl of Śatruleka, the nephew of an Apraca king, is presented in appendix 2 of this book.

32 See Baums 2012, 233–34.

33 Baums 2012, 209–11, 224, 227–33.

34 Salomon and Baums 2007.

35 Legge 1886, 29.

36 Beal 1884, 1:123; Li 1996, 85.

37 Strong 2004, 85–97.

38 Przyluski 1914; Lamotte 1947–50, 152–58.

39 Beal 1884, 1:99; Li 1996, 70–71.

40 Beal 1884, 1:121–23; Li 1996, 84–85. This legend is also recorded in the *Mūlasarvāstivāda-vinaya*; see Przyluski 1914, 510–12.

41 Dunn 2005, 229–30.

42 Beal 1884, 1:112; Li 1996, 78.

43 Beal 1884, 1:47–48; Li 1996: 36. In the northwest, the name Bhallika was assumed to be connected with Balkh, a major city in northern Afghanistan. But other local Buddhist traditions present the two merchants' native lands as such diverse regions as Utkala (modern Orissa), Sri Lanka, or even Burma; see Strong 2004, 76–82.

44 See Falk and Strauch 2014, 54, and the introduction to translation 8.

45 Allon 2014, 22.

46 *Jihonige mahakṣatra(*ve)*; *gadharami*. See Salomon 1999, 141–45, and Lenz 2010, 95–98.

47 British Library fragment 1, avadāna no. 8 (Salomon 1999, 145–49; Lenz 2010, 85–93). This story is summarized in the introduction to translation 7.

48 See the further discussion in chapter 3 (pages 87–88) and the introduction to translation 6.

49 Salomon 1986, 289–90; Przyluski 1914, 513 and n6.

50 Palumbo (forthcoming).

51 See the summary of this story in translation 6f; for further details, see Lenz 2003, 182–84.

52 For further examples, see Errington and Cribb 1992, 10n7 and page 37.

53 Falk 2014.

54 See translation 7b.

55 Sims-Williams and Cribb 1995–96; Sims-Williams 2004.

56 The legends of Kaniṣka as a patron of Buddhism are compiled in Zürcher 1968.

57 Beal 1884, 99–101; Li 1996, 71–72.

58 The site of Kaniṣka's stūpa in Puruṣapura (modern Peshawar, Pakistan) has been identified on the basis of a Gāndhārī inscription found there that refers to "the monastery of King Kaniṣka" (Baums 2012, 246).

59 The starting date of Kaniṣka's era has been a long-standing historical controversy, but the theory of Harry Falk (2001) that it began in 127 CE is now generally considered to be the most persuasive one.

60 See the further discussion of the date of the Senior scrolls in the introduction to translation 2.

61 For an authoritative, though as usual approximate and uncertain, presentation of the

dates of Huviṣka and other Kuṣāṇa rulers, see Sims-Williams and Cribb 1995–96, 101.

62 Baums 2012, 243–44.

63 Salomon 2002.

64 See chapter 3 (pages 88–90) and translation 12.

65 Li 1996, 70; cf. Beal 1884, 1:98.

66 Li 1996, 66; cf. Beal 1884, 1:91.

67 Sachau 1888, 2:11.

68 On this material in general, see Neelis 2011.

69 See the detailed study of these traditions in Nattier 1991 and Lamotte 1988, 191–202.

70 On the early history of writing in India, see Salomon 1998a, 10–14, and further references provided there.

71 Norman 1983a, 10–11; Bechert 1992.

72 Salomon 2009.

73 Salomon 2011.

74 This corpus of early sūtras is referred to in scholarly discourse as the *āgama-sūtra*s. The term refers to the five divisions of the Sūtra-piṭaka (P Sutta-piṭaka), which are usually called *āgama* in Sanskrit and *nikāya* in Pali. For further details on the structure of the sūtra collections, see chapter 3 (pages 84–85).

75 Skilling 1993.

76 On these discoveries in general, see Harrison and Hartmann 2014, vii–xxii, and for specific discoveries, see especially these articles in that volume: for Central Asian manuscripts, Wille 2014; Gilgit manuscripts, von Hinüber 2014; Bamiyan manuscripts, Braarvig 2014.

77 See, for example, pages 168–72 in the introduction to translation 3.

78 Salomon 2011, 167.

79 This problem of scriptural authenticity and accuracy is by no means unique to Buddhism. All religions that rely on a fixed corpus of scripture struggle with the inevitable textual variations, with some traditions taking a more rigid position, others more flexible.

80 For a discussion of this crucial episode, including the several versions and interpretations of it, see Lamotte 1988, 552–56.

81 Since the Gāndhārī language and the Kharoṣṭhī script are almost always used together, the inscriptions or manuscripts concerned have often been referred to, more or less interchangeably, as being in "Kharoṣṭhī" or "Gāndhārī." In this book, as is generally the case in more recent publications, the linguistic designation Gāndhārī is preferred.

82 The name Gāndhārī is not directly attested in ancient documents but was invented by the pioneering philologist H. W. Bailey (1946, 764) to refer what until then had been known as "northwestern Prakrit" or the like. Bailey proposed this term on the analogy of the names of other Prakrit dialects, whose traditional names were based on a geographical term with the addition of a feminine adjectival suffix *-ī*, referring to the understood feminine noun for "language" (*bhāṣā*). Thus, as the local Prakrit of Magadha in northeastern India is called Māgadhī, so, reasoned Bailey, the language of Gandhāra would have been Gāndhārī.

83 In the words of an oft-cited linguist's proverb (attributed to the Yiddish scholar Max Weinreich), "a language is a dialect with an army and a navy."

84 For another example of wide spelling variation, see note 208 in translation 2.

85 This statement disregards the question of the still undeciphered Indus Valley script of the third and second millennium BCE, which has no discernible relationship with the later scripts concerned here.

86 The thorny problems of the origins of the Indian scripts is summarized in Salomon 1998a, 19–31 and 51–54.

87 For the complete history of the decipherment of Kharoṣṭhī, see Salomon 1998a, 209–15.

88 For a specimen of an inscription of this class, see appendix 2.

89 Problems of this kind are particularly common among the avadāna and pūrvayoga stories (samples of which are presented here in translations 6 and 7), because they are casual compositions that were set down by a local monk in a colloquial and extremely compact style.

90 Until recently there was no comprehensive dictionary of Gāndhārī. This situation is now being remedied by the online Dictionary of Gāndhārī (http://gandhari.org/a_dictionary.php) produced by Stefan Baums and Andrew Glass (Baums and Glass 2002b). There is also still no published grammar of Gāndhārī, except in connection with limited groups of texts, such as the Central Asian administrative documents (Burrow 1937).

91 This curious story is explained in detail in Brough 1962, 45–48. It is translated, but without explanation, in Przyluski 1914, 529–31.

92 Salomon 2001, 248–51.

93 Fussman 1989, 486.

94 Brough 1962, 53.

95 On the development and interpretation of the Gāndhārī hypothesis, see Boucher 1998 and 2000.

96 Boucher 1998, 480.

97 Boucher 1998, 499.

98 See the further discussion in chapter 3 (pages 84–85) of the *Dīrghāgama* and its place within the Buddhist canons.

99 See especially Karashima 1994.

100 An extract from this commentary is presented in translation 9.

101 For details of the correspondences and contrasts, see the introduction to translation 9.

102 For the inscription, see the introduction; for further discussion of the scholastic affiliations of the Gāndhārī texts, see chapter 3 (pages 101–2) and the introduction to translation 9.

103 Bailey 1946; Sims-Williams 1983.

104 See pages 99–100 in chapter 3 for a discussion of the notion of a canon in Gāndhārī.

105 For the initial announcement of the Senior collection, see Salomon 2003; for more detailed descriptions, Allon 2007 and 2014.

106 The Bamiyan collection as a whole is described in Braarvig 2014 and Matsuda 2014, while the Gāndhārī component is summarized in Salomon 2014, 6–8. For detailed studies of the Bamiyan manuscripts, see Braarvig 2000, 2002, 2006, and 2016. On

the dating of the Gāndhārī fragments by radiocarbon testing, see Allon, Salomon, Jacobsen, and Zoppi 2006.

107 Allon and Salomon 2000.

108 Strauch 2008; Falk and Strauch 2014.

109 Salomon 1998b.

110 Note that the English word *volume* is derived from Latin *volumen*, "roll" or "scroll," reflecting the use of similar scrolls in classical Europe.

111 For further examples and comments on this pattern, see Allon 2007, 20–21, Salomon 2011, 182–83, and the introductions to translations 2, 5, and 12.

112 For a summary of the collections of Gandhāran manuscripts and the texts that they comprise, see the charts in Falk and Strauch 2014, 55 and 57.

113 Texts with parallels are represented here in translations 1–5, 8, and 12.

114 Translations 6–7 and 9–11.

115 The Sūtra-piṭakas of other lost Indian Buddhist canons evidently had somewhat different contents and arrangements, as far as can be determined from their surviving fragments and from descriptions of them in later Buddhist literature, mostly as preserved in Chinese translation. For example, a given sūtra may appear in different collections in different canons. The contents of the Vinaya-piṭakas and especially the Abhidharma-piṭakas are even more variable across the various schools. For details, see Lamotte 1988, 149–91, and Oberlies 2003.

116 See the description of the *Saṃyutta-nikāya/Saṃyuktāgama* in the introduction to translation 2.

117 See the description of the *Aṅguttara-nikāya/Ekottarikāgama* in the introduction to translation 1.

118 The *Khuddaka-nikāya* (Skt **Kṣudrakāgama*) is the section of the Sūtra-piṭaka most subject to variation across canons, and to some extent even within the Pali canon; see Lamotte 1988, 156–63, and recall the discussion of the *Questions of Milinda* in chapter 1 (pages 24–27).

119 See the summary in Falk and Strauch 2014, 62–64, which is up to date except for the recently identified Gāndhārī *Ekottarikāgama* manuscript from Bamiyan, discussed below.

120 Strictly speaking, one should rather say "correspond to sūtras that in the Pali canon are part of the *Saṃyutta-nikāya*," since we cannot be certain that they were classed the same way in the hypothetical Gāndhārī canon.

121 Translations 3 and 4.

122 In the Pali canon this collection of verses is one of the five sections (*vagga*) of the *Suttanipāta*, which in turn is one of the fifteen works in the *Khuddaka-nikāya*.

123 Falk 2011, 13–15.

124 Translations 5 and 8.

125 These vinaya texts have not yet been fully published but are described in Strauch 2008, 116–18, and Falk and Strauch 2014, 59–60. On the interpretation of the double *Prātimokṣa* text, see in particular Strauch 2008, 116–17.

126 Lamotte 1988, 181.

127 For a summary of the themes of the pūrvayoga and avadāna stories, see Lenz 2010, 8–12.

128 See for example Rotman 2008.

129 Six of these were introduced in Allon and Salomon 2010. A few fragments of a sev-

enth one, the *Sūtra of the Samādhi of Direct Encounter with the Buddhas of the Present* (*Pratyutpannasaṃmukhāvasthitabuddhasamādhi Sūtra*), have been identified in a private collection and are being prepared for publication. This text is particularly interesting as it is among the earliest Mahāyāna sūtras to be translated into Chinese.

130 Baums, Braarvig, Lenz, Liland, Matsuda, and Salomon, 2016.

131 Harrison, Lenz, Lin, and Salomon, 2016.

132 Baums, Glass, and Matsuda, 2016.

133 Strauch 2010, 50–51.

134 Strauch 2010, 29–44.

135 Strauch 2010, 61–62.

136 Of the texts concerned, only the *Perfection of Wisdom in Eight Thousand Lines* is extant in full in Sanskrit, although a Sanskrit version of the *Bodhisattvapiṭaka Sūtra* has recently been discovered, and some small fragments of the *Sūtra of the Samādhi of Direct Encounter with the Buddhas of the Present* (see note 129) and the *Sūtra of the Fortunate Eon* are known.

137 Strauch 2010, 62.

138 This manuscript has not yet been published but is described briefly in Strauch 2008, 120–21, and discussed in detail in Strauch 2014a.

139 Strauch 2008, 121–23.

140 Falk and Strauch 2014, 67–68.

141 See the introduction to translation 5 for details.

142 The British Library manuscript has been edited in Lenz 2003; see translation 4. The Split manuscript is published in Falk 2015.

143 The *Suttanipāta* has been translated many times. The authoritative scholarly translation is Norman 1992; Norman 1985 is an abridged, popular edition of this translation. Bodhi 2017 presents a new translation along with the traditional commentaries.

144 See the introduction to translation 10.

145 The fifth one is not clearly identified. For details see Salomon 1999, 158–63.

146 See the introduction to translation 11.

147 The Bajaur collection also includes three texts, not yet published, that seem to exhibit Mahāyāna characteristics (Falk and Strauch 2014, 71).

148 See Allon and Salomon 2010, 13–17, and Strauch 2010, 25–26.

149 Nattier 2003, 171–92; cf. Strauch 2010, 61.

150 Schopen 1975, 181 = Schopen 2005, 52.

151 But for a partial exception to this statement, see Allon 2001, 224–25.

152 Allon 2001, 22–25. It is for this reason that Mark Allon cautiously entitled his edition of the manuscript *Three Gāndhārī Ekottarikāgama-Type Sūtras*.

153 On these and similar short sūtra anthologies, see the introduction to translation 2 and Salomon 2011, 184–203.

154 See Glass 2007, 21–22, 36–50, and the introduction to translation 2.

155 Hartmann 1999, 127–36.

156 Seven versions are listed in MacQueen 1988, 12–18, to which the Gāndhārī text can now be added.

157 These fragments are presented and their significance evaluated in Jantrasrisalai, Lenz, Lin, and Salomon, 2016. Despite its importance, this manuscript is not presented in this book because the remnants are too fragmentary to allow for a connected translation.

158 Here the Chinese version of the *Ekottarikāgama* is not of much help, because its contents and arrangement are notoriously aberrant in comparison with the other versions.

159 This evolutionary process is described in detail in Salomon 2017.

160 Collins 1990, 96.

161 See Beal 1884, 151–56 = Li 1996, 102–6, and Salomon 2006, 373–74.

162 See, for example, Bareau 1955 and Lamotte 1988, 517–49.

163 See Oberlies 2003 for details.

164 See Allon and Salomon 2000, 273, and Allon 2014, 22–23.

165 Salomon 1999, 166–69.

166 This manuscript has been studied in detail by Mark Allon (2001), and the translations and interpretations presented here are largely based on his edition.

167 Numbers 12+14 in the British Library collection. The double number reflects the fact that two of the component sections of the scroll, which was composed of several sheets of birchbark glued together, had become separated and were initially catalogued and conserved as separate fragments. Only later, when the texts were studied in detail, did it become clear that the two fragments were actually part of the same scroll.

168 The exact number of sūtras is difficult to specify due to the different ways in which they can be presented and enumerated. The modern printed edition by the Pali Text Society numbers 2,344 sūtras, but the text itself refers in a final summary to 9,557 sūtras; see Bodhi 2012: 18–19.

169 The titles applied to this and the other sūtras in the manuscript do not actually occur in the text but are posited on the basis of their contents.

170 Here, as in the other translations, portions of the text that are absent in the manuscript but supplied on the basis of internal or external parallels are indicated in square brackets.

171 For complete lists of the marks (*lakṣaṇa*) of a buddha, see Rotman 2008, 463, and Strong 2001, 42.

172 *Buddha-bayaṇa* = Skt/P *buddhavacana*.

173 For details see the discussion in Allon 2001, 249–53.

174 *Saṅgīti Sūtra* 7.2, translated in Walshe 1995, 502.

175 Here and in the following sentences the verb is in the future tense (*bhaviśasi* = Skt *bhaviṣyasi*), hence literally "Will you be a god?" etc. The verb could be interpreted as a normal future, asking about the Buddha's future lives (as Dhoṇa incorrectly imagines them), but on the basis of the context and many parallels it is probably better understood as the "presumptive future," with the sense of "could you be," "might you be," etc., and this alternative is chosen in the translation. For a complete discussion of the issue, see Allon 2001, 171–74.

176 "General features" (G *ṇimiti* = Skt/P *nimitta*) are the external characteristics or appearances of a sense object that catch one's attention upon perceiving them. "Secondary features" (G *aṇovejaṇa* = Skt/P *anuvyañjana*) are the less distinctive or striking features of an object that are noticed along with or after the general features.

177 A common epithet of the Buddha Śākyamuni, referring to his birth in the Śākya clan, which claimed descent from the Ikṣvākus, who in turn were said to be descendents of the sun.

178 See pages 36, 52, 230, 254, and 262.

179 See chapter 1, note 59.

180 Tests were carried out on two fragments from the Senior scrolls, which yielded probable dating ranges of 129–263 CE for one fragment and 81–244 CE for the other. These results do not provide exact dates since (contrary to the impression often given in superficial media reports) radiocarbon dates provide ranges of probable dates rather than precise years; see Allon et al. 2006.

181 Although the shape and size of the scrolls varies considerably, this is probably a function of the pieces of bark that were available to the scribe or his patron.

182 By Mark Allon in Glass 2007, 19–20.

183 Harrison 1997 and 2002; Salomon 2011, 186–88.

184 A similar example is the famous *Sūtra in Forty-Two Sections*, extant only in Chinese.

185 For details, see the discussion and chart in Glass 2007, 43–46.

186 *Saṃyutta-nikāya* III 22.93–102. These are translated in Bodhi 2000, 949–62.

187 *Saṃyutta-nikāya* I 9.1–14. Translated in Bodhi 2000, 294–304.

188 The preceding arguments are essentially a summary of the detailed discussion in Glass 2007, 26–50.

189 The translations and other materials in this section are based largely on the work of Andrew Glass (2007).

190 This technique is also demonstrated in the story of the disciple Yaśas in the *Songs of Lake Anavatapta* presented in translation 5d.

191 The *Girimānanda Sutta*, translated in Bodhi 2012, 1411–15.

192 *Saṃyutta-nikāya* III 22.33. Translated in Bodhi 2000, 877.

193 This apt term is proposed in Harrison 2008, 219n27.

194 Gāndhārī *ṇivrida* = Skt *nirvidā* = P *nibbidā*. On the several possible translations of this term, see Bodhi 2000, 53.

195 *Saṃyutta-nikāya* III 22.146. Translated as "Engrossed in Revulsion" in Bodhi 2000, 977–78.

196 *Saṃyutta-nikāya* III 22.101. Translated in Bodhi 2000, 959–61.

197 For details see Glass 2007, 35.

198 The sūtras in question are translated in Bodhi 2000, 553–56, and 2012, 1088–89. See Glass 2007, 194, for further details.

199 See the discussion in Bodhi 2000, 35–36.

200 See the discussion of this point on pages 81–82.

201 The translation and analysis presented here is based on the work of Mei-huang Lee (2009).

202 *Saṃyutta-nikāya* IV 35.241–42. These sūtras are translated in Bodhi 2000, 1241–44.

203 Compare, for example, the avadāna of the two parrot chicks who are reborn in heaven in Rotman 2008, 333–36.

204 Compare the remarks in chapter 2 (pages 55–58) and in the introduction to translation 1 (page 107).

205 This type of variation in the location of different versions of a given text is common in sūtra literature generally (Schopen 1997 = 2004, 395–407).

206 See, for example, the brief discussion of the Pali *saṅkassarasamācāro* in Bodhi 2000: 1424–25n188.

207 Here as elsewhere, the titles of the sūtras are added on the basis of their contents or parallels.

208 In this short text the Buddha utters the imperative verb form (second-person plural) "abandon" six times. Among these six occurrences there are no less than five different spellings (*pracajaaṣa*, *pajaaṣa*, *pacaaṣa*, *pacahaṣa*, and *pacaeṣa*, all corresponding to Skt *prajahīta* / P *pajahatha*). This is a classic example of the rough-and-ready character of the Gāndhārī language in the absence of a standardizing authority, as discussed on pages 63–65.

209 Here the full wording is spelled out only for the first and last member of the set of five, which is the typical abbreviating pattern in Buddhist texts. The manuscript says only "This is sensation, this is perception, this is volitional formations" on the assumption that the reader should read "This is sensation, this is the arising of sensation, this is the passing away of sensation," and so forth.

210 This and the preceding sentence were originally omitted by the scribe and were subsequently added by him in small letters above the original line. The scribe was evidently thrown off by the repetition, six times, of the word translated as "because they did not cultivate" (*abhavidatva* = Skt *abhāvitatvāt*), so that his eye skipped from the second occurrence to the fourth one in his archetype manuscript. Later he realized his error and inserted the phrase containing the third instance of this word. This type of copying error, known as *haplography* (from the Greek for "once-writing"), is quite common in all manuscript traditions, but especially so in Buddhist texts due to their highly repetitive style.

211 The phrase translated as "at the right time" (*kaliṇa kalo* = Skt *kālena kālam*) could also be understood to mean "from time to time" or "now and then." Glass (2007, 208–9) translates "day in and day out."

212 The Pali term here, *vetta-bandhana-baddhāya*, is usually translated as "rigging," but since *vetta-* (= Skt *vetra*) means "cane," it might rather refer to the strips of cane with which the boards that make up the hull are lashed together.

213 Here the Gāndhārī text is apparently defective; literally translated, it says only "The ocean, monk, the current of the river Ganges." The translation is supplemented on the basis of the two parallels in Pali and one of the Chinese translations, but the entire phrase is absent from the other four versions out of the seven mentioned in the introduction to this sūtra.

214 As noted in the introduction to this translation, this is evidently a scribal error, and the correct reading should be the "dharma sense-base."

215 This refers to the Buddha's disapproval of those who undertake religious practice in order to gain inferior benefits such as rebirth as a god, instead of the higher goal of liberation from saṃsāra.

216 This explanation involves an etymological play on the word for whirlpool (*avaṭa* = Skt *āvarta*) and the verb "renounces" (literally, "turns back"; *avataḏi* = *āvartate*).

217 One of several possible alternative translations for this problematic phrase is "who has impure intentions and [deceitfully] smiling behavior" (dividing *asuyi-sakapa spera-samayara* instead of *asuyi-sakapa-spera-samayara*); see the comments on this crux in the introduction to this translation.

218 Here and in each of the following phrases the verbs are in the third person rather than the second person, as the context would lead the reader to expect and as is the case in

the parallel texts. This peculiarity is probably the result of miscopying by the scribe, who mechanically repeated the corresponding third-person passage in the preceding text without adapting it to the second-person context here. However, in the interest of faithfully presenting the manuscript text as it stands, I have reproduced the exact wording.

219 The text is translated from the Sanskrit of the *Mūlasarvāstivāda-vinaya* (Dutt 1947, 51).

220 Dutt 1947, 53–57.

221 The introduction and translation are based on Salomon 2000.

222 Ripley 1952, 572.

223 Jamison 1998, 253.

224 Since *khaḍga* (Skt) / *khagga* (P) means "rhinoceros" and *viṣāṇa*/*visāṇa* means "horn," the compound word *khaḍgaviṣāṇa*/*khaggavisāṇa* can be taken to mean "rhinoceros horn." However, *khaḍga*/*khagga* can also mean "sword," so that the entire compound can mean "sword-horn," a nickname for the rhinoceros.

225 The Gāndhārī manuscript itself, as usual, does not bear a title, but I have assumed that this version would have had a title corresponding to that given in the Pali and Sanskrit version.

226 The reconstruction process will be explained below in the section discussing the summary verses (pages 172–74).

227 On solemn resolutions (Skt *praṇidhi*, *praṇidhāna*), see the introduction to translation 5 (page 204).

228 For other stories about solitary buddhas in this book, see the recitations of Mahākāśyapa and Nanda in the *Songs of Lake Anavatapta* (translation 5a–b) and the story of Ājñāta Kauṇḍinya in the previous life stories (translation 6d).

229 See, for example, Norman 1983b; for further references, see Salomon 2000, 8–9.

230 See the introduction to the *Perfection of Wisdom Sūtra* (translation 12, page 337).

231 On the *Dharmapada* in Gāndhārī, see translation 4.

232 The massive commentary on the Pali *Dhammapada* is translated in three volumes in Burlingame 1921.

233 Sutta 122 of the *Majjhima-nikāya*; translated in Ñāṇamoli and Bodhi 1995, 971–78.

234 Compare the similar type of karmic stories (*avadāna*) in the *Songs of Lake Anavatapta* (translation 5).

235 The texts are given below in the original language, where their similarity will again be evident:

Gāndhārī
sarveṣo bhuteṣo ṇiṣae daṃdo
avihesao aṃñataraṃ pi teṣo
*metreṇa citiṇa hitaṇ(*ukampi*
eko care khargaviṣaṇagapo)

Pali
sabbesu bhūtesu nidhāya daṇḍaṃ
aviheṭhayaṃ aññataraṃ pi tesaṃ
na puttaṃ iccheya kuto sahāyaṃ
eko care khaggavisāṇakappo

Sanskrit
sarveṣu prāṇeṣu nidhāya daṇḍaṃ
aviheṭhako anyatare pi teṣāṃ
nikṣiptadaṇḍo trasasthāvareṣu
eko care khaḍgaviṣāṇakalpo.

236 Translated in Jones 1949, 1:302–5.

237 Not to be confused with *udāna*, "inspired utterance."

238 This verse refers to the proper way for a monk to beg for food. He should not care whether the food he gets is delicious or bland, and he should approach the homes where he seeks alms in due order, rather than going directly to those where he has previously gotten tasty meals.

239 It is said in some sources that one can attain liberation of the mind (*ceto-vimutti*) for a while but then lose it; for references, see Norman 1992, 152, and Bodhi 2000, 419–20n308.

240 This verse, like verses 34 and 35, describes a monk who meditates in the wilderness without any fear or concern for its dangers and discomforts.

241 These terms (= Skt *maitrī, upekṣā, karuṇā, muditā*) constitute the four "infinite sublime states" or "pure dwellings" (*brahmavihāra*), a prominent set of ideal mental states.

242 The five obstructions (*nīvaraṇa*) are desire for sense pleasures, malice and hatred, sloth and torpor, agitation and worry, and doubt (*Aṅguttara-nikāya* V 51).

243 The background stories presented in the commentary are conveniently summarized in the notes to Roebuck's translation of the *Dhammapada* (2010, 113–225).

244 See, for example, Brough 1962, xxv–xxix.

245 Among recent translations aimed at a general audience, noteworthy are Carter and Palihawadana 1987 and Roebuck 2010, both of which include helpful extracts from the commentary. The translation of K. R. Norman (1997) provides an authoritative technical rendering for specialist readers.

246 All of these texts are summarized in Roebuck 2010, xxviii–xxxv.

247 See, for example, the list in Harrison and Hartmann 2014, 203.

248 The Sanskrit text was definitively edited in Bernhard 1965–90 but has not been translated.

249 See the discussion in Brough 1962, 34–39.

250 This dialect is known mostly from a large body of official and administrative documents of the Shan-shan (Kroraina) kingdom, which adjoined Khotan to the east. These are partially translated in Burrow 1940.

251 So according to Brough 1962, 28–29 and 44, although Roebuck (2010, xxxviii) disputes this. Similar instances of opposite ordering of sections of a compilation in different sectarian versions have been observed elsewhere, notably in the case of the Pali *Dīgha-nikāya* of the Theravādins versus the Sanskrit *Dīrghāgama* of the Sarvāstivādins, in which the *Brahmajāla Sūtra* is the first and last sūtra respectively (Hartmann 2004, 122–23).

252 The other eight verses are scattered in the chapters "Anger," "The Righteous," "Attention," and "Violence."

253 These problems are analyzed in detail in Lenz 2003 (part I).

254 The details are spelled out in Falk 2015, 26–27.
255 See the discussion on pages 56–57.
256 Brough 1962, xxi.
257 It is largely because of the extensive use of such expansion techniques that the *Udānavarga* is far longer than the other *Dharmapada*-type texts, at nearly one thousand verses.
258 Compare the rejection of Brough's criticism and the more nuanced appreciation of the *Dharmapada* as literature in Roebuck 2010, xlv–li.
259 The translation is primarily based on the Khotan manuscript, which is mostly complete for this section. In the translation of the last thirteen verses, which are also partially attested in the British Library scroll, the translation is a composite, with missing portions in the one manuscript filled in with the reading of the other. Portions of the text that are missing in both manuscripts have been supplied in brackets from the Pali or other parallels. The minor inconsistencies between the two manuscripts alluded to above have been leveled out in this translation, mostly by choosing the more readily comprehensible reading in each case. For full details of the problems involved, see Lenz 2003 (part I). I have also made use of an unpublished translation of the entire Gāndhārī *Dharmapada* from Khotan by K. R. Norman, and the excellent translation of the Pali version of the chapter "The Monk" by Roebuck (2010, 71–74). Faucett 1967 (part 2; the chapter "The Monk," pages 22–23 and 28–30) is a less-scholarly translation of the entire Khotan *Dharmapada* but the only one that has been published.
260 Here "immortality" (Skt *amṛta*) is a synonym for *nirvāṇa*.
261 Apparently the scribe of the Khotan manuscript here repeated verse 5 by mistake.
262 "That" presumably refers to the attainment of nirvāṇa mentioned in the previous verse.
263 The wording for "cultivate friends" (*mitra bhayea*) is virtually identical, not coincidentally, to that of verse 24 in the *Rhinoceros Sūtra*.
264 Because of the ambiguities of Gāndhārī grammar, it is not clear whether the adjectival phrase "pure in livelihood and conscientious" refers to the subject, "a monk," or the object, "friends." In verse 12, the same phrase clearly refers to the monk.
265 An alternative translation for "what he has gotten for himself" (*salāvhu* = Skt *svalābham*) is "one who has more" (= *salābham*). The same ambiguity applies to the corresponding phrase in the following verse.
266 The word translated here four times as "desire" is ambiguous, as it could also mean "karma." The ambiguity arises from the absence of long vowels in Kharoṣṭhī script. The word in question is written *kama*, which could be equivalent either to *kāma* ("desire") or *karma* in Sanskrit.
267 The third line of this verse (*bhikhu viśpaśa mavadi* = P *bhikkhu vissāsa māpādi*), tentatively translated here as "A monk may not be content," is obscure and problematic in all versions of the *Dharmapada*.
268 The phrase translated as "satisfying and liberating" (*aseyaṇe moyaka* = Skt *āsecanaṃ mocakam*) could also be interpreted as "satisfying and nourishing" (*aseyaṇem oyaka* = Skt *āsecanaṃ modakam*). There are several other possible readings and interpretations of this crux in this and the related texts; see Brough 1962, 193.

269 Swallowing a red-hot iron ball is a frequent metaphor in Buddhist sūtras for succumbing to the dangers of saṃsāra.

270 The boat is a symbol for the body, and the (implied) river or ocean through which it travels is saṃsāra. Without the burden of desire and anger, the boat will carry one quickly to nirvāṇa.

271 This verse exemplifies the Buddhist technique of classifying concepts into numerical sets, but by leaving out the referent of the first three sets of five it functions as a sort of riddle. The Pali commentary on the corresponding verse in the *Dhammapada* (370) explains that the first "five," which one must cut off, are the lower bonds (*avarambhāgiya-saṃyojanāni*); the second five, which one must get rid of, are the upper bonds (*uddhambhāgiya-saṃyojanāni*); and the third five, which are to be developed, are the faculties (*indriyāṇi*). Compare the discussion of this set in translation 9. The five attachments that one must pass beyond are attachment to desire, hatred, delusion, pride, and wrong views. (See "spiritual bonds" in the glossary for details of these categories.) The "flood" is saṃsāra; compare the metaphor in note 270.

272 The phrase translated as "being unattached (*asata* = Skt *asaktaḥ*), knows no grief" could also mean "knows no grief on account of what does not exist (*asata* = *asatā*)."

273 The Pali commentary explains that a person who has the outward trappings of a worldly person but the demeanor and discipline of an ascetic can actually be a "monk." The message of this verse is the converse of verse 17, which teaches that a person who acts like a monk may not really be one. As often stressed in Buddhist literature, it is one's state of mind, not one's external actions and appearance, that defines a real monk.

274 The flower of the fig tree (*udumbara*) is proverbial in Buddhist literature for something that is nonexistent or extremely rare.

275 The exact sense of the phrase translated as "this world and the next" (*orapara* = Skt *orapāram*) is a problem that has been extensively but inconclusively discussed by traditional and modern scholars; see, for example, Brough 1962, 202, and Lenz 2003, 72–73. Lenz suggests as a possible alternative translation "[thoughts/considerations] of the world beyond."

276 The first half of this verse is entirely obscure and has different readings in the two Gāndhārī *Dharmapada* texts as well as in the parallel verse in the *Suttanipāta* (v.8; the Pali *Dhammapada* does not contain this verse). Traditional commentators and modern scholars alike have puzzled unsuccessfully over this and the parallel verse that follows. There seems to be some underlying textual corruption, perhaps stemming from a forgotten dialect form, which cannot be recovered—unless, perhaps, this and the similar verses were intended from the very beginning to be obscure or paradoxical!

277 For the five obstructions, see note 242.

278 The five pains (*śalya,* lit. "arrows)" are anger, craving, desire for rebirth, passion, and grief.

279 *Anavatapta* literally means "not heated." According to one Buddhist legend, the lake was so named when a king named Piṇḍavaṃśa performed a great sacrifice there, in the course of which he cooked rice for a vast number of people. The water in which the rice was cooked formed a pit, which gradually cooled off and formed the lake. But in other sources, it is said that the lake is called "not heated" because the mountains surrounding it constantly shield it from the heat of the sun's rays (Salomon 2008, 6).

The actual location of the lake is difficult to determine; in the words of Staal (1990, 275), "It is not clear whether it is a lake with real water or a mythological creation," but he proposes to identify Anavatapta with the lake now known as Rakshas Tal, adjacent to Lake Manasarovar south of Mount Kailash in the high Himalayas.

280 The situation is comparable to that of the *Sūtra of the Log* translated above (translation 2e), which also was incorporated, along with many other originally independent sūtras, into the *Mūlasarvāstivāda-vinaya* and hence is available in the complete Tibetan and Chinese translations of that vinaya as well as in fragmentary remnants in Sanskrit.

281 See the further discussion of this incident below.

282 Although this particular story is not found in other Buddhist texts, Piṇḍola Bharadvāja is notorious in Buddhist literature generally for his gluttony and was sometimes said to have joined the Buddhist community for the free food it provided (see Strong 1979). The compulsive eating of stones described in the *Songs of Lake Anavatapta* seems to be a variant form of these more familiar legends.

283 The verb here is *prasadesa* (= Skt *prasādayata*), the second-person imperative form of the causative stem of the verb *pra-sad*.

284 The Sanskrit root is in fact etymologically related to English "sit" through a common Proto-Indo-European root reconstructed as **sed*; compare also English "sedentary," etc., derived from the Latin cognate *sedeo*.

285 *Prasāda* and the related words also represent an important set of concepts in Hinduism that are related to but distinct from the Buddhist sense. In the theistic context of devotional Hinduism, *prasāda* refers to the pure faith that one feels for a deity, and thence to the rewards that that deity provides in return, roughly comparable to Christian "grace." By a further extension, *prasāda* also refers to an offering of food that is presented to the deity, who then returns it to the worshiper as a sanctified token of his or her favor. On the concept of *prasāda* generally, see Rotman 2009.

286 Gospel of Mark 12:43; Luke 21:3.

287 The terms *avadāna*, *jātaka*, and sometimes also *pūrvayoga*, "previous life stories," briefly introduced in chapter 3 (pages 87–88), are in practice partially interchangeable, and their definitions and applications are somewhat fluid. Examples of early, primitive forms of these genres in Gāndhārī, labeled as *avadāna* and *pūrvayoga*, are presented here in translations 6 and 7.

288 See pages 168–69 above in the introduction to translation 3.

289 Because of its structural similarity to the Pali *Apadāna*, the *Songs of Lake Anavatapta* is often referred to in modern scholarly literature as an *avadāna*, but this term does not actually occur in the text itself. In one of the scrolls that summarize the contents of the Senior collection of Gandhāran manuscripts (see pages 123–26), the extracts from the *Songs* are included in a list of texts referred to collectively as *sūtras*, and this was probably the genre label that was actually applied to it in the northern traditions.

290 Despite the title of this sūtra, it does not contain material typical of the apadāna/avadāna genres. Here the term *apadāna* seems to be used in its more general sense of "distinguished act," with reference to the lives of the previous buddhas (Thomas 1933); see the discussion of these terms and their etymologies in the introduction to translation 7.

291 This passage is translated in Walshe 1995, 199.

292 See pages 91–94.

293 *Vyākaraṇa* also means "grammar" in both Buddhist and non-Buddhist contexts, that is, the analysis of words and sentences. Since words in Sanskrit and related languages are typically built up of complex combinations of separate roots, affixes, and inflections (in contrast, for example, to languages like Tibetan or Chinese), grammar—that is, the analysis of words and language—can be understood as analogous to the analysis of karma, since both involve the isolation and identification of the individual components of a complex whole.

294 See pages 81–82 and 107–8.

295 See pages 123–26.

296 Mahākāśyapa's name is not actually present in the list as it stands, but it can be reconstructed at the lost right end of the relevant line of text (Salomon 2008, 10–11).

297 This number is given instead of the usual five hundred because Ānanda was not yet an arhat and therefore was unqualified to join this group. Unlike the other chief disciples, Ānanda became an arhat only after the Buddha's parinirvāṇa.

298 As shown in Bechert 1958.

299 Compare the discussion of the *Apadāna* in the introduction to the *Dharmapada* translation (page 192).

300 This motif is alluded to, though not directly described, in the text below.

301 For the details of legends about Mahākāśyapa, see Ray 1994, 105–18, Nyanaponika and Hecker 1997, 107–36, Silk 2003, and Tournier 2012. Further information about him and the other disciples can be found in Malalasekere 1937–38, 2:476–83.

302 Translated in Ñāṇamoli 1962, 189.

303 Degener 1990.

304 Rotman 2008, 39–70. In this version, he is known as Koṭikarṇa; compare note 314.

305 Strong 2001, 86.

306 Here both "the Teacher" and "the Victor" are titles of the Buddha. The Gāndhārī text here differs from the other versions, in which Mahākāśyapa says, ". . . nor did I see his disciples." In a well-known episode described in many texts, he exchanged the patchwork garment referred to here with the Buddha when he became his disciple. This important episode is, a little surprisingly, not explicitly mentioned in the text; presumably the author assumed that his audience would know it and understand the significance and associations of the robe.

307 In a famous sūtra in the *Aṅguttara-nikāya* (translated in Bodhi 2012, 109–13), the Buddha designated various of his disciples as the "foremost" in different qualities or achievements.

308 The "marks" (Skt *lakṣaṇa*) are the thirty-two physical characteristics on the body of a "great man" (*mahāpuruṣa*), that is, a buddha or a wheel-turning king (*cakravartin*), such as a thousand-spoked wheel on the soles of his feet, webbed hands and feet, and golden skin. (For further references see note 171.) At the end of his recitation Nanda reports that in this, his last lifetime, he has only thirty of the thirty-two marks; the implied contrast is with his half-brother, the Buddha, who of course has all of them.

309 This is not the monk Kāśyapa but the Buddha who immediately preceded Śākyamuni during the current eon.

310 This refers to a legend, which the author assumed that his audience would know, in

which the three sons of King Kṛki each placed umbrella disks on a stūpa of Buddha Kāśyapa in order of their seniority.

311 In the designations granted by the Buddha to his disciples according to the *Aṅguttara-nikāya* (see note 307), Nanda was foremost among those who guard the apertures of their sense organs rather than, as here, the most handsome one.

312 For a comparison of seven versions of this verse in five different languages, see appendix 1.

313 That is, for the ninety-one eons between the time of Buddha Vipaśyin and the present eon in the time of Buddha Śākyamuni.

314 This episode is intended to explain Śroṇa's nickname Koṭiviṃśa, here understood to mean "twenty crores"; a crore (Skt *koṭi*) is an Indian counting unit equivalent to ten million. The number here implicitly refers to gold or silver coins. Although his nickname is not actually mentioned in our text, it would have been well known to the intended audience. (See also the discussion of his nickname in appendix 1.) In other texts, such as the *Divyāvadāna*, Śroṇa is known as Koṭikarṇa (P Koṭikaṇṇa), *karṇa* meaning "ear." This version of his nickname is explained by a legend that he was born with a jewel in his ear that was worth twenty crores. The original form of the name was actually Koḷivīsa (Bechert 1961, 116), an ethnonym designating him as a member of the Koḷiya clan. But this original meaning was at some point forgotten, leading to various folk-etymological attempts to explain the name.

315 The "effect from the past" (*purima hedu* = Skt *pūrvako hetuḥ*) refers to the beneficial karma produced by his meditations in a previous life.

316 Yaśas means that he is threatened by the terrors of saṃsāra. He is undergoing the experience of "alarm" or "distress" (*saṃvega*) that stimulates one to seek liberation.

317 The image of Yaśas's thirst for liberation and the Buddha's teaching as "sweet Dharma" continues the preceding metaphor of the Tathāgata's "words of deathless nectar."

318 These qualities are reflected in Vāgīśa's name, which means "lord of speech."

319 Kusuma's name means "flower." The word for "jasmine" here is *sumanas*, which is also given as an alternate name for Kusuma in some related texts.

320 See also the discussion of the Gandhāran avadānas in chapter 3 ("Edifying Narratives," pages 87–88) and in the introduction to the previous translation (Avadānas and Related Genres, pages 205–6).

321 Lenz 2010, 99–103.

322 Lenz 2010, 3–14.

323 See pages 81 and 87.

324 One important example of these fragmentary avadānas is discussed above on pages 33–34.

325 Brough 1962, 113.

326 For details and discussion, see Salomon 1999, 71–76, and Lenz 2003, 105–10.

327 Salomon 2009.

328 That we are able to understand them at all is mainly due to the many years of work by Timothy Lenz, on whose work (Lenz 2003, 2010) the translations and interpretations presented here are largely based.

329 See further Lenz 2003, 192–93.

330 See, for example, the story of Koṭikarṇa in Rotman 2008, 39–70.

331 The text, found in the section on schism (*Saṅghabhedavastu*), is published in Gnoli 1977–78, 2:13–14, and translated in Lenz 2003, 98.

332 Based on the suggestions in von Hinüber 2004, 805, a possible alternative translation for this section is "The [other] merchants sank to the bottom. There was help [for them]. He himself brought them here to the shore."
333 Translated in Jones 1949–56, 3:352–53.
334 The full text is given in Gnoli 1977–78, 2:119–33, and translated in Lenz 2003, 226–37.
335 For other studies of the Viśvantara story in Buddhist art, see the references in Lenz 2003, 158n4.
336 See the discussion of this issue on pages 56–59.
337 A possible alternative translation for the uncertain word *aramano* is "was delighted at this."
338 The immediately preceding story was numbered as the second, so the number 4 here may be a slip on the part of the scribe. But the discrepancy may have something to do with the incomplete story 1, which seems to have been a false start by the scribe and might have thrown off his counting of the stories.
339 The second text of Ājñāta Kauṇḍinya's pūrvayoga is edited and translated in Lenz 2003, 87–89 and 198–202, and 2012, 113–15. The translation above is based on a composite text from both manuscripts.
340 For a complete translation see Lenz 2003, 239–41.
341 See page 204.
342 A complete translation of the Sanskrit text is given in Lenz 2003, 81–82, and of the two Chinese versions on pages 244–52.
343 Strictly speaking, Ānanda was Buddha's cousin, but the term "brother" is used here, as often in India, in a loose sense to refer to a related male of the same generation.
344 See pages 33–34.
345 That is, the buddhas.
346 See the discussion of the historical context of this story on page 36.
347 See Nattier 1991, especially 127–28, 150–57, and 243–44.
348 For further comments on this paradoxical situation, see Nattier 1991, 155–56.
349 See page 34.
350 This passage (*sapuruṣasa vado ghinido*) is understood differently in Lenz 2010, 85, as "When a disagreement with a worthy man was taken up."
351 The presentation of stories 6 to 8 is based on Lenz 2010, 73–93. The other avadānas in this group are translated, as far as possible, in Lenz 2010, 53–73 and 93–94.
352 Here the translation differs from that in Lenz 2010, 74: "'Do you have a desire (*to see a magic display)?' Magic was seen; (*it was) excellent." This is one of a great many places in these texts where the interpretation remains uncertain.
353 See Lenz 2003, 89–91, for details and references.
354 This will be explained in the introductions to the first and last sections of the translation.
355 The relevant passage is translated in Beal 1875, 6–16. The *Past Deeds* is text no. 190 in the Taishō *Tripiṭaka*, and the portion that corresponds to the *Many Buddhas Sūtra* is on pages 669a2–672a11.
356 Translated in Jones 1949–56, 1:51.
357 See, e.g., Skilling 1996, 154.
358 Skilling 1996.
359 See translation section 4, "The Eons in Which the Buddhas Lived."
360 A complete translation of the Tibetan version has been published in four volumes

under the title *The Fortunate Aeon: How the Thousand Buddhas Became Enlightened* (Dharma Publishing, 1986).

361 Duan 2009.

362 Baums, Glass, and Matsuda, 2016.

363 See page 207.

364 The radiocarbon dating yielded a span of possible dates with over 95 percent probability (1 sigma) between 206 BCE and 59 CE and a narrower span with a 68.3 percent probability (2 sigma) between 169 and 37 BCE. Whereas a date in the second, or even early third century BCE, is unlikely on historical grounds, a first century BCE date is entirely plausible, especially since we now have evidence from radiocarbon testing that at least one other Gāndhārī scroll dates from the first century BCE at the latest. See page 33.

365 The Sanskrit and Chinese texts have seventeen buddhas compared to fifteen in the Gāndhārī, which does not include Puṣya and Arthadarśin.

366 The name of the second stage does not actually appear in the Gāndhārī text, as the passages where it would have occurred (in sentences 6 through 8 of section 2) happen to fall in places where the manuscript is damaged. It is therefore assumed that its name would have corresponded to that found in the parallel texts.

367 The Gāndhārī name for the third course, *vivaṭana*, resembles the Sanskrit name of the fourth course in the *Mahāvastu*, namely *avivartana* "nonreturning," but without the negative prefix *a-*. Thus the third course of the Gāndhārī list could be understood as "returning" rather than "development," as referring to a stage at which the bodhisattva's success is not yet guaranteed and in which he may still be liable to regressing. But the form of this word is unstable in the various manuscripts of the *Mahāvastu*, and the rendition of the name of the fourth course into Chinese in *Past Deeds of the Buddha* as "transformation" (*zhuan* 轉), suggests that "development" is probably the intended sense of the term. The inconsistencies between and even within the texts concerned is indicative of different ideas current within early traditions as to the correct names of the courses and their meanings. This situation is not at all untypical of the many uncertainties that arose, in antiquity as nowadays, with regard to Buddhist technical terms.

368 *Mahāvastu* 3.249.9–10; translated, inaccurately, in Jones 1949–56, 3.238.

369 The text here is largely reconstructed, but in view of the consistently repeated pattern of this section the reconstruction is virtually certain despite its unexpected content.

370 The passage is translated in Walshe 1995, 250–52, and in Rotman 2008, 337–48.

371 The exception is Tiṣya, who lived only five hundred years while his predecessor Śākyamuni I and successor Vipaśyin both lived for eighty thousand years. This irregularity is probably connected with the instability of the lineage at this point.

372 Maitreya's lifespan is not predicted in this text.

373 The exact number of years in these time periods varies according to different sources and is not always clearly stated, but an uncountable eon is sometimes calculated as 10^{140} years and an eon as 4,320,000,000 years (Strong 2001, 22).

374 Throughout this translation, the names of the buddhas are given in their standard Sanskrit forms. The Gāndhārī forms of their names are sometimes unusual and frequently are spelled inconsistently. For instance, the buddha known as Krakucchanda

in Sanskrit and Kakusandha in Pali is here variously called Kosuda, Kosudha, or Kravasudha.

375 See for example Jones 1949–56, 236–37.

376 In all but one case (Vipaśyin) the phrase "his first assembly" is followed by a gap in the manuscript, but a count of the number of lost syllables shows in every case that there would not have been enough room for the description of a second assembly.

377 This text has not been previously translated. This translation reflects my own efforts, along with a great deal of help from members of the Early Buddhist Manuscripts Project research group.

378 The first verse is entirely lost.

379 After this verse, a set of four verses (7–10) is entirely missing. They must have been on a strip of bark that has been lost.

380 The name of the courses happen to be lost for buddhas 6 through 8, so it is not clear which ones apply to them. The summary verse at the end of the section enumerates the total number of buddhas under whom the bodhisattva followed each course. There the first part of the verse informs us that the Bodhisattva practiced the course of natural character under five buddhas, so we can be sure that he began practicing the second course, the course of the resolution, under the sixth buddha, namely Śākyamuni I. But we do not know where the transition from the second to the third course (development) took place, because, by a stroke of bad luck, the middle of the summary verse is also missing.

381 This entire sentence is lost, but its framework is reconstructed according to the standard pattern.

382 Here the scribe must have omitted the word "out of compassion" (*aṇuapae* = Skt *anukampayā*) by mistake.

383 "Attained the heights of glory" (*yaśo-acugado* = Skt *yaśo'tyudgataḥ*) is an etymological explanation of the Buddha's name Atyuccagāmin (G *acucagami*), literally "he who has gone very high."

384 "Gleamed like the moon on the fifteenth day" (of the lunar month; *cadra paṇaḍaśi-hasi* = Skt *candraḥ pañcadaśyāṃ hāsī*) seems to imply a pun on Śikhin's name (*śi-hasi* ≈ *śikhī*).

385 "Famed in every quarter" (*diśa-viśrudo* = Skt *diśāviśrutaḥ*) is an etymological reference to Viśvabhū's name, which literally means "he who is everywhere."

386 "Sages" and "sage" (*muni*) allude to Konākamuni's name, which can be understood to mean "the golden sage" (Skt *kanakamuni*).

387 The verb translated in each sentence as "went forth" (G *avhiṇikhami* = Skt *abhiniṣkrāntaḥ*) refers specifically to a buddha's abandonment of worldly life.

388 This and the following large numbers are described in the original text in terms of the numerical unit *crore*, or ten million; compare note 314. Thus "five million" is literally "half of a crore" (*adha-koḍi* = Skt *ardhakoṭi*), and "fourteen billion" is stated as "fourteen hundred crores."

389 See pages 101–2 and 47–49.

390 The part of the *Sumaṅgalavilāsinī* that comments on the *Saṅgīti Sūtra* is on pages 3:971–1052 of the Pali Text Society edition.

391 Published in Stache-Rosen 1968.

392 On categorial reduction, see Baums 2014.

393 These texts are paracanonical because, like the *Questions of Milinda*, they are accepted in the *Khuddaka-nikāya* of the Burmese Theravāda tradition but not in the Sri Lankan one.

394 E.g., von Hinüber 1996, 80 and 82.

395 *Dīgha-nikāya* III.246–47; translated in Walshe 1995, 499–500.

396 This intrusive comment looks suspiciously like a marginal comment that had been added by a reader of a previous manuscript and then copied into a later manuscript as part of the main text. As noted on page 142, the insertion of marginal remarks into the text proper is a common phenomenon in all manuscript traditions. However, an army is usually described in traditional Indian literature as having four, not five components, namely elephants, cavalry, chariots, and infantry, so it is not obvious how the five faculties are to be likened to an army. Perhaps—at a guess—the author of this comment had in mind a comparison of the first four faculties to the four elements of an army, with the fifth faculty, wisdom, likened to its general or commander.

397 The meaning and significance of this phrase (... *avhidhamiatasa vivadaṇa*) are uncertain, but there seems to be some reference to an abhidharma interpretation or position. This phrase may also have been a marginal gloss mistakenly incorporated into the main text by a subsequent copyist.

398 Here the scribe has abbreviated the terms of the fifth and sixth cause of argument, which read in full "obstinate in his own views, clings to what is wrong, and finds it difficult to concede" and "has false views and holds extreme views."

399 Translated in Burlingame 1921.

400 Selective compilations of verses of a partially similar type are attested in later stages of Buddhist literature (see Enomoto 2000, 165), but their relationship with the Gāndhārī commentaries, if any, remains to be clarified.

401 See Salomon 1999, 40–42, and Baums 2009, 609–11.

402 The interpretation and translation is heavily indebted to Baums 2009. The passages cited here are analyzed in detail there on pages 373–77 and 501–7.

403 Brough 1962, 144 (v. 159).

404 *Aṇuadiśeṣa-ṇivaṇadhadu* = *anupadhiśeṣa-nirvāṇadhātu*. "Nirvāṇa-without-remnant" refers to a superior, absolute state of nirvāṇa, in contrast to "nirvāṇa-with-remnant" (*sopadhiśeṣa-nirvāṇa*) in which traces of the prenirvāṇa state remain.

405 See Roebuck 2010, xxix–xxx.

406 Compare the comments on the "courses of development" of a buddha on pages 276–79.

407 *Aṅguttara-nikāya* IV 96; translated in Bodhi 2012, 1068.

408 *Yasa ekottariae ṣoḍaśagiehi* = Skt *yathā ekottarikāyāṃ ṣoḍaśāṅgikeṣu*.

409 Namely, the spheres of nirvāṇa with and without a remnant; see note 404.

410 These are explained in Cox 2009 and 2014, 43–46, as well as in Cox's complete edition of the manuscript, now in progress. The analysis and translation presented here are heavily indebted to Cox's studies.

411 See Cox 2009, 56 and 62n9, and 2014, 43.

412 For an important exception in a recently discovered inscription, see Salomon and Marino 2014.

413 Cox 2009, 61.

414 Compare the parallel discussions of the question of whether "everything exists" in the *Kathāvatthu*, translated in Aung and Rhys Davids 1915, 84–87.

415 The complete sūtra is translated in Walshe 1995, 335–50.

416 Here the word *dharmas* does not actually occur in the text, which literally says only "everything exists in all," but it can be assumed on the basis of the Pali commentary on a similar discussion in the Pali *Kathāvatthu*, which explains that in the question "Does everything exist in all?" the unspecified "all" (in the plural form, *sarveṣu*) refers to the dharmas.

417 The example of "impaired faculties" that would have a "future faculty" is unfamiliar and therefore obscure, but it appears to mean that if everything exists in all dharmas, future factors that—it is implied—would produce unimpaired faculties would be present within the impaired faculties, presenting a logical contradiction.

418 The meaning of the word *kaśia* is uncertain, but the context and sequence suggest that it refers to a monk.

419 That is, the states of being as gods, ghosts, humans, and animals.

420 Conze 1978, 7.

421 Williams 1989, 46.

422 Conze 1978, 7.

423 In the fifth chapter of the sūtra, partially preserved on the verso of the Gāndhārī fragment translated here, the discussants are the Buddha and Śakra (Kauśika), king of the gods. Here Śakra, like Śāriputra, is shown to be vastly inferior in intelligence to the Buddha and his wise disciples, as is typically the case for the gods in Buddhist literature.

424 The term in question, Skt *grantha*, properly refers to a unit of thirty-two syllables, equal to one verse in the common *anuṣṭubh* meter, but it is commonly used as a unit of measurement for prose texts as well.

425 Compare Salomon 2011, 181–82; for details of the versions and full bibliographic references, see Conze 1978, 31–74.

426 Translated in Conze 1973.

427 Conze 1978, 1.

428 See, e.g., Lamotte 1954 and Conze 1978, 1–4.

429 Falk 2011, 20.

430 Sander 2000.

431 The eight-thousand-line sūtra was translated into Chinese six more times between the third and tenth centuries.

432 Karashima 2012.

433 See note 451.

434 A complete translation of the colophon is given at the end of this translation.

435 Compare Falk 2011, 20.

436 Besides the examples mentioned here, some though by no means all of the interesting variants are pointed out in the notes to the translation.

437 The five supernatural knowledges are divine sight, divine hearing, knowledge of the minds of others, recollection of previous lives, and magical powers.

438 The text here is incomplete, but the reconstruction of the missing portion is fairly secure. Here Lokakṣema's Chinese translation is similar, but the Sanskrit text reads ". . . should not pride himself of his thought of enlightenment" (*bodhicitta*). Some later Perfection of Wisdom texts combine the two readings as "with the bodhisattva's

thought." This passage has important implications for the history of the Perfection of Wisdom literature (see Schmithausen 1977, esp. page 47), and the Gāndhārī reading provides an interesting new variant.

439 See the comments on this mysterious sentence in the introduction to this translation.

440 The missing part of the text here is supplied from the corresponding Sanskrit, but the Chinese reads "You are the best speaker on the wisdom concerning the body of emptiness," which at least superficially seems more contextually appropriate. But there is no reliable way to know which version (if either) the missing Gāndhārī text corresponded to.

441 The phrase "miraculous display of the Dharma" (*dhaṃma-vigubaṇa* = Skt *dharmavikurvaṇā*) is anomalous and surprising. Here the Sanskrit text reads "all the dharmas of a buddha," and there is no parallel to this passage in Lokakṣema's Chinese version.

442 In Sanskrit, the word that corresponds to the missing word here is "name" (*nāmadheyaṃ*), but the Chinese has instead "mind," which seems more appropriate. This entire sentence is damaged and obscure in the Gāndhārī manuscript, so the translation is highly tentative; it might also mean something like "that mind is neither established nor unestablished" (*[a?]iṭhido ṇa thido*).

443 Although the text is lost here, the amount of space shows that the scribe must have abridged the text by writing only the key words for the next three aggregates (*skandha*), it being understood each one should be inserted into the same formula when the text is recited. Thus the second set would be read out in full as "A bodhisattva who is engaging in the Perfection of Wisdom should not establish himself in sensation. If he establishes himself in sensation, he engages in the production of sensation," and so on. Following the usual pattern of abbreviation in Buddhist manuscripts, only the full texts for the first (form) and the last items (consciousness) of the repetitive set are written out in full. This same pattern occurs in sections 1.14, 17, 20, and 22.

444 Here the Gāndhārī text has a surprising variant in place of "to be grasped" (*grahītavyā*) in the Sanskrit text. The Chinese parallel also differs, with a verb meaning "observe" or "see." Moreover, the Gāndhārī word (*vihatavo*) is ambiguous; it could be interpreted as "to be eliminated" (= Skt *vihantavyā*), as "to be abandoned" (*vihātavyā*), or as "to be dwelt in" (*vihartavyā*). None of these interpretations is very satisfactory, but I have preferred "to be eliminated" on the grounds that a similar verb appears in the preceding sentence in several Chinese translations of the Perfection of Wisdom sūtra (though not in the earliest one by Lokakṣema, the one usually cited here), which describe "the concentration of the ungrasped" as "not to be destroyed by the disciples." In any case, the passage remains obscure, another example of a difficult textual crux.

445 The word translated as "not gone forth" (*aniyada* = Skt *niryāta*) alternates in various versions of the Perfection of Wisdom with a similar word (*anirjāta*) that literally means "not born forth." I suspect that this is not a textual confusion, as sometimes is assumed, but rather an intentional pun on the similar words for "born" (*nirjāta*) and "gone forth" (*niryāta*), which in informal or dialect pronunciation may be indistinguishable.

446 The translation here is based on the Sanskrit and Chinese versions, but in the Gāndhārī text only the first syllable of the expected word "empty" survives, and it is *su* instead of *śu*, as would normally correspond to Sanskrit *śūnyam*. Unfortunately, the correspond-

ing passage later in the paragraph is completely lost, so that we cannot be sure exactly what the text said here.

447 The Gāndhārī text breaks off here, and the rest of the following passage, in which Subhūti explains the positive practice of the bodhisattva in contrast to the preceding negative description, is translated from the Sanskrit version. The remainder of the first chapter (translated in Conze 1973, 87–95), not presented here, concerns other topics such as the meaning of the terms *bodhisattva*, *great being* (*mahāsattva*), and *great vehicle* (*mahāyāna*), followed by further discussions of the nature and actions of a bodhisattva.

448 The translation of the term in question (Skt *prajñāpāramita-prativarṇika*) and related terms such as *prajñāpāramita-pratirūpaka* is controversial. The second member of the phrase could also be rendered as "counterfeit," "imitation," "reflection," etc.; see the discussion in Nattier 1991: 86–89.

449 This sentence seems at first glance strange, as the statement "Form is impermanent," which is here attributed to the teachers of the imitation Perfection of Wisdom, does not conflict with the doctrine of the genuine Perfection of Wisdom. But apparently this is to be understood as referring, in the typically paradoxical way, to a superficial understanding, in the sense that one who ponders impermanence is still reifying impermanence and therefore has not reached transcendent wisdom. The situation is complicated, however (as usual), by the variation among the different texts at this point. Lokakṣema's Chinese translation agrees with the Gāndhārī, but the Sanskrit has instead "They will teach that the impermanence of form is the destruction of form" (*rūpavināśo rūpānityateti upadekṣyanti*). But in the refutation of the initial statement in the following paragraph, the Gāndhārī text has the similar expression "the impermanence of form should not be seen as resulting from the destruction of form," suggesting an underlying sense similar to that of the Sanskrit version. Here, as usual in such cases, it is not possible to determine which formulation is more original or "correct"; this is yet another case of the fluidity and variability of early Buddhist texts.

450 This *peyyāla* abbreviation refers to a complete expansion according to the formula, as seen in the preceding (9–12) and following passages, comparing the amount of merit that one gets by writing and giving a copy of the Perfection of Wisdom to the merit gained from establishing in the fruit of the once-returner, the fruit of the nonreturner, the state of an arhat, or individual awakening, all of the beings in Jambudvīpa, in a billionfold world system, and in as many billionfold world systems as there are sands along the Ganges. In the printed Sanskrit text the corresponding passage is written out in full, covering thirteen pages, whereas Lokakṣema's translation is abbreviated in the same way as the Gāndhārī. In the next paragraph, according to the usual pattern of abbreviating the intermediate members of a repetitive set, comes a final set of comparisons following the same scheme regarding the merit of presenting a copy of the Perfection of Wisdom to an irreversible bodhisattva.

451 An irreversible bodhisattva is one who has progressed to the point that he is certain to attain his goal of buddhahood without regressing to lower stages of development.

452 Here according to the text as it stands, Śakra is apparently still speaking to the Buddha. But this is hardly possible, first because Śakra would always address him as "Venerable Lord" (*bhaṃte bhagava*) rather than just "Sir" (*bhaṃte*), which is the respectful form

of address for an ordinary monk. Moreover, Śakra would surely not presume to tell the Buddha "Thus you should do," as in the succeeding text. In the Sanskrit and Chinese versions this passage is spoken by Subhūti, the foremost teacher of the Perfection of Wisdom after the Buddha himself, but in the Gāndhārī text as it stands he is not introduced here. This is probably due to scribal error. In the Sanskrit, the passage in which Subhūti is introduced as the new speaker begins with the same word, "thus" (*evam*), as the sentence in question here, so that the scribe's eye might have skipped over the earlier "thus" to the next one and thereby omitted a sentence that would have read, according to the parallel texts, "Then Venerable Subhūti said to Śakra, king of the gods, 'Well said, Kauśika, well said!'"

453 The meaning of the Gāndhārī word here, *praṇatia*, is uncertain; the translation follows the corresponding Sanskrit (*prasūtā*) and Chinese correspondents.

454 See translation 11, page 332.

455 Salomon 1999, 12.

456 Details of these materials and summaries of the findings from them are to be found in Allon 2008 and Harrison and Hartmann 2014.

457 See pages 59–68.

458 Falk and Bennett 2009.

459 Salomon 2012, 195.

460 For full references see Baums 2012, 217.

461 Described in Falk 1998, 87–99.

Glossary

Note: Indic-language terms are generally listed in their Sanskrit form followed, where appropriate, by the Pali equivalent.

abhidharma. Literally, "about the Dharma" or "the higher Dharma"; the scholastic analysis and codification of the doctrines of the Dharma as taught by the Buddha in the sūtras. The body of literature in this category constitutes one of the three "baskets" of the Tripiṭaka in the canon of the Theravādins and most other schools.

abhijñā. See *supernatural knowledges*.

abhiniṣkramaṇa. "The Departure"; the flight of the Bodhisattva (the future Buddha) from his father's palace in order to seek enlightenment. Often called *mahābhiniṣkramaṇa*, "the Great Departure."

Abhirati. The paradise of Buddha Akṣobhya.

Achaemenid. The vast empire that ruled Iran and neighboring regions, including Gandhāra and other parts of western India, from the mid-sixth to the early fourth centuries BCE.

adhivacana. A "metaphor" or "metaphorical designation" in Buddhist sūtras.

afflictions. See *āsrava*.

āgama (= Pali *nikāya*). The canonical collections of early, non-Mahāyāna sūtras, grouped according to length and format. These collections are preserved in complete form in Pali and Chinese and fragmentarily in Sanskrit, Gāndhārī, and Tibetan. See *Dīrghāgama*, *Dīgha-nikāya*; *Ekottarikāgama*,

Aṅguttara-nikāya; *Kṣudrakāgama, Khuddaka-nikāya*; *Madhyamāgama, Majjhima-nikāya*; *Saṃyuktāgama, Saṃyutta-nikāya.*

aggregates (*skandha*). The five physiological and psychological constructs that constitute the illusory sense of individual personality: form (*rūpa*), sensation or feeling (*vedanā*), perception or discrimination (*saṃjñā*), volitional formations or mental constructions (*saṃskāra*), and consciousness (*vijñāna*).

Ajātaśatru. The king of *Magadha* who ruled during the lifetime of the Buddha and became one of his main patrons.

Akṣobhya. A buddha who was a major cult figure in the early Mahāyāna. See also *Abhirati.*

anāgāmin. See *nonreturner.*

Ānanda. Among the Buddha's most prominent disciples, Ānanda served as his permanent attendant and recalled the text of all of his sūtras after the parinirvāṇa.

Aṅguttara-nikāya (P). See *Ekottarikāgama.*

anuśaya. "Negative proclivities" or "contaminants"; enumerated as sensual passion (*kāmarāga*), resentment (*pratigha*), views (*dṛṣṭi*), doubts (*vicikitsā*), pride (*māna*), becoming (*bhava*), and ignorance (*avidyā*).

anuṣṭubh. The simplest and commonest Indian meter, consisting of four quarters of eight syllables each. Also called *śloka.*

Apadāna. A verse text contained in the Pali *Khuddaka-nikāya* (see *Kṣudrakāgama, Khuddaka-nikāya*) consisting of 614 recitations by the Buddha and his disciples in which they reveal the karma from their previous lives. See also *avadāna.*

Apraca. An Indo-Scythian dynasty ruling in the region of *Bajaur* around the beginning of the Common Era.

arapacana. The name of the alphabetic order of *Kharoṣṭhī* script, after its first five letters, *a-ra-pa-ca-na.*

arhat. Literally, "worthy one"; honorific term for a person who has eliminated all of the afflictions (*āsravas*) and thereby is destined to achieve nirvāṇa at the end of his or her worldly life. See also *nonreturner*; *once-returner*; *stream-enterer*.

Aśoka (r. ca. 269–232 BCE). The great emperor of the *Mauryan dynasty* and legendary patron of Buddhism. He is credited with transforming Buddhism into a pan-Indian religion.

āsrava. The obstacles to the attainment of arhatship, variously translated as "taints," "depravities," "afflictions," or "evil influences." They are typically enumerated as three, namely desire (*kāma*), becoming (*bhava*), and ignorance (*avidyā*); sometimes a fourth, (wrong) views (*dṛṣṭi*), is added.

avadāna. A legend illustrating Buddhist principles, particularly the workings of karma. Avadānas typically consist of a story of a past life, a story of a present life, and an explanation of the karmic relationships between the two. See also *pūrvayoga*.

āyatana. See *sense-bases*.

Bactria. The ancient region corresponding to modern northern Afghanistan and southern Uzbekistan, ruled by Greek kings in the third and second centuries BCE.

Bactrian. The ancient language of Bactria, an eastern member of the Middle Iranian family, written in an adapted form of the Greek alphabet.

Bajaur. A frontier region in modern northern Pakistan along the Afghan border.

bhadrakalpa. The "Fortunate Eon," the period of cosmic history (*kalpa*) in which we are now living. It is called "fortunate" because it is predicted that a total of one thousand (or 1,004) buddhas will live during it.

bodhipākṣikadharma. A set of thirty-seven "dharmas conducive to enlightenment," comprising the four foundations of mindfulness (*smṛtyupasthāna*), the four correct strivings (*samyakprahāṇa*), the four bases of supernatural powers (*ṛddhipāda*), the five spiritual faculties (*indriya*), the five powers (*bala*), the seven factors of enlightenment (*bodhyaṅga*), and the eightfold path (*aṣṭāṅgikamārga*).

bodhyaṅga. The seven "enlightenment factors," namely mindfulness (*smṛti*), investigation of phenomena (*dharmavicaya*), energy (*vīrya*), delight (*prīti*), tranquility (*praśrabdhi*), concentration (*samādhi*), and equanimity (*upekṣā*).

Brāhmī (script). The dominant script of ancient India, used everywhere except in Gandhāra and the far northwest. Brāhmī is the parent of all of the modern Indian and Indian-derived scripts. See also *Kharoṣṭhī*.

Buddhist Hybrid Sanskrit. A form of mixed Sanskrit with many features of *Prakrit*, characteristic of Buddhist literature of northern India during the early centuries of the Common Era.

Campā. An ancient city along the Ganges in northeastern India (near modern Bhagalpur, Bihar), capital of the kingdom of Aṅga.

contaminants. See *anuśaya*.

defilements (*kleśa*). A general term for the psychological defects that prevent liberation; one becomes an *arhat* by eliminating the defilements. The defilements are enumerated variously, for example, in a list of six: desire, hatred, pride, ignorance, wrong views, and doubt.

Devadatta. The Buddha's depraved cousin who tried to subvert the saṅgha and assassinate the Buddha.

dhāraṇī. A protective spell containing magic words and phrases that do not correspond to normal language. See also *rakṣā*.

dharma, dhamma. This complex term has two main senses: (1) The teachings of the Buddha conceived as a comprehensive whole; here spelled *Dharma*. (2) The constituents, factors, or elements of existence; phenomena; spelled *dharma*.

Dharmaguptaka. One of the traditional eighteen schools of early Buddhism that was particularly prominent in Gandhāra. Several of the Gāndhārī manuscripts apparently belong to the Dharmaguptaka tradition.

dharmarājikā. Literally, "the Dharma king's," an epithet applied to stūpas that were reputed to have been built by King *Aśoka*.

dharmas conducive to enlightenment. See *bodhipākṣikadharma*.

Dīrghāgama, Dīgha-nikāya. The canonical collection (*āgama*) of long sūtras.

disciple (*śrāvaka*). A person who hears the teaching directly from a buddha.

Ekottarikāgama, Aṅguttara-nikāya. The canonical collection (*āgama*) of short sūtras arranged in numerical categories. The title means literally, "The collection that increases one by one."

emptiness (*śūnyatā*). The Mahāyāna principle that all phenomena have no inherent reality.

enlightenment factors. See *bodhyaṅga.*

five supernormal powers. See *supernatural knowledge.*

Gāndhārī. The ancient *Middle Indo-Aryan* vernacular dialect of Gandhāra, which became a major language of Buddhist literature.

Gotama (Pali = Skt Gautama). The name by which the historical Buddha is commonly referred to in the Pali tradition; compare *Śākyamuni.*

Heaven of the Thirty-Three Gods (*Trāyastriṃśa*). One of the six levels of heaven, ruled over by *Śakra,* king of the gods.

Heir of the Sun (*ādityabandhu*). Epithet for Śākyamuni Buddha.

Huviṣka (r. ca. 150–90 CE). An emperor of the *Kuṣāṇa* dynasty; son and successor of the great *Kaniṣka.*

Indo-Aryan. The dominant language family of north and central India since ancient times. See also *Middle Indo-Aryan*; *Old Indo-Aryan.*

indriya. (1). The five sensory faculties: sight, hearing, smell, taste, touch. (2) The five spiritual faculties: faith, energy, mindfulness, concentration, and wisdom.

infinite sublime states (*apramāṇa*). Epithet of the four "brahma dwellings" (*brahmavihāra*): loving kindness (*maitrī*), compassion (*karuṇā*), joy (*muditā*), and equanimity (*upekṣā*).

inspired utterance (*udāna*). A brief statement, typically in verse form, stimulated by a spiritual realization; usually attributed to a buddha or solitary buddha. (Not to be confused with *uddāna, summary verse.*)

Jambudvīpa. Literally, the Rose Apple Isle or Black Plum Isle. In traditional Indian cosmology, this corresponds to the known world, i.e., India.

jātaka. "Birth stories," legends telling of the previous lives of the Buddha when he was a bodhisattva, recorded in a Pali collection of 547 stories. See also *Vessantara-jātaka*.

jātismara. Literally, "life-memory"; the ability, possessed by highly developed persons, to remember one's past lives.

kalpa. A cosmic eon; an immensely long period of creation and evolution, alternating with intermediate periods of dissolution and destruction.

Kaniṣka (r. ca. 127–50 CE). The greatest emperor of the *Kuṣāṇa* dynasty and one of the most prominent royal patrons of Buddhism.

Kāśyapa. The buddha who preceded the "historical" Buddha Śākyamuni. Not to be confused with Mahākāśyapa, sometimes also called Kāśyapa, one of the Buddha's leading disciples.

Kāśyapīya. One of the traditional eighteen schools of early Buddhism.

Kauśika. Nickname of Śakra, king of the gods.

Kharoṣṭhī. The script, principally derived from Aramaic, that was used in ancient Gandhāra to write the *Gāndhārī* language. See also *Brāhmī*.

Khotan Dharmapada. A Gāndhārī manuscript discovered in Central Asia in 1892.

Khotan Saka (Khotanese). An ancient language of the Iranian family; the *Saka* dialect spoken in the region of Khotan in Central Asia. Khotanese literature includes many translations of Indian Buddhist texts.

Khuddaka-nikāya. See *Kṣudrakāgama*.

Kizil. A major site of Buddhist caves, paintings, and manuscripts on the northern rim of the Tarim Basin in the Xinjiang Uyghur Autonomous Region, China.

Kosala. A powerful kingdom of central north India (in modern Uttar Pradesh) at the time of the Buddha. See also *Śrāvastī*.

kṣatriya. A member of one of the four traditional social classes of ancient India, consisting of kings, warriors, and the nobility.

Kṣudrakāgama, Khuddaka-nikāya. The canonical collection (*āgama*) of miscellaneous short sūtras.

Kuru. A mythical paradise situated far to the north of *Jambudvīpa.*

Kuṣāṇa. A dynasty and empire of Central Asian nomadic origin that ruled a vast territory in northern India, eastern Afghanistan, and southern central Asia from the first to third centuries CE.

lakṣaṇa. Literally, "mark" or "characteristic"; the thirty-two major and eighty minor signs that distinguish the body of a buddha.

lower bonds. See *spiritual bonds.*

Madhyamāgama, Majjhima-nikāya. The canonical collection (*āgama*) of medium-length sūtras.

Magadha. The dominant kingdom of northeastern India at the time of the Buddha.

Māgadhī. The vernacular *Prakrit* dialect of *Magadha,* believed to have been the language in which the Buddha originally preached.

Mahābhārata. One of the two great Sanskrit epics of the Brahmanical/Hindu tradition. See also *Rāmāyaṇa.*

Mahāmaudgalyāyana. Along with *Śāriputra,* one of the Buddha's two most prominent disciples. He was the foremost of the disciples in supernatural powers.

Mahāsāṅghika. One of the traditional eighteen schools of early Buddhism, often associated with the early development of the Mahāyāna.

Mahīśāsaka. One of the traditional eighteen schools of early Buddhism.

Majjhima-nikāya. See *Madhyamāgama.*

Māra. The personified spirit of desire and death; the opponent and rival of the Buddha.

Mauryan dynasty. The greatest dynasty of early India, ruling from Magadha from the late fourth to early second centuries BCE. See also *Aśoka.*

Menander. An Indo-Greek king of the second century BCE, known in Indian languages as Milinda. He is celebrated in the Pali text Questions of King Milinda (Milindapañha).

Meru. The holy mountain at the center of the world according to Buddhist cosmology.

Middle Indo-Aryan. The secondary stage of development of the languages of the *Indo-Aryan* family, including Pali, *Gāndhārī*, and *Māgadhī*. See also *Old Indo-Aryan, Prakrit.*

Milinda. See *Menander.*

Mūlasarvāstivāda. A prominent school of Buddhism in northern India, closely affiliated with the *Sarvāstivāda* school, although their precise historical relationship is uncertain and controversial. See also *Mūlasarvāstivāda-vinaya.*

Mūlasarvāstivāda-vinaya. The massive vinaya literature of the *Mūlasarvāstivāda* school, extant in Sanskrit, Chinese, and Tibetan, and incorporating many legends and *avadānas.*

nāga. A serpent-like demigod, associated with rain and bodies of water.

Nālandā. A great Buddhist monastic and educational complex that flourished in the second half of the first millennium and early second millennium. Situated in modern Bihar (ancient *Magadha*).

negative proclivities. See *anuśaya.*

nidāna. The preface to a sūtra, reporting the place and occasion on which it was spoken by the Buddha.

nikāya. Literally, "group" or "compilation." (1) One of the five divisions of the sūtra basket (compare *Tripiṭaka*) according to the Pali canon; see *āgama.* (2) A Buddhist initiation lineage or scholastic tradition.

Nirgrantha. A rival sect to the early Buddhists, the ancestor of the Jain religion.

nonreturner (*anāgamin*). A person who has reached the third of four stages toward enlightenment; see also *arhat*; *once-returner*; *stream-enterer*). A nonreturner is destined to achieve the final goal without being born again as a human being and is instead reborn in the highest spheres of existence and attains enlightenment there.

obstructions (*nīvaraṇa*). The five obstacles to leading a successful spiritual life: craving, malice, sloth, agitation, and doubt. See also *obstructions of the mind* (*āvaraṇa*).

obstructions of the mind (*āvaraṇa*). Equivalent to *obstructions* (*nīvaraṇa*).

Oḍi. An Indo-Scythian kingdom of the first century CE in the Swat Valley of northern Pakistan.

Old Indo-Aryan. The early stage of development of the languages of the *Indo-Aryan* family, represented by Vedic and classical Sanskrit. See also *Indo-Aryan*; *Middle Indo-Aryan*.

once-returner (*sakṛdāgamin*). A person who has reached the second of four stages toward enlightenment (see also *arhat*; *nonreturner*; *stream-enterer*) and is destined to have only one more lifetime as a human being before achieving the final goal.

pains (*śalya*). Literally "darts"; the causes of suffering in saṃsāra, usually listed as five: internal corruption, thirst, becoming, craving, and grief.

parinirvāṇa. The Buddha's final passing from the cycle of rebirth.

Pāṭaliputra. The capital of *Magadha* in the time of the *Mauryan dynasty*, situated along the Ganges River near modern Patna, Bihar.

perfections (*pāramitā*). The six virtues that are gradually developed and attained by a bodhisattva: generosity (*dāna*), conduct (*śīla*), forbearance (*kṣānti*), energy (*vīrya*), meditation (*dhyāna*), and wisdom (*prajñā*).

piṭaka. Literally, "basket"; one of the three main divisions of the Buddhist canon or *Tripiṭaka* ("three baskets"), namely *sūtra*, *vinaya*, and *abhidharma*.

pleasures of the five senses (*kāmaguṇa*). Sights, sounds, smells, tastes, and tactile sensations.

Prakrit. Traditional generic term for various dialects of *Middle Indo-Aryan* language group.

prajñā. Wisdom; profound insight into the true nature of being. Compare *prajñāpāramitā*.

prajñāpāramitā. The perfection of wisdom: (1) The complete attainment of *prajñā*. (2) The body of Mahāyāna sūtras that teach *prajñā*.

praṇidhi, praṇidhāna. See *solemn resolution*.

Prasenajit. The king of *Kosala* during the time of the Buddha.

pratyekabuddha. See *solitary buddha*.

Puruṣapura. The capital of Gandhāra; modern Peshawar.

pūrvayoga. Stories about previous lives. See also *avadāna*; *jātaka*.

Rājagṛha. The original capital of *Magadha* in the time of the Buddha; modern Rajgir, Bihar.

rakṣā. Literally "protection," a class of Buddhist apopotraic texts, usually containing *dhāraṇīs*.

Rāmāyaṇa. One of the two great Sanskrit epics of the Brahmanical/Hindu tradition. See also *Mahābhārata*.

Saka. (1) Ethnic designation of nomadic tribes from Central Asia who settled in northwestern India from the first century BCE; see also *Scythian*. (2) The name of their Iranian language. See also *Khotan Saka*.

Śakra. The king of the gods according to Buddhist theology.

sakṛdāgamin. See *once-returner*.

Śākyamuni. "The sage of the Śākyas," the title by which the historical Buddha is usually referred to in northern Buddhist tradition. See also *Gotama*.

Śākyas. The clan, settled in the borderlands of modern India and Nepal, into which the Buddha Śākyamuni was born.

saṃyojana. See *spiritual bonds*.

Saṃyuktāgama, Saṃyutta-nikāya. The canonical collection (*āgama*) of short sūtras arranged according to topics.

saṅgīti. A communal chanting of the Buddhist scriptures.

Śāriputra. Along with *Mahāmaudgalyāyana*, one of the Buddha's two most prominent disciples. He was the foremost of the disciples in wisdom (*prajñā*).

Sarvāstivāda. One of Buddhism's traditional eighteen schools, which was particularly prominent in Gandhāra and northern India. See also *Mūlasarvāstivāda.*

satrap. Title for a regional governor in the Iranian and Indo-Scythian kingdoms. See also *stratega.*

Scythian. Greek equivalent of *Saka.*

sense-bases (*āyatana*). Collective term for the sense organs (eye, ear, etc.), which are the six internal sense-bases, and their objects (sights, sounds, etc.), the six external sense-bases.

Shrine of Many Sons (*bahuputracaitya*). Site of a sacred tree near the city of Vaiśālī, where the local people went to pray for the birth of sons and which the Buddha sometimes visited.

śloka. See *anuṣṭubh.*

solemn resolution (*praṇidhi, praṇidhāna*). A pious vow, typically uttered by a person who has just performed a meritorious deed, declaring the karmic result that he or she hopes to attain thereby. Such vows are often inspired by an encounter with a buddha or a *solitary buddha.*

solitary buddha (*pratyekabuddha*). A buddha who has perceived the truths of the Dharma and achieved enlightenment through his own insight but does not choose to teach it to others.

spiritual bonds (*saṃyojana*). The harmful mental states that keep one bound in saṃsāra. The bonds are divided into the five *lower bonds* (*avarabhāgiya-saṃyojanāni*), namely false view of self, doubt, attachment to rules and vows, desire, and malice, and the five *upper bonds* (*ūrdhvabhāgīya-saṃyojanāni*), namely craving in the form realm, craving in the formless realm, pride, distraction, and ignorance.

Śrāvastī. The capital of the kingdom of *Kosala,* where the Buddha often taught.

srotāpanna. See *stream-enterer.*

stratega. Title of a general or military governor in the Iranian and Indo-Scythian kingdoms. See also *satrap.*

stream-enterer (*srotāpanna*). A person who has reached the first of four stages toward enlightenment. See also *arhat*; *nonreturner*; *once-returner.*

stūpa. A domed structure built over a relic of the Buddha or other items associated with him. A stūpa is usually surmounted by a vertical shaft bearing a series of disks representing umbrellas.

Sudaṣṇa. An alternative name of Viśvantara/Vessantara, hero of the *Vessantara-jātaka*.

summary verse (*uddāna*). A verse that functions as a mnemonic summary by listing the sections or topics of a larger text or portion thereof. (Not to be confused with *udāna, inspired utterance.*)

śūnyatā. See *emptiness*.

supernatural knowledges (*abhijñā*). Five special powers attributed to highly developed persons: magical power (*ṛddhi*), divine hearing (*divyaśrotra*), knowledge of the minds of others (*paracittajñāna*), the recollection of previous lives (*pūrvanivāsānusmṛti*), and divine sight (*divyacakṣu*).

sūtra. A discourse or sermon spoken by the Buddha. The collections of sūtras (see *āgama*) constitute one of the three "baskets" of the *Tripiṭaka*.

Tathāgata. Frequent title of the Buddha, which can be interpreted either as "Thus-Come One" (*tathā-āgata*) or as "Thus-Gone One" (*tathā-gata*).

Taxila (*Takṣaśilā*). A major city of northwestern India in antiquity (modern Pakistan), mentioned as the capital of Gandhāra in Buddhist texts.

Theravāda. The conservative school of Buddhism that prevails in Sri Lanka and Southeast Asia; the only surviving school of the eighteen traditional schools of Buddhism.

Thirty-Three Gods. See *Heaven of the Thirty-Three Gods*.

Tocharian. An ancient Indo-European language of Central Asia, spoken on the northern rim of the Tarim Basin. Many Buddhist texts were translated into Tocharian.

Tripiṭaka. "The three baskets," the traditional designation for a complete Buddhist canon. The three "baskets" are *vinaya*, *sūtra*, and *abhidharma*.

udāna. See *inspired utterance*.

uddāna. See *summary verse*.

upper bonds. See *spiritual bonds*.

Vajrapāṇi. Guardian spirit of the Buddha, depicted with a thunderbolt (vajra) in his hand (pāṇi).

Vajrayāna. The tantric form of Buddhism.

Vessantara-jātaka. The last and most popular of the *jātaka* stories, extolling the virtues of generosity as exemplified by the hero, Prince Vessantara (Skt Viśvantara). See also *Sudaṣṇa*.

vihāra. A Buddhist monastic residence.

vinaya. The laws of monastic discipline. The texts concerning vinaya constitute one of the three "baskets" of the *Tripiṭaka*.

Vipaśyin. A buddha of the remote past, the sixth in sequence before Śākyamuni.

vyākaraṇa. Literally "analysis"; an explanation, usually by a buddha, of the workings of karma.

wheel-turning king (*cakravartin*). A righteous ruler who conquers the entire known world.

Xuanzang. A Chinese Buddhist pilgrim who traveled in Central Asia and India from 629 to 645 CE and left a detailed description of Buddhist life and practices there.

yakṣa. A kind of demigod or spirit associated with trees and forests; often beneficent toward human beings, but sometimes dangerous.

Bibliography

Allon, Mark. 2001. *Three Gāndhārī Ekottarikāgama-Type Sūtras: British Library Kharoṣṭhī Fragments 12 and 14*. Gandhāran Buddhist Texts 2. Seattle: University of Washington Press.

———. 2007. "The Senior Manuscripts." In Glass 2007, 3–25.

———. 2008. "Recent Discoveries of Buddhist Manuscripts from Afghanistan and Pakistan and Their Significance." In *Art, Architecture and Religion along the Silk Roads*, edited by Ken Parry, 153–78. Silk Road Studies 12. Turnhout, Belgium: Brepols.

———. 2014. "The Senior Kharoṣṭhī Manuscripts." In Harrison and Hartmann 2014, 19–33.

Allon, Mark, and Richard Salomon. 2000. "Kharoṣṭhī Fragments of a Gāndhārī Version of the Mahāparinirvāṇa-sūtra." In Braarvig 2000, 243–73.

———. 2010. "New Evidence for Mahāyāna in Early Gandhāra." *The Eastern Buddhist* 41: 1–22.

Allon, Mark, Richard Salomon, Geraldine Jacobsen, and Ugo Zoppi. 2006. "Radiocarbon Dating of Kharoṣṭhī Fragments from the Schøyen and Senior Manuscript Collections." In Braarvig 2006, 279–91.

Aung, Shwe Zan, and Mrs. Rhys Davids. 1915. *Points of Controversy or Subjects of Discourse: Being a Translation of the Kathā-vatthu from the Abhidhamma-piṭaka*. London: The Pali Text Society.

Bailey, H. W. 1946. "Gāndhārī." *Bulletin of the School of Oriental and African Studies* 11.4: 764–97.

Bareau, André. 1955. *Les sectes bouddhique du petit véhicule*. Publications de l'École française d'Extrême-Orient 38. Saigon: École française d'Extrême-Orient.

Baums, Stefan. 2009. "A Gāndhārī Commentary on Early Buddhist Verses:

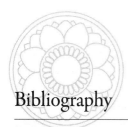

British Library Kharoṣṭhī Fragments 7, 9, 13 and 18." Ph.D. dissertation, University of Washington.

———. 2012. "Catalog and Revised Texts and Translations of Gandhāran Reliquary Inscriptions." In Jongeward et al. 2012: 200–251 (chapter 6).

———. 2014. "Truth and Scripture in Early Buddhism: Categorial Reduction as Exegetical Method in Ancient Gandhāra and Beyond." In *Buddhism across Asia: Networks of Material, Intellectual and Cultural Exchange, Volume I*, edited by Tansen Sen, 19–38. Singapore: Institute of Southeast Asian Studies.

Baums, Stefan, Jens Braarvig, Timothy J. Lenz, Fredrik Liland, Kazunobu Matsuda, and Richard Salomon. 2016. "The Bodhisattvapiṭakasūtra in Gāndhārī." In Braarvig 2016, 267–82.

Baums, Stefan, and Andrew Glass. 2002a. *Bibliography of Gāndhārī Studies.* https://gandhari.org/a_bibliography.php.

———. 2002b. *Dictionary of Gāndhārī Studies.* https://gandhari.org/n_dictionary.php.

Baums, Stefan, Andrew Glass, and Kazunobu Matsuda. 2016. "Fragments of a Gāndhārī Version of the Bhadrakalpikasūtra." In Braarvig 2016, 183–266.

Beal, Samuel, trans. 1875. *The Romantic Legend of Sâkya Buddha: From the Chinese-Sanscrit.* London: Trübner & Co.

———. 1884. *Si-yu-ki: Buddhist Records of the Western World, translated from the Chinese of Hiuen Tsiang (a.d. 629).* 2 vols. London: Trübner & Co.

Bechert, Heinz. 1958. "Über das Apadānabuch." *Wiener Zeitschrift für die Kunde Süd- und Ostasiens und Archiv für indische Philosophie* 2: 1–21.

———. 1961. *Bruchstücke buddhistischer Verssammlungen aus zentralasiatischen Sanskrithandschriften.* Vol. 1, *Die Anavataptagāthā und die Sthaviragāthā.* Deutsche Akademie der Wissenschaften zu Berlin, Institut für Orientforschung, Veröffentlichung 51; Sanskrittexte aus den Turfanfunden 6. Berlin: Akademie-Verlag.

———. 1992. "The Writing Down of the Tripiṭaka in Pāli." *Wiener Zeitschrift für die Kunde Südasiens* 36: 45–53.

Bernhard, Franz. 1965–90. *Udānavarga.* 3 vols. Abhandlungen der Akademie der Wissenschaften in Göttingen, Philologisch-historische Klasse, ser. 3, nos. 54, 187; Sanskrittexte aus den Turfanfunden 10. Göttingen: Vandenhoeck & Ruprecht.

Bodhi, Bhikkhu. 2000. *The Connected Discourses of the Buddha: A Translation of the Saṃyutta Nikāya.* Boston: Wisdom Publications.

———. 2012. *The Numerical Discourses of the Buddha: A Translation of the Aṅguttara Nikāya*. Boston: Wisdom Publications.

———. 2017. *Suttanipāta: An Ancient Collection of the Buddha's Discourses and Its Commentaries*. Somerville, MA: Wisdom Publications.

Bopearachchi, Osmund. 1990. "Ménandre Sōter, un roi indo-grec. Observations chronologiques et géographiques." *Studia Iranica* 19: 39–85.

Boucher, Daniel. 1998. "Gāndhārī and the Early Chinese Buddhist Translations Reconsidered: The Case of the Saddharmapuṇḍarīkasūtra." *Journal of the American Oriental Society* 118: 471–506.

———. 2000. "On *Hu* and *Fan* Again: The Transmission of Barbarian Manuscripts to China." *Journal of the International Association of Buddhist Studies* 23: 7–28.

Braarvig, Jens, ed. 2000. *Buddhist Manuscripts, Volume I. Manuscripts in the Schøyen Collection*. Oslo: Hermes Publishing.

———, ed. 2002. *Buddhist Manuscripts, Volume II. Manuscripts in the Schøyen Collection*. Oslo: Hermes Publishing.

———, ed. 2006. *Buddhist Manuscripts, Volume III. Manuscripts in the Schøyen Collection*. Oslo: Hermes Publishing.

———. 2014. "The Schøyen Collection." In Harrison and Hartmann 2014, 157–64.

———, ed. 2016. *Buddhist Manuscripts, Volume IV. Manuscripts in the Schøyen Collection*. Oslo: Hermes Publishing.

Brough, John. 1962. *The Gāndhārī Dharmapada*. London Oriental Series 7. London: Oxford University Press.

———. 1968. *Poems from the Sanskrit*. Harmondsworth: Penguin Books.

Burlingame, Eugene Watson, trans. 1921. *Buddhist Legends: Translated from the Original Pali Text of the Dhammapada Commentary*. 3 vols. Harvard Oriental Series 28–30. Cambridge: Harvard University Press.

Burrow, T. 1937. *The Language of the Kharoṣṭhi Documents from Chinese Turkestan*. Cambridge: Cambridge University Press.

———, trans. 1940. *A Translation of the Kharoṣṭhi Documents from Chinese Turkestan*. James G. Forlong Fund 20. London: Royal Asiatic Society.

Carter, John Ross, and Mahinda Palihawadana. 1987. *The Dhammapada*. New York: Oxford University Press.

Collins, Steven. 1990. "On the Very Idea of the Pali Canon." *Journal of the Pali Text Society* 15: 89–126.

Conze, Edward. 1973. *The Perfection of Wisdom in Eight Thousand Lines & Its Verse Summary*. Bolinas CA: Four Seasons Foundation.

———. 1978. *The Prajñāpāramitā Literature*. The Reiyukai Library, Bibliographia Philologica Buddhica, Series Maior 1. Tokyo: The Reiyukai.

Cox, Collett. 2009 [2013]. "What's in a Name? School Affiliation in an Early Buddhist Gandhāran Manuscript." *Bulletin of the Asia Institute* (new series) 23: 53–63.

———. 2014. "Gāndhārī Kharoṣṭhī Manuscripts: Exegetical Texts." In Harrison and Hartmann 2014, 35–49.

Degener, Almuth. 1990. *Das Kaṭhināvadāna*. Indica et Tibetica 16. Bonn: Indica et Tibetica Verlag.

Demiéville, Paul. 1924. "Les versions chinoises du Milindapañha." *Bulletin de l'École française d'Extrême-Orient* 24: 1–258.

Dharma Publishing. 1986. *The Fortunate Aeon: How the Thousand Buddhas Became Enlightened*. 4 vols. Berkeley: Dharma Publishing.

Duan, Qing. 2009. "A Fragment of the *Bhadrakalpasūtra* in Buddhist Sanskrit from Xinjiang." In *Sanskrit Manuscripts in China: Proceedings of a Panel at the 2008 Beijing Seminar on Tibetan Studies: October 13 to 17*, edited by Ernst Steinkellner, 15–39. Beijing: China Tibetology Publishing House.

Dunn, Ross E. 2005. *The Adventures of Ibn Battuta*. Berkeley: University of California Press.

Dutt, Nalinaksha. 1947. *Gilgit Manuscripts*, vol. 3, pt. 1. Srinagar: Research Department.

Enomoto, Fumio. 2000. "The Discovery of 'the Oldest Buddhist Manuscripts'" [review article on Salomon 1999.] *The Eastern Buddhist* 32.1: 157–66.

Errington, Elizabeth, and Joe Cribb. 1992. *The Crossroads of Asia: Transformation in Image and Symbol in the Art of Ancient Afghanistan and Pakistan*. Cambridge: The Ancient India and Iran Trust.

Faccenna, Domenico. 1964. *A Guide to the Excavations in Swat (Pakistan) 1956–1962*. Rome: Department of Archaeology of Pakistan / Istituto italiano per il Medio ed Estremo Oriente.

Falk, Harry. 1998. "Notes on Some Apraca Dedicatory Texts." *Berliner indologische Studien* 11/12: 85–108.

———. 2001. "The Yuga of Sphujiddhvaja and the Era of the Kuṣâṇas." *Silk Road Art and Archaeology* 7: 121–36.

———. 2005. "The Introduction of Stūpa-Worship in Bajaur." In *Afghanistan: ancien carrefour entre l'Est et l'Ouest*, edited by Osmund Bopearachchi and Marie-Françoise Boussac, 347–58. Indicopleustoi: Archaeologies of the Indian Ocean 3. Turnhout, Belgium: Brepols.

———. 2011. "The 'Split' Collection of Kharoṣṭhī Texts." *Annual Report of the*

International Research Institute for Advanced Buddhology at Soka University 14: 13–23.

———. 2014. "The First-Century Copper-Plates of Helagupta from Gandhāra Hailing Maitreya." *Annual Report of the International Research Institute for Advanced Buddhology at Soka University* 17: 3–26.

———. 2015. "A New Gāndhārī *Dharmapada* (Texts from the Split Collection 3)." *Annual Report of the International Research Institute for Advanced Buddhology at Soka University* 18: 23–62.

Falk, Harry, and Chris Bennett. 2009. "Macedonian Intercalary Months and the Era of Azes." *Acta Orientalia* 70: 197–216.

Falk, Harry, and Seishi Karashima. 2012. "A First-Century *Prajñāpāramitā* Manuscript from Gandhāra—*parivarta* 1 (Texts from the Split Collection 1)." *Annual Report of the International Research Institute for Advanced Buddhology at Soka University* 15: 19–61.

———. 2013. "A First-Century *Prajñāpāramitā* Manuscript from Gandhāra—*parivarta* 5 (Texts from the Split Collection 2)." *Annual Report of the International Research Institute for Advanced Buddhology at Soka University* 16: 97–169.

Falk, Harry, and Ingo Strauch. 2014. "The Bajaur and Split Collections of Kharoṣṭhī Manuscripts within the Context of Buddhist Gāndhārī Literature." In Harrison and Hartmann 2014, 51–78.

Faucett, Lawrence W. 1967. *Seeking Gotama Buddha in His Teachings: An Analytical Arrangement of Passages from the Earliest Scriptures of Buddhism*. San Marcos, CA [published by the author].

Fussman, Gérard. 1989. "Gāndhārī écrite, Gāndhārī parlée." In *Dialectes dans les littératures indo-aryennes*, edited by Colette Caillat, 433–501. Paris: Institut de civilisation indienne.

———. 1993. "L'Indo-Grec Ménandre ou Paul Demiéville revisité." *Journal asiatique* 281: 61–138.

Glass, Andrew. 2007. *Four Gāndhārī Saṃyuktāgama Sūtras: Senior Kharoṣṭhī Fragment 5*. Gandhāran Buddhist Texts 4. Seattle: University of Washington Press.

Gnoli, Raniero. 1977–78. *The Gilgit Manuscript of the Saṅghabhedavastu: Being the 17th and Last Section of the Vinaya of the Mūlasarvāstivādin*. 2 vols. Serie orientale Roma 49. Rome: Istituto italiano per il Medio ed Estremo Oriente.

Gokhale, Balkrishna Govind. 1982. "Early Buddhism and the Urban Revolution." *Journal of the International Association of Buddhist Studies* 5: 7–22.

Harrison, Paul. 1997. "The *Ekottarikāgama* Translations of An Shigao." In *Bauddhavidyāsudhākaraḥ: Studies in Honour of Heinz Bechert on the Occasion of His 65th Birthday,* edited by Petra Kieffer-Pülz and Jens-Uwe Hartmann, 261–84. Indica et Tibetica 30. Swisttal Odendorf, Germany: Indica et Tibetica Verlag.

———. 2002. "Another Addition to the An Shigao Corpus? Preliminary Notes on an Early Chinese Saṃyuktāgama Translation." In *Shoki Bukkyō kara Abidaruma e: Sakurabe Hajime Hakushi kiju kinen ronshū* 初期仏教からアビダルマへ: 櫻部建博士喜寿記念論集 (Early Buddhism and Abhidharma Thought: In Honor of Doctor Hajime Sakurabe on His Seventy-Seventh Birthday), 1–32. Kyoto: Heirakuji Shoten.

———. 2008 [2010]. "Experimental Core Samples of Chinese Translations of Two Buddhist Sūtras Analysed in the Light of Recent Sanskrit Manuscript Discoveries." *Journal of the International Association of Buddhist Studies* 31: 205–49.

Harrison, Paul, and Jens-Uwe Hartmann, eds. 2014. *From Birch Bark to Digital Data: Recent Advances in Buddhist Manuscript Research. Papers Presented at the Conference Indic Buddhist Manuscripts: The State of the Field. Stanford, June 15–19, 2009.* Beiträge zur Kultur- und Geistesgeschichte Asiens 80; Denkschriften der philosophisch-historischen Klasse 460. Vienna: Österreichische Akademie der Wissenschaften.

Harrison, Paul, Timothy Lenz, Qian Lin, and Richard Salomon. 2016. "A Gāndhārī Fragment of the *Sarvapuṇyasamuccayasamādhisūtra.*" In Braarvig 2016, 311–19.

Hartmann, Jens-Uwe. 1999. "Buddhist Sanskrit Texts from Northern Turkestan and Their Relation to the Chinese Tripiṭaka." In *Collection of Essays 1993. Buddhism across Boundaries: Chinese Buddhism and the Western Regions*, 107–36. Sanchung: Foguang Cultural Enterprise Co. (Revised ed. published as *Sino-Platonic Papers* 222 [March 2012], edited by John R. McRae and Jan Nattier. Taipei, Taiwan: Fo Guang Shan Foundation for Buddhist and Culture Education. http://sino-platonic.org/complete/spp222_indian_chinese_buddhism.pdf.)

———. 2004. "Contents and Structure of the *Dīrghāgama* of the (Mūla-) Sarvāstivādins." *Annual Report of the International Research Institute for Advanced Buddhology at Soka University* 7: 119–37.

Hinüber, Oskar von. 1996. *A Handbook of Pāli Literature*. Indian Philology and South Asian Studies 2. Berlin: Walter de Gruyter.

———. 2004. [Review of Lenz 2003.] *Journal of the American Oriental Society* 124: 803–5.
———. 2014. "The Gilgit Manuscript: An Ancient Buddhist Library in Modern Research." In Harrison and Hartmann 2014, 79–135.
Hofinger, Marcel. 1982 and 1990. *Le congrès du lac Anavatapta (vies de saints bouddhiques): Extrait du Vinaya des Mūlasarvāstivādin Bhaiṣajyavastu.* 2 vols. Publications de l'Institut orientaliste de Louvain 28, 38. Louvain-la-Neuve: Université catholique de Louvain, Institut orientaliste.
Horner, I. B. 1963. *Milinda's Questions.* 2 vols. Sacred Books of the Buddhists 22–23. London: Luzac. (Reprint ed., 1996: Oxford: The Pali Text Society.)
Hultzsch, E., ed. 1925. *Inscriptions of Aśoka.* Corpus Inscriptionum Indicarum 1. Oxford: Clarendon Press.
Jamison, Stephanie. 1998. "Rhinoceros Toes, Manu V.17–18, and the Development of the Dharma System." *Journal of the American Oriental Society* 118: 249–56.
Jantrasrisalai, Chanida, Timothy Lenz, Qian Lin, and Richard Salomon. 2016. "Fragments of an Ekottarikāgama Manuscript in Gāndhārī." In Braarvig 2016, 1–122.
Jones, J. J., trans. 1949–56. *The Mahāvastu.* 3 vols. Sacred Books of the Buddhists 103. London: Luzac and Co.
Jongeward, David, Elizabeth Errington, Richard Salomon, and Stefan Baums. 2012. *Gandharan Buddhist Reliquaries.* Gandharan Studies 1. Seattle: Early Buddhist Manuscripts Project.
Karashima, Seishi 辛嶋 静志. 1994. *Jōagonkyō no gengo no kenkyū—onshago bunseki o chūshin to shite* 長阿含経の原語の研究一音写後分析を中心として [*A Study of the Original Language of the Chang ahan jing: Focusing on an Analysis of the Transcriptions*]. Tokyo: Hirakawa Shuppansha.
———. 2012. "Was the Aṣṭasāhasrikā Prajñāpāramitā Compiled in Gandhāra in Gāndhārī?" *Annual Report of the International Research Institute for Advanced Buddhology at Soka University* 16: 171–88.
Konow, Sten. 1929. *Kharoshṭhī Inscriptions with the Exception of Those of Aśoka.* Corpus Inscriptionum Indicarum 2.1. Calcutta: Government of India Central Publication Branch.
Lamotte, Etienne. 1947–50. "Alexandre et le Bouddhisme." *Bulletin de l'École française d'Extrême-Orient* 44: 147–62.
———. 1954. "Sur la formation du Mahāyāna." In *Asiatica: Festschrift Friedrich Weller zum 65. Geburtstag gewidmet von seinen Freunden Kollegen und Schülern*, 377–96. Leipzig: Otto Harrassowitz.
———. 1988. *History of Indian Buddhism from the Origins to the Śaka Era.*

Translated by Sara Webb-Boin. Publications de l'Institut orientaliste de Louvain 36. Louvain-la-Neuve: Université catholique de Louvain, Institut orientaliste.

Lee, Mei-huang. 2009. "A Study of the Gāndhārī Dārukkhandhopamasutta ('Discourse on the Simile of the Log')." PhD dissertation, University of Washington.

Legge, James. 1886. *A Record of Buddhistic Kingdoms: Being an Account by the Chinese Monk Fâ-hien of His Travels in India and Ceylon (A.D. 344–414) in Search of the Buddhist Books of Discipline.* Oxford: Clarendon Press.

Lenz, Timothy. 2003. *A New Version of the Gāndhārī Dharmapada and a Collection of Previous-Birth Stories: British Library Kharoṣṭhī Fragments 16 + 25*. Gandhāran Buddhist Texts 3. Seattle: University of Washington Press.

———. 2010. *Gandhāran Avadānas: British Library Kharoṣṭhī Fragments 1–3 and 21 and Supplementary Fragments A–C.* Gandhāran Buddhist Texts 6. Seattle: University of Washington Press.

Li, Rongxi. 1996. *The Great Tang Dynasty Record of the Western Regions.* BDK English Tripiṭaka 79. Berkeley: Numata Center for Buddhist Translation and Research.

MacQueen, Graeme. 1988. *A Study of the Śrāmaṇyaphala-sūtra.* Freiburger Beiträge zur Indologie 21. Wiesbaden: Otto Harrassowitz.

Malalasekera, G. P. 1937–38. *Dictionary of Pāli Proper Names.* 2 vols. London: J. Murray.

Matsuda, Kazunobu. 2014. "Japanese Collections of Buddhist Manuscript Fragments from the Same Region as the Schøyen Collection." In Harrison and Hartmann 2014, 165–69.

Ñāṇamoli, Bhikkhu, trans. 1962. *The Guide (Netti-ppakaraṇaṃ) According to Kaccāna Thera.* Pali Text Society Translation Series 33. London: Luzac & Company.

——— and Bhikkhu Bodhi, trans. 1995. *The Middle Length Discourses of the Buddha: A New Translation of the Majjhima Nikāya.* The Teachings of the Buddha. Boston: Wisdom Publications.

Nattier, Jan. 1991. *Once Upon a Future Time: Studies in a Buddhist Prophecy of Decline.* Nanzan Studies in Asian Religions 1. Berkeley, CA: Asian Humanities Press.

———. 2003. *A Few Good Men: The Bodhisattva Path according to The Inquiry of Ugra (Ugraparipṛcchā).* Studies in the Buddhist Tradition. Honolulu: University of Hawai'i.

Neelis, Jason. 2011. *Early Buddhist Transmission and Trade Networks: Mobility and Exchange within and beyond the Northwestern Borderlands of South Asia*. Dynamics in the History of Religion 2. Leiden: Brill.

Norman, K. R. 1983a. *Pāli Literature, Including the Canonical Literature in Prakrit and Sanskrit of All the Hīnayāna Schools of Buddhism*. A History of Indian Literature, vol. 7, fasc. 2. Wiesbaden: Otto Harrassowitz.

———. 1983b. "The Pratyeka-buddha in Buddhism and Jainism." In *Buddhist Studies, Ancient and Modern*, edited by Philip Denwood and Alexander Piatigorsky, 92–106. Collected Papers on South Asia 4. London: Curzon Press.

———, trans. 1985. *The Rhinoceros Horn and Other Early Buddhist Poems: The Group of Discourses (Sutta-nipāta)*. Pali Text Society Translation Series 44. London: Pali Text Society.

———, trans. 1992. *The Group of Discourses (Sutta-Nipāta)*. Vol. 2, *Revised Translation with Introduction and Notes*. Pali Text Society Translation Series 45. Oxford: Pali Text Society.

———, trans. 1997. *The Word of the Doctrine (Dhammapada)*. Pali Text Society Translation Series 46. Oxford: Pali Text Society.

Nyanaponika Thera and Hellmuth Hecker. 1997. *Great Disciples of the Buddha: Their Lives, Their Works, Their Legacy*. Boston: Wisdom Publications.

Oberlies, Thomas. 2003. "Ein bibliographischer Überblick über die kanonischen Texte der Śrāvakayāna-Schulen des Buddhismus (ausgenommen der des Mahāvihāra-Theravāda)." *Wiener Zeitschrift für die Kunde Südasiens* 47: 37–84.

Palumbo, Antonello. Forthcoming. *The Invention of the Buddhist Monarch: The Avadāna of Indravarma in the Kalpanāmaṇḍitikā Dṛṣṭāntapaṅkti of Kumāralāta and the Development of Buddhist Ideals of Kingship in Ancient Gandhāra*.

Przyluski, J. 1914. "Le nord-ouest de l'Inde dans le Vinaya des Mūlasarvāstivādin et les textes apparentés." *Journal Asiatique* ser. 11, vol. 4: 493–568.

Ray, Reginald. 1994. *Buddhist Saints in India: A Study in Buddhist Values and Orientations*. New York: Oxford University Press.

Ripley, S. Dillon. 1952. "Territorial and Sexual Behavior in the Great Indian Rhinoceros, a Speculation." *Ecology* 33: 570–53.

Roebuck, Valerie. 2010. *The Dhammapada*. Penguin Classics. London: Penguin Books.

Rotman, Andy. 2008. *Divine Stories: Divyāvadāna, part I*. Classics of Indian Buddhism. Boston: Wisdom Publications.

———. 2009. *Thus Have I Seen: Visualizing Faith in Early Indian Buddhism*. New York: Oxford University Press.

Sachau, Edward. 1888. *Alberuni's India: An Account of the Religion, Philosophy, Literature, Geography, Chronology, Astronomy, Customs, Laws, and Astrology of India about A.D. 1030*. 2 vols. London: Trübner & Co.

Salomon, Richard. 1986. "The Inscription of Senavarma, King of Oḍi." *Indo-Iranian Journal* 29: 261–93.

———. 1998a. *Indian Epigraphy. A Guide to the Study of Inscriptions in Sanskrit, Prakrit, and the Other Indo-Aryan Languages*. South Asia Research Series. New York: Oxford University Press.

———. 1998b. "Kharoṣṭhī Manuscript Fragments in the Pelliot Collection, Bibliothèque Nationale de France." *Bulletin d'Études Indiennes* 16: 123–60.

———. 1999. *Ancient Buddhist Scrolls from Gandhāra: The British Library Kharoṣṭhī Fragments*. Seattle: University of Washington Press.

———. 2000. *A Gāndhārī Version of the Rhinoceros Sūtra: British Library Kharoṣṭhī Fragment 5B*. Gandhāran Buddhist Texts 1. Seattle: University of Washington Press.

———. 2001. "'Gāndhārī Hybrid Sanskrit': New Sources for the Study of the Sanskritization of Buddhist Literature." *Indo-Iranian Journal* 44: 241–52.

———. 2002. "A Fragment of a Collection of Buddhist Legends, with a Reference to King Huviṣka as a Follower of the Mahāyāna." In Braarvig 2002, 255–67.

———. 2003. "The Senior Manuscripts: Another Collection of Gandhāran Buddhist Scrolls." *Journal of the American Oriental Society* 123: 73–92.

———. 2006. "Recent Discoveries of Early Buddhist Manuscripts and Their Implications for the History of Buddhist Texts and Canons." In *Between the Empires: Society in India 300 BCE to 400 CE*, edited by Patrick Olivelle, 349–82. South Asia Research. Oxford: Oxford University Press.

———. 2007. "Dynastic and Institutional Connections in the Pre- and Early Kuṣāṇa Period: New Manuscript and Epigraphic Evidence." In *On the Cusp of an Era: Art in the Pre-Kuṣāṇa World*, edited by Doris Meth Srinivasan, 267–86. Brill's Inner Asian Library 18. Leiden: Brill.

———. 2008. *Two Gāndhārī Manuscripts of the Songs of Lake Anavatapta (Anavatapta-gāthā): British Library Kharoṣṭhī Fragment 1 and Senior Scroll 14*. Gandhāran Buddhist Texts 5. Seattle: University of Washington Press.

———. 2009. "Why Did the Gandhāran Buddhists Bury Their Manuscripts?" In *Buddhist Manuscript Cultures: Knowledge, Ritual, and Art*, edited by

Steven Berkwitz, Claudia Brown, and Juliane Schober, 19–34. Routledge Critical Studies in Buddhism. London and New York: Routledge.

———. 2011. "An Unwieldy Canon: Observations on Some Distinctive Features of Canon Formation in Buddhism." In *Kanonisierung und Kanonbildung in der asiatischen Religionsgeschichte*, edited by Max Deeg, Oliver Freiberger, and Christoph Kleine, 167–207. Österreichische Akademie der Wissenschaften, philosophisch-historische Klasse, Sitzungsberichte 820; Beiträge zur Kultur- und Geistesgeschichte Asiens 72. Vienna: Verlag der Österreichischen Akademie der Wissenschaften.

———. 2012. "Gandhāran Reliquary Inscriptions." In Jongeward et al. 2012: 164–99 (chapter 5).

———. 2014. "Gāndhārī Manuscripts in the British Library, Schøyen and Other Collections." In Harrison and Hartmann 2014, 1–17.

———. 2017. "On the Evolution of Written *Āgama* Collections in Northern Buddhist Traditions." In *Research on the Madhyamāgama*, edited by Dhammadinnā, 239–68. Dharma Drum Institute of Liberal Arts Research Series. Taipei: Dharma Drum Publishing.

Salomon, Richard, and Stefan Baums. 2007. "Sanskrit Ikṣvāku, Pali Okkāka, and Gāndhārī Iṣmaho." *Journal of the Pali Text Society* 29: 201–27.

Salomon, Richard, and Joseph Marino. 2014. "Observations on the Deorkothar Inscriptions and Their Significance for the Evaluation of Buddhist Historical Traditions." *Annual Report of the International Research Institute for Advanced Buddhology at Soka University* 17: 27–39.

Salomon, Richard, and Gregory Schopen. 1984. "The Indravarman (Avaca) Casket Inscription Reconsidered: Further Evidence for Canonical Passages in Buddhist Inscriptions." *Journal of the International Association of Buddhist Studies* 7: 107–23.

Sander, Lore. 2000. "Fragments of an Aṣṭasāhasrikā Manuscript from the Kuṣāṇa Period." In Braarvig 2000, 1–51.

Schmithausen, Lambert. 1977. "Textgeschichtliche Beobachtungen zum 1. Kapitel der Aṣṭasāhasrikā Prajñāpāramita." In *Prajñāpāramitā and Related Systems: Studies in Honor of Edward Conze*, edited by Lewis Lancaster, 35–80. Berkeley Buddhist Studies Series 1. Berkeley: University of California.

Schneider, U. 1982. "The Calcutta-Bairāṭ Edict of Aśoka." In *Indological and Buddhist Studies: Volume in Honour of Professor J. W. de Jong on his Sixtieth Birthday*, edited by L. A. Hercus et al., 491–98. Canberra: Australian National University, Faculty of Asian Studies.

Schopen, Gregory. 1975. "The Phrase *sa pṛthivīpradeśaś caityabhūto bhavet* in the *Vajracchedikā*: Notes on the Cult of the Book in Mahāyāna." *Indo-Iranian Journal* 17: 147–81. Reprinted in Schopen 2005, 25–62.

———. 1997. "If You Can't Remember, How to Make it Up: Some Monastic Rules for Redacting Canonical Texts." In *Bauddhavidyasudhākaraḥ: Studies in Honour of Heinz Bechert of the Occasion of His 65th Birthday*, edited by Petra Kieffer-Pulz and Jens-Uwe Hartmann, 571–82. Indica et Tibetica 30. Swisttal-Odendorf, Germany: Indica and Tibetica Verlag. Reprinted in Schopen 2004, 395–407.

———. 2004. *Buddhist Monks and Business Matters: Still More Papers on Monastic Buddhism in India.* Studies in the Buddhist Traditions. Honolulu: University of Hawai'i Press.

———. 2005. *Figments and Fragments of Mahāyāna Buddhism in India: More Collected Papers.* Studies in the Buddhist Traditions. Honolulu: University of Hawai'i Press.

Silk, Jonathan. 2003. "Dressed for Success: The Monk Kāśyapa and Strategies of Legitimation in Earlier Mahāyāna Buddhist Scriptures." *Journal Asiatique* 291: 173–219.

Sims-Williams, Nicholas. 1983. "Indian Elements in Parthian and Sogdian." In *Sprachen des Buddhismus in Zentralasien*, edited by Klaus Röhrborn and Wolfgang Veenker, 132–41. Veröffentlichungen der Societas Uralo-Altaica 16. Wiesbaden: Otto Harrassowitz.

———. 2004 [2008]. "The Bactrian Inscription of Rabatak: A New Reading." *Bulletin of the Asia Institute* 18: 53–68.

Sims-Williams, Nicholas, and Joe Cribb. 1995–96. "A New Bactrian Inscription of Kanishka the Great." *Silk Road Art and Archaeology* 4: 75–143.

Skilling, Peter. 1993. "Theravādin Literature in Tibetan Translation." *Journal of the Pali Text Society* 19: 69–201.

———. 1996. "The Sambuddhe Verses and Later Theravādin Buddhology." *Journal of the Pali Text Society* 22: 151–83.

Staal, Frits. 1990. "The Lake of the Yakṣa Chief." In *Indo-Tibetan Studies: Papers in Honour and Appreciation of Professor David L. Snellgrove's Contribution to Indo-Tibetan Studies*, edited by Tadeusz Skorupski, 275–91. Buddhica Britannica, series continua 2. Tring, U.K.: Institute of Buddhist Studies.

Stache-Rosen, Valentina. 1968. *Dogmatische Begriffsreihen im älteren Buddhismus II: Das Saṅgītisūtra and sein Kommentar Saṅgītiparyāya.* Sanskrittexte aus den Turfanfunden 9. Berlin: Akademie-Verlag.

Strauch, Ingo. 2008. "The Bajaur Collection of Kharoṣṭhī Manuscripts: A Preliminary Survey." *Studien zur Indologie und Iranistik* 25: 103–36.

———. 2010. "More Missing Pieces of Early Pure Land Buddhism: New Evidence for Akṣobhya and Abhirati in an Early Mahayana Sutra from Gandhāra." *The Eastern Buddhist* 41: 23–66.

———. 2014a. "The Evolution of the Buddhist *rakṣā* Genre in the Light of New Evidence from Gandhāra: The **Manasvi-nāgarāja-sūtra* from the Bajaur Collection of Kharoṣṭhī Manuscripts." *Bulletin of the School of Oriental and African Studies* 77: 63–84.

———. 2014b. "Looking into Water-pots and over a Buddhist Scribe's Shoulder: On the Deposition and the Use of Manuscripts in Early Buddhism." *Asiatische Studien / Études asiatiques* 68: 797–830.

Strong, John. 1979. "The Legend of the Lion-Roarer: A Study of the Buddhist Arhat Piṇḍola Bharadvāja." *Numen* 26: 50–88.

———. 1983. *The Legend of King Aśoka*. Princeton, NJ: Princeton University Press.

———. 2001. *The Buddha: A Short Biography*. Oxford: Oneworld Publications.

———. 2004. *Relics of the Buddha*. Princeton, NJ: Princeton University Press.

Thomas, Edward J. 1933. "Avadāna and Apadāna." *The Indian Historical Quarterly* 9: 32–36.

Tournier, Vincent. 2012. "Matériaux pour une histoire de la légende et du culte de Mahākāśyapa: une relecture d'un fragment de statue inscrit retrouvé à Silao (Bihar)." In *Autour de Bāmiyān: De la Bactriane hellénisée à l'Inde bouddhique*, edited by Guillaume Ducœur, 375–413. Archaeologia Afghana, série scientifique 1. Paris: Association for the Protection of Afghan Archaeology / De Boccard.

Walshe, Maurice. 1995. *The Long Discourses of the Buddha: A Translation of the Dīgha Nikāya*. Boston: Wisdom Publications.

Wille, Klaus. 2014. "Survey of the Sanskrit Manuscripts in the Turfan Collection (Berlin)." In Harrison and Hartmann 2014, 187–211.

Williams, Paul. 1989. *Mahāyāna Buddhism: The Doctrinal Foundations*. The Library of Religious Beliefs and Practices. London: Routledge.

Zürcher, Erik. 1968. "The Yüeh-chih and Kaniṣka in the Chinese Sources." In *Papers on the Date of Kaniṣka*, edited by A. L. Basham, 346–90. Leiden: E. J. Brill.

Image Credits

fig. 1 (British Library pot): © The British Library
fig. 2 (British Library scrolls in pot): © The British Library
fig. 3 (British Library fragments 16–19): © The British Library
fig. 4 (British Library conservators): © The British Library
fig. 5 (Senior scroll 19): © The British Library
fig. 6 (Manikiala stūpa): © Christian Luczanits
fig. 7 (coin of Menander): © Pankaj Tandon
fig. 8 (Shinkot reliquary): Archaeological Survey of India, published in *Epigraphia Indica* 19 (1937).
fig. 9 (silver reliquary of Indravarma): Miho Museum. Previously published in JAOS 116 (1996): 419.
fig. 10 (Tīrath footprint inscription): author
fig. 11 (Kaniṣka): © Christian Luczanits
fig. 12 (donors in Central Asian dress): Isao Kurita, *Gandharan Art II: The World of the Buddha*, figure 51.
fig. 13 (Trojan horse): © Trustees of the British Museum
fig. 14 (Herakles/Vajrapāṇi from Haḍḍa): © Deborah Klimburg-Salter. From *Buddha in Indien* (Vienna, 1995), 122, fig. XV.
fig. 15 (Roman glass from Begram): © RMN-Grand Palais / Art Resource, NY
fig. 16 (coin of Kaniṣka): © Trustees of the British Museum
fig. 17 (rock carvings and inscriptions from Hodar): © Heidelberg Academy of Sciences and Humanities

fig. 18 (Kuthodaw slabs): © Kuthodaw Pagoda Project
fig. 19 (folio from Bamiyan): © Norwegian Institute of Philology
fig. 20 (Senior 24 as found): © The British Library
fig. 21 (British Library fragment 1): © The British Library
fig. 22 (Senior pot and lid): © Robert Senior
fig. 23 (Senior index scroll 8): © The British Library
fig. 24 (upper right corner of Senior scroll 5): © The British Library
fig. 25 (Senior scroll 5, before unrolling): © The British Library
fig. 26 (Senior scroll 5, after conservation): © The British Library
fig. 27 (Kizil, *Sūtra of the Log*): © Staatliche Museen zu Berlin—Museum für Asiatische Kunst
fig. 28 (Indian rhinoceros): © Krish Dulal
fig. 29 (*Rhinoceros Sūtra*, debris box): © The British Library
fig. 30 (Khotan *Dharmapada* scroll): Institute of Oriental Manuscripts of the Russian Academy of Sciences, St. Petersburg
fig. 31 (portion of British Library scroll 1): © The British Library
fig. 32 (British Library scroll 1 as originally found): © The British Library
fig. 33 (sleeping women): © Trustees of the British Museum
fig. 34 (*Viśvantara-jātaka*): © Trustees of the British Museum
fig. 35 (*Dīpaṅkara-jātaka*): © Trustees of the British Museum
fig. 36 (*caitya*): © Staatliche Museen zu Berlin—Museum für Asiatische Kunst
fig. 37 (British Library scroll 9): © The British Library
fig. 38 (Śatruleka reliquary): © Staatliche Museen zu Berlin—Museum für Asiatische Kunst

Index

B

E

M

necessity of, 135
parable of log for teaching, 139
in Perfection of Wisdom sūtras, 336, 337–38
on repulsiveness (*aśubha-bhāvanā*), 129, 387n190 (*See also* body, impurity of)
solitary, 179
wisdom and, 193
meditations, four, 135, 149, 150, 151, 346, 353
memorization, 97, 106, 113, 167, 243–44, 295–96, 310
Menander, 24–27, 34, 380n27
Menander, donor of Gandhāran reliquary, 375, 377
merchant class, 222, 223, 225, 237–38
merit
from copying texts, 82
field of, 204
from interring texts, 121
from publishing scripture, 54
pure heart and, 204, 370
rebirth and, 221, 222
from relic dedication and donation, 21, 45, 375
from solitary buddhas, caring for, 162, 247–48, 249
from teaching perfection of wisdom, 346, 353–58
in viewing Buddha's footprints, 31
Meru, Mount, 259, 260
metaphors and similes
agricultural, 204
carpenter's adze handle, 136, 151–52
clear water, 203
crossing to other shore, 238
deathless nectar, 224, 395n317
for five faculties, 304, 399n396
floods, 196, 392n271
flower on fig trees, 196, 392n274
great caravan leader (*mahāsārthavāha*), 238
of hen, double, 136, 150, 151
hot iron ball, swallowing, 195, 392n269
jewels, 238
in "The Parable of the Log," 141, 142–43, 153–55
sand on bank of Ganges, 346, 353, 356, 357, 402n450
for sense bases, 142–43, 153, 154, 155
ship on dry land, 136, 152
snake shedding skin, 196–97
teaching by, 139
meter, 400n424
anuṣṭubh (*śloka*), 206
jagatī, 213
Milindapañha. See *Questions of Milinda*
mind
beneficial dharmas and, 135–36, 149–52
calm, 114, 193
enlightened and unenlightened, distinctions between, 165
fixation of, 161, 163, 164–65, 175, 176–77, 181
focused/concentrated, 195, 223, 271, 304, 316
four efforts and, 111–12, 117–19
guarding, 179
liberation of, temporary and permanent, 167–68, 390n239
liberation of Nanda's, 142, 154
one-pointedness of, 131, 145–46
in Perfection of Wisdom sūtras, 336–38, 345, 347–48, 349, 353, 401n442
pure, 140, 203, 218, 220, 221, 222, 228, 371
restraint of, 193
as sense-base, 143, 153
mindfulness
as enlightenment factor, 118
four foundations of, 135, 149, 150, 151
mnemonic summaries, 173–74
monasticism
curriculum of, 92, 93, 94, 97, 310, 312
decline of, 47
and laity, symbiosis of, 249
oral and written texts in, 97
royal patronage and, 17
and secular authority, relationship between, 22, 34–35

About the Author

PROFESSOR RICHARD G. SALOMON of the University of Washington is a leading figure in the field of early Buddhist studies. He directs the Early Buddhist Manuscripts Project and is editor-in-chief of the Gandhāran Buddhist Texts series published by the University of Washington Press.

Also Available from the *Classics of Indian Buddhism* Series

Divine Stories (2 vols.)
Divyāvadāna Parts 1 and 2
Andy Rotman

"The Buddha was a skillful and inveterate storyteller who understood the enduring power of narrative to entertain, engage, and enlighten. In his beautiful translation, Andy Rotman ensures the transmission of these divine and very human stories to a new generation of readers."
—Ruth Ozeki, author of *A Tale for the Time Being*

Nāgārjuna's Middle Way
Mūlamadhyamakakārikā
Mark Siderits and Shōryū Katsura

"Authoritative, vivid, and illuminating."—Graham Priest, author of *Logic: A Very Short Introduction*

Also Available from Wisdom Publications

The Suttanipāta
An Ancient Collection of the Buddha's Discourses
Together with Its Commentaries
Bhikkhu Bodhi

This landmark volume in the Teachings of the Buddha series translates the *Suttanipāta*, a text that matches the *Dhammapada* in its concise power of expression and its centrality to the Buddhist tradition.

Buddhist Teaching in India
Johannes Bronkhorst

"A most welcome addition to the growing literature on early Indian Buddhism."—Charles Prebish, Redd Chair in Religious Studies, Utah State University

In the Buddha's Words
An Anthology of Discourses from the Pāli Canon
Bhikkhu Bodhi
Foreword by the Dalai Lama

"It will rapidly become the sourcebook of choice for both neophyte and serious students alike."—*Buddhadharma*

The Buddhist Philosophy of the Middle
Essays on Indian and Tibetan Madhyamaka
David Seyfort Ruegg
Foreword by Tom Tillemans

"Without a doubt, the articles collected here will greatly advance this philosophical tradition finding its rightful place as one of the treasures of human thought and reflection."—Ernst Steinkellner, University of Vienna

Sexuality in Classical South Asian Buddhism
José Ignacio Cabezón

"Over a distinguished career, José Cabezón has produced a range of studies that have enriched and broadened our knowledge of the Buddhist tradition. Here, in what will be regarded as his most important work, he masterfully explores the multiple worlds of Buddhist sexuality. A learned combination of compendium and critique, this book immediately becomes the standard work to which all readers will turn."—Donald Lopez, University of Michigan

About Wisdom Publications

WISDOM PUBLICATIONS, a nonprofit publisher, is dedicated to making available books about Buddhism for the benefit of all. We publish works by ancient and modern masters across Buddhist traditions, translations of important texts, and original scholarship. We also offer books that explore East-West themes, which continue to emerge as traditional Buddhism encounters modern culture in all its complexity. Our titles are published with an appreciation of Buddhism as a living philosophy, and with a commitment to preserve and transmit important works from Buddhism's many traditions.

You can contact us, request a catalog, or browse our books online at our website. You can also write to us at the address below.

Wisdom Publications
199 Elm Street
Somerville, Massachusetts 02144 USA
Telephone: (617) 776-7416
Fax: (617) 776-7841
Email: support@wisdompubs.org
www.wisdomexperience.org

Supporting the *Classics of Indian Buddhism* Series

The volumes in the *Classics of Indian Buddhism* series adhere to the highest standards of accuracy and readability, making them works that will stand the test of time both as scholarship and as literature. The care and attention necessary to bring such works to press demand a level of investment beyond the normal costs associated with publishing. If you would like to partner with Wisdom to help make the series a success, either by supporting the meticulous work of translators and editors or by sponsoring the publication costs of a forthcoming volume, please send us an email at cib@wisdompubs.org or write to us at the address above. We appreciate your support.

Wisdom is a nonprofit, charitable 501(c)(3) organization affiliated with the Foundation for the Preservation of the Mahayana Tradition (FPMT).